George Washburn Smalley

London Letters and Some Others

In Two Volumes. Vol. I

George Washburn Smalley

London Letters and Some Others
In Two Volumes. Vol. I

ISBN/EAN: 9783744688949

Printed in Europe, USA, Canada, Australia, Japan

Cover: Foto ©Thomas Meinert / pixelio.de

More available books at **www.hansebooks.com**

LONDON LETTERS

AND SOME OTHERS

BY

GEORGE W. SMALLEY

IN TWO VOLUMES

VOL. I.

PERSONALITIES—TWO MIDLOTHIAN CAMPAIGNS

NEW YORK
HARPER & BROTHERS, FRANKLIN SQUARE
1891

TO

WHITELAW REID

UNITED STATES MINISTER TO FRANCE

My Dear Reid:

The letters here reprinted were written to the *New York Tribune* —or the greater part were—during your editorship of that journal. I am much indebted to you for leave to use them, and inscribe them to you in testimony of the respect and regard with which I remain,

Yours sincerely,

GEORGE W. SMALLEY.

London, *September* 12, 1890.

CONTENTS OF VOLUME I.

	PAGE
PERSONALITIES	1
Prince Bismarck	3
Count Herbert Bismarck	12
The Dismissal of Prince Bismarck	19
The German Emperor	29
Léon Gambetta	34
Louis Blanc	43
Lord Beaconsfield	52
Mr. Delane	61
Darwin in Westminster Abbey	69
The Darwin Memorial	76
Mr. Fawcett	81
Mr. Forster	94
Lord Iddesleigh	106
Mr. Bright	113
Lord Carnarvon	146
Lord Hartington	152
Lord Randolph Churchill	161
Mr. Balfour	178
Mr. Chamberlain	183
Mr. John Morley	199
Lord Rosebery	205
Lord Spencer	209
Lord Ripon	214
Mr. Lowell	217
Mr. Phelps	224
John Stuart Mill	232
George Eliot	241
Thomas Carlyle	249
The Carlyle Memorial	264
Mr. Hayward	270
Lord Houghton	279

	PAGE
Lord Shaftesbury	286
Matthew Arnold	289
Mrs. Procter	303
Laurence Oliphant	306
Robert Browning	309
The Master of Balliol	320
Lord Lytton	326
M. Renan and Marcus Aurelius	332
Gustave Doré	338
Carlo Pellegrini	344
Mr. Watts	347

TWO MIDLOTHIAN CAMPAIGNS 353
 Mr. Gladstone in 1879 355
 Mr. Gladstone in 1884 385
 Beyond Midlothian 423
 Mr. Gladstone's Politics 440

PERSONALITIES.

PRINCE BISMARCK.

[BERLIN, *March* 19, 1888.]

My only glimpse of Prince Bismarck this week was in the Reichstag. His public appearances are now rare, and even the presence of his carriage in the streets is enough to attract a crowd. From my windows in the hotel I could see the Prince's palace in the Wilhelmstrasse, and whenever his carriage entered or left the gates a company of the curious followed it. As he drives at a good pace, they had to follow fast if they counted on a look at the inside passenger. The custom is one which is perhaps peculiar to Berlin. People in London collect, often in large numbers, opposite the gates of Buckingham Palace to see the Queen, or on the pavement over against the entrance to Marlborough House in patient expectation of the exit of the Prince or Princess of Wales. I cannot recollect to have seen any of these eager throngs pursuing on foot the objects of their loyal adoration.

The Reichstag had been summoned to hear a message from the new Emperor, and there was some hope that it would be read by Prince Bismarck. Our Minister, Mr. Pendleton, was kind enough to take me with him to this ceremony; one of many friendly acts for which I have to thank him. Arriving a few minutes before the hour, we found no signs of excitement in the Leipsigerstrasse or about the plain, large edifice where the Imperial Parliament is, for the present, content to sit. They are erecting a great building for its permanent home, destined to be, some years hence, magnificent. Nobody in Berlin is ever in a hurry about anything. The hall itself was empty. It is not splendid, but respectable in appearance, with a general tone of reddish brown in its decorations. There are seats for rather more than three hundred members, in pairs, desks for each pair in front of the seats, with two inkstands sunk in each desk. The President's tribune rises high in the middle of one of the longer sides; below it the tribune from which any orator so minded addresses his fellow-legislators; below that a small desk for the official reporters, of whom four might use it at the same time. On the right of the President are seats for Ministers, also raised above the level of those who are not Ministers; on the left other seats equal in elevation, whether for more Ministers or for ex-Ministers I did not make out. These seats and tribunes fill the whole of one of the longer sides of a hall which is a parallelogram in shape. Seats and desks occupy all the space to the opposite wall, curving in rows so that the occupant may always face the President. There are galleries at either end of these two longer walls; at one end royal and diplomatic boxes, at the other the tribunes of the general public, separated in each case by square pillars and raised well above the level of the house. The seats in the body of the hall are in light brown leather; the walls are painted brown, but of a ruddy hue; the woodwork is everywhere brown; the walls also panelled in brown; the cornice, or rather cove, is in brown, and the roof is in glass more or less painted in brown.

By half-past two some two hundred members have arrived and the public galleries are half full. They remain half full during all the proceedings, which seem to have no great interest for the people of Berlin. Possibly the people of Berlin are aware that this highly respectable Imperial Parliament is not the final arbiter of the destinies of the German Empire, whether for weal or woe. The centre of political power is not here, so the centre of political interest is elsewhere; whether at Charlottenberg with the dying Emperor, or in the Palais Radziwill in the Wilhelmstrasse where lives the Imperial Chancellor, may be a question. It is not here in the Reichstag, at any rate; not even when the Imperial Chancellor puts in a formal appearance. The members have, nevertheless, a business-like look. They are a stalwart body; with for the most part good gray heads on their bodies, and would be the more distinguished in aspect if they wore fewer spectacles. It may be the spectacles which stamp on them as a body a slightly pedantic air, as of a body of professors. The House of Commons looks, even in these degenerate days, like a gathering of men of the world; of men who spend their lives, whether in country or city, on a high level, and who take large views of affairs; with their eyes set well apart in their heads. They have not derived their opinions, Liberal or Tory, from books; they are not parochial. The German analogue for parochial is Particularist. A man who regards the concerns of his own province, or even kingdom, more than he regards the concerns of the Empire, is a Particularist. What business has he in an Imperial Parliament? Yet there are many such; nay, I thought I detected this provincial stamp on some men who would resent the application of such a name to them.

The defect of the Germans, if we are to believe Mr. Matthew Arnold, is a defect of civic courage. Perhaps, but I suspect an American would discover in them a want of practical politics. I do not use that phrase on this occasion as a synonym for "the machine," or anything like it. It is a colloquial way of saying that they are without that political training which comes from long and responsible connection with public affairs, beginning with municipal and ending with imperial affairs. They see the thing next to them with painful distinctness; beyond it, little or nothing. I speak of the average; the best of them belong to a totally different class. But I confess, as I looked upon the Reichstag and thought over the history of its contentions, and of the Prussian and other disputes that had preceded it, it seemed to me an assembly of amateurs. No German Parliament is comparable in efficiency to the House of Commons or to the

Congress at Washington. What is here efficient is the Crown. It is the kingly principle, the imperial principle, by which fifty millions of Germans, though with universal suffrage, and triennial Parliaments, and the power of the purse in their hands, are really governed.

There is time enough for these and other reflections while the House assembles. Nobody seems to know whether Prince Bismarck is coming himself or not. But while the President, who has the air of a man about to deliver a sermon, is conversing sedately with a group of deputies on the steps of his pulpit, a dark young man enters at his right from a door in the rear, and lays a large red portfolio on the shelf in front of the ministerial seat nearest the tribune. Just beneath stands a tall man of slender build, in an undress uniform of dark blue and red, his smooth-shaven face scored all over with fine lines, the nose aquiline and thin, eyes sunken, forehead lofty and broad and deeply thoughtful, a palpable brown wig on his head; the whole figure slightly stooping; an air of refinement and delicate firmness marking him out among the sturdy personages near him. That is the first soldier of Europe, Count von Moltke, and the seat below which he stands is that of Prince Bismarck, who enters a moment later.

It was all but two-and-twenty years since I had seen Prince Bismarck. In 1866 he was fifty-one; he is now seventy-three, wanting some days, and they are years that make a difference. They have left a mark even on this man of iron. He is grayer and stouter, and the lines in his face are as if burnt in; the scars that corroding time has left. They are visible even in his photographs; his scorn of insincerities is far too deep for such flatteries as artists in black and white are wont to practise. They are visible even from the box where I sit, as the light from the ceiling falls full on his upturned face. He strides heavily in; it is but a step from the door to the spot where the scarlet portfolio is waiting for him, but the weight of the step is what first strikes you. It is not lassitude; it is sheer physical

bulk. He stands six feet two, and his frame is the frame of
a giant. He is broad and square in the shoulders and deep
chested; the arms are big; the legs are big; and that part
of the body which is intermediate between the legs and
chest is big, yet not gross. He is as heroic in his physical
proportions as in his character. The head is set on the
shoulders and almost into them with a singular solidity and
closeness. The man is all of a piece; body and mind, as it
were, fused and welded together. Faithful as are many of
the photographs, I remember none which brings out strongly the helmet-shape of the head. It is the head of Pericles:
domelike in its amplitude as well as in its curve, with a
breadth at the temples which its towering height cannot
disguise; and far overhanging the steel-gray eyes, which
look out as from caverns, deep fringed with gray eyebrows.
There is no regularity of feature or of contour. The nose
is short and carelessly moulded; the mouth you must imagine, for a gray moustache shades it; the jaw is the jaw—
well, of Prince Bismarck, and of him alone. The stamp of
power, of irresistible force, is on face and figure; into this
one human form has Nature for once collected all her irrepressible energies, and subdued them to his overmastering
will.

The impression I get as I gaze from a distance only recalls the impression of twenty years ago, when I sat in his
study and listened to him till long past midnight, and mentally noted down features and the fleeting, flashing expressions that lighted them up. The changes are many and
they are nothing; age has brought with it increase of
strength; he looks more like a giant than he did then. He
is in uniform, but not in the white of the cuirassiers, which
is still, I believe, his favourite costume. He wears a single-
breasted, dark blue frock, reaching halfway from the waist
to the knees, silver-buttoned to the throat; collar and deep
cuffs of what, from this distance, looks like tarnished silver
lace, gray in tone, with broad edges of bright yellow. The
star of the Black Eagle glitters on the blue coat, and a

whole tier of other orders stretches clean across the breast. As he opens with his right hand the scarlet portfolio, which contains the royal message, the left rests on his sword hilt,— an attitude that gives rise to reflections. Never, that I heard of, did the Chancellor enter Reichstag or Landtag in any but a soldier's dress; once, at least, I saw him arrive in jack-boots, and even to-day he wears spurs.

It was for the Chancellor that the House had been waiting. As soon as he was in his place the President rang his bell; some brief formalities were briefly got through, and Prince Bismarck was at once on his feet. A murmur of cheers greeted him. With a bow to his audience and another to the President he began reading, holding the message on a folio sheet in his hand. He read in a strong voice, audible everywhere, I judged, throughout the hall; deliberately, with marked emphasis on some sentences. It was the Emperor's first message to the Imperial Parliament; the hand of the Chancellor who counter-signed and now delivered it to its destination visible in every line. What could be more like him than these thanks—"imperial thanks"—offered in the name of the late Emperor to the Reichstag, which had voted those last millions of money and men while the Emperor was still living? The voice rang out clearest of all in the final words, "Trusting in the tried love of the whole people and their representatives for the Fatherland, we leave the Empire's future in God's hand." Cromwellian hypocrisy? Cromwellian if you like, but hypocrisy, no. For if anything be true of this stern statesman, as of his dead master, it is that both of them ever had a simple faith in the God of whom they avowedly stand in fear. "We Germans fear God, and nothing else in the world beside." The confession, and perhaps also the boast, seem to belong to a past age, but of the genuineness of both I, for my part, have no doubt.

The message ended, the scene changed. Prince Bismarck sat down, and the President rose; the deputies still all up-standing as while the imperial message was reading. The Prince sprang up too, and the President spoke briefly. All at once, in the middle of his speech, as he mentioned the Emperor, there came a cry from the body of the hall which seemed like a signal. The President took it up and called, German fashion, for cheers. The whole assembly, raising each man his right arm to its full length, shouted out the deep, guttural "hoch" which does duty for our hurrah. "Again," cried the President, and then, "again," so that the three cheers were duly given, and given with a solid heartiness of voice and manner that befitted the place and occasion — German to the core. I cannot remember to have looked down ever before on a Parliament thus expressing itself in cheers; still less with these strange but fine salutes.

As this scene and the President's brief harangue ended, once more Prince Bismarck rose and, to everybody's delight, began to speak. To everybody's astonishment, also, this Minister of the German Empire appeared all at once as a mouthpiece of Parliaments. He asked leave, in quiet tones, to consider himself charged by the House to communicate the thanks of the Reichstag to those foreign Parliaments which had expressed their sorrow and sympathies in the grief that had fallen upon the German nation. He spoke for not more than three or four minutes, but it was a very different business from the mere reading of the message. Orator, perhaps, he is not, but no man excels him in the faculty of so saying what he wishes as to impress his thought and his will — there is the real point — on his audience. Words are to him weapons. In great crises, they are words which three millions of soldiers are ready to enforce. On an occasion like this, hardly more than ceremonious, there is still the trace of the manner of the master of many legions. Nothing can be said or done at such a time in an ordinary manner. The blackness of death still hangs over Berlin— her streets and the hearts of her people still in mourning; the shadow of a coming tragedy blending with that which is not yet past.

As before, the voice easily filled the hall, and it had that vibration which comes from the direct appeal of one man to many before him. There are hard tones, as you might guess, in Prince Bismarck's register, but it is a full, deep voice, rising and falling not too abruptly, capable of expressing emotion. I have heard it when it sounded like a command for a cavalry charge. When he used to speak to a hostile Parliament, as often befell in old days, it was the hoarse summons of an angry sovereign to his rebellious subjects. To-day, of course, everything goes smoothly. The Prince concerns himself little about gesture or any purely oratorical art. He stands erect behind his closed portfolio. The right hand swings carelessly, almost continually, by his side, the arm at full length, the fingers sometimes contracted, more often loose, and the hand quite open. The left again, all unconsciously, finds its way to the sword hilt. The head is thrown well back. The face is in profile from where I sit, and he looks for the most part straight forward, but turns once or twice to our box, and then the light from his eye, with the light from above glancing on it, is opalescent. Of fatigue or illness I could see no trace. I heard afterward that the Prince was really ill, and that his doctors had given him tonics, or whatever it may have been, to brace him up for this afternoon's work.

He is cheered from time to time. When he sits down a few deputies go up, some of them timidly, to congratulate him. He shakes hands with some of them. One who comes from near the door bows almost to the ground. With him the Prince, who bows in return rather stiffly, omits to shake hands. He tarries a moment in his seat. As he rises the group about him divides swiftly and leaves him an open road to the door. He bows again; one rapid inclination of the head to either side in response to all the salutes, and strides off, still erect, the step firm but not less heavy than when he came, the steel scabbard of his long cavalry sword ringing sharp against the brown oak. The door opens, as a door opens on the stage, wide before him, with invisible hands. He fills it as he passes through; the broad shoulders, the towering form, the kingly head of this king of men are set in a frame for one instant, then vanish. He has done what he came to do: done it in that rapid, workmanlike, decisive way of his; with energy, with authority; done it, though no great matter, once for all, and with the dignity befitting the occasion. Every one feels that in this first message from an Emperor, so soon to be an Emperor no more, there is something solemn, and it has been solemnly delivered. In all, Prince Bismarck has not been twenty minutes in the chamber, but as he passes out it is as if another chapter in history had been transacted—another leaf turned in the book of fate.

COUNT HERBERT BISMARCK.

[BERLIN, *March* 19, 1888.]

NEXT after the Imperial Chancellor, the most interesting personage among German statesmen is his son, Count Herbert von Bismarck, Foreign Minister of the German Empire. He is the rising hope of the Germans; the man to whom they look to continue that imperial policy which his father founded and established; to keep Germany what Prince Bismarck has made her. In the funeral procession of Friday no figure was more remarked. In European politics no Minister is more studied by other Ministers. I suppose even in far-off America, happy enough to concern itself little with the details of European diplomacy, you may like to know what manner of man he is.

Count Herbert has long been known in London, where he was for some years secretary to the German Embassy. He was a favourite in society. The liking of Englishmen for Germans is, as a rule, subject to qualifications. Both in politics and in their personal relations there has long been a kind of friction between these two peoples, so closely connected by race and by their rulers. Perhaps the prejudice which sprang up when the House of Hanover first came to the throne has never died away. No nation really likes being governed by foreign kings and queens. The English have visited this natural resentment on the people from whom for nearly two hundred years they have borrowed their kings and queens. They make exceptions, but then they like a man not because he is a German, but in spite of his being German. Count Herbert von Bismarck was one of the exceptions. Remark also that he went to London at a time when England was getting ready to give up her long coquetry with France, and revert to her natural ally. The English Minister who most decisively turned his face to Germany was perhaps Lord Rosebery, when he held, for all too brief a period, the portfolio of Foreign Affairs in Mr. Gladstone's last Government. And it happens that Lord Rosebery and Count Herbert are intimate friends. The beginnings of the change go farther back; as far as the Congress of Berlin in 1878, when Lord Beaconsfield was indebted in no slight degree to Prince Bismarck for his victory over Prince Gortchakoff.

With all this—all his popularity and all the tendencies of the times—I am not sure that London took Count Herbert very seriously. His reputation there was for a long time a social reputation. The smart world laid hold of him. He belonged, not exclusively, but still belonged, to a set. One of his nearest friends was the present Viceroy of Ireland. Lord Londonderry was not then supposed to occupy himself with politics or to cherish political ambitions. He lived the life which so many others in England, high in rank and social position—two things which by no means always go together—and caring much for amusement, have always led. In their company, and much other like it, the young German was to be seen at races, at parties, in Rotten Row, at Four-in-Hand meets, at the clubs most frequented by the most gilded English youth, at the best houses in town and country alike, whether in England or Scotland. That he was, during this butterfly period, quietly devoting himself to real work may be guessed. He had been the same, or something like it, in Berlin, before he came to London. In that sedate capital, too, Count Herbert—or rumour is a more idle gossip than usual—had found means of enlivening his leisure. Whether in London or Berlin or elsewhere, this butterfly period passed. After he had quitted England his English friends began to perceive that he had destined himself for a serious career. His father had discovered his real abilities. He was sent to the Hague as Minister; a quiet place, with little to do, unless you believe with the French, who will believe anything, that the all-grasping Chancellor was then meditating the absorption of the Netherlands into the German Empire. The Hague, in any case, was a spot from which it was possible for a young man to study Europe and fit himself for the great duties which lay before him.

I had met Count Herbert Bismarck in London, and I had a desire to see him in Berlin in a position and circumstances so totally unlike those of London. He was so good as to lend himself to this wish of mine. If I were to adopt the phrase of the Germans, who take an official and even solemn view of whatever happens in connection with the official world, I should have to say that I had an audience of the German Foreign Minister. The Foreign Office adjoins the Palais Radziwill, where father and son live together. Count Herbert made an appointment to see me at four o'clock Monday afternoon. When I gave my name to the concierge at the gate, I found one more proof of that amazing thoroughness with which here in Berlin the least details are worked out. I have had many appointments during the last week with official personages to whom, under the ægis of the one who became my protector, I had to apply for those favours without which a journalist is helpless. In no case did I ever arrive without finding that my errand had been explained beforehand. In the same way I now perceived that the concierge, and then the ushers in the outer chamber, and then some other higher official, knew that I was coming, and I was passed on from one to the other without a question or any delay. "His Excellency is engaged with the French Ambassador, but will receive you in a moment," was the final message which met me on the threshold.

The threshold was an anteroom where sat two French officers in full uniform, and their presence denoted that it must be General Billot, the special envoy from France sent to attend the Emperor's funeral, who was closeted with the

Minister. The Frenchman came out in five minutes or so: a short, broad, smiling man, with as much gilt lace and as many decorations as it was possible for one man of his superficial area to carry on his person. The smiles, the orders, the bows, the civil speeches he addressed to the Minister, who came out with him, the general glitter of his appearance and amiability of his manner—what could all these mean if not friendly relations between France and Germany? But not on such civilities do the friendships of nations depend. If you do not care about General Billot, albeit a soldier of distinction in his own land, accept him as a contrast, not unkindly, to the more famous German who towers above him. Count Herbert is all in black, morning costume, not a decoration of any kind, not a touch of colour, except the gold pin that fastens his black scarf. He stands well over six feet, and like his father is broad and strong and soldierly in bearing. Dark brown hair and dark brown flashing eyes and sweeping dark brown moustache, straight, strong features, the wide forehead of his father, the Prince, full at the temples like his—these are the things that first strike you.

He begins talking at once, and in English; another point of resemblance to the Prince, whose English is racy and idiomatic, though less fluent than the son's, who has lived in England to some purpose. This talk went on for an hour, with hardly an interruption, and this it is which I should like to repeat to you, but must not, except here and there a sentence. But the impression of it as a whole on the hearer —that I may describe, and it confirms all I have heard in London and here in Berlin of the transformation in Count Herbert. He is, in fact, Foreign Minister and something more. He is Prince Bismarck's right hand, and chief of staff. "My father likes me to help him"—that was his own account of the matter, in the simple, direct speech, going straight to the mark, which characterises these two men; them, and few other Germans. There can be no doubt what this means. The Imperial Chancellor is training his son in the business of governing the German Empire. What a business, and what training! I do not imagine that the Chancellor spares his son more than he spares others under him; probably less; and people in Berlin will tell you that the iron Minister has used up men by the score. What is certain is that he never spared himself. There is no hour of day or night when you may not find him at work. One of the officials nearest him in official rank was asked to dine by a diplomatist. "I cannot," he answered. "I regret to decline, but I am obliged, since I have been in the Foreign Office, to make it a rule to refuse invitations except to Court. I never know at what moment I may be wanted." The business of the State before everything—that is the motto in Germany.

What I heard from such persons likely to know as I have met here is that Count Herbert, who began late, has developed great aptitude for work, and especially for that varied and difficult work which has been his father's for so long a time, and which can only be called governing an empire. It is sometimes said in England that next after the Prime Minister, the most powerful man in the kingdom is the Prime Minister's private secretary. He knows everything, he is in all the secrets, his influence with his chief must be decisive on a vast number of questions, personal questions especially. Well, Count Herbert is Prince Bismarck's private secretary, in this English sense, as well as his colleague in the Ministry. The conduct of foreign affairs, which is his special department, is of course shared with the Chancellor, who indeed may be said to be for many purposes sole Minister. Cabinet, in the English meaning of the word, there is none. An English Prime Minister may be, and sometimes is, voted down in his own Cabinet. The imagination refuses to picture Prince Bismarck as the hero of such a scene. He is much more in the position of the President of the United States, with a group of able clerks about him, adorned with the title of Cabinet Ministers. The will which impresses itself on Germany is the will of a single man. For the despatch of business nothing could be more convenient than this confidential relation of father and son. "You can have no idea," said an ambassador, "how quickly things are done in the Berlin Foreign Office. It is only because Count Herbert is so close to the Chancellor, knows his mind, knows what he wants and does not want, and can and does, if in doubt, consult him instantly." I heard from Count Herbert himself a sort of converse to that remark. He was speaking of Mr. Pendleton. "We see much less of him here at the Foreign Office than we should like. Our relations with your country are so friendly that the interests of Germany and America require little discussion, and Mr. Pendleton is a man of business, and the discussion is soon over." And I heard with pleasure, which all Americans will share, that Mr. Pendleton's diplomatic reputation and social position in Berlin were alike all that he or we could wish.

Of America Count Herbert von Bismarck spoke in the tones of that friendship which is traditional in German diplomacy. With him, at any rate, it is also hereditary, for Prince Bismarck has often expressed it—yes, and proved it more than once. He spoke of the five millions of Germans in America—nay, he was more accurate than that—"nearly five millions" was his phrase—with a double affection; they were both his countrymen and ours. He spoke of the late Emperor and the present; of his father; of his own friends in England; of the tributes that had come from abroad to the memory of the late Emperor, which he warmly acknowledged; and of many other things, all which I must pass over in silence. The stream flowed on full and strong for an hour. He sat at his great desk in the large audience and business room—for it is both in one—masses of urgent-looking papers about him; affairs pressing; but all the while talked with his whole mind and with complete absorption in the one subject that occupied him for the moment. He resembled in that every very able man I have ever met. There can be perhaps no very able man in public life deficient in that power of entire concentration of thought. What he

I.—2

had to say he said with the energy, the deep sincerity which alone makes any serious talk ever effective. Once or twice as he turned in profile the almost hidden mouth and the curves of the sculptured chin had a likeness to Napoleon's—the real Napoleon's. A deep fire burned in the dark brown eyes. He used words in a way which few foreigners ever attain to,—the Emperor's malady, for example, was "such a cowardly disease."

Over and over again, I thought as I listened and looked—Who would recognise the Herbert Bismarck of English drawing-rooms of a few years ago? Great duties, great responsibilities have set their seal upon him, elevated his character, brought out his inner qualities and capacities, done him that service they do to every man whom they do not crush. He may or may not have in him the transcendent genius, the commanding nature and gifts of his father. Time will show, and Count Herbert is still young. But this I will say, that after having met most of the first men in Europe, it seems to me the list has now to be enlarged to include the name of Count Herbert von Bismarck. I saw him on such terms that for the liberty I take in this account of my visit, I owe him excuses. If he will remember that, whether in private or public, he is a great figure in the imperial life of Germany, yet still unfamiliar to those in America for whom I write, he will, I trust, forgive my indiscretions.

THE DISMISSAL OF PRINCE BISMARCK.[1]

I.

WHAT EUROPE THINKS OF IT AND WHAT IT REALLY MEANS.

[LONDON, *March* 22, 1890.]

THERE was a reception on Thursday at the private residence of Sir Philip Currie, the permanent Under Secretary at the Foreign Office. Sir Philip now lives in that mansion opposite Hyde Park, just beyond the Marble Arch, once possessed by the late Mr. Beresford Hope and then known as Arklow House. It was filled on Thursday with the smart London world, including almost every diplomatist, domestic or foreign. I asked one of the most eminent of these latter —not a German—what he thought of Prince Bismarck's retirement. He answered—

"It is a disaster of which we see the beginning. No man can foresee the end."

This wise and experienced Minister expressed in that sentence his own opinion and the opinion of Europe. This opinion of Europe includes even that of France. If Prince Bismarck cares for a tribute to his genius and character and influence, he has but to turn to the French press. He was execrated in France as the Minister who had contrived and accomplished the humiliation of that great country. None

---

[1] These accounts of Prince Bismarck's dismissal, written on the morrow of that event, are conjectural in tone but sprang, nevertheless, from authority which I then thought sufficient, and they have since been confirmed in every essential particular. They have a higher sanction, also, were it permissible to say whose.

the less does France deplore his loss. I quote the two journals which on international questions speak with most weight, *Le Temps* and, pre-eminently, *Le Journal des Débats*. The consequences of Prince Bismarck's resignation are incalculable, says the former. The *Débats* declares that the presence of Prince Bismarck in office was a guarantee for the peace of the world. No finer nor truer homage was ever offered to a departing statesman.

Why does he depart? The murmur of innumerable conjectures has filled Europe for a week. The most plausible and the most foolish guesses are put forward with equal confidence. I omit most of them. If ever the public are allowed to see those eighteen folio pages of large German manuscript in which Prince Bismarck set forth his reasons for resigning, even then they would probably have to read between the lines for the true meaning of what must be one of the most remarkable State papers ever penned. No man is more a master of the difficult art of putting stern purposes into smooth words. It is certain that neither age—Prince Bismarck will be seventy-five next Tuesday week—nor ill-health, though he is a martyr to neuralgia and otherwise far from well, had anything to do with his resignation. His iron frame has long been racked with maladies which never shook his constancy. The political reverses of the last election broke up his majority in the Reichstag. But Prince Bismarck has governed Germany before now, as he governed Prussia before there was a Germany, in the face of a hostile parliamentary majority. The elections, we may be sure, gave him little concern.

He is supposed to have parted company with the Emperor on social questions. Here we get a little nearer to the truth. It is probable, it is almost certain, in spite of some denials which ought to be authoritative but are not, that the Emperor and Prince Bismarck were not at one in that Socialistic policy which the Emperor so suddenly adopted and so rashly proclaimed. M. Clemenceau, with his penetrating perception, has defined the Emperor as a young and restless sovereign, who under his soldier's uniform seems at this moment a prey to the mystical dreams of Christian Socialism. A true description as far as it goes, and it helps to explain the antagonism between this Soldier-Socialist and the Chancellor, whose statesmanship has never been of the stuff that dreams are made of. The Emperor believed that he could control Socialism by putting himself at the head of the Socialist movement. He took command, as he thought, of the Social army when he summoned the Labour Conference at Berlin. Prince Bismarck warned him that he would strengthen, not weaken, a movement which aimed ultimately at subverting Imperial authority. The elections have shown that he was right.

But neither does this disagreement explain Prince Bismarck's decision. If there be any single difficulty or detail to which his resignation can be traced, it is probably the refusal of the Emperor to accept Prince Bismarck's view of the relations between himself as Prime Minister and his colleagues. Prince Bismarck desired the other Ministers to be primarily responsible to him. The Emperor insisted that they were responsible only to the Crown. That difference, technical in form, goes to the root of the difficulty.

For the real question at issue between these two men was which of them should rule Germany. Long ago Prince Bismarck said, "Prince William will be his own Chancellor." He detected—it was not even then difficult to detect—the masterful spirit of the young Prince, between whom and the throne there were then two lives. The prophecy has come true, perhaps a little sooner than its author expected. Others, too, have seen the crash coming. "The next Chancellor crisis," said a well-known diplomatist last autumn, "will be the last." Nor is Prince Bismarck the man for half-measures. He would either govern Germany or not govern it, and his loyalty to his Sovereign is such that he would leave it absolutely to his Sovereign to choose between these two alternatives. The Sovereign has chosen, and the Chancellor disappears.

That is the real truth. It is the simplest solution which is the right one. He who created the German Empire and bore sway over it from the hour of its birth till now, has vanished. Yesterday there was a Prince Bismarck. To-day there is only a Duke of Lauenburg.[1] Yesterday Germany—the Germany of Prince Bismarck—was the arbiter of Europe, the guarantee of the peace of the world. To-day there rises upon the horizon a new Germany, under a new ruler, and no man can predict what the day may bring forth. The first specific danger is the weakening of the Triple Alliance. If it be not weakened its object may be altered. It has been a league of peace; it may become an instrument of war. The German Emperor is before all things a soldier; he is credited with vast ambitions; and his first act is to choose a soldier to conduct his negotiations with Europe.

If General von Caprivi were really Prince Bismarck's successor, the choice would be ominous indeed. But Prince Bismarck leaves no successor. The title of his great office may pass to another, but to transfer his authority in Europe, his prestige, his unrivalled tact, his experience, his commanding influence, is beyond the power of the Emperor. General von Caprivi is reported to be able, versatile, and skilled in business. But he with whom Europe has now to deal is not General von Caprivi, but the Emperor. Youth succeeds to age, the soldier to the statesman, the hereditary to the chosen ruler. For twenty-five years the will of Prince Bismarck has been the most powerful factor in Europe. Yes; but it was an instructed and rational will—a force wielded with an ever-present sense of responsibility. The will of the boy-Emperor, what is that? Who knows? Force of character he has, courage he has; but who answers for his prudence, and what is an experience of eighteen months? What all men see is that he is imperious,

[1] It now seems that, under the strong pressure put upon him by his Imperial master, Prince Bismarck has accepted the Dukedom of Lauenberg. Meanwhile it was the occasion of one of his latest pleasantries—that the name might be useful as an incognito when he was travelling abroad.

domineering, arbitrary even beyond the ordinary Hohenzollern measure; and they ask mournfully, What has he ever said or done that sounds or seems like a guarantee of peace?

True, in one of his two farewell letters to the great Minister whom he dismisses to private life, he has a phrase for peace. "I am resolved," says the Emperor, "to take as the inspiration of my action your wise, energetic, and pacific policy." It is a phrase for which Europe is not ungrateful. But there has been an Emperor before now who said that his Empire was peace. What is best in these Imperial rescripts is their acknowledgment of Prince Bismarck's services. Seldom has a sovereign bowed so low before a subject. Never was any reverence better deserved. The Dukedom of Lauenburg, a Field-Marshalship of the German Army, Imperial homage to him who put the Imperial crown on the first and greatest German Emperor's head— these are all worthy of the Emperor and worthy of Prince Bismarck. But it is the grave fear of Europe for the future which Prince Bismarck is not to guide, that is the loftiest homage of all. It is the admission that his incomparable genius has been beneficent even when it wrought in blood and iron.

II.

THE EMPEROR'S RESOLVE TO RULE ALONE.

[LONDON, *March* 29, 1890.]

The conjectures of last week have become the certainties of this, and it now has to be said that Prince Bismarck was dismissed by the Emperor; not, of course, in terms, but only in fact. Personal relations between the Emperor and the Chancellor are of a kind which excludes the notion of incivilities on either side. But the autocratic young sovereign has many methods at his disposal, any one of which would suffice to relieve him, with every due form of politeness, from any further continuance of services which have become irksome to him.

Many are the stories still current, and many the versions of the incident on which the crisis finally turned. All of them cannot be true, and all of them cannot be without foundation. All point to one conclusion: Prince Bismarck has been sacrificed to the Emperor's ambition, to his passion for personal rule, to his longing for glory, to his belief in his own all-sufficing power of insuring the good of the country, which, for good or for ill, he is resolved to govern alone. Never since William the Second came to the throne has he lost an occasion of making himself seen, heard, and felt, at home and abroad. Undoubtedly he had produced an impression on public opinion. He had persuaded Europe that it had a new force in international politics to deal with, that the young German Kaiser had both character and ability. It was not enough. Between the Emperor and Europe still towered the gigantic figure of the great Chancellor. The servant overshadowed the master, and the master resolved to get rid of the servant. Germany has hitherto meant Prince Bismarck; it was henceforth to mean the Emperor.

What matter the means by which such a change as that is effected? But it is I believe true, as I said last week, that the direct issue between the Emperor and the Chancellor was raised by the Emperor on the question of ministerial responsibility. All Ministers were to report to the Emperor in the first place, and no longer through Prince Bismarck in the first place. The point cannot be made too clearly nor its importance overestimated. Prince Bismarck has been Prime Minister of Germany. He has made and unmade all other Ministers, always observing forms and acting nominally as the agent of the Emperor, but with the real power in his own hands and the real responsibility for everything resting on him. All Ministers have reported to him, and their communications with the Sovereign have been carried on through him. No other system prevailed during the long reign of this boy's grandfather, or the few short months while his father lay on that sick-bed which was his throne. It was under this system first that Prussia became first among the German States, and then that Germany was created, solidified, and established on the rock which is now the immovable foundation of the German Empire.

All this method of doing business presently became odious to this Emperor. He struck at the root of it by insisting that Ministers should send reports to him direct. Prince Bismarck ceased from that moment to be Prime Minister; he became the mere equal of his colleagues, and sank into a mere head of department. He had been Chancellor; he became a clerk. He had ruled the Empire and the Emperor; he was now to be ruled. He preferred resignation to servitude and disgrace, and that is the true history of this crisis.

The existing system being broken up, Prince Bismarck pointed out the impossibility of working the new one. "I, at any rate, cannot work it," he said; and to convince the Emperor of the sincerity of his protest he offered, as it was meant that he should offer, his resignation, which the Emperor instantly and eagerly accepted.[1] The past services of his foremost subject, the coming perils to his country, counted for nothing with this imperial egotist. Here was the man who stood in his way. He must go. He is gone, and all the sunlight there is falls full and falls fiercely on the headstrong boy who wears the German crown, with no Bismarck to intercept its rays or to reflect its splendour.

You will look in vain in German papers for the facts. There have been hints of the truth, but the penalties for telling too much truth in Germany are heavy, and even private speech is fettered. "Do not come to Berlin now," writes a friend; "no man here, even to his wife, dare say what he thinks. The little Emperor hears every word uttered by the humblest." It was said elsewhere that Berlin received the

---

[1] The Emperor sent twice to Prince Bismarck's residence to demand his resignation in writing. It had, at first, been tendered orally.

news of the Chancellor's fall with indifference. "Oh no!" says another friend, in his German way. "It was a thunder-stroke which left us stunned."

By last Wednesday the Berliners had recovered a little, and I suppose the Emperor himself heard the cheers which saluted Prince Bismarck as he passed to and from the Palace for his last audience before his final retirement to Friedrichsruh. Multitudes filled the streets and thronged about the Palace gates, and about the gates of that other palace in the Wilhelmstrasse which has been the Chancellor's home but is his home no longer. They saw him come out from his leavetaking of the Emperor; erect and smiling, say the papers, and there are inane inferences that the interview must have been agreeable. Do people suppose Prince Bismarck the kind of man who wears his heart upon his sleeve for these and other daws to peck at? The parting was decorous, and perhaps something more, for even an Emperor is human and he was parting with the subject to whom he owes it that he is Emperor.

Prince Bismarck said in 1866: "You in America cannot understand how deep is that loyalty which I feel to my Sovereign." We may be sure that he feels it still, amid all the just resentment, the righteous anger, the forebodings, the anxious doubts that fill the mind of the pilot who quits his ship with the breakers all about her. A Prussian is quite capable of cursing his Kaiser one moment and kneeling to him the next. But as between Emperor and Chancellor, whether in the Royal Palace or the palace in the Wilhelmstrasse, it is certain no high words passed. Events are not transacted in that way. If all the world had been admitted to this last interview they would have seen a piece of high comedy well acted, and nothing more. The tragedy is acted in private only, but nobody need be misled because appearances are kept up.

Europe looks on and wonders that Prince Bismarck is allowed to fall with so few demonstrations of gratitude or regret from his own countrymen. Parliament meets and adjourns day by day without a word.¹ There is no stir in any great German city nor any sign of protest among the German people. The baser souls rejoice. The Emperor, whose voice is never long silent, cries aloud that the course of the ship is still the same, so "Full steam ahead!" Yes, the course may be the same but not the hand that steers the ship, and the boldest hold their breath. The perils that beset Germany at this moment are internal rather than external. There are forces at work which threaten disintegration to the Empire. The young Emperor thinks it wise to encourage them, heeds no warning, despises all counsel but his own, takes no thought of the past, and believes in a future guided by himself as vicegerent of God on earth. A monarch in that mood is himself the greatest peril to his country.

Count Herbert Bismarck's resignation followed naturally upon that of his father. He had been his father's right-hand man, and was looked to as his successor in some distant future. He was personally liked by the Emperor and was trusted in business. It does not seem to have occurred to the Emperor that Count Bismarck would stand or fall with his father. "Why not stand or fall with me?" his wondering majesty is reported to have asked. He held out against the son's resolve to share the father's fate, offered him leave of absence, and declined to accept his resignation. But the Count was firm, and the Emperor at last had to own that fidelity to a father might be as strong a motive as loyalty to a sovereign.

Finally, it is the hour for us Americans once again to remind ourselves of one other thing; that Prince Bismarck has been a steadfast friend to America through his whole public career. He kept Prussia benevolently neutral when Napoleon tried to organise a European cabal in favour of the Southern Confederacy. But for Prince Bismarck in Germany and Disraeli in England, that perfidious scheme might have succeeded. "I never would listen to it," said Prince

---

¹ The Reichstag has since found courage to express its regret.

Bismarck. "When the Emperor asked my counsel I set my face against it as an act of enmity to the United States, and I had only to remind the King that friendship with the United States was a policy traditional with Prussia from the day of Frederick the Great." In lesser matters he was equally staunch. He renounced and rebuked his own officer in Samoa sooner than tolerate acts leading to a possible quarrel with the United States, and his hand is visible throughout the Samoan Treaty; a hand then, as ever, outstretched in cordial goodwill to America and Americans.

THE GERMAN EMPEROR:

HIS NOTIONS OF DIVINE RIGHT, OF INFALLIBILITY, OF SOCIAL-
ISM, AND OF PILOTING A SHIP.

[LONDON, *May* 31, 1890.]

MINGLED with those expressions of sympathy for the German Emperor which his accident on Sunday has called forth are some other expressions which, if he read or heard them, he would hardly think sympathetic. The cheapest moral is drawn first, that an Emperor who cannot drive an English gig may yet overturn the coach of state. Even that would not have been said a year ago. But a good deal has happened since last spring, and other illusions than those cherished by Prince Bismarck have melted away. It is still the fashion to offer compliments in public, but no longer compliments only. Never, probably, since the world began has there been a people so ready with its advice to the rest of the Universe as the English. The boy-Emperor of Berlin is now coming in for his share. He is told this morning rather solemnly that he talks too much—an opinion from which nobody is likely to dissent—and especially that he talks too much about Divine Right. He said at Königsberg—

"We Hohenzollerns accept our crown only from Heaven, and are responsible to Heaven only for the performance of its duties. I, too, am animated by this view, and am resolved to act and to govern on this principle."

How strangely it sounds in our American ears; less strange to Europeans in general; least strange of all to the Germans. It is not the principle which the Germans object to; it is the continual assertion and reassertion of it by their Emperor which is beginning to tell upon their heretofore somewhat leathery nerves. "The Teutons," said a Frenchman, "have no nerves; they have sinews." They are beginning to have nerves; the sinews are beginning to vibrate. This Imperial voice echoes through the Fatherland day and night like the shriek of a railway whistle. "If he were so sure of his Divine Right would he think it needful to say so much about it?" asks one humble student of imperial human nature. Probably he is sure of it. Whether he is sure that others are sure of it, is another question.

Sure or not, their faith will hardly be strengthened by these ear-piercing blasts on the Imperial trumpet. No political observer has yet proclaimed his belief that the throne of the Hohenzollerns is tottering. But if it were, would it be long upheld by these Imperial methods? They are the methods now in common use to spread the sale of a particular soap. A Tory journal sees fit to remark that this young man has adopted the pushing, self-advertising ways of an American candidate for office. It tempts one to stop long enough to ask whether English candidates for office are pre-eminently distinguished by retiring modesty; long enough but not longer. A sense of humour is not a German, any more than it is a French, characteristic. There are Frenchmen who have it and there are Germans who have it. In each case they are the exceptions. But a sense of humour is one thing, and sensitiveness to ridicule is another.

The ridicule heaped on this boisterous Emperor has hitherto been confined, for the most part, to the Chancelleries of Europe, to Courts, to Cabinets; but in those high precincts it has never been silent since the date of the Imperial visits to St. Petersburg, to Constantinople, to Vienna, and elsewhere. In vain did Prince Bismarck warn his master. The master was too headstrong to accept a warning from anybody, or to believe in anybody's wisdom but his own. Go he would, and did. The visits were so many failures; each for a different reason, but each decisively a failure.

The statesmen and diplomatists, the sovereigns and courtiers of Europe, looked on at first with amazement, then with derision at this unheard-of spectacle. By the time the German Emperor had completed his tour he had sown the seeds of distrust of himself and his policy broadcast over Europe. Some fell by the wayside in Germany as he came and went, and they too are springing up and blossoming and ripening rather rapidly into a kind of fruit such as no man likes the taste of in his own mouth. And now, while this singular harvest is coming to maturity, the Sower of it has already another crop in the ground.

The doctrine of Infallibility is a perilous one even for a Pope. For an Emperor it is certainly more perilous. He must be, as Cardinal Newman said of the greater potentate, not merely infallible, but infallibly certain that he is infallible. And the domain of Papal infallibility, even as matter of dogma, is confessedly limited. The German Emperor clearly believes his to be unlimited. You must go very far back into history before you can hear such a voice as this at Königsberg:—

"I am in a position to make the welfare of every individual and every Province in my Kingdom my own care. I know very well where in each case the shoe pinches, and what has to be done for you, and I have formed my plans accordingly."

What is that but the attitude of an all-wise and all-powerful Providence? Yet William the Second of Germany is, after all, human. His divine commission may confer on him some of the attributes of Divinity but not Divinity itself. When, therefore, he presents himself to his people in this omniscient and omnipotent character, he gives rise to expectations which he may find it difficult to fulfil. He has perhaps already discovered some of the inconveniences attaching to the part he plays. The Labour Conference answered neither to the anticipations of its august author nor to those of the German Socialists. He was prepared to be, for certain purposes and to a certain extent, their leader. They were prepared to accept him as a leader, but on condition that he should make himself known first as a Convert. There is nothing novel in the character of Convert. Mr. Gladstone—another great man who has notions about the delegation of Divine authority—has figured as a Convert for the last four years. But the Emperor declined the rôle offered him. His Labour Conference came to nothing, and Prince Bismarck has said nothing better adapted to anger his Imperial master than when he described the summoning of that European assemblage as a *coup d'épée dans l'eau*.

Yet, failure as that was, the confident young Kaiser launches the phrase above quoted with a cheeriness of demeanour that might have been justified, though hardly, if success and not failure had attended his previous effort. Such a speech will again be thought by the poorer classes to range the Emperor on their side. The effort of Socialism, of German Socialism most of all, is to take from those who have and give to those who have not. That is, in effect, what the poor will understand their present ruler to mean. When Faust wants money and applies to the Devil, and gets it, and presently discovers that the Devil has plundered an old woman in his behalf, and remonstrates, His Satanic Majesty replies with coolness and force that he cannot create money, and that if he pays Peter he must rob Paul to do it.

It is a reflection which disturbs no Socialist; it is the basis, for example, of Mr. Henry George's whole scheme of social ethics and social progress. The Emperor has simply aroused hopes which he will find it impossible to gratify, and stirred passions which he will vainly strive to allay except by methods akin to those of the Devil and of Mr. Henry George. What he would give to one he must first take from another. He certainly does not mean to do anything of the kind. He would no more undertake anything in the nature of a redistribution of property than intrust the keeping of order in Berlin last May to the workmen on strike. But he alarms society and he exasperates the enemies of society at the same time. There is not a Minister in Europe who would applaud such a policy as that; not a tyro in politics who does not perceive how foolish it is.

The Königsberg discourse is, on the whole, the least wise of the many which it has pleased the present Majesty of Germany to deliver; the impression made by it the most unfavourable to him. Taken with all that has gone before, it produces a feeling of uneasiness none the less real because so little is said about it. The Emperor is thought to have ability and nobody denies to him great powers of work, genuine patriotism, sincerity of purpose, devotion to his business of governing, and great aptitude for the administrative parts of it. But he is regarded as a sovereign who is swayed by his impulses and not as one who acts from well-considered and settled principles. To remove the distrust he has roused nothing less would be adequate than long years of prudent rule.

You remember Mr. Tenniel's cartoon in *Punch*, "Dropping the Pilot." Prince Bismarck, in cap and pilot coat, is going down the ladder of the great ship; the Emperor looking over the side. Seldom if ever has Mr. Tenniel drawn a finer picture. The face and figure of Prince Bismarck are full of strength and nobility; the grave, manly feeling and character are depicted with astonishing dignity and force. The little Emperor looks more little than ever as he peers over the rail, the Imperial crown on his head, a smirk of complacent satisfaction on his features. The whole story is told with a degree of imaginative power of which Mr. Tenniel is capable, and I know not who else. Prince Bismarck saw it and was pleased, which was natural. But the Emperor also saw it and was pleased; and it is a revelation of his true nature that he should have found pleasure in it. To the pathos of the situation, to its tragic meaning, to its reproach upon his own flightiness and self-sufficiency, he was insensible. He thought himself the chief figure, he was the captain, his great Chancellor but a mere pilot after all, and he had sent him about his business. You can almost see the movement of the lips ready to cry out, "Full steam ahead!" His infatuation is complete.

LÉON GAMBETTA.

[LONDON, *January* 2, 1883.]

GAMBETTA was the one man of great position in France who had in a supreme degree the saving grace of common sense. Nothing is so rare in a country where politics are conducted on straight lines. Now, if ever, is the moment to repeat the saying of one of the few Frenchmen who had an eye for the essential faults of his compatriots. "The greatest service," said he, "that could be done to France would be to abolish out of the language two words—*logique* and *principe*." The latter word does not, or in his mouth did not, signify principle, but the formula. When a Frenchman talks of a *principe*, he means some neat phrase in which he has embodied for the moment his most eager prejudice and his most damaging criticism on his nearest foe. Then it serves him for a rule of conduct, usually with disastrous results. He is the slave of it, and there is not much good in being the slave of anything. Gambetta was the one French statesman who understood what Burke meant when he said that the essence of politics is compromise. In France, and in the master hand of the great man who is dead, it became Opportunism. No word has brought greater reproach on him. It ought to be inscribed on his tomb as an epitaph and a eulogy.

In different words but in a similar sense I once heard Gambetta pronounce his own eulogy and the summary of his character. The memory of it goes back to the days when Gambetta was perhaps at his greatest, not to 1870 and 1871—to the period of his Dictatorship and his heroic resistance to what he knew was inevitable defeat—but to the days when he organised France against the Reactionist conspiracy of the Seize Mai. In those memorable months from May to November 1877, it was he, as Carlyle said not more truly of Mirabeau, who, when old France was shaken from its basis, as if with his single hand held it toppling there, still unfallen. It was the one hour of deadly peril through which the French Republic has passed, and this one man saved it from utter wreck. The elections of October were his work. The majority was his majority, the 363 Republicans of the Assembly were his men. So well did Messrs. de Broglie and Fourtou know where their danger lay that they set even the criminal law in motion against Gambetta. Long afterward the Duc de Broglie was asked if he really meant or expected to convict and imprison the Republican chief for saying that Marshal MacMahon must either submit to the will of France or resign. "Certainly," answered the Duke. "But with what object?"—"I meant to fasten on him the stigma of legal guilt, and so discredit him that he should become thereafter *un homme impossible.*"

As it turned out, it was not Gambetta but the Duc de Broglie who became impossible. When the Assembly met in November, the conspirators knew that there remained to them but one resource, a *coup d'état;* and to that Marshal MacMahon could not be brought to consent. The step resolved on by Gambetta to turn out the Ministry was a motion for a commission of inquiry into the acts of Ministers. On that motion a four days' debate took place, and on the fourth day it was closed by a speech from the Duc de Broglie and a reply from Gambetta. The Assembly at that time was sitting at Versailles. Half Paris streamed out to the portals of the palace. The streets of Versailles were filled with troops. The doors of the palace were guarded. Deputies had to make their way between files of soldiers, and the soldiers at that time were believed to be ready to act against the Assembly if only a leader could be found. Gambetta himself was supposed to be in danger of military arrest. The project of seizing him had been discussed and put aside as too full of peril. Even M. de Fourtou, resolute as he was unscrupulous, did not care to have all Paris on his hands.

I had met Gambetta a day or two before in one of the street cars which plied between the railway station and the palace, and Louis Blanc had introduced me to him. I asked him about the debate and he told me that if I wanted to hear him I should have to stay over the week—"supposing I am allowed to speak." When the day came the throng at Versailles was great, the difficulty of approaching the doors was extreme. I had a promise of a seat, but no ticket, and without a ticket nobody was allowed to pass. On ordinary days, and during all previous days of this debate, the public had been permitted to enter freely as far as the anteroom of the Chamber. Finally a deputy took me under his protection, and by dint of some parleying with the officer in command we got past the bayonets.

There had not been such a day in France since the Convention, or since the 18th Brumaire. That day's vote was to decide whether the Republic should go to pieces and some despotism or other be set up on its ruins. That the vote would be against the Ministry was known, but whether the Ministry and Marshal MacMahon would submit was not known. In the tribunes not a seat was vacant. In the corridors and bureaux of the Chamber the excitement was at fever heat. Deputies, journalists, Ministers, great bankers, ambassadors, generals, senators, were gathered in knots, and the din of talk was tremendous. Outsiders were offering £20 for a place to hear. It was by sheer good luck and the unwearied kindness of an editorial friend that I found a seat just as the President's bell rang. M. Grévy, now President of the Republic, that day preserved to him by the man he has since but ill-requited, was then President of the Assembly.

The Duc de Broglie mounted the pulpit which the French call a tribune as soon as some formal business was over, and spoke for an hour and a half. Gambetta was in his seat, never quiet for an instant. Some colleague or other was always coming up to him, a few words were exchanged, the great man rolled about in his chair, gestured, gesticulated, every movement full of intense energy. Twice or thrice he interrupted the Duc de Broglie, whose elocution, like his diction, was measured, elaborate, every effect calculated in advance. Refined in manner, intellectual, cultured, cold, malignant, the Duke was precisely the opponent to rouse Gambetta. As he was descending the stairs on the right of the tribune, Gambetta, shouldering his way through the cluster of deputies at the foot, was already mounting on the left. Once in the tribune he had directly confronting him, in the hemicycle beneath and on the first bench, the whole body of Ministers whom he was about to assail and overthrow.

The Chamber echoed for some minutes with cheers. The Right cheered the orator who had just finished. The Left and Left-Centre, on that day united by a common danger and perfectly at accord, applauded Gambetta; there was a stir and movement everywhere, and through the closely packed galleries ran murmurs almost loud enough to be called cheers. Gambetta waited. He looked to better advantage in the tribune than anywhere else. You no longer observed his want of commanding stature, the heaviness of his figure about the waist, or the coarseness of his complexion and hands, which in the distance looked merely high coloured. The broad shoulders were those of a giant, and the powerful head rose well out of them, albeit in common attitudes his neck seemed short. The head was thrown back, the blood ran freely through the arteries which feed the brain, the long black hair fell low, the single eye glowed and flamed. If ever there was a born orator, a man with authority and sympathy, here he was.

With the first note of that mighty voice the vast audience grew still. Almost the first word, as I recollect the opening sentence, was a blow. The speech of the Duc de Broglie had been a singularly ingenious and totally misleading version of the policy and purpose of his Ministry. Gambetta pierced the fine-spun net with a word—*son très habile et très perfide discours*—and the house thrilled to the word *perfide*, which everybody felt exactly characterised the Duke's performance. It went to the verge of parliamentary permissibility, but it was not challenged. Then came an apostrophe to the Duke. You pretend to serve a cause but how have you served it? When you set your foot on France, when for five months you left no art untried to corrupt, oppress, terrify, and coerce the electors of every department, did you think what a heritage of infamy you would leave to your children? You stand here to-day to defend it—*il vous est facile d'apporter ici avec votre élégance de grand seigneur vos épigrammes longuement préparées*—but it is to France you have to answer, and epigrams are not enough. And then came the sentence I referred to above as Gambetta's own account of himself: *Je suis un homme de mon temps; vous n'êtes pas un homme de votre temps.*

And so he went on, the speech gathering in volume and force as it proceeded. Gambetta in his quieter moments was rapid enough; he spoke in public and in private with extreme velocity, but when he became impassioned the words followed each other at such a pace that only the singular distinctness of his articulation made them audible at all. The voice was sonorous, full, and varied; liable, like Mr. Bright's, to become husky, but while at its best, musical and deep. The gesture was large and free, sometimes violent; not always stately but always significant and despotic. When he was roused the movement of the head became frequent, the hair was tossed away from the forehead, the chin was uplifted, the nostrils expanded like those of a man who opens his lungs to a fresh breeze. That piercing glance swept from side to side and missed nothing as it roamed over the upturned faces. The Monarchists on the right had shown themselves disposed at first to interrupt, but of interruption Gambetta, contrary to his habit, would take no notice other than a defiant and scornful look. So presently that section of the hall grew quiet again.

The one great storm which broke out was toward the

middle of the speech. During the long contest Gambetta had somewhat confidently foretold the election of the full number of Republican deputies to whom the party stood pledged, 363. When the returns came in, the number proved considerably less—I think in all 310. As the orator touched upon the figures he was taunted with this falling off. Without an instant's pause he flung the answer full in the face of the Ministers who sat in front of him. "True; but we failed to allow for fraud and robbery"—of the ballot boxes, that is. The whole Right rose in tumult. But Gambetta for once was cool. He leaned back against the President's tribune behind him, squared his shoulders, said not a word, and regarded the raging sea beneath him. Far on the back bench somebody was heard shouting at the top of his voice some insulting epithet. "That, perhaps, is a deputy for Vaucluse who interrupts," cried Gambetta. And it was. The frauds and ministerial pressure had notoriously been more flagrant in the Vaucluse than in any other department. The four deputies elected were nobodies, and new men, but Gambetta in these first few days of the session had found time to make himself acquainted with the faces of his foes, and so turned on them with a retort the more crushing because of the civil scorn with which it was uttered. That of itself is no bad specimen of the immense pains he took to master the political facts of every new situation.

The speech was but just over an hour long. I have always been disposed to think it the greatest single effort of oratory I ever heard. Five years have passed and the impression is hardly less vivid in my own mind than it was the next day, though I am only too well aware that the difficulty of conveying it to others is much greater with the lapse of time. The broad outlines one can still reproduce; the more delicate lights and shades of that strangely picturesque scene are hardly to be caught. I asked Gambetta's friends who had heard him often if he had ever made a greater speech. "Never," was the uniform answer. He was then thirty-nine years old and his oratory answered exactly and fully to that maxim of the great orator of Greece who demanded first, second, and third as the condition of successful speaking—energy. But I don't conceive that any of us at the moment thought of Gambetta as an orator. No critical attitude could be taken or kept till afterward. It is not meteorological observations that you care about at the height of a hurricane in mid-Atlantic. The consummate art, the finish of diction, the argumentative weight, the perfection of delivery and method of the speech, became impressive to you after the speech was done. But at the moment it was the tremendous sincerity, earnestness, and force of the man which absorbed everything else. It was not a debate, it was a battle, and this man was leading the legions of France, his life in his hand, and the life of the Republic bound up with his. That crowded and brilliant assembly, those benches where sat the deputies of the Republic, those galleries where the beauty and chivalry of France, her youngest loveliness and her oldest nobility, were gathered—over all these passed the spell of that resistless eloquence and far more resistless force of character, and of that all-surrendering devotion which during that hour inspired orator and audience alike.

I will add this only, that the speech, though devoted to the destruction of a corrupt Ministry and so necessarily aggressive in form, contained a programme. Gambetta never was content with mere criticism, which he pronounced sterile, however useful. His mind was constructive. He said of himself, "I am a man of government. A year of real power is worth more than a life of opposition." He hungered for power, and his enemies, of whom no man had more, accused him of ambition. No doubt he was ambitious, but his ambition was to make a free and powerful France, independent of King or Pope, self-teaching and self-governing. And nothing in this magnificent speech was more obviously genuine and more terrible to its victims than the final sentence in which he denounced the guilty schemes of the Duc de Broglie as the offspring of personal and selfish lust for rule: "Yours is not ambition of power; it is gluttony of office."

Well, he is dead. He leaves behind him men of ability, of experience, of knowledge, strong Ministers, adroit politicians, leaders of this section and that, in his own party and in other parties. But the one statesman in whom capacity for affairs was blended with profound views, dies with Gambetta. The little house at Ville d'Avray holds all there was in France of real political genius. His disappearance changes the face of European politics and diplomacy, and there is but one other man of whose death the same could be said. It is not the hour to draw a parallel between Gambetta and Bismarck, but I suppose Frenchmen will consider, and rightly consider, that among the many tributes offered to Gambetta none is more striking than Prince Bismarck's avowed conviction that Germany is safer to-day because Gambetta is dead. The Dictator of Tours had done his work; the new chief of the Republic, it is certain, would never have suffered France to enter upon her war of revenge at an inopportune moment. It is equally certain that he would not have suffered her to falter when the moment came. His voice would have been the trumpet note heard in every corner of her territory. His policy, whether foreign or domestic, never lost sight of that one ultimate aim which every Frenchman cherishes, and which he has done so much to make possible.

It is far more honourable to Gambetta that he was dreaded by one set of his own countrymen as much as by the Germans. The Socialistic Communism of France once looked to Gambetta as its leader in a war against property and society. The chiefs of that gang have avenged their stupid mistake by an implacable animosity. Probably nothing has done more to enlarge the confidence of wise and honourable men in Gambetta than the vindictive calumnies and insults of M. Rochefort and his accomplices. Gambetta, in fact, was always for legal means and patriotic ends. In opposition under the Empire his counsels were steadily against violence. Many years later, by way of antidote to his misunderstood remark about the *nouvelles couches sociales*, he said, "There is no social question; there are social questions." His career is cut short, as Mirabeau's was, but his life was long enough to save the honour of his country, to secure by incredible exertions and skill the legal establishment of the Republic in 1875; to protect that Republic, as we saw, against what but for him would have been a successful conspiracy against it two years later. Perhaps he did a still greater service when he uttered the phrase which for the rest of the century to come will be the motto of French Liberals: *Le clericalisme —voilà l'ennemi.* For it is to Gambetta more than to any one else that France, awakening to new life in a generation educated by State schoolmasters, will owe her emancipation from the rule of the Romish priest.

LOUIS BLANC.

[LONDON, *January* 16, 1883.]

IF ever a man lived free from stain, it was he who has just died. All his life long the fierce light of passionate political, and still more passionate social controversies beat upon him. He made innumerable enemies; he was the object of innumerable calumnies. Not one of his enemies hated the *man*, not one of the calumnies touched his private worth. He plunged into every conflict of his time. From the first he made himself felt as a formidable antagonist. He attacked with fearlessness the classes and creeds which were then, and still are, the most powerful in modern life. His criticisms went to the root of the existing social organisation, which he strove to dissolve and reconstruct. His theories were destructive to the idea of property as at present held, and to the processes by which property is accumulated. For forty years he was a foe to every government and form of government which maintained its power in France. Even after 1870, which saw a Government republican in form rise on the ruins of the Empire, Louis Blanc preserved his attitude of reserve and distrust. It was a Republic, but it was not his Republic. And again, after the Constitution had been voted which baptized the new *régime* and gave it the sanction of the coveted name Republican, it was not socialistic and therefore not to his mind. So late as the autumn of 1877, after the decisive overthrow of the royalist conspiracy which went by the name of the Seize Mai Ministry, with the Duc de Broglie at its head, I heard Louis Blanc say, "Yes, thank God for the defeat of that intrigue, but it is only the beginning of the end." And not long after: "Wait till we get a real Republic; then you'll see what we shall do." The Extreme Left, the group to which he has always belonged in the Chamber and of which he was president, is a minority, and necessarily a minority. It has practically been in opposition to every Republican Ministry, which has not prevented it from saving many of those Ministries at critical moments from disaster. Louis Blanc allowed himself in most cases to vote with his colleagues, but if the vote involved upholding a policy or a measure which he thought unsound, the utmost pressure had to be used to secure his adhesion. If he had followed his inclinations he would have let any Ministry go to pieces sooner than swerve a hair's breadth from his loyalty to the most abstract principle. The doctrine of Opportunism was distasteful to him, yet he lent a substantial support to M. Gambetta, with whom he had, at any rate, among other points of sympathy, a hearty detestation of clericalism.

Thus he had against him from the beginning to the end, Government, Society, the Church. He was hated and feared. His pen was never idle; his books, his letters, his newspaper articles were read from one end of France to the other. His voice, while it was allowed to be heard in his own country, had an echo from every quarter. He was never forgotten and could never be despised. All possible means were used to discredit and crush him. But none of his enemies was quite stupid enough to suppose that any disparagement of Louis Blanc's private character would find credit with the people.

But that merely spotless purity is, after all, negative. He had much more than that. He had the most positive private virtues. He was not only unselfish, he was generous in a rare degree. He was devoted to something more than an idea. He became the benefactor of those whose place in the world and share of the world's possessions was less than in his view it ought to be. He never thought it enough to plead their cause; to devote his life to their advancement.

Always a poor man, he gave lavishly. I do not think he always gave wisely. Nobody who knocked at his door was ever sent empty away.

He gave on a much greater scale than this, and with prodigal recklessness of his own interests. A story of his financial experience with his *History of the French Revolution* will show to what lengths he allowed his sympathies with the supposed troubles of others to carry him. He made a contract with a publisher for 300,000 francs, out of which a certain sum was to be paid him yearly; the balance on the conclusion of the work. After some years the publisher came to him with a pitiful story of depression in business, lessening sales of the early volumes, and loss of all profit; in short, he declared that the price first offered was greater than the publication could support, and besought Louis Blanc to forego 100,000 out of the 300,000 francs. A cooler piece of impudence would perhaps be found with difficulty in the annals of the publishing trade. Legal claim this man of business had none; of morality the less said the better. But it was precisely the sort of appeal which Louis Blanc could not resist; an appeal (no matter how unfounded) at once to his sympathies and his sense of justice. He assented, and with a stroke of his pen made M. Pagnerre, then a rich man, a free gift of the 100,000 francs. I believe I am right in saying that Louis Blanc had not at that moment a dollar in the world except what he was earning from day to day. Emboldened by his success the man of business presently made another attempt, repeating the old story, and finally inducing his victim to abandon another large sum to him— either another 100,000 francs or 50,000. And so it happened that when Louis Blanc had finished his great work, to which he devoted eighteen of the best years of his life, he was not a penny the richer for it. He had parted with his property in the book, and he had received during the writing of it just enough to keep body and soul together.

Charles Sumner used to say that the first volume of this History was one of those profoundly philosophical studies which mark an epoch in literature and in the development of human intelligence. Nobody had traced the causes of the Revolution to their deeper sources, or with such wide knowledge of men, events, books, and the movement of thought. Of the later volumes, the other eleven, it is to be said that they contain a fuller narrative of events than any other single history then written. But like every other French history of that period, it is a pamphlet. Louis Blanc, by some strange caprice of Fate, became the apologist of Robespierre, and his History is Robespierrist throughout. He does full justice to no one else, and he does far more than justice to the man who, in his eulogist's conception, was the incarnation of the revolutionary spirit. Starting with a preconception of this sort, he has written a misleading book. He does not so much defend the worst acts of Robespierre—for example, the Orange Commission, the Loi du 22 prairial, the murders of Danton and the Dantonists—as colour them, and too often deny Robespierre's responsibility for them or culpability for them. The book must be read, therefore, with constant reference to the writer's prepossessions and with unfailing caution on the part of the student. But it must be read.

So must many other books of his, and among them the three collections of his *Letters on England*. These cover a large portion of the time he spent here in exile. They deal for the most part—as the conditions of French journalism, which is, in its best mood, really more serious than almost any other, permitted them to deal—with subjects of more than ephemeral interest. He made a study of England; knew its history, social organisation, and current daily life, both political and personal, as few foreigners have known it. His letters are composed with the care he gave to everything he wrote—never slovenly, or hurried, or superficial, or gossiping. There are, on the whole, perhaps no ten volumes about England more instructive, nor many more readable.

I first met Louis Blanc soon after I came to live in London, and the friendship which grew up between us lasted without a break till his death. His life in London was the life of a student. He passed the day among his books in the quiet little house in Upper Montagu Place, or in the British Museum. It was in the Museum that he wrote his *History of the French Revolution;* and there alone, he used to say, could the Revolution be fully studied. Beginning with the collection made by John Wilson Croker, and sold by him when he found himself forestalled by Alison in his project of a history of that period, the Museum has since bought pretty much everything it could lay hands on. It has a mass of rare pamphlets and contemporary literature not to be found in the National Library at Paris. It has not, of course, the archives which repose in the various departments of State, and the want of acquaintance with them is evident in Louis Blanc's work. I suppose he might have returned to Paris if he had wished, but nothing would induce him to set foot on French soil so long as it lay under the yoke of Napoleon the Third. It was the Republic of '48 which had driven him from France but it was the Bonapartist Empire for which he reserved all his resentment. He pardoned the injustice done to himself; the outrage upon his beloved France he would pardon never.

That will serve as well as anything for the keynote to his public character, or to one rare and attractive side of his character. He was the most disinterested of men. His great fame has been won by a life filled with sacrifices, one after the other, of almost everything that brings fame to a man. It is not that he was careless of honour and reputation or ever affected a superiority to applause. He valued it, coveted it, hungered for it, and sacrificed it all the same. Praise pleased him as it pleases a child, as it pleases most simple natures. But with a passion for popularity he was for ever doing, and consciously doing, the most unpopular acts. By birth he belonged to the upper middle class, and his life was given to strengthening the hands of a class below his own, intensely hostile to it, whose idea of rising is to pull down whatever is above it. The bent of his mind was naturally toward culture. Nobody could have made more admirable contributions to purely elegant literature; nobody was more academic, more capable of the last refinements and polish which are the results of a leisure devoted to making the most of one's natural gifts. But from his first article in a newspaper to the last page of his History he made himself the servant of an idea. He was fond of society, of salons, of conversation, of art, and he turned away from them all to preach a gospel which in the hands of less scrupulous practitioners would surely put an end to them all.

His socialism—for I may as well say the inevitable word about it at once—was very far-reaching in theory, yet with him I always thought it less theoretic than sympathetic. In his stringent analysis of the existing social structure he found faults enough, and not in the structure only but in the whole scheme and idea which were the foundation of it. He had drunk deep at the half-poisoned fountain of Rousseau. He thought for himself, boldly, clearly, with singular power of logic, with endless critical ingenuity, and his socialism, as I said above, was essentially of a destructive kind. He would not have destroyed a fly himself; he invariably refused to apply on any great scale the subversive principles he announced in his books. He never foresaw and hardly ever admitted the consequences which others drew from them, and the results to which his so-called disciples would have made them contribute. What in truth underlay these utopian speculations was not so much a reasoned conviction as a passionate pity. He could not witness the misery of the poorer classes without longing to relieve it. His books on social questions were a cry of distress. When his heart was touched his head became its instrument. No doubt he had argued himself into the belief that the organisation of society was radically faulty and radically unjust. He described himself as hungering for justice, and it was a true description. But a passion for all the gentler virtues lay just as deep in his being. Charity, mercy, infinite compassion and affection for whoever was weaker or poorer or less gifted and happy than himself were the constant motives of his acts and thoughts.

His books, whether historical or political or socialistic, are all one long panegyric on the people. An American reader is liable to forget that the word people does not mean in his mouth what it means with us—the whole people. These pæans are sung in honour of a class, and that the lowest class of all. Louis Blanc's faith in the people was not in the true sense a democratic faith. He was not for the rule of a majority. The people meant with him in theory the whole sum of the population of France excluding the nobility, the aristocracy, the clergy (albeit springing mostly from the soil), the professions, the whole middle class in whose hands are the wealth and the property accumulated by successful industry. The artisan and the peasant were the people. They were a majority, it is true, but there never has been a moment since '93 when the peasantry was revolutionary in the social sense. It was the artisan, and above all the artisan of Paris, to whom Louis Blanc looked as the arbiter of the destinies of France. Paris was to give law to the rest of the country, and the Paris working men to give law to Paris. He was for the rule of the section which had accepted his doctrines. But when the people of Paris appeared in the streets in 1848 and invited him to govern the country, he shrank back appalled from the task; and he was appalled with reason. Of the particular charges brought against him, and on which he was expelled from France, he was not guilty. But he was certainly a danger to any Government of which he was not the head, and the choice lay between his dictatorship and his exile. Such is the irony of fate. Louis Blanc believed in a Republic without a head, and because he would not govern his mere presence made a Republic impossible.

Those who have once met Louis Blanc in society or at his own house will not forget the charm of his manner. To those who have been fortunate enough to meet him often, the memory of it will remain as among the best life has had to offer. It may be said in one sense that his manner never varied. He had the same kindly and polished greeting for visitors of every rank. It was never cold. To his friends it was affectionate, whether you had seen him yesterday or not for many months. His eye was as beautiful as a woman's, with that luminous depth which betokens a profoundly sympathetic nature. He was something more than sympathetic; he was a man to be loved. His conversation was varied, imaginative, abounding in reminiscence and anecdote, every now and then lighting up the remotest depths of a subject with flashes of penetrating intelligence. He was in earnest, but never heavy; serious, but free from gloom; the life of a dinner-table and a delightful companion in private. From everything like pretence or affectation he was absolutely free. It was too much his custom to take sombre views of affairs, especially the affairs of his own country, for which he had a love that knew no bounds. But of the men who were mismanaging France he had little to say that was hard, nothing that was uncharitable; while of his personal enemies he hardly ever spoke with severity. He had to bear during the last eighteen months of his life acute and unremitting torment. It never disturbed the serenity of his temper nor checked his interest in public matters. To the last he was at work for others. I saw him in September; sadly altered in face, but then as ever the same simple, genuine, heroic nature that for so many years I had admired, and that I now think I never admired enough.

A word only about his funeral, which I went to Paris to attend, not to describe. The people were true to their true friend. Every effort was made by the Reds to prevent a popular demonstration. Of late years Louis Blanc, like almost every sane and honest Radical, had been hated by the insane and unscrupulous faction which seeks again to set up the Commune in blood and fire. The political brigands who have usurped a name once respected made a good many people believe that they had Paris—the Paris of the Faubourgs —behind them. It was one service which Louis Blanc did in his death to expose this imposture. The Paris which had over and over again given him its suffrages had not forsaken him to follow the blind guides who proclaim themselves its new leaders. All the efforts to keep people at home failed. The streets were thronged from the Rue de Rivoli to Père la Chaise. The feeling of grief among the spectators was unmistakable and profound. The presence of Ministers and senators and deputies, the many associations and deputations who came from all parts of France, the crowns of *immortelles*, the wreaths of white and violet which covered his coffin and hearse, the military guard, the official conduct of the ceremony by the Government of the Republic—all these were marks of deserved honour, and a late acknowledgment of the neglect in which the Republic had left one of its founders. But they were all nothing compared to the homage offered by the vast multitude of that same people for whom Louis Blanc had toiled in life.

Mr. Morton's presence was much remarked. He was the only member of the Diplomatic Corps who was at the funeral, and I for one was not sorry that it should be so. Others could have had little sympathy with Louis Blanc, either personally or as ambassadors of monarchical powers. But Mr. Morton rightly felt that the American Republic ought to be represented when one of the foremost Republicans of Europe was laid to rest. Our Minister was at the house which Louis Blanc occupied, and from which the procession started, wrote his name in the list of mourners, followed in his carriage to the cemetery, and stood by the grave. America is well served when she is served by an envoy who makes clear on a great occasion like this that his sympathies and those of his country are with the Liberal cause, and those who serve the Liberal cause.

LORD BEACONSFIELD,

AS SEEN AT A GUILDHALL BANQUET.

[LONDON, *November* 11, 1879.]

ONE Guildhall banquet differs from another Guildhall banquet in glory; differs also in the degree of public expectation which attends upon the speeches of Her Majesty's Ministers to whom the banquet is given, and who have more or less to say according to circumstances. Perhaps that of yesterday was among the most brilliant because curiosity was at its height. Never were invitations more eagerly sought. A friend in authority kindly offered me a card, and so I found myself at six o'clock on Monday evening in the midst of the great throng which gathered to listen to the Prime Minister's words of wisdom.

Our country was represented last year at this ceremony by Mr. Welsh, who, being Minister and Envoy Extraordinary, and of unusual height, made a conspicuous figure among the great personages of the day. Last night the sovereignty of the Republic was impersonated by Mr. Hoppin as Chargé d'Affaires. He refrained from describing himself as Minister, though if personal merit were to count he might have marched up the aisle in the blaze of such glory as illumines the possessor of full diplomatic rank. He was among the earliest arrivals. It is doubtful whether any of the many city officials who act as heralds on this occasion had ever before heard of a Chargé d'Affaires. They could make nothing of the title so modestly announced and in their distress their sonorous voices sank to a whisper, so that the crowded ranks of city squires and city dames between whom he advanced were unaware that a Plenipotentiary of the United States was their fellow-guest. When Count Munster, the German Ambassador, walked in, he was much cheered. It is permitted to us to hope that an American diplomatist would not have been less warmly greeted had his presence been made known with equal distinctness.

Of these heralds there were, I should say, some eight or ten in all, and they were often as much at fault about English titles as about American. When Ministers began to arrive some of them were announced by their ministerial titles, some by their personal titles; some with the proper handle to their names, some without; and all with a pleasing variety in the use of aspirates. Thus we heard of the Right *H*onourable Mr. Cross, and of the Right Honourable the First Lord of the Admiralty. The Marquis of Salisbury was shorn of his Most Noble. The ex-Prime Minister of Belgium was introduced as ex-Envoy. Sir Evelyn Wood, the hero of the Zulu War, was announced at one end of the aisle as Sir General Wood, and at the other as General Evelyn Wood; all these proclamations being in duplicate or triplicate. He was greatly cheered, which led a friend at my elbow to remark that the British public knew how to distinguish a real from a sham hero. Five minutes later came Lord Chelmsford, for whom the cheering was not less hearty; whereupon my friend desired leave to withdraw his previous remark. He was immensely pleased with his cheers; so, for that matter, was Sir Evelyn Wood. Still more so was Sir Charles Whetham, outgoing Lord Mayor; and as he had been soundly hissed all day during the procession of which he formed part, he can hardly be blamed for enjoying the contrast. He has been a most unpopular Mayor, but one rather likes to hear that he took his punishment cheerfully and waved his lace handkerchief in response to the groans that followed him all along the route.

Meanwhile streamed in city dignitaries and invited guests of all ranks and of no rank. Humility was no safeguard against the perilous honour of a promenade up this avenue in a glare of light, with hundreds of curious eyes bent on you. The men with wands, in their zeal to thin the crowd at the entrance, urged everybody along. If, however, you gave your name as Mr. Jones, you were in no danger of hearing that modest patronymic echoed along your path. The hall resounded with great titles; each herald shouting louder than the other for an earl or duke. But he quite lost his voice when the commoner came. The number of men in uniform is very great and the blaze of scarlet suggests that the army is in high favour with the city. It is depressing to be told that most of these warriors are peaceful burgesses who assume this martial panoply by virtue of being Deputy-Lieutenants of the Tower Hamlets.

Two ladies were cheered. One was Lady Salisbury, to whom the Woman's Rights people owe thanks for asserting the precedence of her sex. She would not walk behind her husband nor yet by his side; but when the name of the Foreign Secretary was thundered out at the lower end of the great hall, Lady Salisbury was already well on her way up the aisle, swinging along with pride of port and a certain jollity of face which seemed to imply that her ladyship looked upon this solemnity as devised for her personal amusement. Lord Salisbury hurried after but failed to overtake her. She it was who first shook hands with the Lord Mayor, whose three-cornered hat provided her with a fresh occasion for mirth; and when Lord Salisbury came in, a bad second, the intelligent foreigner from Belgium was clearly in doubt whether the "terrible Marquis" or his quick-footed wife was the real Cabinet Minister.

The Lord Chancellor had passed in just before, certainly to a foreigner the most picturesque figure of all, preceded as he was by the whole staff of sticks-in-waiting walking backward and bowing low, and by his own staff bearing, one the mace, and another the velvet bag with the great seal, and a third the heavy train of his lordship's velvet robe. Lord Cairns's powerful face looks out from the voluminous wig which descends upon his shoulders. The contrast I should draw is not between him and the nobody of no name who has gone before, but between him and the great Duke of Northumberland. A great noble he of Northumberland assuredly is with his long descent and vast possessions, and he looks every inch the heir of a hundred earls, with his shapely features and perfect manner. He is Lord Privy Seal, too, yet his name is never heard in politics. What he is and all he is, he is by birth. Lord Cairns is an earl of yesterday, but he has made himself Earl and Lord High Chancellor by his own powers and personal gifts, and that is not a bad thing for a man who started in life as a north of Ireland lawyer.

Last of all Lord Beaconsfield came also. It is three-quarters past the dinner hour; but that delay and the long succession of dignitaries who have preceded him seem to have been contrived to render his entry the more impressive. And impressive it is in all ways. I verily believe the guests would rather have gone without their dinner than without this sauce to it. The whole hall rises for him; the applause is deafening; the greeting such as he is rightly proud of. It was a common remark that Lord Beaconsfield was looking uncommonly well. So he was; so long as he thought people were looking at him. The condition of this great man's health is an affair of State, and is discussed very much as Louis XIV's bodily welfare was discussed when he changed his shirts in public. Lord Beaconsfield does not change his shirts in public. He finds it less embarrassing to effect from time to time an exchange of what are sometimes called his principles. He has, however, his physical peculiarities, and one who sees him from time to time is able to guess near enough at his actual health. When he made his entry into the Library of the Guildhall, I stood near the door. I could see him pull himself together and compose the muscles of his face till the desired expression was attained. All resemblances, says a great physiognomist, lie in the eyes and mouth. Individual expression lies there too, and the brief space during which Lord Beaconsfield was advancing up the aisle was not too brief for a good look at these features. They quite confirmed the good reports from Hatfield which I recently mentioned. A strange fire burned in his eyes. The jaw and lips were set fast. For those two minutes no man's face was more full of energy, no step firmer than his, septuagenarian as he is, with four years added to the seventy. He wore his Windsor uniform of dark blue with embroideries in gold, with pendent sword, and on his breast that matchless and priceless star of diamonds inclosing the ruby cross of the Garter which fills all meaner breasts with envy. To the Lord Mayor he bowed low; and again to the Mayoress, accomplishing the double obeisance without any too perceptible stiffness or audible creaking of the joints.

As the procession from the Library to the Banqueting Hall slowly made its way about the tables there was no fault to find with his bearing. There are few actors who make up better, or who play their parts more perfectly so long as they are on the stage. When he stood up to speak amid the cheers of the nine hundred guests greeted him, he received the applause with quite admirable dignity. He was too great a man to be moved by these natural expressions of respect. Not even a bow acknowledged them; he stood as upright as the inveterate stoop of his shoulders permitted. No more did he acknowledge by a single word the overdone panegyrics of the Lord Mayor, but began at once what he had to say, which, nevertheless, was so little that it would not have suffered from a brief exordium of politeness. In his contempt for commonplace civilities there was a touch of almost regal manner. It is of the essence of royal good breeding to show, and I presume to feel, a certain indifference to the feelings or comfort of all lesser persons; not because a king may not be kind-hearted but because the distance which separates him from his greatest subject is simply infinite. Had Lady Beaconsfield been living it would hardly have surprised anybody to see her husband give her his arm to dinner, as a king does to his wife. In her absence he took in the Lady Mayoress, as required by Guildhall etiquette. It seems to be Guildhall etiquette, also, that the guest of the evening should not be placed on the Lord Mayor's right hand, nor even next to the host on the left. Lady Salisbury was on the Lord Mayor's right. The Lady Mayoress sat next to the Lord Mayor, and on her left sat the Prime Minister. He did not finally settle himself in his chair till after some fumbling with the cards that lay on his plate and the plates near by, as if perplexed by his position.

During dinner he sat for the most part silent. During his speech he had recourse at intervals to the glass of claret, or it may have been port, which was in front of him, which was full when he began and empty when he finished. His voice was strong enough to reach through the hall, with the help of a singularly elaborate and patient articulation of each syllable that he uttered. But it was hollow; it seemed to be fetched by a succession of calculated efforts from somewhere in his throat, and was husbanded as if he had only a limited supply which might run out if not used with economy. He has very much the trick of mouthing his words which Mr. Irving has in his least happy moments. It is as if the muscles of the tongue were weak and did not invariably respond to the will of the speaker; as if at times it required two distinct exertions, or even more, to bring that unruly member in contact with the palate. If you had heard him for the first time you would not have said this man is a great orator. But you could not listen to a sentence without perceiving that he had a consummate knowledge of the art of speaking in public, and consummate cleverness in making the most of his knowledge.

He rose knowing that not England only, but all Europe and all the civilised globe—since there is no part of it where England has not a foothold and a meddling hand—were waiting for long promised disclosures. Then, if ever, was the moment to prove to the world that he is sincerely sensible of his responsibilities; that those who accuse him of treating grave affairs as a game do him a real injustice; that he is in earnest; that he has a patriotic regard for the commonwealth, and not merely a deep pleasure in the exercise of personal power; that he seeks to administer an empire on settled principles; that he recognises the right of the people to pass judgment on its rulers; that he, too, is of opinion that governments derive their just authority from the consent of the governed. Even if he be not sincere, he had an opportunity to appear sincere at little or no cost to himself.

He threw the opportunity away. His speech was solely remarkable for what it did not contain. On no single question did he speak fully or frankly. On the most urgent he said not a single word. To the appeal which all England, his own party not less than his opponents, had addressed to him, he responds by a silence which seems the silence of contempt—the silence of a man who declines to answer a question because it is put by a man who has no right to an answer. He says to the English people: Mind your own business; plant and reap; stick to your lasts, to your furnaces and looms, to your ships and factories; leave politics to your betters; I will govern you. With every disposition to discover some other meaning in this astonishing discourse, none other is discoverable. Those of us who heard it could scarce believe our ears. The keenest scrutiny, applied to it since can extract nothing else from it. In the papers of this morning there is one general outburst of criticism. It is not the pique of baffled curiosity; it is the resentment of serious men who feel that they are being trifled with; of patriots who fear for their country under a prolonged dictatorship.

When he came to refer to the murder of the English Envoy in Cabul his tones grew so solemn, his attitude so impressive, there was in his manner such excellent mimicry of pathos, that one who did not know what philosophy he can bring to the endurance of woes not his own would surely have believed that he was beholding the symbols of a genuine sorrow. But what is genuine in the man is his intellect and his courage; together with his scorn for men whose intellect is kept in subjection to settled convictions, and whose courage is not sufficient to overrule conscience, or to disregard such facts as happen to be inconsistent with an effective statement.

Later in the evening Lord Beaconsfield paid Sir Stafford Northcote the compliment of supposing that his speech on finance was occupying the attention of the audience. He leaned back in his chair, his mask slipped off for a moment, the light from the great chandelier above streamed full on his face, and you saw what he was like when not posing for the gallery. The cheeks grew hollow, the tint of his skin waxlike, the lips relaxed, the cavernous jaws fell slightly apart, the carefully trained curls on the left of the brow slid out of place, the fire sank low in his eyes, the whole face aged painfully in a minute. If ever a human countenance looked weary and bored and scornful, Lord Beaconsfield's was that countenance at that moment. Perhaps he felt that his speech had fallen flat, in spite of the cheers; perhaps he did not care whether it had or not, but was simply tired and sleepy and wanted to have done with this pageantry and get home. This state did not last; as soon as Sir Stafford gave signs of ending his heavy speech, his chief was once more aware of his public, and alert. He resumed his war paint as nimbly as he had quitted it. When you once begin to study a remarkable face the study soon becomes a fascination. There was nothing else to interest one, unless Lord Salisbury's acid civilities to the Lady Mayoress might be called interesting; but I stayed on to the last.

And to the last the weary old man preserved his air of fresh serenity. He followed the Lady Mayoress dutifully out to the drawing-room. He endured without any show of resentment the congratulations of a few pushing admirers. The ever-faithful Montague Corry presently brought him his cloak, a romantic garment of cloth, very short and lined with fur; then the two put their backs to the wall as if to defy all comers till the Prime Minister's carriage should be announced. He had not long to wait before the far cry from outside the door, "Lord Beaconsfield's carriage coming up!" was passed on to him by a dozen clamorous yet reverential voices. With a last salute to the company he put on his cocked hat—a laced and plumed piece of headgear of the kind known as a fore-and-aft hat—and limped away between a double hedge of liveried attendants and spectators of every degree. Not even his brougham is like an ordinary man's brougham; it is not a brougham at all but a single coach of ancient fashion, swung high in the air on C springs; carriage, horses, and servants all very smartly turned out. The ever-faithful followed his chief into the coffee-coloured interior. The footman closed the door and climbed up behind, but, his foot catching, came down headlong faster than he went up. There was a cry among the crowd, for it looked as if the man would be drawn under the wheels, and there was a rush to rescue him, but he was already in the arms of a big policeman and presently was righted and thrust up into his perch. All this took a minute or two; during which Lord Beaconsfield sat immovable and uninterested. Then carriage and horses and footman and coachman and Prime Minister and private secretary vanished into the darkness. The play was played out and not for another twelvemonth will the curtain be rung up again on this stage. Lord Beaconsfield was good enough to assure the company that he should in all probability again be the chief performer at the twelvemonth's end. Perhaps this was only an oracular pleasantry; perhaps his lordship had never read that sound maxim of Mr. Hosea Biglow, "Don't never prophesy onless ye know."

MR. DELANE.

[LONDON, *December* 2, 1879.]

MR. DELANE's death is an event to which no journalist can be insensible. Had it occurred a few years ago the loss would have been not less momentous to the public than to the profession of which he was the recognised head. But Mr. Delane resigned the editorship of *The Times* in 1877; resigned it after long struggle against a chronic disease of a peculiarly depressing character, with which few men would have contended under such a burden of toil and responsibility as lay upon him. He had sustained it only too courageously and far beyond the limit which ordinary prudence and the counsels of friends would have set. But he probably cared little for life without power. For some years he must have known very well that he was risking his life by continuing at his post. For five-and-twenty years he had been in the doctor's hands; and was, perhaps, as intractable a patient as ever vexed the soul of a kindly physician. In one respect he and the late Mr. Raymond had something in common. Neither of them would ever believe that any stress of work could be too much for them, or that the will of a resolute man was not stronger than any physical malady. Both of them paid the penalty of their mistake by a premature death. Mr. Raymond went down at a blow. Mr. Delane toward the last did parley a little with his enemy. He took now and then a vacation, and less than three years ago made a trip of some duration to a continental watering-place, freeing himself meanwhile absolutely from all connection with the office. But his earlier vacations were hardly vacations, except in name. Paying a visit in the extreme north of Scotland, some distressing blunder would bring him back by express train, a flight of peremptory telegrams from station to station preceding his arrival. And his continental holiday was so much too late that it was the direct cause of his determination to retire altogether from his post. I wrote to him on his return to ask if the current rumours of his resignation were true. This was his answer:—

> I grieve to say that the report you mention respecting myself is entirely well founded. I returned from Homburg this year so little the better for a few weeks abroad as to leave me no solid hope of ever returning to work again. After thirty-seven years' hard work it is not perhaps to be wondered at. During all that long career I have been cheered by the kindness of the press, to whom I owe and feel the liveliest obligations. Pray accept a large portion for yourself.

I do not strike out the reference to myself, though, with his invariable kindness, he has spoken as if I had been able to do him some service, and it is a pleasure to me that he did so speak. The indebtedness was wholly on my side, save so far as he might choose to consider himself under an obligation for the goodwill to him and admiration of his character which I cherished. Personal regrets have no place in the attempt to estimate a great public character, yet I cannot but say how deeply I feel Mr. Delane's loss. Such acquaintance as I had with him was not intimate. I have no possible claim to write of him as a near friend; yet there are few near friends whose death would be a more grievous shock. In certain ways I owed him much. I have had some personal kindness to thank him for, which I shall not forget, and what I owe to him professionally is a debt of much larger dimensions. If anybody chooses to think it heightens my estimate of his character and capacity and public services, that is only another reason for frankness in stating it.

We all knew lately that he was very ill. Since the date of that letter he has lived in seclusion on his place at Ascot

Heath, his health steadily failing. He was often too ill to see the friends who had gone down from London to call on him. For the first time in his life he had leisure to enjoy the domestic pleasures which were dear to him, and which he had so long sacrificed to the requirements of duty. And on Saturday, November 22, he died. There was no reason to be surprised by the news of his death. But the surprise is always the same when it comes.

The European world has long been agreed in reckoning *The Times* the first journal in the world. In Europe there has been none to dispute its pre-eminence, whether in England or on the Continent. It might be hard to say at what date the paper first acquired an unquestioned supremacy. Possibly it was before Mr. Delane's time, but no matter. If it were, that proves, not the excellence of *The Times*, but the inferiority of its rivals. The paper as we know it to-day, as all Europe knows it or knew it down to his death, was the creation of Mr. Delane. Its previous half century of existence had given it a commercial basis, but it was still contending with *The Morning Chronicle* for a controlling influence in England. Judged by the modern standard it was neither a very able journal nor a great newspaper. The leaders of Sterling, which gave it the name of the Thunderer, would now be thought discreditable to a provincial penny paper of the lesser sort. The profession of journalism did not exist. The methods of journalism, as we understand them, did not exist. I don't refer to the transformation which has occurred in the methods of collecting news. There was as much room for enterprise before telegraphs and railways as since — perhaps more. But neither *The Times* nor any other journal was organised on the editorial or on the news side as every important journal is now organised. The making of newspapers was in its experimental, not to say embryonic stage. Perhaps nobody but a journalist can accurately measure the extent of the change, but the public reaps the benefit of it though it may not have followed the process.

Down to a very late period in the history of English journalism *The Times* led the way in this transformation, and that is only saying that Mr. Delane led the way. What Carlyle said of Sterling with exaggeration may be said of Mr. Delane with strict accuracy. For five-and-thirty years he *was The Times*. And the measure of Mr. Delane's ability and of his work is to be found in the advance from *The Times* of 1840 to *The Times* of 1870. That advance, or, as I called it before, that transformation, is in my judgment the most signal fact in the history of journalism. It may be said that no one man is the sole agent in any great work—the influences of the time work with him, and he is in a sense only the exponent and agent of those influences. True, but that does not modify our opinion of any great man, because it applies to all great men. Mr. Delane was as much the author of this transformation in journalism and in *The Times* as Prince Bismarck was the author of the German Empire. For the improvements made in some departments Mr. Delane may divide the credit with some of his colleagues. But for the organisation of the intellectual power of the paper, for the elevation of its intellectual tone, for the building up of the vast authority it wielded, for, in one word, the editing of *The Times* in the right sense of the word, the credit belongs to him and to him alone. On this and kindred points there is a great deal to be said, but I wrote at some length on them at the time of his resignation and I will not repeat the views then expressed. I do not hold them any less strongly now than then; what has since occurred strengthens them. Some notion of the range and value of Mr. Delane's work may be got by comparing the paper as it was under him and as it now is, with its editorship in commission.

The quantity of work he did was prodigious—work of the purely editorial kind. He seldom or never wrote a leading article in his own paper. But in one sense he was the author of most of them. It was he who chose the topics and dictated the treatment of them. He had an able staff about him of practised writers—and these also he chose—whose main business it was to put into readable shape the ideas and views which they received from their chief. Of course I do not mean that he supplied more than the scheme of the articles which these gifted writers worked out. He took care—and it was one of the secrets of his power and of the freshness and vigour of these leaders—that measures should be advocated by men who believed in them. When the paper changed sides another writer took up the subject. No man was expected to argue against his own convictions. The best men are not to be had on those terms, nor will the best men do their best work under conditions exposing them to such humiliations.

The routine and method of the editorial office varied little. To the last Mr. Delane wrote his own letters. I never received from him a letter not in his own handwriting from beginning to end; nor ever saw one that he had dictated. One reason of his keeping to the old habit may have been that he wrote exceedingly good letters. They were always straight to the point, with never a word too much. In many other ways he adhered to his early customs—in none more conspicuously than in his hours of work and the nature of the control he exercised over the daily production of the paper. He was at the office by ten, or, if dining out, before eleven every evening. He never left it till the paper had gone to press and the first complete printed sheet had been placed in his hands. Nothing was there which had not had his sanction. A map of the whole lay in his mind before it went to the stereotyper. He was not of those editors who think the "make up" of a great journal may be safely left to the night-foreman of the printing-office.

Mr. Delane's activity ranged over every department of the paper. I do not think he cared deeply about anything except politics, including under that head the whole course of public affairs throughout the civilised world. But he supervised everything. The quantity of proof he read is something incredible. Literature, art, music, commercial news, trade reports, military and naval intelligence, the money article, the long series of letters from abroad, law reports—nay, the very police reports and local items—passed, however rapidly, under that all-scrutinising eye and cool judgment. He used to say the great thing was to know what to keep out of the paper. Another favourite phrase with him will be found embodied in the note below; which again will show the sort of pains he took. It refers to the letter I wrote to *The Times* on Mr. Dana's rejection by the Senate as Minister to England. Mr. Delane took the trouble to strike out of it a personal phrase or two and a closing paragraph in which I had expressed a rather free opinion upon one or two of the senators who had most contributed to the contumely put upon Mr. Dana. These criticisms in no degree helped the argument, they surely would not have been to the taste of the English public, and Mr. Delane did a service both to Mr. Dana and to me by his expurgations. I wrote to thank him for it, and he answered:—

I am very much flattered at your taking so well the excisions I ventured to make from your letter. I believe it is only those of our own profession who are so tolerant of criticism or who concede so readily that a second pair of eyes will see better than the first " how it will look to-morrow."

And since it has sometimes been said that Mr. Delane showed himself careless about correcting mistakes committed in the paper or atoning for injuries done to individuals, I will quote one more letter—one which explains itself:—

I did not receive your letter until late this evening, as I was, according to my ordinary habit, out of town on Saturday, or I should have written at once to express my regret that injustice had been done to ——, and to beg that you would redress it in your own language. I think a contradiction would be more effective if it came from you, signed with your name, and it is my desire to make the contradiction as effective as possible.

He was as good as his word, and I have to say that I never

appealed in vain to his sense of justice, whether for myself or another, nor ever knew him reluctant to give a hearing to the advocate of an unpopular cause, no matter how obscure, or to the opponent of his own views. It was part of his theory of editorship that both sides should be heard.

They say he was inconsistent, which is true. It is a fault he shared with the public for whom he undertook to speak. He did not think it his duty to be wiser or more tenacious of opinion than the world. That theory of a journalist's duty which consists in swimming with the stream is not perhaps the highest, but it may at least be said of Mr. Delane that he was consistent in his inconsistency. His perception of public opinion, his quickness in discovering its changes of mood, his knowledge of the world about him, his judgment of character, were all marvellous. He lived much with men, was deep in the secrets of Ministers, often called in as adviser both in public and private business, was trusted often and never betrayed his trust. Personally he was a capital type of Englishman, both in appearance and character. Meeting him in the early afternoon in Rotten Row you would take him for a country gentleman. Probably no man in Europe made up his mind so decisively on so many questions during each day. I do not think he cared much for advice. He had the confidence in himself which most men of genius for affairs have. And in Printing House Square he ruled with a rod of iron. There never was a great editor or great administrator of any kind who did not. As much velvet as you please on the gauntlet but the steel beneath is the essential thing. Yet he was considerate to his subordinates in every possible way, aware that personal considerateness is perfectly consistent with rigid discipline and ruthless judgment upon their work in the interest of the journal. Men stayed long upon *The Times* and wrought for it zealously. They were not lightly chosen nor lightly dismissed.

Mr. Delane had another point of resemblance with Prince Bismarck. He trained no successor. He had under him, indeed, an accomplished lieutenant, thoroughly familiar with the details of the office and probably the most capable man at the moment of his retirement to take command of the ship. But that was not the view of the proprietors, and Mr. Delane himself perhaps took little thought of the deluge that should come after him. The amiable and cultivated scholar who nominally holds the post of editor is understood to conduct *The Times* in accordance with the views of its chief owner, a man of cautious mind, noted for a dry conservatism in most matters not ecclesiastical, and zealous in these last. Mr. Delane could not have held office a day without power. It has always been understood that he was absolute master; perfectly independent and perfectly despotic. It was in Mr. Walter's power to dismiss him; it was not in his power to edit *The Times* so long as Mr. Delane was editor. If the passage purporting to give an extract from Mr. Delane's will be authentic, he leaves legacies to Mr. Walter in company with other well-known writers and workers on *The Times*, of all whom he speaks as his colleagues. Authentic or not, the passage accurately describes the relations which Mr. Delane conceived to exist between the chief proprietor of the paper and himself. They were colleagues. There was a partnership between the two; a partnership of a kind not unknown in other commercial enterprises; in which one member of the firm supplies the capital and the plant, the other supplying the special knowledge by which these are made productive. Mr. Walter is known as a man of considerable ability; of undeniable business talents; a sufficient member of Parliament. If he is to be considered as a journalist the best proof of his capacity in that profession must be sought in the sound judgment which led him to confide the unchecked control of *The Times* to Mr. Delane.

DARWIN IN WESTMINSTER ABBEY.

[LONDON, *April* 26, 1882.]

"LAID in death among his peers in Westminster Abbey by the will of the intelligence of the nation," is the remark of Darwin's greatest pupil upon the burial of his master. Undoubtedly that is a true account of the matter. Professor Huxley knows, as we all know, that the Dean of Westminster and the advisers of the Dean gave a willing assent to the proposal that Darwin's body should rest beneath the arches of St. Peter's. But the Dean was only the official mouthpiece of the nation. The solemnity of to-day was appointed with one mind by all classes of men, by men of all creeds and schools of thought. Of recent funerals in the Abbey none has been more notable than this in circumstance and character. Perhaps few were ever known anywhere to which the sincere grief and reverence of a greater number of high-minded men and women lent a deeper impressiveness.

Four policemen guarded the closed gateway into Dean's Yard. At the entrance to the cloisters more policemen; at each angle, at each doorway, and at the foot of the stairway leading up to the chapter-house there were both police and officials of the Abbey. In company with a friend I found my way through this thicket of constables a little past eleven this Wednesday morning. Everybody was expected to show his card pretty frequently. Similar precautions were taken at the other entrances to the Abbey. The number of admissions issued was carefully restricted—necessarily so, I suppose—and a rigid order was maintained in the distribution of visitors throughout nave and aisles and choir. There was much eagerness to be present and the precautions against a rush of the unprivileged public were the usual ones. If for no other reason, Westminster Abbey stands in a neighborhood capable of pouring forth at any moment the human contents of some of the foulest slums in London.

The hour of the funeral was noon. Holders of chapterhouse tickets were expected to arrive not later than half-past eleven. At that hour a company of perhaps 200 people had assembled. The coffin was placed in the cloister arcade through which lay the approach to the chapter-house — a coffin of plain oak, one heard, but of which all one could see was a pall of black velvet and thick wreaths of flowers. The passages of the Abbey, never well lighted on the best of days, were obscure with the dull gray haze of an air soaked with moisture. A true London morning—no rain, but the constant menace of rain; no glimpse of sun between the soft masses of cloud; hardly a gleam of daylight through the latticed windows, or within the gray-green enclosure of the cloisters or past the smoke-stained buttresses and pinnacles of the chapel.

One's first look at the group in the chapter-house showed how brilliant—if one may use such a word—was the company gathered to pay the last tribute to Darwin. Some of the greatest names in England belonged to the men who clustered at the top of the steps. The ten nearest are the pall-bearers; life-long friends and disciples of Darwin some of them: Mr. Huxley, whose resolute face is softened by the sense of a double bereavement, by the loss of his leader and his comrade; Sir Joseph Hooker, Mr. Spottiswoode, President of the Royal Society; Sir John Lubbock, the Duke of Devonshire, the Duke of Argyll, the American Minister, Lord Derby, Mr. A. R. Wallace, and Canon Farrar. The last name gives rise to the same reflections which come to everybody who thinks for a moment of the significance of the burial of Darwin in Westminster Abbey. What has Darwin to do with the Abbey or the Abbey with him?

What place has a dignitary of the Church of England by the coffin of the foremost man of science of his age? Dean Stanley used to say the Abbey was something more than a church, that it was the fitting tomb of the heroes of England—their resting-place and monument; and so it is. England, or so much of England as is modern and liberal, would have cried out at the exclusion of Darwin from the national shrine. And I suppose we may take Canon Farrar's presence and his share in the ceremonial as an act of personal respect and of ecclesiastical compensation. It is not twenty years since divines of the Church of England anathematised Darwin as a heretic—to use no harsher term. Her advocates said then what a Roman Catholic advocate has said since Darwin's death—that a man capable of inventing a theory which led straight to atheism must be knave or fool or both. The relative intelligence of the devotees of the two Churches—of Rome and of England—may be measured by the breadth of their divergence to-day on this point.

The Duke of Argyll, all orthodox as he is in religion, has hold enough on science to explain his presence here. But what does Lord Salisbury's homage mean? The Tory statesman concerns himself with chemistry but he belongs to the Middle Ages none the less, and to the party of mediævalism. His presence may be deemed an honour to Darwin; it is certainly honourable to himself. Nor were Lord Salisbury and the Canon the only distinguished persons whose presence at this solemnity gave rise to comment. At least three other members of the late Lord Beaconsfield's Cabinet were there: Sir Stafford Northcote, Sir Richard Cross, and Mr. W. H. Smith. Both the members of each of the two great Universities of Oxford and Cambridge, all four Conservatives, were among the mourners for Darwin. This is no place for politics and still less for theology, but how happens it that Conservatism in public life bestows this marked regard on the greatest Radical of the age? This is, as a German writer has aptly said, Darwin's century. What makes it Darwin's century if it be not the discovery of a great principle or law, the truth of which can by no ingenuity be reconciled with the theories affirmed by the Church? The staunchest defenders of Church and State are nevertheless here—nay, Oxford herself is here in the persons not only of her two members of Parliament, but of her Chancellor (none other than Lord Salisbury himself), her Vice-Chancellor, and the most eminent of her heads of colleges, the Master of Balliol—not a few of her best professors as well. Is this the Oxford "steeped in sentiment, whispering from her towers the last enchantments of the Middle Age, the home of lost causes and forsaken beliefs and impossible loyalties," on which Mr. Arnold pronounced his imperishable panegyric? Again I say, it is honourable to these types and incarnations of Tory reverence for the past and Tory dread of the future that they seek thus to offer their tribute to Darwin. But this is a tribute which is more than a token of homage; it is a token of defeat, and the visible sign of the ascendancy of the new over the old.

Our Minister is here as representative of the United States, and General Merritt, our Consul-General, stands near. Mr. Lowell is representative of literature also, one may say, of which the representatives are fewer than might have been expected. There were many men who have a high place in letters, but a higher out of it, whom I do not include; but of the men one thinks of instinctively as above all things writers and among the foremost of living writers, there were not many. I saw neither Mr. Tennyson nor Mr. Browning, neither Mr. Froude nor Mr. Trevelyan, neither Mr. Ruskin nor Mr. Matthew Arnold. When I have mentioned Mr. Lecky, Mr. John Morley, and Sir Henry Maine, I have named all whom I saw who can be described as in the front rank. The exception to this remark is again that of a man at least as eminent in the domain of science as of literature, Mr. Herbert Spencer. That Mr. Spencer should take any part in, or even be present at, a religious ceremony might well surprise his friends. But his personal attachment to Darwin, his loyal admiration for him as a teacher, his strong wish to leave no mark of reverence unshown, overcame in the end his well-known scruples against ecclesiastical observances. It is almost needless to add that deputations attended from great scientific societies, and that men of science came from all parts of the kingdom to the funeral of the one man of science in whose presence all jealousies and all rivalries were silent. It was thought odd that but two members of the Cabinet, Lord Spencer and Mr. Childers, represented the Government. Lord Sherbrooke, Lord Aberdare, the Speaker of the House of Commons, and many another political notability walked side by side with the presidents of the College of Surgeons, and of the Physical Society, the Geographical, the Geological, the Linnæan—I suppose all the great scientific bodies.

The one great representative body conspicuous by its absence was the Royal Family. In life, as Professor Huxley says, they had ignored Darwin, and they ignore him now that he is dead. Continents vie with each other in doing honour to the great man who is buried to-day. In England everything that is illustrious pays him a last tribute of reverence, royalty excepted. Sometimes a king or queen who cannot be present in person sends a lord-in-waiting, a goldstick, an aide-de-camp—some sort of functionary or other—to be respectful by proxy. Not even that cold civility was thought due to Darwin by the Queen, or by the Prince of Wales, or by any single member of the family which occupies the throne. It does not matter to Darwin. It matters a little to them—not perhaps very much, but it is one thing left undone the doing of which would have strengthened, as the omission of it weakens, in whatever degree, the attachment of Englishmen to their rulers.

At twenty-five minutes to noon the coffin was taken up, the pall-bearers ranged themselves on either side of it, the procession formed in the rear and moved round the aisle of the cloisters leading to the Abbey. At the entrance came a long halt, and we were permitted to stand where a draft of air swept keenly through the corridor. The coffin and pall-bearers had passed on; some church officials appeared to be arranging themselves in the gap which their advance had left. Presently the great men in front, Lord Salisbury, Lord Spencer and the rest began to cover themselves, and soon the whole procession was covered and stood, not very much at ease, looking out through the arches into the green court. This lasted for a quarter of an hour, but just at the stroke of twelve the head of the column passed through the narrow doorway and into the south aisle.

The south aisle and the centre of the nave and choir had been kept clear; everywhere else was a throng of humanity, almost all in black. Between these dense masses the procession slowly took its way, along nearly the whole length of the nave, entering the choir through the door of the screen which divides and degrades the church. The coffin was placed beneath the lantern at the steps of the altar; the pall-bearers took seats on either side, the rest of the followers passed on and into the chancel and stood there during the service. Daylight as it was, of the London sort, the gloom between the walls of the choir was heavy and throughout the choristers' seats candles were lighted; with the effect of mingling daylight and candlelight in the most singular manner. From where we stood in the chancel looking past the open space beneath the lantern the choir beyond looked like a lighted tomb; or like the *chapelle ardente* which is so marked a feature of Catholic burials on the Continent.

The service was the usual one for the burial of the dead, in its most elaborate form, with choral music and processional chants and deep-voiced canons intoning the given sentences. Then the company reformed, the coffin was borne back, and about the grave at the extreme eastern end of the north aisle gathered most of the mourners of the family, and of the greater circle of friends and followers of the dead. The organ played Beethoven's Funeral March, then another by Schubert, and another canon read the remainder of the service. There were phrases here and there which fell strangely on the ear, but the swell of the deep notes of the organ soon covered them. The men who composed the burial literature of the Church of England did so in a spirit of sincere belief, and the sincerity saves it even when the belief is less than it was. The inscription on the coffin-plate read: "Charles Robert Darwin. Born February 12, 1809. Died April 19, 1882." That too was sincere; the simple record of the beginning and ending of a simple and noble life. If there be anything to add to it, let me quote again from Mr. Huxley:—

"He found a great truth trodden under foot, reviled by bigots and ridiculed by all the world; he lived long enough to see it, chiefly by his own efforts, irrefragably established in science, inseparably incorporated with the common thoughts of men, and only hated and feared by those who would revile but dare not. What shall a man desire more than this?"

Not much, perhaps, unless it be that his epitaph should be written in just such words as these; echoed as they are through a world which with rare unanimity decrees to Darwin a pure and permanent fame.

THE DARWIN MEMORIAL,

UNVEILED BY PROFESSOR HUXLEY, THE PRINCE OF WALES,
AND THE ARCHBISHOP OF CANTERBURY.

[LONDON, *June* 14, 1885.]

EVEN amid the excitement of the Ministerial crisis people in London have found time to be interested in one or two matters which have no relation to politics. Chief among them was the ceremony of unveiling the Darwin Memorial Statue last Tuesday. The ceremony was a simple one. There was no pageantry, nor any of the outward splendour which attracts a smart company or a great multitude of sightseers. But few spectacles have been more impressive.

The memorial is the complement of the honour paid to Darwin at his burial in Westminster Abbey; itself a scene of the most singular attractiveness. That was three years ago. Immediately afterward, as Professor Huxley reminded us on Tuesday, a public meeting was held in the rooms of the Royal Society, to consider what further steps should be taken "to honour the memory of the man who, without fear and without reproach, had successfully fought the hardest intellectual battle of these days." The meeting resolved to ask for subscriptions for a statue and their appeal went out over all the world. There is hardly a country, great or small, in Europe which did not respond; nor were the United States backward. Mr. Huxley tells us that Sweden sent in more than two thousand subscriptions, from all sorts of people, from the bishop to the seamstress, and in sums from £5 to twopence. So the order was given for the statue, the execution of which was intrusted to Mr. Boehm. The memorial committee proposed to the Trustees of the British Museum to set up this image of Darwin in the great hall of the Natural History Museum at South Kensington. The Trustees accepted the offer. The statue was put in its place, and this meeting of Tuesday was convoked to receive it with due homage to the memory of the illustrious dead.

Invitations were addressed to all the chief men of science in England, and to many whose fame has nothing to do with science. Professor Huxley was there on Tuesday as chairman of the committee, perhaps also as President of the Royal Society, to hand over the statue to the Trustees. The Prince of Wales, one of the Trustees, was there to receive it on behalf of his colleagues. Among the company that clustered on the steps and platform were the Lord Steward (Lord Sydney), Lord Cadogan, whom rumour appoints to the Viceroyalty of Ireland; Lord Sherbrooke, Lord Houghton, Lord Acton, Sir Henry Rawlinson, one of the greatest Orientalists of his time; Mr. Browning, Mr. Flower, the superintendent of the Museum; Sir Richard Owen (who can hardly have enjoyed all the arrangements), three sons of Darwin, and the Master of Christ's College, Cambridge — Darwin's college. I break in upon the enumeration of names to ask you to notice how carefully they had been chosen, and with what utter disregard of mere rank or fashion this assemblage had been made up. The men of rank above named are all men who have an official connection with the Museum, or other claims to be present wholly irrespective of their rank. Next came Admiral Sir B. J. Sullivan and Vice-Admiral Mellersh, two of the three surviving officers with whom Darwin sailed in the memorable cruise of the *Beagle;* Sir Joseph Hooker, ex-President of the Royal Society and I suppose the first of English botanists; Lord Aberdare; Professor Newton, the classical archæologist; Mr. Bond, Principal Librarian of the British Museum; Sir William Gull, one of the most fashionable and, notwithstanding that, one of the best physicians in London; Sir Joseph Lister, the most original surgeon of the day, and author of the antiseptic treatment of wounds, the discovery which has revolutionised surgery; Sir James Paget, perhaps the most gifted operating surgeon in England; Mr. Lecky, and Mr. Herbert Spencer.

Besides all these, there were three men whose presence is even more worthy of note. Archdeacon Farrar was one, whose *Life of Christ* is said to have surpassed *Uncle Tom's Cabin* itself in circulation. The second was the Dean of Westminster. The third was the spiritual Head of the Church of England, the Archbishop of Canterbury. There he stood on the platform, by the side of the Prince, and at the very feet of Darwin. He had an air of apostolic humility which sat well on him, and which suited well the circumstances in which he appeared. All men must have felt the significance of his coming, but not one word was publicly said which could seem ungracious in the presence of this act of homage from the Church to the great man of science who has shaken to its foundations the authority of the Church. If it be a step toward that reconciliation of which so much is said between Science and Religion, it is, so far as the Church of England is concerned, an act which savours more of submission than of toleration. It is a recantation of the anathemas once pronounced on Darwin; it is, at least, a recognition of his rightful position in the intellectual world. It is, I am tempted to say, a concession to Darwin of co-ordinate authority in matters of faith, or which were once of faith. This time it is the Church which has gone to Canossa. The great hall of the Natural History Museum is less inclement than the snow-covered courtyard of the Castle where Hildebrand kept Henry three days waiting, and so much softer are the manners of modern days that the Archbishop stood something less than half an hour before the marble effigy of his victorious foe. But the light which beat upon him has made him a visible figure for centuries to come.

The whole ceremony was among the shortest on record.

Punctually at noon the Prince of Wales walked up the hall amid cheers, mounted the steps, accompanied by Mr. Huxley and others who had gone to the front door to receive him, shook hands with others of the company, and signified his readiness to begin. Mr. Huxley unfolded his sheet of printed proof and read his brief address. The veil fell from the statue. The audience applauded. Mr. Huxley in a few closing sentences committed the memorial to the care of the Museum Trustees. The Prince of Wales, in sentences not less few, accepted it, and the solemnity of the day was over before the clock had struck the quarter.

Professor Huxley's address is much too condensed to be condensed again. He is one of the not too numerous men of science with a definite sense of literary form, and with a power of expression which places him, quite independently of his scientific position, among the first writers of his generation. He has summed up the case for Darwin in a sentence. Darwin was one of those rare ministers and interpreters of nature whose names mark epochs in the advance of natural knowledge. "Whatever be the ultimate verdict of posterity upon this or that opinion which Darwin has propounded, whatever adumbrations or anticipations of his doctrines may be found in the writings of his predecessors, the broad fact remains that since the publication and by reason of the publication of the *Origin of Species*, the fundamental conceptions and the aims of the students of living Nature have been completely changed." Then upon the uncovering of the statue came these words:—

It only remains for me, your Royal Highness, my Lords and Gentlemen, Trustees of the British Museum, in the name of the Darwin Memorial Committee, to request you to accept this statue of Charles Darwin. We do not make this request for the mere sake of perpetuating a memory; for so long as men occupy themselves with the pursuit of truth the name of Darwin runs no more risk of oblivion than does that of Copernicus or that of Harvey. Nor, most assuredly, do we ask you to preserve the statue in its cynosural position in this entrance hall of our National Museum of

Natural History, as evidence that Mr. Darwin's views have received your official sanction, for science does not recognise such sanctions, and commits suicide when it adopts a creed. No; we beg you to cherish this memorial as a symbol by which, as generation after generation of students of Nature enter yonder door, they shall be reminded of the ideal according to which they must shape their lives, if they would turn to the best account the opportunities offered by the great institution under your charge.

The dignity of that is worthy of all admiration, while as for the diction, the whole passage may be commended to the student as a model. What the Prince of Wales had to say was said with tact and good feeling, very audibly, in the slight German accent which is one of the peculiarities of the heir to the English throne. After that there was no further ceremony, unless the conversation which broke the gathering on the platform into groups may be called a ceremony. The Prince said a word, as his way is, to everybody whom he knew; singling out Mr. Boehm to congratulate him on the success of his work. Mr. Huxley had already expressed his admiration of the power of artistic divination which enabled the sculptor to place before us so characteristic a likeness of one whom he had not seen. The statue deserves that praise and something more. There is in it that sculptural quality without which a statue may be a good portrait but cannot be a work of real art. The seated figure, with its bent head and easy pose, has the power which comes of simplicity; as Darwin himself had. Mr. Boehm's greatest success is perhaps to be seen in the stamp of patient observation and reflection which the face bears; it is the record in marble of Darwin's intellectual life.

MR. FAWCETT.

[LONDON, *November* 11, 1884.]

MR. FAWCETT's death was sudden in the sense that few people knew he was in danger, or even seriously ill. His constitution, once very strong, had been shaken by the long typhoid illness which brought him near death two years ago. So slow was his convalescence at that time that months after his reappearance in the world he used to describe himself, half seriously, as a wreck. But presently he seemed to regain all his old vigour, and I suppose only his nearest friends knew how delicate he really was.

Fawcett's friends always spoke of him as a man to be loved, and no doubt they were right, but to those outside of that circle he seemed pre-eminently a man to be respected. What has been said of him since his death proves how universal the respect was, and how high was the opinion the world had formed of his character and abilities. It is sometimes said the world takes a man at his own valuation, and this is perhaps true enough in Fawcett's case. It would be hard to name a man who had a more complete confidence in himself. This confidence was not a vain egotism. It sprang from a reasoned conviction. He had a habit of judging by the dry light of reason, and he applied this process to himself as to other subjects of interest. He had no doubts about anything. He was as sure of himself as of a proposition in geometry. His mind had a mathematical cast which to a certain extent unfitted him for politics. He argued in straight lines, and lacked the flexibility which is in most cases a condition of success in English public life. When he had demonstrated that a thing ought to be on principle, he became impatient of those who would have shown him it was impossible in the circumstances, or premature. He had a contempt for practical politics, though he would have been very much surprised if you had told him so. Before he took office he was a thorn in the side of the Liberal Government, to which he thought himself a friend. He was a candid friend, unsparing in reproof, in rebuke, in exhortation, in the preaching of sound doctrine, regardless whether his friends would endure sound doctrine or not. He was one of the two or three Liberals who defeated Mr. Gladstone's Irish University Bill in 1873, an incident which shook the Ministry and prepared the way for its overthrow in 1874. He early took up the cause of India, and came to be known by and by in the House as Member for India. When he took office in 1880 it was with a reservation in favour of India. He was to be free to speak his mind on that subject, and to abstain from voting for any Government measure for India of which he might not approve. His services to the natives of Hindostan were considerable, but it may be doubted whether he ever brought himself to admit that India is, after all, a military dependency of Great Britain, or to understand what Pascal meant when he said, though with irony, that truth varies with the meridian, and that there is hardly any justice or injustice which does not change its nature as you change the climate. He applied Western ideas to Eastern communities. And yet this very stubbornness of intellect made him a useful man in a country where the word principle is unpopular in politics. None the less it often misled him. A man who applies the differential calculus to the solution of political problems is sure to arrive at some queer results. He was a partisan of woman's suffrage, and of something very like equality between the sexes. As Postmaster-General he employed large numbers of female clerks in post and telegraph offices. His friends speak of the experiment as a success. I should like to ask them how many telegrams they get in which there is not a mistake, and whether they think the general business of the Post-Office is done more or less accurately since women came to have a large share in it. The female mind may by and by be educated into habits of precision, but the education is carried on at the expense of the service and of the public. Fawcett was a not less enthusiastic partisan of what is called proportional representation, or the representation of minorities; an idea born of impatience at the rule of the majority, and fruitful of fantastic schemes the permanent adoption of which would make government by majority impossible.

Fawcett's blindness has made him an object of general sympathy. No words can be too strong to express the admiration due to the cheerful fortitude with which he faced that calamity when it came upon him. Everybody knows that his sight was destroyed by the accidental discharge of a gun. Two small shots struck him; each penetrated an eye and vision was gone for ever. The calamity that would have crushed most men was the key to Fawcett's success. It developed his amazing energy of character, and it concentrated his aims. He was then twenty-five and reading for the Bar. He instantly gave up the Bar and resolved on politics, and politics with him meant a seat in the House of Commons and ultimately a place in the Government. But it meant also that he was to be the chivalrous champion of every cause that wanted a champion, if he happened to believe it a good cause. He refused all concessions to what is commonly called his infirmity, for people seldom spoke in plain terms of his blindness. He pursued his studies, wrote books, was chosen Professor of Political Economy at Cambridge. He delivered lectures. He stood for Parliament and was repeatedly unsuccessful. His friends urged him to give up his ambition for public life. He had little or no money. He refused, and said he should win in the end. Brighton, after once rejecting him, chose him in 1865, but turned him out in 1874; since which he has represented Hackney.

At first, in spite of the kindness felt toward him, Fawcett was anything but a success in the House. To put it bluntly, he bored honourable members. The House does not like professors, and Fawcett lectured. As years went on he got the ear of important sections of the Chamber, and still more important sections of the public. His logical faculty, his obvious sincerity, his earnestness, his argumentative powers, his mastery of his subjects, his convincing way of stating his case, made the impression they could not fail to make. He became a power in the House, and in the Liberal party. It was seen that some place must be found for him, and when in 1880 Mr. Gladstone formed his present Administration, he made Fawcett his Postmaster-General. The post has often carried with it a seat in the Cabinet. Fawcett remained outside the Cabinet to the day of his death. It was commonly said that his blindness stood in the way. It would have been necessary to confide Cabinet papers and other Cabinet secrets to Fawcett's secretary—perhaps to more than one secretary. His secretary was his other self, his confidant, adviser, fellow-student, wife, everything one human being can be to another. The closeness of the relation between them would have had the effect of making Mrs. Fawcett a Cabinet Minister as well as her husband. She deserved every trust that could be placed in her, but a Prime Minister may be excused for hesitating to extend to the Cabinet the principle or practice of woman's rights.

Fawcett's refusal to allow himself to be beaten by his blindness was shown in many ways. A friend who was with him at Cambridge at the time of his accident has described to me his first walk. He struck at once into his old stride, which was rapid and powerful. "Don't do that, Fawcett," cried his friend; "you will come to grief."—"No matter," answered Fawcett, "I have got to learn to do without eyes, and I may as well begin at once." And on he went. He skated, he rode, he fished. He rode fourteen miles on horseback the day before he was taken ill. I have heard him describe his salmon-fishing in Scotland with all the zest of the keenest sportsman. He had of course a man with him in fishing. He dined out constantly, and was a favourite guest in many country houses. As a talker he had the defect of his blindness; he could not watch the faces of the company and he talked too long—lectured sometimes, as he did in the House—and his voice was strong enough to bear down all opposition. But his talk was often admirable, and his genial good-humour and wonderful spirits and energy conciliated everybody. Awkward things sometimes happened, however. A knot of men were conversing one evening after dinner in a certain smoking-room; among them Fawcett and a well-known member of the House, popular but no genius. Let us call him Robinson. Presently Robinson got up, said good-bye, the door opened and closed, and there was a pause. "Robinson is a good fellow," resumed Fawcett in his resonant tones, " but what an awful fool he is." And Robinson was still there.

MR. FAWCETT IN THE POST-OFFICE.

[*November* 20, 1884.]

Among the many eulogies on Mr. Fawcett not the least curious comes from the Secretary to the Post-Office, Mr. Stevenson A. Blackwood. A society journalist, who at one time was a post-office clerk, had said rather curtly that Mr. Fawcett was crotchety and difficult to get on with and was disliked by those who had to work with him. Mr. Blackwood, who is the permanent head of this great department, declares all this story baseless. The heads of every branch of the office regarded Mr. Fawcett with respect and affection. He looked carefully after the personal interests of those under him, and if he had to overrule anybody, did it with considerateness. Nor was his blindness, Mr. Blackwood assures us, an impediment to the transaction of business.

This testimony is gratifying so far as it goes. But there is a sentence in Mr. Blackwood's letter which raises a different question. The respect and affection which he and his colleagues had for Mr. Fawcett was such as can, in Mr. Blackwood's opinion, "be rarely won from their subordinates by the parliamentary chiefs of public departments." That is a very significant remark. I should be disposed to add that it could, as a rule, only be won by the parliamentary chiefs who give way to their so-called subordinates. The public seems often to take for granted that the parliamentary chief is the real chief; that the Post-Office is ruled by the Postmaster-General, the Navy by the First Lord of the Admiralty, the War Office by the Secretary of State for War, and so on. This is true in a strictly limited sense. On some great questions the head of a department has his way, or the Cabinet takes a decision. In other matters this country is governed by permanent clerks, and the Post-Office is a very good example of the way in which a permanent clerk like Mr. Blackwood governs. Time was when the Post-Office was penetrated with a spirit of efficiency, when reforms were welcomed, when abuses were remedied and defects made good with alacrity. The public interest, and not the interest or convenience of the department and its clerks, was considered. It would be rash to affirm that the same state of things exists now. *The Times* said not long ago that experience had confirmed the doubt whether St. Martin's-le-Grand (headquarters of the permanent Post-Office clerks) were as open-minded as it was inclined to be little less than half a century ago. It is rare to see such a sentence of condemnation passed on a great public office by the leading journal of Great Britain. But it is deserved.

The truth about Mr. Fawcett's administration of the Post-Office has not been quite correctly stated. He has been much praised, perhaps not too much, but for the wrong things. He devoted his energies to what I may call side issues. He enlarged the facilities for investing in savings banks, here a branch of Post-Office business. He fought for the Post-Office monopoly against telephones, successfully resisted for a long time the general introduction of the telephone, finally saw his policy was mischievous and gave way. He flooded the offices, telegraph offices included, with women, with the result that the telegraph service of England is talkative and inaccurate. He established the Parcels Post, which is irresponsible, irregular, and at present insolvent, but which may easily be so improved as to be invaluable. But the real business of the Post-Office is the collection, transmission, and delivery of letters and papers. If Mr. Fawcett gave much attention to perfecting this work, to keeping up the standard of efficiency, to promoting speed and punctuality, his efforts yielded but a poor result. The Post-Office for some years past has not been improving; it has deteriorated. I suspect Mr. Fawcett was very much in the hands of his subordinates in these essential matters. It would not be fair to charge upon him the spirit of obstruction, the love of routine, the steady opposition to reform, the acquiescence in delay and decay which mark the present rule in the British Post-Office. As Mr. Blackwood is the permanent executive and ruling spirit at St. Martin's-le-Grand, it is he who must be held responsible.

I have often talked over Post-Office matters with Mr. Fawcett, especially the American mail service. A plain statement of some of the most inveterate faults used to astonish him. Afterward he looked into the question for himself, and I believe really meant to sweep away the anomalies and absurdities of the existing contract system—a system under which, out of fourteen fast ships plying regularly between England and New York, the British Post-Office employs exactly four. But Mr. Blackwood and the steamship ring were too strong for him. When the old contract was renewed for a year, I wrote to Mr. Fawcett to say how sorry I was he had not been able to look into the question himself as he had meant to. From what I had heard him say and from what I knew of his capacity for mastering a subject, and his impatience of imbecilities, I felt sure he would have insisted on a sweeping reform if he had inquired into the existing system. To my astonishment I got a letter from him saying that there was no subject he had more carefully considered than the American mails, and that he was much disappointed at finding himself obliged to continue the old arrangement. Rumour has it that the Treasury overruled Mr. Fawcett, who was, for his part, ready to try the American plan. Whether he yielded to the authority (decisive in all matters) of the Treasury, or to the diplomacy of Mr. Blackwood, I cannot say. What is certain is that Mr. Blackwood has publicly expressed his satisfaction with the present system, and the fair inference is that he, as well as the ring companies who profit by it, did his best to maintain it in all its magnificent inefficiency.

Perhaps I may give another example of the obstructive power of the permanent clerk. My talks with Mr. Fawcett about the Post-Office touched on other points than the American service. He was good enough to propose to me to write to him personally whenever I had a complaint to make or a suggestion to offer. I did so several times. I always got an answer from Mr. Fawcett himself, and a promise to look into the matter. Then my letter apparently went through the usual routine. It was handed over to the particular branch of the Post-Office which was in the habit of dealing with similar topics. Some weeks or months later an inspector would call to make personal inquiry into the matter. More weeks would elapse, and then would come an official letter expressing with elaborate civility the regret of the secretary that I should have been put to inconvenience, and his grief that it had not been found practicable to make the change I desired in the rules of the office. Or sometimes there would be an assurance that every effort would be made to avoid delay, or whatever it was, in future. Of actual practical redress or remedy, none. Occasionally there was an improvement which lasted a few weeks; then things went on as before.

It did not seem worth while to trouble Mr. Fawcett for so slight a result as this, so I gave up writing to him except when there seemed a chance of bettering the American service. I am certain he did what he could. I suspect he sometimes believed he had insured some reform. But Mr. Blackwood and his fellow-clerks were too powerful to be overruled when they were really bent on having their own way. Nor do I mean to make a single reflection upon Mr. Blackwood's honesty of purpose. I do not doubt he does what he thinks best for the department. The difficulty with him is that he seems to think the convenience of the department the first thing to be considered. The convenience of the public, which the department is created to serve, is a secondary matter; if, indeed, it does not sometimes drop out of sight altogether.

I have entered upon a large subject but I must leave it on the threshold. I certainly do not mean it to be inferred from what I have written that Mr. Fawcett was below the average of Postmasters-General. He was above the average. Nor do I mean that the Post-Office itself is the worst in the world, or even in Europe. Much of its work is well done, some of it admirably. But I think it could be demonstrated that whereas once the British Post-Office was foremost in conforming to the constant demand for improvement, in readiness to accept new ideas and try new plans, it is now one of the most backward. There are more reasons for its sluggishness than the permanent-clerk reason. But whatever the reason be, the fact remains that in many points many European postal services are now superior to the English, which formerly was superior to them all.

THE POST-OFFICE WITHOUT MR. FAWCETT.

[*October* 12, 1885.]

The so-called sixpenny telegram system came into operation on Thursday, October 1, and the public seems by this time to have found out that it is a very doubtful "boon" indeed. We used to pay a shilling for a message of twenty words, addresses free. We now pay sixpence for twelve words; addresses are counted as part of the twelve words, and have to be paid for. If the message exceeds twelve words, each extra word is charged one cent. Addresses in England are so prolix, and composed often of so many words, that despatches in which even only the address of the receiver is given are with difficulty compressed into the departmental limit. The effort to do it produces confusion, and despatches are either so imperfectly addressed that they cannot be delivered, or are so abbreviated in the text that the receiver is no wiser than before. If on the other hand you throw parsimony to the winds, and do not strenuously apply your mind to the saving of halfpence, your telegram becomes dearer than under the old rate.

What was needed was a telegram of ten words for sixpence, addresses free. That would have been a real convenience and a real "boon." The Post-Office said they could not afford it, and published reams of figures to prove that it cost tenpence on an average to transmit each despatch under the old system. The best answer I know to that is to be found in a speech of Mr. Grimston, a distinguished man of business who was chairman of one of the two great telegraph companies which the Post-Office absorbed. His company used to charge five shillings for a despatch of twenty words from London to Manchester. The public complained. Mr. Grimston in reply told his shareholders that the actual cost of transmission for every such message was three shillings and sixpence. No doubt he had figures which proved it, just as the lightning calculators of St. Martin's-le-Grand now have figures which prove that it costs tenpence. It is this sort of nonsense which the Post-Office clerks of Rowland Hill's time produced with equal gravity when they wanted to convince themselves that penny postage would be the ruin of the department. It cost a shilling to send a letter to Liverpool; the Post-Office would be elevenpence out of pocket on each letter if Rowland Hill had his way. Well, Rowland Hill had his way in spite of all the clerks and permanent magnates of the Post-Office of the day. If there had been a Rowland Hill to insist on real sixpenny telegrams, the public would have got them instead of the sham reduction now palmed off on them, and the Post-Office would presently have been as proud of the good work which somebody else had forced it to do as it is now of its penny postage.

During all the discussion which preceded the new tariff, the Post-Office officials had ever two pleas in their mouths; the telegraphs are only beginning to pay their way, and the Treasury, which is supreme over Post-Office and everything else in England, will not tolerate more than a certain fixed amount of probable loss. Yes, my permanent friends, we all know all that. We know you bought, or, as the phrase goes here, took over the telegraphs at an exorbitant price, enormously beyond their real value. This has hampered you ever since and you are welcome to the admission, for who was it who promoted this bargain, who sanctioned it, who agreed to the price, who was "done" by the shrewder men of business who owned and managed the old companies? Who but these same permanent officials who now plead their own incompetence and folly in bar of the permanent demand for telegrams at a fair price? The public officialdom of that day was incarnated in the person of the late Mr. Scudamore, just as it is to-day in the person of the present Mr. Stevenson Blackwood, the eminent revivalist who rules the Post-Office and Postmasters-General with a rod of iron.

Lord John Manners, to his credit be it said, stood out against his despotic subordinate. He tried his best to induce the House of Commons to sanction a scheme of free addresses. But Lord John Manners had just succeeded to place as a member of Lord Salisbury's Government, then existing on sufferance of the House of Commons, whose Liberal majority was still for many purposes intact. Mr. Shaw-Lefevre, his predecessor, had yielded to the peremptory persuasiveness of the permanent people. He had committed himself to the principle of taxed addresses, and when Lord John Manners tried to reverse it Mr. Shaw-Lefevre sounded once more the Liberal war-cry, and put on the party screw, and signalised his submission to his own clerks by a House of Commons triumph over common sense and the convenience of the public. And once more the public was made to understand that it exists for the convenience of the Post-Office. The deluded persons who hold that the Post-Office exists for the convenience of the public were left where they ought to be—in a minority. The idea that they are the servants of the people, and not their masters, is one which no permanent official I ever heard of in England has grasped. Anybody who propounded that notion inside the walls of the Post-Office would soon find himself outside.

To get a conception of this spirit you have only to read the rules and regulations which the Post-Office puts forth. The Czar of all the Russias does not address his subjects in a more despotic tone. The public "must" do this and must not do that. There is perhaps no odder instance of the sway which this idea bears than the attempt of the department to make the public do its bookkeeping for it. A year or two ago the Post-Office issued an order that the senders of telegrams should stamp them. The object seems to have been to have a check on the office clerks who received pay for messages. In most London offices this new commandment was ignored. People ran into an office with their messages, put down message and shilling together, and ran out. In small local offices in the provinces the rule was enforced strictly; the postmaster was forbidden to send an unstamped message. Growing bolder, the department began to enforce its rule in London. I have handed in a message for New York at the West Strand Office, one of the chief in London, and the manager has refused to transmit it, though paid for, unless I put on stamps to the amount of the sum paid. An impertinent little printed placard was displayed in telegraph offices: "The public are *required* to affix stamps to telegrams, just as they are required to affix stamps to letters." Who is the respectable telegraph clerk, one would like to know, who "requires" thirty-five millions of Englishmen to do his work for him? And now on the new forms appears an italic sentence: "Stamps *must* be affixed by the sender." You may not care much about the bad manners of this, but when you meekly attempt to obey the order of your master your difficulties begin. The rules for counting are numerous and complicated. To understand them is given to few; to master them perhaps to none. Formerly you put on your shilling stamp as you were told to, and at least knew what task was set you. But whether your message of to-day ought to be stamped sixpence, or sevenpence-halfpenny, or eighteenpence two farthings, is more than the unassisted human intelligence can make out. Probably this is what the Post-Office and Treasury have foreseen, and what they hope is that their victim, in despair of solving the puzzle they have set him, will recklessly affix a shilling stamp to a sevenpence-halfpenny message and go his way—whether rejoicing or not is to them a matter of the most complete indifference.

MR. FORSTER.

I.

HIS REVOLT AGAINST THE CAUCUS.—HIS ORATORY.—HIS CAREER.

[LONDON, *August* 3, 1885.]

AMONG the worst things that can be said of the Caucus in England is that it tries to banish independence from public life. It has declared war, for example, on Mr. Forster, who, among living English statesmen, is one of the most independent, as he is one of the most Liberal in the best sense of the word. He has been for nearly a quarter of a century a representative of Bradford in the House of Commons. He has been a great personage there and before the country at large. He has been a Cabinet Minister. Some of the most beneficent reforms in this generation are identified with his name. The most beneficent of all, the Education Act of 1870, was his work. Few men have done so much for Liberalism, or are to-day better exponents of the cause which bears that name, or likely to be better servants of it. Yet he is ostracised by the so-called Liberal Association of Bradford.

Under the new Franchise Act Bradford is split up into divisions, and Mr. Forster can never again be member for the whole borough. He has to say good-bye to the constituency which has stood by him through five-and-twenty years. In order to render some account to them of his long stewardship, he asked the Liberal Association to summon, in the usual way, a meeting of the Liberal electors of the town.

They refused. The refusal seems to me an act of spitefulness of which they will some day be heartily ashamed; an act which illustrates and condemns the spirit in which the Caucus is now worked. It could have no other result than to impose on Mr. Forster the duty of calling together his own meeting. Even the little politicians who compose this association could not imagine they would be allowed to stand between the people of Bradford and the member for Bradford. They could annoy. They could not embarrass. And so on Saturday some 5000 citizens of this great Yorkshire town assembled to hear the farewell speech of their representative.

Mr. Forster often says of himself that he is no orator. His speeches, it may be, lack some of the art which goes to the most finished oratory but the best of them are singularly impressive. It is evident that the speaker knows the secret of his own strength. He is well advised in putting aside the artifices by which the rhetorician seeks to persuade or convince. This naturalness of manner is worth all the hackneyed tricks of the trade. Simplicity and directness of speech are qualities which will never lose their force with an English audience, or an American either. Homeliness of phrase, indeed, is a thing which many a practised speaker strives after in vain. To Mr. Forster it comes without effort. In vigour nobody excels him. He said of himself on Saturday, characteristically, there is some life in the old dog yet, and some fight left in the old man. It is astonishing to be reminded that Mr. Forster is nearer seventy than sixty years old.

He has declared the secret, or one secret, of his strength as a statesman. In early manhood his life was rather solitary; he had time to read and to think, and he then formed those political opinions which he has spent the last twenty-five years in advocating. These are days when people tell you that convictions are superfluous and principles at a discount, and they point to shining examples of young men, and some old, who go fast and far in politics without either.

But if a thing is valuable in proportion to its rarity, the man who has both does well to cling to them. In great crises, or on great matters of policy, the note of sincerity is worth all the rest, and by sincerity I do not mean the sincerity born of the moment, to be succeeded by a different sincerity the next. Lifelong adherence to settled views is still a recommendation to the public. "Thou'rt a trimmer," screamed out somebody from the Bradford audience. The charge has been heard before. It dates from the days when Mr. Forster angered the Dissenters by what they thought needless concessions to the Church in the Education Act. Mr. Chamberlain, once the bitterest critic of Mr. Forster and still hostile to him, has supplied an answer to that stale charge, which was of his own begetting. Mr. Chamberlain pronounced the Education Act the greatest legislative achievement of the generation. Mr. Forster modestly says he has had more credit for it than he deserved. He has had less. It would have been done without him, he says, though not quite so soon. But he admits it would have been dangerous to wait.

No man can say how dangerous. A statesman is bound to look into the future. Undoubtedly Mr. Forster saw household suffrage in the counties coming; in the boroughs it had already come. He knew as well as anybody the enormous peril of an extended franchise without education. If he had not secured the passage of the Education Act in 1870 by those concessions for which he was criticised, who can say when any such act would have become law? But fifteen years have elapsed, and the generation then coming to a teachable age has grown to manhood and finds the ballot in its hand almost before the spelling-book. The proportion of uneducated voters among the two millions just enfranchised cannot be computed exactly, but is known to be formidable. Years must still elapse before the Education Act can have its full effect. But had there been none, what would have been the prospect in England? The government of this country would have been in the hands of ignorant men. It is Mr. Forster's merit to have prevented this, in a measure; to have modified the conditions under which an uneducated democracy, but for him, would have acceded to power. It will be a lasting claim on the gratitude of England, and once the malignity of faction has passed away, it is a claim which all England will recognise. Mr. Forster himself does not make it. He passes over the subject in three or four sentences. But he will lose nothing by that.

No more will he forfeit any part of his claim on us for what he did in our behalf during the Rebellion because he shares it with others,—with Mr. Bright and Mr. Cobden, and with the great northern constituencies in England and the English working men. The same is true of Mr. Forster with reference to household suffrage; the reform was not due to him exclusively, or perhaps mainly, but his share in it was a large one. Then comes Ireland. I know how useless it is at present to ask Irishmen to do justice to Mr. Forster's efforts in their behalf. His voice and all other voices will be drowned in cries of coercion and buckshot. But when these have died away it will remain true that to Mr. Forster's efforts was due in great degree the securing to the Irish tenant that fixity of tenure which was one of the things the Irish tenant most cared for. Perhaps you will not refuse to read what Mr. Forster himself says of the state of things that led up to coercion: "I was in Ireland to see that men were not murdered, to see that they were not ruined because they did what was right, to see that they were allowed to earn their living without interference by others." These are not very inhuman objects, but the power to accomplish them was wanting till the first Coercion Act had been passed. Then followed the long contest between Mr. Forster and Mr. Parnell, which ended with the arrest of the latter and the break-up of the power of the Land League.

You know why Mr. Forster resigned the Chief Secretaryship for Ireland. If he had been the Halifax some men call him, he would have stayed in office, and when he was out he would have trimmed his sails to any breeze that would have carried him back to the Cabinet. But the cry against him in the Bradford Caucus and elsewhere is that he will not blindly follow the party leader. He has taken an independent line on various questions. He has censured the Egyptian policy, or no policy, of the late Government; the policy, as Gordon called it, of a log drifting out to sea. He still censures it. The chances in the new division of Bradford for which he is to stand are, they say, against him, but not for that does he bate a jot of his straightforwardness in opposing what he thinks wrong. It would be easy for him to make his peace with the Bradford Caucus. They censured him at the time when he voted to censure the Government, and they are doing what they can now to turn him out of Bradford. But Mr. Forster neither retracts nor apologises. He restates the case against the Gladstone Government without bitterness but with unanswerable force.

Nor does he promise to be more amenable to discipline for the future. He declines to walk under Lord Rosebery's umbrella, whether Mr. Gladstone or anybody else holds it. There is this about umbrellas, he observes, that if they are so very big as that would have to be, they come down before your eyes and you do not see where you are going. "And I must speak out," adds he; "I have not such confidence in Mr. Gladstone's foreign policy that I can undertake to follow him wherever he leads." On most points of what is supposed to be the Liberal programme for the future, Mr. Forster is at one with the party and will rejoice to work with the party. But he well knows, though he does not say so, that it is his duty to lead as well as follow; to state his convictions freely; to try to make them the convictions of his fellow-Liberals. He is grateful to Bradford for its long support. "Again I thank you," he says, "and I thank you for this more than for anything else, that for the long time I have been your member I have not been your mere delegate, not your mere mouthpiece, but your representative, doing what

I thought to be right; and upon no other condition will I serve you in the future." That is an expression of the best and highest and most honourable spirit in the public life of England.

You hear machinists on the one hand, and speculative publicists on the other, complain that Mr. Forster is breaking up the Liberal party. Nothing could be more absurd. The Liberal party in England will cease to be Liberal when it is controlled by the local managers whose one idea of Liberalism is obedience to the behests of Birmingham. It has always hitherto tolerated and encouraged independence. It embraces many sections and shades of opinion. Its hold upon the people is due to the breadth and flexibility of its organisation. Narrow it and make it mechanical, and you will soon see the limits of its power.

II.

HIS DEATH AND HIS CLAIMS TO THE GRATITUDE OF HIS COUNTRY.

[LONDON, *April* 6, 1886.]

It is eight months since Mr. Forster was attacked by the illness which ended fatally yesterday afternoon at a quarter to one. He has been a considerable figure in English public life for more than thirty years; since 1870 he has been a great one; since 1880 one of the very greatest. You may roughly estimate the place he held by the space he occupies this morning in *The Times*, which devotes six columns to his biography and a leading article to the consideration of his life. I assume that the leading facts of his career are known, and touch only on certain passages, and on the more marked traits of his character.

There have been six great questions in which Mr. Forster took a deep interest and a great part: The relations of England to the United States during the Civil War; the Colonies; Reform; Education; the Ballot; Ireland. The two with which his name, at least of late years, has been most closely identified are education and Ireland. And it is by a cruel irony of fate that his death occurs in the very week when the Irish question is once more to be brought forward in the House of Commons in its very broadest form, by the newest and greatest convert to Home Rule.

Hardly a word can be necessary to an American audience on Mr. Forster's services to the American cause from 1861 to 1865. We all knew then, and we shall never forget, that of the small band who pleaded in England the cause of Freedom and the Union, Mr. Forster was one of the foremost. We had no better friend. Mr. Bright excepted, we had not one who wrought for us so steadily, so ably, with so much success. He spoke in the House, he spoke from many a platform to many a great popular audience; his labours in public and private were incessant. We owe to him not a little of that ardent sympathy with the Republic and that loyal friendship of race which kept so much of Lancashire and the North of England on our side. Into no cause did Mr. Forster throw himself with more heart and soul than into that in which, as he believed, and has ever believed, the interests of England and the interests of America were alike involved.

This was at the very outset of his Parliamentary career, which, beginning with his election for Bradford in 1861, continued to the last. He was member for Bradford for just a quarter of a century. Within four years of his entrance into the House of Commons, he became Under Secretary for the Colonies, a post which probably gave to his mind that strong bent toward great Imperial questions which ever after distinguished him. He never swerved from his advocacy of a close union, in spirit if not in form, between the mother country and the colonies. He extended this doctrine till it embraced English-speaking countries the world over. He had a clear vision of Anglo-Saxon supremacy and a perfect belief that England and America, united in a common policy, could not only control the commerce but keep the peace of the world. He was for Imperial Federation, as the phrase now runs, and meetings to advance that cause were among the last at which he was present. The Colonists well know what a friend they had in Mr. Forster, and his name was a household word on the banks of the St. Lawrence and by the wooded shores of Sydney harbour.

His contributions to the cause of Reform and extension of the Franchise began with the struggle of 1866, which produced the Reform Bill of 1867. They continued down to the passage of the last Reform Act of 1884. Of every measure for enlarging the share of the people in the government of the country he was an advocate. The one measure of which he had entire charge personally was the Ballot Act, which he carried through the Commons in 1871, and over the heads of the Lords in the year following.

But it was the Education Act of 1870 which was the chief constructive work of Mr. Forster's life. His belief in the English people was a reasoned belief. He was a Radical, not a fanatic. He perfectly understood that the triumph of democracy in America was a triumph of enlightenment, of popular knowledge, of educated good sense. He foresaw that the day when the still unenfranchised masses of English people would have the vote was near. He sought to provide for its arrival. As Minister of Education (under the cumbrous official title of Vice-President of the Committee of Council on Education), he brought in and carried the great measure of 1870. It was a bill which for the first time recognised and undertook to enforce the responsibility of the State for the schools. The principle that underlay its complicated provisions was simple and efficient. The State was not to create schools; it was to accept those which existed, see that a local authority should establish others where needed, and assume the duty of guaranteeing a proper standard of teaching by a system of inspection. This bill created the School Board, in a word; and the School Boards of England have been and are the best agents of that instruction for her youth which gives the best promise for her political future.

He had to carry his bill in the teeth of the most strenuous and bitter opposition from two sets of foes. The Church attacked it because it threatened Church authority over education. The Dissenters attacked it because it yielded too much to the claims of the Church. The parsons denounced measure and author as infidel. The Nonconformist ministers assailed both as mere tools of existing ecclesiastical ascendency. Time has vindicated Mr. Forster and proved the soundness of his views. Nobody now dreams of repealing his act.

It was on the formation of Mr. Gladstone's Ministry in 1880 that Mr. Forster became Chief Secretary for Ireland. Earl Cowper was Viceroy, but Mr. Forster governed the country. How he governed it is a question on which Irish Nationalists and Englishmen differed widely at the time. But other questions are now to the front. Mr. Forster's conduct is matter of history, and not of present controversy. The winter of 1880-81 was one of the most gloomy in the history of Ireland. The Land League was rising into power, and, as Mr. Gladstone said, crime dogged its footsteps. Mr. Forster bent all his energies to cope with organised outrage. It was too much for him or for anybody with only the ordinary powers of law, and therefore it was that he obtained from Parliament those extraordinary powers for the suppression of crime by an act to which those who profited by crime gave the nickname of Coercion Act. Then and during the whole session which followed Mr. Forster became the target for Irish attacks. He was assailed in the House of Commons with a cool, persistent, calculating ferocity without precedent, and never since surpassed by its inventors. He might have escaped these attacks as the Irish Secretary in the late Government escaped them, by abandoning all effort to enforce the law and leaving the country at the mercy of the League. He did not so construe his duty. He waged war on outrage, on murder, on agrarian crime of every degree. The storm of insults that daily howled about him in the House never turned him from his one purpose of restoring social order in Ireland. He was accused of imprisoning 900 suspects, and keeping them in prison without trial. Whoever else may accuse him, accusation would come with a poor grace from us in America who during the war locked up nearly 40,000 men on suspicion of disloyalty, and seldom thought of trying them.

A duel was going on between the League and the Government—or, if you like, between Mr. Parnell and Mr. Forster—which ended for the time by the retirement of Mr. Parnell into the peaceful seclusion of Kilmainham Gaol. The power of the League was broken. So great had it become that if Mr. Forster had not locked up Mr. Parnell, Mr. Parnell might soon have locked up Mr. Forster. That a worse fate did not befall the Chief Secretary was due to the merest chance; or, as some would say, to Providential interposition. The history of the plots to murder Mr. Forster came out in the investigation of the Phœnix Park tragedy. Nobody will forget the assassins who looked into the window of the railway carriage at Westland Row where sat Mr. Forster's wife and daughter, before whose eyes they meant to kill him. They did not, simply because he had driven to Kingstown instead of taking the train.

In Dublin they show the stranger—I was shown it a fortnight ago—the bridge on which Mr. Forster was to have been murdered, and over which he actually drove while an accident detained the car with a white horse which should have preceded him as a signal to his assassins. These were but two attempts out of many.

Mr. Forster made one retort in his singularly forcible and sagacious speech at Bradford which may rank with the best of its kind. The Irish went to St. George's Hall to silence the man who had charged Mr. Parnell with complicity with agrarian crime. They interrupted Mr. Forster, after their manner, with savage yells. He bore it till the interruptions threatened to put an end to his speech. Then he turned to the gallery where the Irish were massed, and said, "As you did not succeed in murdering me in Ireland, you will have to hear me in England." The roar of cheers which followed showed the Parnellites that they had no choice but to be silent; and for the rest of the evening silent they were.

Mr. Forster knew well enough his life was aimed at, but went his way with a tranquil courage which even among his Irish enemies was not without its admirers. When he resigned on account of the Kilmainham Treaty, to which he refused to be a party, he had cleared the ground for his successor. It is the fashion among those who do not like him to say he failed. Ask Mr. Parnell, and the other leaders of the Land League which Mr. Forster shattered, what *they* think.

To the memorable scenes that followed in the House of Commons I need refer but briefly. The attack on Mr. Parnell as one who connived at outrage and murder made a profound impression on the country, and it remained unanswered at the time save by a counter attack from Mr. Parnell on Mr. Forster's administration of the law. The Irish, I suppose, will never forgive the man whom they so long assailed. He was hated to the last; that was his reward for two years of devoted service and heroic effort to secure to Ireland the rights which we most value in America. He was, of course, an opponent of Home Rule; "no Home Rule," they say, were the last words that passed the lips of the dying statesman.

"He was a man," said Mr. Gladstone in his eulogy upon Mr. Forster, "upon whom there can be no doubt that Nature had laid her hand for the purpose of forming a thoroughly genuine and independent character." It was this very genuineness and independence which brought him sometimes into collision with his colleagues. Mr. Forster was incapable of compromising with his conscience. He took immense pains to be right; he studied and mastered his subject; there were no difficulties before which his industry shrank; then, once convinced, he was adamant. Mr. Gladstone resented at the time Mr. Forster's resignation and his statement of the causes of his resignation, but he now lifts himself high enough to say that his Chief Secretary for Ireland administered his great office in a spirit of self-sacrifice and genuine philanthropy. That is not an adequate tribute, but it covers and repels the charges which the Irish Nationalists used to bring against him.

Patriotism was with Mr. Forster a passion; his love of freedom intense; his conception of duty unbending. He had humour and good humour, and he bore with singular stoicism the invective which the Irish heaped upon him. When he spoke, he spoke to the point. Of rhetoric he had little; of grace or finish of style, almost none; but he had a power of clear statement and an energy of intellect which made his speeches impressive. At times he was eloquent— the eloquence which comes from directness and picturesqueness of speech, from sheer intensity of conviction, and from burning sympathies. In the House he was an effective debater. On the platform at Bradford he could rouse a wild enthusiasm. He cultivated none of the arts of the drawing-room; men often thought him rough, but appeal to him for a service and he was kindness itself. Amid the pale shadows which flit through modern public life, Mr. Forster was a solid and vigorous individuality; a force in politics; a man who had to be reckoned with; who could not be cajoled; who was stubborn for the right. He was a type of Englishman who would have made his mark in any period of English history; one of that great middle-class from which so many of the best of them have sprung. He dies unhappily at the very moment when his experience, his sagacity, his fearlessness might have been of most service to the country he profoundly loved.

LORD IDDESLEIGH.

[LONDON, *January* 15, 1887.]

IN all the long biographies of the late Lord Iddesleigh which papers of all kinds publish, you will look in vain for good anecdotes of him. His was not a life which lent itself to gossip. What is said of him is for the most part well said. Justice is done to his purity of character, his fine sense of honour, his unselfishness, his genuine abilities, his services to his party and to the State. If there be a point on which our English friends do not seem to care to dwell, it is Sir Stafford Northcote's share in the Treaty of Washington. That has never been a popular business here, and it was always thought that Mr. Gladstone showed much cleverness in putting one of the Conservative leaders on a Commission whose labours were foredoomed to a cold acknowledgment in England. The coldness would have become rancorous party hostility and pertinacious opposition, had not Sir Stafford compromised his party by his adhesion to the Treaty. And it really is odd that one of the few stories about him should relate to his visit to Washington, and should consist chiefly in a friendly reminiscence of the fact that he was photographed in boots which, to the American eye, were excessively thick.

Lord Iddesleigh was not what is called a society man, but there were many houses in London where he was to be met more or less frequently. At some he called with old-fashioned polite regularity once a year. Then, instead of limiting himself to the conventional twenty minutes and discussing the weather, he stayed for an hour or longer, and talked exceedingly well. A good deal depended on the encouragement he got from his hostess, but he had far too much of the stately courtesy of the generation to which he belonged to let it be seen in any case that he was paying a visit as a mere formality. He would not discharge a social obligation as if it were a bill of exchange. As a talker he had no great reputation. He did not care to shine, and he lacked that confidence of manner and assertiveness of tone on which the reputation of so many talkers so much depend. He preferred an audience of one or two. If he had a listener to his mind his conversation was often very good. It was the talk which came from a full mind; if anything, his mind was, for the purposes of mere success in life, too full, his interests too various, his estimate of the relative claims of conflicting or competing subjects not decisive enough. He did not resolve on politics till he was thirty-seven. He had been in his youth a scholar—not using the word too strictly—knew his classics, cultivated literature, not, as Sydney Smith said, on a little oatmeal, but on six thousand a year sterling. He shot, rode, did most of the things which well-born young English country gentlemen commonly do. To the last his tastes remained eclectic. His Edinburgh address showed he had kept up his reading, and even his thinking, on subjects which have nothing to do with party politics. He came near being a financier of a high order. In that, as in the more strictly political part of his career, it was thought that Mr. Gladstone's influence was harmful to him. He never quite emancipated himself from the private secretaryship, and the spell which Mr. Gladstone knows how to cast on those who once come into close contact with him remained on Sir Stafford to the last. His private life was far more complete for all this miscellany of interests. Probably his public life was less concentrated, less earnest, less successful.

Lord Carnarvon publishes a letter on Lord Iddesleigh which contains two rather striking points. "In the bitterest crisis of the bitterest political struggle of recent years," writes Lord Carnarvon, "I remember his saying to me, 'I never rise in the House of Commons without a kindly feeling to Gladstone.'" Precisely, and that was one of the traits in Sir Stafford's amiable character of which his own party complained most loudly. I said that he never freed himself from the spell which Mr. Gladstone cast upon him. This is confirmation enough. Then adds Lord Carnarvon: "His love of literature was great, and almost the only personal difference of opinion in these many years that I can now recall was over a disputed passage of Chaucer." The two men were colleagues, each holding high office in the State. Most Englishmen will think it slightly ludicrous that two Cabinet Ministers should be losing their tempers over a crabbed line in an early English poet.

Pity more of them do not care more about poetry and other things than politics and potatoes. The fault of Englishmen, of most Englishmen, in public life is the limitation of their intellectual interests. Sir Stafford was in 1885 one of the few men left in the House of Commons who could cap a classical quotation, just as Mr. Gladstone is now almost the only man who ever ventures on a line from Virgil. The culture of Fox and his Whiggery are vanishing together. Lord Carnarvon is a charming example of the survival of letters in a statesman, yet he is almost as lonely in the House of Lords as Sir Stafford was in the lower Chamber. The peers who have a strain of learning do not speak; Lord Sherbrooke, for example; and those who speak most often have little learning beyond the domain of the practical. The late Lord Derby has left no successor. Of the present Lord Derby, it was his father himself who said that a blue book had more charm for him than Homer had.

I speak of Lord Iddesleigh as I knew him late in his life; earlier I did not know him at all except as one knows a Minister in the House of Commons from the gallery, or a personage one sees across a drawing-room. For some years past, and while he was still in the House of Commons, I met him pretty often. When the door opened and the servant announced Sir Stafford Northcote, there was always a slight stir in the company. A group of English men and women are seldom wholly insensible to the approach of a Cabinet Minister. The signs of interest are slight but sufficient. The figure which entered was not very tall, not what a soldier would call well set up, not in itself remarkable for dignity or distinction. The large head, square in front, was striking enough, and the eyes might have been fine if you could have got behind the spectacles; but the full grayish white beard, trimmed almost to a point, always seemed to pull the head down. It drooped, and the hands either hung loose or were clasped about his hat, if hat he happened to have, so that the air of the whole man was a little deprecating. He seemed just the least doubtful whether he should come in or not, and as if he had not made up his mind, or as if the servant with his announcement had made it up for him.

That was your first impression. A second look showed you how wrong you were. You had mistaken outward signs for inward uncertainty; of which there was none. What you too rashly thought timidity was gentleness and refinement of manner. The younger Englishman—not all, but some—enters a room as if it belonged to him, or as if he were going to annex it and all it contained. Not so Sir Stafford. He was rather carelessly dressed, too, but whatever you thought of his dress or of details in his appearance, you never were in the least doubt that there stood before you an English gentleman of the best period; or of the best which anybody now knows by personal experience and observation. He assumed no authority, he seemed never to care to assert that which rightfully belonged to him. Yet he was certainly not the kind of man with whom other men thought they might take liberties. He was clear, accurate, judicious, not brilliant, humourous at times, always sincere, always interesting. Of late he was depressed, even melancholy, and roused himself with an effort. One of the staunchest of friends, said his friends. It was possible to think it had been better for Sir Stafford had he been a staunch enemy also. He always seemed to hold it beneath him to engage in a personal contest.

His reputation in the House of Commons has suffered by little fault of his own. It might be said that the degeneration of the House could be traced by the decay of Sir Stafford's authority. He would not change with the times. He undertook, as he supposed, to lead a House composed of men who were, in a measure, like himself; of men who respected the traditions of the House, and of the class which till lately gave the tone to its proceedings. Certainly he never expected to have to face a mutiny in his own ranks. Into that unhappy business I do not now wish to go far. The story of the Fourth Party, of the long guerilla war they carried on against their nominal chief, of the final triumph of Lord Randolph Churchill and banishment of Sir Stafford to the Lords, is known of all men. This is not the moment to attack, still less to defend, Lord Randolph. He had taken for his motto: *Autres temps, autres mœurs*—and added to himself, other men also. But the notion that has become current about Sir Stafford's leadership does him injustice. He lacked, indeed, pugnacity, the delight in conflict for conflict's sake. The Donnybrook Fair doctrine, whenever you see a head hit it, was not his. He missed opportunities which a less scrupulous man would have seized. He abstained from retorts that sprung naturally to less delicate lips. It is impossible to conceive of Sir Stafford Northcote, under no matter what provocation, addressing an opponent across the table—even in an undertone—as "You —— old humbug." It has never been recorded of him that, in reply to a proposal from a rather distinguished member of his party to speak on a pending question, he asked what was the use of being leader if he could not keep such a —— old fool as ——'s mouth shut. He kept his best retorts for the table. A friend told him that the defeat of the Ministry on the Budget had been arranged by the Ministry themselves. "No," said Sir Stafford, "if they had arranged it, it would have failed." Had he but said this sort of thing at times from the Front Bench, it might have been less easy to oust him from the leadership of his party.

But for legitimate opposition as he understood it, Sir Stafford was a singularly capable man. I have seen him fence with the Old Parliamentary Hand on a question of procedure, and pink his man. I have heard him sum up a debate in which the greatest debater of the House had made one of his most telling speeches, and reply to him point by point, with triumph. At critical moments his eye kindled, his voice reached easily to the gallery and filled the chamber with its rather harsh resonance; he had energy of manner and abundant intellectual resource. Certainly he lacked dash and devil, and for a party in a militant mood he was by no means an ideal chief. He never mastered, or perhaps never accepted, the maxim that the business of an Opposition is to oppose. That, I think, was the first cause of the cabal against him. It is the fashion to speak of Lord Randolph Churchill as having intrigued and conspired against his chief from motives of personal ambition. Lord Randolph is probably not deficient in personal ambition, but he is before all things, or was, a party man. His idea of the duty of the leader of a party in opposition was to turn out the Ministry; to attack, harass, annoy, diminish, and finally overturn the reigning majority. In season and out of season was his motto, and all is fair in war, his doctrine. Sir Stafford Northcote did not adopt that doctrine, and because he did not the Fourth Party was formed, and took up very much the position adopted by the *francs-tireurs* in the German war; a kind of land privateers.

This much and no more will I say on a subject fitter for some other occasion. Nor will I go into Lord Iddesleigh's Foreign Office administration. He came to that enormously difficult post much too late in life. He had no natural bent for foreign affairs. He had not the physical strength, or flexibility, or quickness which fit a man to deal with an intolerable accumulation of business, due in a measure to the faulty organisation of the office. No wonder Lord Iddesleigh failed to make an impression on continental Cabinets. But it was, after all, only an episode in his life, and the verdict of his countrymen on his life as a whole is one of which his family and friends have every right to be proud.

MR. BRIGHT.

I.

THE LIBERAL LEADER AS HE APPEARED IN 1866 AND AGAIN
IN 1882.

[LONDON, *March* 9, 1889.]

It was to Mr. Sumner that I owed my first introduction to Mr. Bright. They were old friends, and any one who at that time—it was in 1866—presented himself to the great Englishman with a letter from the Massachusetts Senator was sure of being kindly received. Mr. Bright was to speak in Birmingham on the new Reform Bill, and I went down from London, as I have often done since and shall never do again, to hear him. I believe I came over from the continent on purpose; at any rate, I got to Birmingham but just in time for the speech in the Town Hall, in the evening. When it was over I sent Mr. Sumner's letter to Mr. Bright, and was asked to the room where he was discussing the situation with a number of local celebrities.

There had been a great outdoor meeting of fifty thousand people, or more, that day. The Town Hall holds perhaps five thousand, all standing except in the galleries and on the platform. The first I had missed. The second gave me my first notion of what English enthusiasm and English cheers were like. Mr. Bright had been welcomed as nobody else in those days was welcomed. He was the idol of Birmingham, which was then, as it still is, the home of the most convinced, intelligent, and rational Radicalism in all England. On the question of the new Reform Bill he and his constituents were at one. It was a Middle Class franchise which that bill proposed, and of the middle classes Mr. Bright has ever been the champion and representative. They include, at least in the Midlands, the better class of artisans, and of these the hall was full. They had been stirred, as Bright alone knew how to stir them, by the last sentences of his speech; one of the finest and most characteristic of his perorations. Their hurrahs were still echoing in the corridors and dimly-lighted passages about the hall, as I took the hand which Mr. Bright held out to me.

It was not a moment to forget—the moment in which one of the wishes of a lifetime was granted. Among Englishmen then living there was none whom I more cared to see; no orator whom, judged by his reported speeches, I thought his equal; no Englishman who had done the same kind of service to his country and to ours; none whose political mission had a character so apostolic as his. It was a long time ago and I, like the Birmingham artisans, was full of enthusiasms, all of which I hope I have not outlived.

With this feeling of more than admiration for Mr. Bright, it was my good fortune to see him first in all the illumination of one of his great popular triumphs. What Burke said of Conway came into mind instantly as I looked at him, "Hope elevated and joy brightened his crest," a quotation from his favourite Milton. His manner, even amid these trumpet blasts, never lost its simplicity—it was in pure simplicity that lay so much of its incomparable charm. The flush of triumph did not intoxicate him. You hardly saw a trace of the deep feeling which surely filled his soul, save in the luminous glow of his eyes. I stammered out some compliment about his speech. "Yes," he said, "it was a good meeting, was it not?" There was not much time to talk. The hour was late. The day had been a fatiguing one, his health was none too strong. He asked about Sumner affectionately, and about some matters in America, with the keen interest he ever had in things American. He was pleased that an American had come to Birmingham to hear him speak. He asked me to pay him a visit at Rochdale. The others looked on, I thought curiously, while these few sentences were spoken.

It was a low room, rather crowded, with two jets of gas flickering in the face of the orator. His hair even then was gray, though abundant, the complexion florid, and the rather irregular but powerful features gave you at first sight an impression of singular force and firmness of character. So did the whole man. The broad shoulders, the bulk of the figure, the solid massiveness of this masterful individuality, the immovable grasp of his feet upon the firm earth, his uprightness of bearing, the body knit to the head as closely as capital to column—all together made the least careful observer perceive that here was one in whose armour the flaws were few. He looked straight at you, not as if he meant to or by an effort of will but with the natural directness of a child or an animal—there was neither fixedness nor flinching but perfect frankness.

Neither then nor since, during the two and twenty years I have known him, did I ever see an expression on his face which did not bear the stamp of sincerity. No man hated pretension or falsity of any kind more than he. It was obvious he could hate. There were lines in his face which never came there by peaceful reflection. He was of those who think they do well to be angry against baseness and injustice, against oppression and privilege. It was the spirit of the Old Testament quite as much as of the New. His mission was in a measure one of destruction; he had spent his life in uprooting abuses; in thundering against tyrannical institutions; in denouncing laws and law-makers who stood between the people and prosperity. The passion for justice was not stronger in him than the hatred of injustice.

You may say that all these things were not likely to be visible in the first five minutes, nor were they. What I mean is that Bright's face answered to the conception one had formed of it, and that long familiarity never changed the first impression of that first interview. If we are to accept Arnold's classification of civilising elements into Greek and Hebrew, there is no doubt where Bright belongs. It was the Hebrew element which dominated him. Isaiah was his prophet, and I have seen him at times—mostly in public, but sometimes also in private—when the lightnings of his eye might have flashed from the sternest of Hebrew messengers from the Most High. A good photograph of him has often an air of benignity, and an air of benignity belongs to him, but he does not wear it always. The broad arch of the forehead, the crown of hair set far back on the head, the beautiful gray eyes, the gentle manner, find their contrast in the perverse curve of the mouth and the strongly, heavily moulded jaw. He was a saint, if you like, but a saint who belonged to the church militant. He was a man of peace, always in arms to prevent you from going to war.

The word reminds me of the interview which among all those I had with Mr. Bright was, next after the first, most impressive to me. It was the morning after he resigned office on account of the bombardment of the forts at Alexandria. I called on him at his rooms in Piccadilly. He occupied the same for many years on the second floor of the house numbered 132. It has lately been pulled down to make way for a smart new block. He had the whole of the second floor, and the room in which he sat and worked and received visitors was large and comfortably furnished, with an outlook into Green Park. It was a sunny July morning; brighter than is often to be seen in London; the sun streaming in through the three large windows. Bright was in his dressing-gown; a garment to which, like Carlyle, he was much attached; not a fashionable short smoking-jacket, but an ample robe that fell below his knees. He was not given to conventional speeches, but he said as the door opened, "Ah, you are very good to call on a Minister out of office." His tone and look were both of depression. I said his resignation would be regretted as much in America as in England, and that, if he cared to say anything in addition to what was known, his friends would be eager to hear it. "No," he answered, "I have nothing to say." So we talked for two or three minutes about the weather and the last dinner party, and I rose to go. "Sit down," he said, and forthwith began on his resignation and the Egyptian business generally. Much of what he said was for the public and was published at the time; some can never be published. He was extremely agitated; the tears were sometimes in his eyes. It was a crisis in his life. He longed to be useful. He liked office. The Chancellorship of the Duchy of Lancaster suited him perfectly. There was no administrative or departmental work, which he hated; there was a salary, £2000 a year, which he did not object to draw, and there was a seat in the Cabinet, with all the authority and dignity which Cabinet rank confers. Mr. Gladstone and he were united by almost lifelong ties. His attachment to his chief was as strong as it is possible for such an attachment to be. He said—

"You know something about the relations between us. You know what I expected from his Government. You know what it costs me to part from it and from him."

"Then why resign?"

He got up from his chair, walked to the window, and stood there looking out on the green fields and blue sky. Then he turned, walked back with a flushed face and flaming eyes, and burst out—

"Do you think I am going to be party to an act like the bombardment of Alexandria? If it were just, if it were necessary, I should hate to be responsible for it in the least degree. But it is not just, it is not necessary. It is a wanton and wicked outrage on a nation which has a right to be free. I have borne witness against war all my life long. I abhor it. None of our wars have been just. There has not been a just war since William the Third, except your war to put down the Rebellion. My legacy to my children is a message of peace. Do you think, do you think, at my age I am going to be false to all my principles, to go back on all my record, to retract all I have said, to sanction such an act as this, to leave my children a heritage of shame and disgrace, to leave behind me for them the memory that their father was a traitor and a renegade? Never!"

His voice was hoarse with passion, with the passion of a great nature stirred to its depths. The smooth tones had become rough and hard. He spoke with all the energy of sorrowful indignation at a great wrong which he was powerless to prevent. He had tried to prevent it and failed, and grief and righteous anger surged and boiled within him. I had never, anywhere, on the platform or in the House, known him in this mood, nor heard such tones, nor seen such gestures. He went on—

"I have spoken to nobody as I speak to you. Of course I have protested. I have argued, entreated, remonstrated, all in vain. I believe I threatened. It was equally vain. I appealed to Gladstone. He listened but I could not move him. I do not censure him; not a word of what I say about the war is meant for censure on Gladstone. There is no purer soul than his. He believes himself right. Nothing would induce him to fire a shot if he did not. But I must judge for myself. I resigned three days ago, but it is only this morning the world is allowed to know it. I could not sleep for the roar of those English guns at Alexandria. It is the end of my public life. I never shall take office again. My work is done."

To hear him was distressing. Nothing could be more pathetic than the situation in which he found himself. It was breaking his heart to break with Mr. Gladstone. To make up his mind to that had been a sore struggle. But he had quitted the Ministry and there was no going back.

At the same time, it was clear that the merits of the Egyptian question played but a little part in the tragedy. What swayed him was not so much his conviction of the wickedness of this particular war, if war it could be called, as his conviction of the wickedness of all war. His horror of bloodshed was as deep as any feeling of his nature. He hated war—hated it for its cruelty, and also, I think it must be said, because it interfered with the course of trade and the growth of a nation's prosperity. Lord Palmerston said of him that if an enemy landed at Dover, Bright would make a calculation whether it was cheaper to let him in or drive him out. The epigram has been quoted often. I quote it again, to say I think it a cruel slander. There was no more ardent patriot than Bright. He loved his country and his countrymen and believed the welfare of both dependent on peace. He shrank from the reproach he knew Alexandria would bring on his country. It was one more precedent for violence, and therefore it was that with all the passionate energy of his nature he strove, and strove vainly, for peace.

II.

MR. BRIGHT'S READING.—HIS TASTE IN POETRY.—HIS PLACE IN SOCIETY.—HIS TALK.

Mr. Bright was not a man of wide reading or general culture. He knew nothing of any language but English, and not much of any literature, English and American excepted. He had no knowledge of science, nor deep feeling in art. He was a type of his class—the middle class; with some of its narrowness of interest, and all its virtues, and with his own surpassing genius in addition to all. To those who despise culture, his name and the limitations of his mind will serve as an argument to the end of time. He deserves a better fate than that; and there is a far truer thing to be said of him, namely, that he perfectly understood how to make the most of his intellectual gifts. No Latin or Greek, but the best English of his time. He is not an argument for narrowing culture and limiting studies, unless you find another mind like his on which to try the same process.

Everybody has heard that Milton—perhaps next after the Bible—was the book he most cared for. That of itself impairs the force of the narrowing argument, for Milton is saturated with the classical spirit, and with classical lore. He who knows Milton well cannot be wholly ignorant of antiquity. Bright knew by heart the poems, or nearly all the poems. The prose had no particular attraction for him; the *Areopagitica*, and one or two other pieces, excepted. What is remarkable is that there should be so little trace of Milton's diction in Bright's prose. It is remarkable, but not inexplicable. He studied the poet wisely; not for imitation, but for inspiration. He copied neither Milton nor anybody else. He learnt from him many secrets of style, which he used in his own way, not in Milton's. There is little in the structure of Bright's sentences, any more than in his choice of words, to remind you of the author of *Paradise Lost*. What he caught from him, if he had it not already, was the elevation of tone which is alike remarkable in the poet and in the orator. "He nothing common said or mean," may be affirmed of both; if an alteration in Marvell's fine line be permissible. In every speech, as in the whole life of this carpet-weaver of Rochdale, there is the note of distinction. He stands apart. He breathes the upper air. No man is more remote from the sordid or common; none more hostile to the vulgarity of thought amid which he passed his life.

But if Milton, why not Shakespeare? I once asked Mr. Bright if it was true that he did not read Shakespeare. He said—

"It is true I don't read him."

"Will you tell us why?"

He gave the very oddest reason I ever heard.

"It is the dialogue that spoils him for me. The break from sentence to sentence, the question and answer, the continual interruption of the thought, divert the attention and impair the interest. The flow of thought is not sustained; the style goes to pieces."

There is no arguing with this, nor did I want to argue; but the answer may stand as an intellectual novelty. The Bible he knew well; and if Bright's own incomparable style now and then suggests any original, it is the greater prophets of the Old Testament. Whether his reading was very various, even among English poets, may be doubted. It is singular that, next to Milton, the one whom he most quoted should be George Wither. I have his own authority for it. He said to me once: "If you come across a quotation in any speech of mine which you don't recognise, it is probably Wither." He could hardly explain what it was that attracted him to this obscure writer, for obscure he is, and hardly more than two or three of Wither's poems hold their place in literature.

Late in life Bright read, I think, not very much except current writings on subjects that were nearest to him. He knew the latest pamphlet on Ireland, and the newest popular arguments for Free Trade. He had a habit, which was not critical, of mentioning these ephemeral writings in some speech of his own, with unstinted praise. No advertisement could be so effective. He sold countless thousands of Mongredien's treatise by such an allusion: and other thousands of a poor history of England. He was not critical. Even Milton had not formed his taste in poetry. He pronounced a panegyric on such very mediocre verse as is to be found in the *Epic of Hades*. Mr. Lewis Morris's popularity, such as it is, dates from that sentence.

Between Mr. Bright and Mr. Gladstone contrasts were more numerous than resemblances, but no contrast was stronger than between their habits of reading. Mr. Gladstone has read, and does read, widely in at least half a dozen languages; and his reading of the best books is continuous. Both of them read the last thing before sleeping. Mr. Gladstone reads Homer. Mr. Bright read, not even his beloved Milton, but the last pamphlet somebody had sent him. And yet Mr. Gladstone's English style is one of his weak points, and Mr. Bright's English style one of his strong points. What a natural genius in the use of words he must have had!

What he liked, I have always thought, in poetry—at any rate, in modern poetry—was the sentiment, rather than the poetry. There is no evidence that I know of that he cared much for the delicate art of Lord Tennyson, or for Matthew Arnold in all his force and purity. His favourite among living or recent writers of verse was Mr. Whittier. Mr. Bright and Mr. Whittier had much in common. Both were members of the Society of Friends. Both were Abolitionists, and there were other likenesses on which I need not dwell. Mr. Whittier's anti-slavery verse had endeared him to his English co-religionist, whose enthusiasm embraced much more than the anti-slavery verse of the American poet. He admired the simplicity, the courage, the fervour in a holy cause, the faith in great things, which are among Mr. Whittier's best gifts. He admired him altogether, quoted him, talked of him with delight. One night at dinner—I may be indulged in saying that it was at my house—Mr. Bright turned the conversation to Mr. Whittier. The ladies had gone to the drawing-room.

"Of course you read Whittier."

"Yes, I have read him."

"But I mean, read him often. Do you mean to say you don't know him by heart?"

"No, not much by heart."

"Not his best things? Don't you know 'Snowbound'? can't you repeat it?"

And upon a general admission from the four or five who were present that no one of them could repeat it, Mr. Bright's eye kindled, he got up, walked to the fireplace, put his back against the chimney-piece, and declaimed the whole poem.

I can see him as he stood there, his beautiful face lighted up with the glow about him, and the deeper glow within him; his voice subdued to the size of the room, but not less rich, deep, melodious, and true than if rolling out to thousands; his gesture, not frequent but decisive, and sometimes dramatic. Mr. Whittier never heard his own poetry so recited. I thought I should tell him of the scene. I never did, but I hope somebody will tell him now. When Mr. Bright had finished, we went upstairs. He carried Whittier with him, and talked of him to the ladies as he had talked to us; not, as I said before, critically, but with deep feeling, and real apprehension of what is best in him.

Nor did it end there. Mrs. Procter, the delightful young lady of eighty, as Mr. Lowell called her, was one of the company, alert, fresh, energetic, keen-witted, as she always was. I think Whittier was new to her; not familiar, at any rate. She listened intently. When the company broke up she drove Mr. Bright home—gave him a lift, is the phrase here. I saw her again not long after, and she told me that he repeated Whittier to her in the carriage all the way to Piccadilly; and when they had arrived, kept it standing a minute or two in front of his door while he finished what he had in hand.

In the society of London Mr. Bright was a unique figure. Needless to say he never was a man of fashion. There was a long period during which the world of fashion held aloof from him. It ended before he became a Cabinet Minister and Privy Councillor. The Tribune of the People, as some of his friends used to call him, had ceased to be thought dangerous by the Classes. He was asked often to all sorts of houses and to all sorts of entertainments. While breakfasts were the fashion, he went to breakfasts. I think your friend Mr. Choate of New York will remember meeting him at breakfast, and walking home with him across Hyde Park. Mr. Bright, I know, remembered Mr. Choate, and asked about him more than once afterward; he was charmed with the American's manner and talk, and quite forgave him for being a great lawyer. Lawyers, great or little, were not as a rule favourites with him.

He was not often, I think, to be seen at parties, but dined out rather frequently. His curiosity about the great world came late in life, but it came. He had a curious exactitude, and when he was asked to dinner—as years ago was the custom—for quarter to eight, used to arrive at quarter to eight, while his hostess was putting the last touches to her toilette. His habit had this advantage, that he could hear the names of the guests as they were announced at the door of the drawing-room. If he did not hear, or if any one came in whom he did not know, he used to interrogate the friend nearest to him eagerly—"Who is that?" And if he failed to recognise the name—"Who is she? Tell me something about her."

To mere conventionalities he paid but scant respect. It was his habit to wear a black velvet waistcoat long after other people had ceased to wear them. I cannot remember ever to have seen one in London except his. It did not matter what he wore. There was no truer gentleman in the company—a phrase which is detestable, but has a meaning not easy to express briefly otherwise. There was no courtlier personage than this Quaker; none whose manners were more perfect. If there had been no standard of good manners he would have created one. It could not be said of him that "manners maketh man"; the reverse was true. "The gentleman," said Emerson, "is a man of truth;" the word "is a homage to personal and incommunicable qualities." Swift said, "Whoever makes the fewest persons uneasy is the best bred in the company." Mr. Bright's simplicity was such that a stranger who was disconcerted by meeting him must have been timid indeed.

Many years ago I took the late Dr. Ripley to see him. Dr. Ripley was a man of the world as well as a man of books, and admired Mr. Bright, and was most desirous to see him yet a little nervous at the prospect of the meeting. We had an appointment, and found him at breakfast in rooms he then occupied in Clarges Street. When the interview was over, Dr. Ripley's first remark was, "How completely Mr. Bright puts you at your ease." He had been, nevertheless, in one of his Hebraic moods. Something had angered him which had appeared in a certain London newspaper. He talked of it a minute or two, but finally ended with, "What does it signify what such a paper says? It was never anything but Palmerston's strumpet!" That will give you a notion how far his freedom of speech in private exceeded at times the freedom of his speech in public; which also exceeded, perhaps, that of any other great orator of his day.

His talk, always delightful, had many qualities. If any one thing could be said to characterise it more than another, it was directness. Perhaps downrightness would be a more descriptive word. He said what he thought. Out it came, no matter to whom or about what he spoke his mind. It was impossible to take offence. There was not an atom of malice in him; for all his power of contempt and power of invective.

There was a dinner during which India was discussed. A very eminent man of science expressed some strong opinions in favour of holding India by the sword, without much regard to the rights of the natives. Mr. Bright's opinions are well known. He turned on the eminent man of science, who was also a man of high spirit, and told him in a few sentences what he thought; made him and the company see that his opinions, whatever their merits, were not according to knowledge. It was done with energy, unsparingly, but with unruffled sweetness of tone and manner. "I never," said the eminent man of science, contemplatively, as we walked upstairs, "I never before realised how much pleasure a man may have in being told he is a fool." Mr. Bright of course had used no such word, but he had perhaps conveyed the impression.

There is at least one distinguished American who will recall an occasion when a still stronger word was in fact used. It was in the lobby of the House of Commons, and the American had just been introduced to Mr. Bright as a friend of Mr. Greeley, who was still living. "Ah," said the great Free Trader, "does your friend Mr. Greeley still cling to that idiotic doctrine of Protection?" He had, and often expressed, a real regard for Mr. Greeley in other characters, but for Mr. Greeley, or for anybody else, as Protectionist, he had a kind of holy abhorrence.

Another American was told of this little outburst, and the same evening met Mr. Bright at dinner. He was still in the combative mood—on that subject he was always combative and always scornful—and he began on it across the table.

"Well, Mr. Bright," answered the American, "when I talk on Protection with a Free Trader, I always begin by admitting that I am an idiot." It was a doubtful thing to say, but Mr. Bright, though perplexed for a moment, took it in good part, and the conversation turned.

He preserved his seriousness of thought in the most frivolous society. Nobody had more humour, or lightness in hand, but if the subject was serious, or interested him deeply, he said his say seriously, or, as in the story I am going to tell you, bore his testimony unflinchingly. In the days of Mr. Gladstone's earlier unpopularity — for society had prejudices against him long before he took Home Rule in hand—Mr. Bright was once dining at the same table with a certain Princess. Her Royal Highness made a remark disparaging to the Liberal leader. Mr. Bright turned to her gravely. "May I ask you, ma'am, have you any children?"

"Yes; why do you ask?"

"Let me beg of you, ma'am, to take them at the first opportunity where they may see Mr. Gladstone. When they see him, say to them that they are in the presence of the Englishman to whom God has permitted to do greater service to his own country than almost any other in his time."

Of Mr. Bright's home life I have little or nothing to say. I paid a visit to Rochdale in 1866, two months after his invitation was given, but it was too hurried to be of much avail. I had to arrive and leave the same morning, on my way to Liverpool for the steamer. But at least I saw One Ash, his home, and the owner of it in his library. Neither Rochdale, nor the suburb or environs where Bright's house stands, would be attractive but for him. His house was of brick, of no great size, nor anything other than what might be expected of a Quaker mansion. His family clung to the tastes and habits of his religion, and of his people. There was nothing gay but the bindings of his books, which I think had been given him. Nor can I repeat the talk, for it happened to be altogether about private matters.

III.

HIS ORATORY.—HIS METHOD OF PREPARATION.—SOME OF THE
SECRETS OF HIS SUCCESS.

[LONDON, *March* 27, 1889.]

Among many speeches of Mr. Bright's which I have heard, one which is not the greatest has left the deepest impression. It was delivered in October 1873, to his constituents of Birmingham. He had been very ill for nearly three years, his life had been in danger, his reason threatened. It was the second illness of the kind he had had to endure. Never a hard-working man, in one sense of the word, hating and altogether neglecting the drudgery of departmental business, he nevertheless put a great strain upon his mind. The interest he took in a great question shook him to the centre. His nature was sympathetic, emotional, passionate. To keep himself under control when deeply stirred cost him great efforts. He had, moreover, a meditative mind; he brooded upon great subjects, and thought out, as few Englishmen do—for it is not an English habit of mind, or not the habit of most English statesmen—the principles which governed a case, or on which a policy was based. The religious mood, too, was with him just as much a political mood as anything else. He wrestled with his subject in the watches of the night; with tears and prayers, perhaps; certainly with the most strenuous thought of which he was capable, and with a sense of responsibility and anxious care which never left him. Whenever he spoke, he lifted politics from a lower to a higher level.

All this told upon his strength. In the winter of 1870, then President of the Board of Trade in Mr. Gladstone's first administration, he broke down. So critical was his condition that his doctor ordered him out of London instantly. The doctor had been summoned in the morning, Mr. Bright went to Norwood the same afternoon, and his voice was not again heard in public till the autumn of 1873. He had resigned office, and resumed it again in August of that year; not in his old post, which demanded too much work, but in the sinecure of the Chancellorship of the Duchy of Lancaster.

In the October following he once more met his constituents, who, meantime, had re-elected him without a contest, on his new acceptance of office. The desire to hear him was great. No ordinary hall — not even the Town Hall of Birmingham, large as it is—could contain the multitude of his friends and supporters. It was arranged that he should speak in Bingley Hall, a kind of market, a mere covered area, where fifteen thousand or twenty thousand persons might stand and listen. For oratorical purposes it was as ill adapted as the Waverley Market in Edinburgh, where Mr. Gladstone tried his voice so sorely. Mr. Bright's friends felt it to be a doubtful experiment, with his health still less firm than of old, but he was resolved to make it.

The welcome they gave him as he entered was enough to shake the most iron nerve, and it possibly shook his. When he came to speak, his voice was hardly his own; the emotion of the moment mastered him and us. He began, in vibrating tones, with a reference to his long illness, and to the generous forbearance of his constituents during the four years of his absence. There was nothing in the words he used which, as you read them, explains the effect they produced, but before the few sentences on this subject were ended many of these hard-faced hearers were in tears. I believe—indeed, I think I afterward heard Bright admit—that, so afraid was he of breaking down with his own emotion, he said less than he meant to say. I have read the speech this morning. So simple, so reserved, are the opening sentences that, but for my memory of the scene, I should almost say that they expressed inadequately what he wished his constituents to understand. They do not give up their secret; they do not account for the uncontrollable agitation which swept over that great body of men. There is nothing in the printed page to suggest the pathos of the speaker's voice and look. But I read on to the end, and this is the end:—

"For me the final chapter is now writing. It may be already written; but for you, this great constituency, you have a perpetual youth and a perpetual future. I pray Heaven that in the years to come, when my voice is hushed, you may be granted strength, and moderation, and wisdom to influence the councils of your country by righteous means, for none other than righteous and noble ends."

The pathos of that would touch the coldest, and to read it on the morning of Bright's death turns the pathos into tragedy. The final chapter was fifteen years more in writing; years filled like those which had gone before with generous words and high aims; beneficent in example and in influence; a pure life and a noble life if ever there was one.

Many and many of the best known passages in Bright's speeches might be quoted as splendid examples of purity in diction. It is not to rhetorical ornamentation that they owe their effect, but to the absence of it. No diction is more perfect; none would be more impossible to imitate; it seems the natural expression of the thought of the speaker. It is, of course, not natural; it is the result of immense pains. Bright made no secret of his methods. He almost never spoke offhand. He prepared carefully, and used notes freely. The framework of the speech was put together like a mosaic; passages were written out and committed to memory. Mr. Carl Schurz will recollect hearing Bright himself discuss and explain his own method one night at dinner. Others were there whose authority in such matters has weight. There were, I think, no two opinions. Bright, at any rate, thought no speech could be too fully wrought out in the speaker's mind in advance of delivery. He dwelt on the difficulty of dovetailing the written passages into the fabric so that none should find the joints, and he quoted Brougham as a good instance of an orator who failed to conceal the art with which his speeches were constructed.

"Though I have spoken much," says Mr. Bright in a

letter, "I am not sure that I am qualified to teach even what I have practised with some show of success." He tells his correspondent, however, what his own practice has been:—

"When I intend to speak on anything that seems to me important, I consider what it is that I wish to impress upon my audience. I do not write my facts or my arguments, but make notes on two or three or four slips of notepaper, giving the line of argument and the facts as they occur to my mind, and I leave the words to come at call while I am speaking."

This last is in substance the advice which Mr. Pitt gave Lord Mornington, who consulted him about speaking. It is misleading, and has misled more students of oratory than one. Mr. Pitt had a copious vocabulary and was never at a loss for a word. Few men at the start are thus endowed. Mr. Bright cautions his correspondent against relying too much on his advice, and the caution is sound, though not for the reason which Mr. Bright modestly suggests to him. What is good for the practised orator is not always good for the novice.

Mr. Bright, by practice and also by study of which he says nothing, has acquired not merely what is called command of language, but one of the most perfect styles known in the history of oratory. Neither practice nor study, nor both, would have availed to attain to this perfection without that natural genius which is born with some men and not with others. But even Mr. Bright does not trust to the words coming at call in critical passages. "There are," he says, "occasionally short passages which, for accuracy, I may write down, as sometimes also—almost invariably—the concluding words or sentences may be written." The very passages, that is, on which his fame as an orator rests, have been written. That is a very different thing from writing out and committing to memory a whole speech; "a double slavery which I could not bear." Mr. Everett bore it, and other orators have borne it.

They knew, I suppose, what best suited them; how they

could best produce the effect they wanted to produce. I have heard Mr. Bright discuss this subject, and I hope some day to return to it. To suppose that, because he is against writing except in passages, he is against careful preparation, would be an entire mistake. "To speak," he says, "without preparation, especially on great and solemn topics, is rashness and cannot be recommended." I do not imagine that he ever thought the general preparation of a lifetime of public speaking on great and solemn topics sufficient. Each great speech has had a special preparation of its own.

Emerson says in the Preface to his *Parnassus* that he has sometimes inserted a poem for the sake of a single line, perhaps even for a word. There are passages in Bright where a single word is a lesson in oratory. Such is the famous one on the Crimean War in the House of Commons, when, in the winter of 1855, news was anxiously awaited from the trenches before Sebastopol:—

"Many homes may be rendered desolate when the next mail shall arrive. The angel of Death has been abroad throughout the land; you may almost hear the beating of his wings."

The student of style may well ask himself what would have been the effect of that sentence had the orator used some other word than "beating." It would have been so easy, for any but a man of genius, to have taken the fatal step from the sublime to the ridiculous. As it stands, the sentence is a very daring one to have been spoken in the House of Commons. The House is impatient of oratory, of enthusiasm, of deep feeling, of anything but what is businesslike and commonplace. It listened to Bright with something more than admiration. There was a reverence for him even in the days when he stood almost alone, and in those later days when he was the head of a hated minority.

It was not eloquence alone that subdued this critical, censorious body. It was not even character alone. Bright was the equal of their best men on their own ground. There was no better debater, if you consider mere debating by itself; nobody who could hit harder; nobody who kept more strictly to the business in hand, or who knew more about it. When Palmerston sneered at him—it was in another Crimean debate—as a peace-at-any-price man, he answered: "I am not afraid of discussing the war with the noble Lord on his own principles. I understand the Blue Books as well as he, and I say it with as much confidence as I ever said anything in my life, that the war cannot be justified out of these documents." Nothing suited the House better than such a declaration; they felt the solid earth beneath the speaker's feet, and beneath their own.

And it was by such a declaration that he led them to that almost incomparable peroration which every American schoolboy ought to know if he does not, beginning, "I am not nor did I ever pretend to be a statesman," and ending, "Let it not be said that I am alone in my condemnation of this war, and of this incapable and guilty Administration. And even if I were alone, if mine were a solitary voice, raised amid the din of arms and the clamour of a venal press, I should have the consolation I have to-night—and which I trust will be mine to the last moment of my existence—the priceless consolation that no word of mine has tended to promote the squandering of my country's treasure or the spilling of one single drop of my country's blood."

There are many parts of the speeches on America which the American, whether schoolboy or statesman, knows, in more senses than one, by heart; both for their value to us at the time, and for their rhetorical beauty. On them I need not dwell even for a moment.

What Emerson said of poetry may also be said of oratory —of the best oratory—that it teaches the enormous force of a few words, that it requires that splendour of expression which carries with it the proof of great thoughts; and that every word should be the right word. I commend this Crimean passage to the student. If he will master the sense of it without committing to memory the words, and will then try to write out the sense in his own words, he will have had a lesson which ought to profit him. Or let him try to take these sentences to pieces and reconstruct them, or forget a word and try to replace it. The topic is full of interest, but I discussed it twenty years ago and have written much about it since, and I will add a word on one other point only.

Bright's speeches were never frequent, and rarity always adds to the value of a thing. Neither in the House of Commons nor on the platform was he, at any time since the repeal of the Corn Laws, to be heard very often. It was an event when he spoke in the House, and when he delivered an address at Birmingham there were pilgrimages from far and near. He disliked parade, ostentation, fuss, as much as any man could, but he never shrank from the affectionate greetings of his constituents. The infrequency of his public appearances was due, however, to other causes than indolence or love of seclusion. He understood that great efforts must be made at long intervals, and that one great speech is worth a score which just fall short of being great. I once heard an admirer of Mr. Gladstone claim for him a superiority to Mr. Bright, because he had spoken so much more than Mr. Bright. There are half a dozen bores in English public life who might be ranked above him for the same reason. If Mr. Gladstone's speaking fails to attain to the very highest excellence, it is probably because of its copiousness, as well as from the extraordinary complications of his style. His exuberance is irrepressible; it is magnificent, but it is not always oratory. Bright avoided extremes. He valued directness of speech. The majesty of Chatham, the sonorous pomp of Pitt, the luxuriance of Burke, the elaborate artifice of Brougham—none of these were his, but to none of them, perhaps to no orator who ever lived, was he inferior in those qualities which are the vital force of oratory, nor in all its literature is there anything more admirable than his august simplicity.

IV.

ENGLISH PUBLIC OPINION AFTER MR. BRIGHT'S DEATH.

[LONDON, *March* 28, 1889.]

Without, or almost without, distinction of party, and with genuine and deep grief, the English people are signifying everywhere, and in many ways, their sense of what they have lost in John Bright. It is natural to turn to the press for the most complete expression of the general sorrow, but I apprehend that his death is felt most keenly in the humble homes and among the humbler classes of this country. If ever they had a friend, it was Bright. To him more than to any other of his generation, they owe it that their condition to-day is one of some content and reasonable comfort. They owe to him and to Cobden together untaxed food, but they have to thank him almost alone for the breaking down of the spirit of class monopoly, which before his time was the one intolerable burden upon their life. They owe their political enfranchisement to him, not directly, but indirectly. He was the real author of Mr. Gladstone's bill of 1866, and of Disraeli's of 1867. Neither gave the vote to the working man, nor was the giving of it then possible. But they made the speedy giving of it inevitable, and given it was, in truth, from Mr. Bright's own hand, if not by his act.

All this they know well, but in the English press you hear little of it. The most grateful classes are not the articulate classes. Even the middle class, of which Mr. Bright was the lifelong champion, are under less obligations to him than those below them. But it is their voice which is mostly heard to-day. No class or condition is quite silent. The Queen had a real regard for her great subject, whose loyalty to the crown and personal respect for the Queen have been often declared. Some of the last messages which reached One Ash before his death came from the Queen, and from the Prince and Princess of Wales. They know—

or if they do not, their advisers do—that Mr. Bright's influence was the chief among those which averted revolution, or, at any rate, which have made revolution peaceful instead of violent. So do those very privileged classes whose privileges he attacked, and either destroyed or diminished. Until of late years they denounced him fiercely. Of late years they have covered him with eulogies, and none to-day are more ready to wreathe his memory with laurel.

As for the English press, it has done its present office well. Mr. Bright had no great admiration for the London press, which he regarded as in the main the defender of whatever is powerful, whatever is established, whatever has wealth, precedent, or prerogative on its side. He had to carry on the great contests of his life with but little help from the most powerful of these papers, at the most critical moments. But they lift themselves to do him justice, and the provincial press, as often happens, surpasses that of London.

They both claim him as a typical Englishman—and so he was—and they see clearly that in the higher range of his character he was not typical, but unique. They say of him without stint that he was perhaps the only English statesman of the first rank in public life whose honesty, whose sincerity, whose perfect single-mindedness and entire devotion to interests other than his own or his party's, have never once been questioned amid all the conflicts of a stormy political life. They do justice to his rigorous conception of duty; they recognise the apostolic character of his political mission; they acknowledge what to most of them seems one of his chief titles to lasting renown—the success of every reform identified with his name. Nothing is here respected by the majority so much as success. They are not insensible to the loftiness of his aims, or to the religious fervour of his public aspirations, any more than to his incomparable genius as an orator, or to the truth of his private life and personal character. He is still, even to the disappointed Radicals, the Tribune of the People of earlier days; always their advocate, never their flatterer.

The Tories, perhaps less disappointed, as things are going, speak with no trace of bitterness of those days when he thundered against Pluralists and Sinecurists in Church and State; against monopoly in land and monopoly in legislation; against the adulterous origin, as he called it, of Spiritual Peers; against the military and naval services as a gigantic system of outdoor relief for the aristocracy; against Protection, when protection meant, as it did here, dear food for the people; against almost everything which the Tories then held sacred. What they now hold sacred, Mr. Bright himself would have been perplexed to define with accuracy.

No doubt they are grateful to him for his refusal to follow Mr. Gladstone in his Home Rule crusade. No doubt, also, some of the more extreme Home Rulers find it hard to refrain from expressing by his open grave some of the animosity they felt and expressed toward him in the later years of his life, even when the end of his life was in sight, and even though Ireland never had a truer friend. One of the leading Home Rule journals of Ireland, even to-day, speaks of him as a "crank." It is the sole exception that I have seen to the general and successful wish of this party to forget all recent controversies, and to remember only the beauty, and splendour, and purity of Mr. Bright's whole life.

There is, perhaps, no part of his great career so little dwelt on in proportion to its importance as his immense services to America. Few Englishmen care to remind themselves how much need there was for them, or to own how all but universal in public life and in society was English sympathy with the Pro-slavery Rebellion in America. There was no period in Mr. Bright's history when he had more need of courage; none when to be in the minority was to be more hated; none in which his finest qualities shone more brightly. If the English do not choose to acknowledge it, there is a reason the more why we should render him full tribute. A nation's gratitude cannot now repay the debt which the nation then incurred. Living, he would have been the nation's guest, had health permitted him to cross the Atlantic, at President Hayes's invitation. Dead, the nation which mourns for him cannot declare its homage too publicly or too solemnly. To the last, America was dear to him. What he did for the extinction of slavery and the saving of the Union was one of his most precious reminiscences, and there was no subject on which he discoursed with more eloquent delight.

V.

THE TRIBUTE TO MR. BRIGHT IN THE HOUSE OF COMMONS.

[LONDON, *March* 29, 1889.]

What the House of Commons feels itself able to do in honour of the memory of John Bright, it has done this afternoon. It has kept strictly within the unyielding limitations of precedent; transgressed no rule; forgotten no custom; sacrificed something less than an hour of its often squandered time. There has been no ceremony, and even the poor compliment of adjourning was thought outside those traditions by which the House abides on such occasions. Yet the homage which the House offered to its great Member has been, on the whole, not unworthy of it or of him. It would have pleased him because it was simple; touched him because it was genuine. There have been a few brief speeches, and nothing more. But they were the unanimous voice of the House, and it was enough.

Even in their grief the English are business-like. The House met at the usual hour and transacted the usual routine business. There was from three to four no sign that anything unusual was to occur, except that more strangers than usual were waiting outside the crowded, narrow quarters allotted to them. Inside, the Members' benches were for an hour almost empty. None of the leaders of either side were present until the questions began, and one or two of the collisions, now daily, took place. The Members were mostly in black. It was four o'clock when Mr. Smith came in, and a quarter past before Mr. Gladstone appeared. By that time the questions were nearly over and the House had filled. Both front benches were crowded. Mr. Gladstone sat, as usual, between Sir William Harcourt and Mr. Morley, his head sunk between his shoulders. Beyond him were Mr. Chamberlain, Sir Henry James, and Lord Hartington, all together at the end of the bench.

By half-past four the last question had been asked, and the last wrangle between interrogating Irishmen and reluctant Ministers had worn itself out. There was a pause. The House grew suddenly silent, expectant, almost anxious. Mr. Speaker, in his clear, resonant voice, said gravely, "The First Lord of the Treasury." Mr. Smith rose and stood by the table. The whole House uncovered as it uncovers for majesty alone; this time for the majesty of death.

The First Lord was in black; very pale; his voice uncertain; his manner that of a man on whom is laid a burden too heavy for him. He began nervously, with stumbling sentences, clearly trying not to show, but to conceal, emotion. His ten minutes' speech had almost no oratorical merit except that of sincerity, the word which during its delivery was oftenest on his lips. Mr. Bright had been almost a lifelong opponent of the party whose leader was now pronouncing a panegyric on him; but leader and party were agreed that his motives had ever been pure, his convictions firm, his loyalty absolute and complete. They lament him, and would follow him reverently to his grave.

Amid the muffled cheers which swelled through the House as Mr. Smith ended, Mr. Gladstone rose. He, too, was all in black; his face was almost as white as the shirt-front which his low waistcoat left open; a carelessly knotted, narrow, black necktie straggling across the shirt. He leaned with both hands on the box resting on the table in front. A moment before Mr. Smith spoke, Mr. Gladstone had been talking and laughing with the men about him, but this mood had passed, and he had grown all at once silent and stern. He began easily, but in a tone which deep feeling had subdued; his voice was not strong; the lower notes were husky; the muscles and chords of the throat not at all moments entirely under his control. No empty chamber could be so still as this thronged house, listening for his first words. The most careless spectator, if there were one, could not but feel that he was looking on at a great scene of historic grief. The soft, gray twilight of the London afternoon fell on rows of strong, sad faces which friend and foe turned upon the great Liberal leader.. There he stood, greatest of living orators, to pronounce the last eulogy upon an orator even greater than himself, his lifelong friend, his comrade, his colleague; the man who bore him, perhaps, a truer and longer affection than any other. He spoke in the very chamber which for almost fifty years had echoed to Mr. Bright's voice, amid the thronging memories of many conflicts and many triumphs. What he said you will have otherwise; the impression of what he said and the points of his speech are all I can try to convey. The House seemed always to be waiting for something that never came.

It was a noble eulogy. Complete it certainly was not; it contained hardly a sentence which fixed itself in the memory. Mr. Gladstone's manner was almost more than his words. He spoke throughout with a grave dignity that was pathetic. There was no stint in his praise, no conscious withholding of the honour that was his friend's due; yet it was less the friend than the colleague and chief who spoke. The passage about recent differences is sufficient as far as words go, yet it was not quite free from a sense of effort; it was more the doing of a duty than a spontaneous outburst. Far finer were the sentences in which he dwelt on Mr. Bright's and Mr. Cobden's renunciation of popularity during the Crimean War: "I felt profoundly, and have never ceased to feel what must be the moral elevation of men who, having been nurtured through their lives in an atmosphere of popular approval and enthusiasm, could at a moment's notice consent to part with the whole of that favour which they had heretofore enjoyed, and which their opponents might have dreamed was to them as the very breath of their nostrils." Finer still, perhaps, were the words in which he described Mr. Bright's eloquence as the loftiest that has sounded within these walls during this generation. That generous acknowledgment of his great rival's supremacy touched the House profoundly. So, in lesser measure, did the tribute to Mr. Bright's repugnance to office; the tribute to character deeper than eloquence, deeper than intellect; the tribute to his life's great services, as recorded in the progress of his country and the prosperity and happiness of the people.

When Mr. Gladstone sat down the murmur of cheers was but faint. The House seemed hardly to know whether to express what it felt or not. Lord Hartington followed briefly, weightily, sincerely—speaking with more signs of emotion than might have been expected from a man singularly self-contained. Then, in the absence of Mr. Parnell, Mr. Justin McCarthy spoke for the Irish. He manfully owned their debt to Mr. Bright, and he ended with the most eloquent sentence of the day, claiming for himself and his friends "the right to lay an Irish wreath on this great Englishman's grave." With that, all the leaders of all the parties had spoken. But there followed a few words from Mr. Chamberlain, as Mr. Bright's colleague in the representation of Birmingham—measured, perhaps memorised words, not wholly wanting in feeling or in fitness.

So ended a scene that had lasted less than an hour, and the House passed almost at once to business, the members streaming out into the lobby as the Speaker was heard calling for the orders of the day.

VI.

HIS RELATIONS WITH MR. GLADSTONE AND MR. CHAMBERLAIN.—PORTRAITS.—THE SENATE.

[LONDON, *April* 6, 1889.]

Conventionality is carried in this country to great lengths; as it is in some other countries. What was said of Mr.

Gladstone's eulogy on Bright in the House of Commons is an example. There was but one opinion in the lobby—that the speech, though elevated in tone and full of fine things, was not, as a whole, up to the mark. Mr. Gladstone's friends said so quite as freely as his political opponents. But behold next morning the press without distinction of party praises the eulogy without stint and without qualification. Those who dislike the Liberal ex-Prime Minister seemed more anxious to suppress criticism than those who usually applaud him whatever he does. Yet there is such a thing as history, and the truth must in the end be told. I will quote one remark. "Mr. Gladstone," said one of his admirers, " was plainly longing all through his speech to break out on Home Rule. It is Home Rule and nothing else which occupies his mind. Everything gives way to it; personal friendships as well as political interests and other political questions. He knew well that Bright had stood as a lion in his path. *Felix opportunitate mortis* meant—all unconsciously to Mr. Gladstone himself—that it was time he went."

You may say that this is a hard judgment. I think it is, but it is by no means the judgment of this one man. I know nothing that better shows how all-engrossing is the question of Home Rule than the relations between Mr. Gladstone and Bright since it came to the front, and also the relations between Bright and those Liberals who followed Mr. Gladstone into the Home Rule camp. I say nothing of the Irish. But it was felt by the Gladstonians in 1886 that, more than any other single influence, Bright stood between them and victory. His was the most inspiring personality of all those which were on the side of the Union. Old Liberals hung back from the polls when they were asked to vote against the convictions of him to whom they had so long looked as a leader. His Liberalism was of far older date than Mr. Gladstone's. The purity of his motives was beyond question: neither politics nor political ambition had any share in determining his course. He has never been forgiven, and when he died, although he had ceased to take an active part in this or any other burning subject, it was felt by the Home Rulers that their chances of a near triumph were better than before.

It is to be said, also, that through Mr. Gladstone's speech there runs another note which jarred on the House. There was something of officialism about it; it was the Prime Minister discoursing on one of his colleagues, almost as if the colleague were a subordinate. Again it is to be said that Mr. Gladstone was certainly unconscious of his tone, but other people felt it, and it added to the general want of complete content with the speech as a tribute to one who, whatever he may have been in the Cabinet or in his Department, was in the House of Commons the equal of any one.

There is a story that may throw light on Mr. Gladstone's mood. He had occasion some years ago to read to the House part of a correspondence which had passed between himself and Bright. He read out the beginning of Bright's letter to him, "My dear Mr. Gladstone." The letter in fact began, "My dear Gladstone." The Prime Minister had inserted the "Mr."

Mr. Chamberlain said something the other day in the House of Commons about thirty years' friendship between him and Bright. There was, however, a long time when that friendship was not thought by common friends of both to be very close on either side. It has been hinted that Bright's letters to his son, and perhaps to others than his son, would disclose the real truth. For many years there was reason, there were several reasons, for divergence between them. There were many subjects on which they held hostile opinions. Mr. Chamberlain is a root-and-branch man. Mr. Bright's conservatism went down to the foundation of things,—to those very foundations which the younger man would disturb; will still, if he has his own way, and in spite of his temporary alliance with Toryism, disturb. Then they were both members for Birmingham, and Bright's name had lent lustre to that constituency long before Mr. Chamberlain had been heard of outside parochial politics.

The ambition of the younger man but ill brooked an inferior position, and his position could be nothing but inferior while the elder man lived. However, anything like an open rupture was avoided and of late years the feeling between them grew more kindly; more kindly than the public who heard or read Mr. Chamberlain's speech in the House of Commons might suppose. Not the warmest admirer of the present member for Birmingham could think that effort worthy of him.

Mr. Shaw-Lefevre publishes some reminiscences of Bright in office. It was he who was Secretary to the Board of Trade while Bright was President of that Department, and was, he tells us, in daily contact with him. But this daily contact between Mr. Shaw-Lefevre and Bright has not added much to our knowledge of the latter. It was known before that the great orator took little interest in departmental questions, but it may surprise the public to hear that he left them almost entirely to Mr. Shaw-Lefevre. A story is given of an interview between the President of the Board of Trade and the Elder Brethren of Trinity House. Mr. Shaw-Lefevre tells us that Bright posed before them as a Conservative statesman who had a regard for ancient institutions. It is desirable to treat the ex-secretary of a public department, and everybody else, with civility, but it is difficult to conceive Bright as "posing" before anybody, or for any purpose whatever. There never was a man whose bearing in all the circumstances of life was more simple and genuine. But when we find Mr. Shaw-Lefevre gravely telling us that Bright on one occasion did not agree with him, and on another gave him solid assistance, it is time to turn elsewhere for illumination.

For portraits of Bright you must go to the photographers. There are several photographs which are excellent. Engraved on wood in the English illustrated papers they are considerably less excellent. Sir John Millais painted him, but the portrait is not one of his best. Full as it is of technical merits, it misses the true character of the man who sat for it; misses, most of all, that massive force, that constant suggestion of power, of solidity, of strenuousness, which every observer was impressed by. It has some of Bright's simplicity but all too little of his strength. It has been engraved, and most of the better qualities of the picture have disappeared in the engraving. None the less did the too-enterprising publishers dispose of some two thousand "artist's proofs" to the confiding British public at six guineas apiece. As the plate was "steeled" before any impressions were printed off, there are, properly speaking, no proofs at all; artist's or other.

The late Frank Holl painted him, and that too was a picture which had its admirers, yet falls far short of justice to the subject. Holl, like Millais, painted with force and fidelity what he saw, but it is no mere accurate transcript of the superficial facts of face and figure which can adequately render a character like Bright's. The deeper truths of it are not so much as suggested. A caricature of him by the late Carlo Pellegrini has just been published, but Carlo Pellegrini is for once totally at fault, and has given us not a glimpse of the Bright known to others. It is a caricature of qualities and expressions which were not his. A very good bust of him by Sir J. Boehm is in the possession of Lord Rosebery, for whose sake Mr. Bright consented to sit to the sculptor.

Finally, I ask to be allowed to express for myself—it is a purely personal opinion which can compromise nobody else—my regret that the American Government and American Senate should have thought it imprudent to send a word of sympathy to Bright's family and countrymen. "I do not know," said Mr. Gladstone in the House of Commons, "that any statesman of any time has ever had the happiness to receive on his removal from this passing world honours and approval at once so enthusiastic, so universal, and so unbroken." What would the Liberal leader have said had he known that no word of sorrow was to come from Washington; that the Senate of the United States would shelve a resolution in Bright's honour? For us he braved unpopularity, he courted obloquy. For him we have not the courage of so poor a thing as a compliment to his memory.

He died a private citizen, it is true, and a Government composed of private citizens is, it may be, a body too awful to remember the existence or acknowledge the death of one who was not at the moment in receipt of public pay. Precedent? It would be time to talk of precedent when another Rebellion had put the Union in peril, and another John Bright had pleaded the American cause. Government? We owe it in some measure to Bright that we still have a Government. The Senate? Let us speak of the Senate with respect, and impute no motives. The motives of these gentlemen matter chiefly to their own consciences. But it is to be said plainly that their act brings upon their country the reproach of such ingratitude to one of its benefactors as the best motive cannot excuse. The Irish? I say it is to the everlasting honour of the Irish race that their chosen orator in the British Parliament claimed the right to lay an Irish wreath on the grave of this great Englishman. Why should Americans have been willing to claim less?

It matters not to him. The best friend we ever had on this side of the Atlantic is gone. He sleeps just as peacefully in the little Rochdale burial-ground as if we had covered the sod with flowers, or offered him the nation's homage that was his due. There are no means of knowing what has been said or thought at home these last few days, but the hour will come when Americans will lament the cold silence of those who might have spoken for them, and that blank page in the records of the Senate will be thought the least honourable in all its history.

I.—10

LORD CARNARVON:

HIS PLACE IN PUBLIC LIFE. — HIS GIFTS. — HIS PERSONAL
CHARACTER.

[LONDON, *July* 2, 1890.]

HE was never, says one of his biographers, what is called a robust politician. It is meant as a criticism: his friends may well be content to let it stand as a eulogy and an epitaph. Mr. Caine may perhaps be named as a type of the robust politician, or one type, and Sir William Harcourt as another. Lord Carnarvon certainly had not much in common with either of them. In these days, when the caucus outside and obstruction inside the House of Commons are two recognised instruments of practical politics, it can be a reproach to no man that he retains a preference for earlier methods. What is said about his lack of robustness does not, indeed, refer to either of these matters, but they serve just as well as illustrations of what the robust politician will accept as a condition of his political existence and prosperity. By no stretch of the imagination is it possible to conceive of Lord Carnarvon as taking any part in the coarser work of public life. "He carried scrupulousness and sensitiveness in public life almost to a fault," says the same writer. If they be faults, this fourth Earl of Carnarvon had them. There are, perhaps, still a few natures to whom they would seem virtues.

He thrice resigned high office—that is why we are asked to believe that Lord Carnarvon was not a robust politician. He resigned in each case because his colleagues in the Cabinet had resolved on measures which he thought wrong, measures to which he was opposed on principle; measures in each case of such import that, if wrong, they could not but be deeply injurious to his country. The robust politician, of course, would not have resigned; he would have swallowed his scruples, put his principles away for safe keeping till a more convenient season, clung to his place in the Ministry; and from his place in Parliament would have stoutly defended the measures he had stoutly opposed in the Cabinet. Thus, and not otherwise, if you accept this view of public duty, can the government of this country, or of any country, be carried on. We may agree or disagree with Lord Carnarvon in each or all of the three cases. But no man doubted then, or doubts now, that he acted in each case from conviction, from a reasoned conviction, and that he resigned because it was to him morally impossible to do otherwise.

He had, nevertheless, statesmanlike qualities of a kind none too common, now or ever. You have only to look across the Canadian border to see one proof of this. He was the author of the Dominion of Canada, perhaps the most successful of many recent English experiments in colonial policy. Lord Durham had conceived the idea thirty years before. Lord Cardwell had worked on it later, but it fell to Lord Carnarvon as Colonial Minister in 1867 to carry the bill through Parliament. The political economists, with Mr. Lowe, now Lord Sherbrooke, at their head, were aghast. One part of the general scheme was the proposal of a guarantee for an intercolonial railway. Mr. Lowe and his fellow-doctrinaires said there was no demand for such a railway; it could not be built; it would never pay, and so on. But Lord Carnarvon had a trait of character not less valuable sometimes than the robust pedantry of the disciples of Adam Smith; he had faith and imaginative energy enough to believe even in something not tangible or visible. He carried his measure triumphantly, with results now known of all men and recognised even by the doctrinaires.

If he were an impracticable politician, how came it that

Disraeli twice sought his services as Minister, and that Lord Salisbury, with two resignations staring him in the face, again in 1885 offered him office and a seat in the Cabinet? Lord Carnarvon resigned in 1867 because he was not prepared to hand over the government of this kingdom to the working classes. The working classes of this kingdom were, at that time, almost wholly uneducated. The Education Act came thirteen years later. They were without knowledge and without political experience or training. The author of the Reform Bill of 1867 was Mr. Disraeli. Was his a name to inspire confidence? Mr. Disraeli returned to power seven years later, and Lord Carnarvon came back with him again, as Minister for the Colonies. He remained Minister for the Colonies for four years. Early in 1878 Lord Beaconsfield thought himself appointed by Providence to preserve the Turkish Empire from the encroachments of Russia, and ordered the British fleet to the Dardanelles. Such a step meant, in all probability, war, and to such a war Lord Carnarvon would not be a party. Nor would Lord Derby; the two resigned for the same reason, though Lord Derby's retirement came a little later.

From 1878 to 1885 Lord Carnarvon was out of office; then Lord Salisbury wanted a man of character and capacity as Lord-Lieutenant of Ireland, and once more turned to his old colleague. The Tory party were about to enter upon a novel experiment in Irish policy; a man was needed whose name should be a guarantee to the country of sincerity. The experiment was tried. It may well enough be that the new Viceroy went further than the Prime Minister wished or expected him to go. The Parnell interview took place; one of the most curious incidents in the perplexed records of Anglo-Irish politics. After it had become public and a controversy had arisen over it, Lord Carnarvon resigned the Viceroyalty. It was supposed, and said, that his experience in Dublin had converted him into a Home Ruler, and that he would no longer work with a Government which he could not convert. There is just enough foundation for that supposition to make it entirely misleading. The story, as told at the time and repeated since, is inaccurate. But Lord Carnarvon's public life in the ordinary sense of the words there came to an end. His service to the State had been long and useful and honourable.

There was, however, a more interesting personage than Lord Carnarvon the Minister, and that was Lord Carnarvon himself. He was one of the most delicately modelled figures of the period. It must be admitted that he belonged to the Classes; that he came of patrician stock; was, indeed, by descent, of the very flower of the English nobility, with the blood both of the Herberts and the Howards in his veins. He had almost everything a man can have; almost all the gifts of fortune were his; and of all he made a noble use. He was admirable in all the relations of life. He had culture of a kind now becoming unhappily each year more rare. He did not disdain the classics, which he knew well; not as a German professor knows them, but as part of the literature of the world which ministers to the growth of a man's mind. Translations of the *Agamemnon* and the *Odyssey* into English were the fruit of his political leisure. He wrote on various subjects, edited the new *Chesterfield Letters* with an excellent preface, had much learning in history, and a tinge of ecclesiastical learning also that coloured his whole life.

There were few more devoted Churchmen and perhaps none more free from intolerance, whether in the Church itself or in private life. It seemed to him no part of his duty to preach the gospel to those who did not care to hear it, or to insist on ecclesiastical observances for those to whom they were unmeaning or tedious. It sometimes happens in England that your host, if himself an attendant upon the religious services of Sunday, feels bound to urge the attendance of others, as if responsible for their spiritual welfare so long as they are his guests. Lord Carnarvon was free from that. Everybody was his own master at Highclere Castle; not the least hint toward church-going was offered to any one. The

Archbishop of Canterbury might be one of the party, yet the freedom was none the less complete. If you asked, as a matter of civility, whether this great prelate might not expect others to go to church with him, you were told that nothing whatever was expected or desired except that each should follow strictly his own inclination, and this was said with a sincerity which made its meaning unmistakable. There were prayers at the Castle and a Sunday evening service, but at these also you were entirely free to be present or not.

In such points, and in many others, there was in Lord Carnarvon's ideas and conduct something that seemed of the last century rather than this: an unfailing courtesy, a considerateness for the opinions of those about him, a forgetfulness of self, that were all delightful. So much did he care for the outward observances and opportunities of religion, that he conceived it possible not many years ago to open, and keep open during the week, the churches of London, as the Roman Catholic churches of the Continent and here too are open. He wrote a letter on this subject to the Archbishop; a letter so penetrated with devout goodwill to his fellow-men that, whatever you thought of his scheme, you liked the man all the more for having imagined it and written about it as he did. He had that gift of expressing himself daintily which seems to belong to men of certain temperaments, and not to others. Some years ago he put up a monument on the battle-field of Newbury; not far from which stands Highclere Castle with its magnificent view over the spreading fields and woods of Hampshire. It is a plain obelisk of gray granite, with inscriptions in various tongues on the four sides of the base. The one in English runs, as nearly as I can remember, thus: "In memory of Viscount Falkland and of those who fell on either side in the Battle of Newbury, this monument has been set up by those to whom the rightful authority of the Crown and the liberties of the subject are alike dear." It would not be easy to collect into a single sentence a neater tribute to both parties in a great civil war.

This neatness and finish were characteristic of Lord Carnarvon in his talk. The scholar and the man of the world were always contending in his speech; or rather, each contributed to the brilliancy of the other. His long contact with great affairs gave weight to what he said, and his studies and natural taste gave it form. Sometimes his manner was nervous — from ill-health, I always thought. He was a martyr to gout, which became neuralgic gout. Ill or well, he had the most constant amiability; he had for all those who knew him the irresistible attractiveness which is felt only under the influence of a beautiful nature. If he did not belong to the last century, as I said, he belonged to that generation which has passed, or is only too rapidly passing. It had qualities which the new has not; very admirable qualities which seem to die with those who possessed them, and seldom to reappear; and of this generation Lord Carnarvon was an admirable example.

LORD HARTINGTON.

I.

SOME NOTES ON HIS POLITICAL METHODS.

[LONDON, *July* 1, 1886.]

How is it, I hear some Americans ask, that Lord Hartington alone, or almost alone, among Liberal Unionists, escapes personal attack? Every other Liberal who has declined to follow Mr. Gladstone in his new departure is assailed, and assailed bitterly. Mr. Goschen, Sir George Trevelyan, Mr. Chamberlain, Mr. Bright himself—all are targets for many a shaft shot from the new fortress of their old friends. They are not merely opposed, which nobody would complain of —they are abused, and in many cases the abuse is of a sufficiently angry kind. Why does Lord Hartington escape?

Well, there is one obvious answer. Lord Hartington abuses nobody. He is a man who thinks it possible to engage in politics and to oppose his adversaries without the help of what Lord Beaconsfield called the ornament of debate, invective. Nobody can have heard him, or have read him, without being struck by this peculiarity; for, unhappily, it is a peculiarity, though he is not alone in it. He treats his opponents on the platform or in the House of Commons as he would treat the party of the other part—if I may borrow a phrase from the lawyers—in a business controversy. He attacks their principles, controverts their arguments, and does not think or say that a man who holds views different from his own on Home Rule is a traitor, or a scoundrel, or a maniac.

It is tolerably obvious, also, that Lord Hartington would not care a straw if all these names were bestowed on him. Like other members of the Gladstone Government, he was persecuted by the Irish during the debates on Coercion, and at other convenient seasons. Occasionally, some Tory tried his prentice hand at "drawing" Lord Hartington. I have seen this pastime, and I know no more entertaining spectacle. Mr. Healy or Mr. Biggar, or perchance Mr. Callan, let loose his budget of insults on the Secretary for War. Mr. Gorst may have joined in. The storm raged, and sharp-edged missiles flew across the House. There on the front bench sat the object of them, his legs drawn up and his hat drawn down over his eyes. He might be asleep. His imperturbability is so complete that, watch him as you may, you cannot see a muscle move or a nerve twitch. Mr. Disraeli used to assume indifference; he was often stung by sarcasms, and when he came to reply showed that he had been stung. Being a consummate comedian, his assumption of indifference answered perfectly as long as he kept it up. His face was not a book wherein men might read the strange matters he was meditating, but a mask.

Lord Hartington is not a comedian and has no occasion to wear a mask. His indifference is not feigned, it is real, and he has no need of the hat over his eyes, whether as a shield or a disguise. It took our Irish friends some time to find this out. Quick-witted as they are, they were slow to perceive that here was a man on whom their bitterest taunts and most ferocious vituperation made absolutely no impression—that he really and truly did not care what they thought or said. One moment he would hear himself branded as a murderer; the guilty colleague of Lord Spencer in sending innocent men to the gallows. The next he would be answering a question in an unmoved tone. I do not think he was even shaken by the delicate innuendoes levelled at him as the brother of Lord Frederick Cavendish. So, after a while, it came to be understood among the Parnellites that nothing was to be got by badgering Lord Hartington, and they let him alone.

There are, as I said, others among the public men of England who abstain habitually from violent personalities, or from imputing low motives to their antagonists. Mr. Gladstone is one, though Mr. Gladstone's passionate enthusiasm for the business in which he has now embarked has led him to say some strange things, not in his usual manner. But there is absolutely nobody so careless as Lord Hartington about what is said of him. Mr. Gladstone notoriously is not. He cannot sit still under fire. Old Parliamentary Hand as he describes himself, and is, the veriest novice in the Chamber is more master of himself under provocation than is Mr. Gladstone. Anybody can draw him; nobody is too insignificant, no topic too trivial, to be treated seriously, and often very vehemently, by this Grand Old Man. Lord Hartington answers to the description of the late Mr. Rufus Choate. He is as cool as a couple of summer mornings. If he answers, he answers without heat.

Look at the speech Lord Hartington made yesterday at Cardiff. He went down there in behalf of Mr. Brand, a Unionist, who is contesting that borough against Sir Edward Reed, its present member, and a Gladstonian. The local Gladstonian paper welcomed him with the remark that nothing could be more mean or contemptible than his coming on such a mission. Lord Hartington's reply reminds one of what Wendell Phillips told Charles Remond when he called Washington a scoundrel. He said the word was not descriptive. Lord Hartington made answer to the local editor that the Unionists were advocating the opinions held only a few months ago by the whole Liberal party, and, if they had not been able to change them, they might be wrong or mistaken, but could hardly be described as mean or contemptible. He attributed no evil motives to those who, unlike himself, had changed, but suggested that they might be as forbearing as himself. "For, in my opinion, there can be nothing contemptible in adhering to opinions which you had deliberately thought out, and on the strength of which you had recommended yourselves to the constituencies of your fellow-countrymen."

A later passage in the same speech has—what is very rare with Lord Hartington who seldom talks of himself—an autobiographical interest. He had been replying to Mr. Gladstone, and quoting some of the hard things Mr. Gladstone had said of the Parnellite party—that their doctrine was the promulgation of the gospel of plunder, for instance. Why does he quote them? To answer Mr. Gladstone, for one thing; to ask, for another, whether men whom Mr. Gladstone described as marching through rapine to the dismemberment of the Empire may safely be trusted with the government of Ireland. But not for the purpose of casting discredit or opprobrium on men with whom he is engaged in political controversy. "I do not think," says Lord Hartington, "I have ever denounced them. At all events, I am quite certain I have never been capable of denouncing them in nearly as strong terms as those employed about them by Mr. Gladstone. I have opposed them to the best of my ability, and though I do not admit that their weapons of warfare are legitimate, I have not thought there was much in complaint or denunciation, and I have endeavoured without complaint or denunciation to do my best to withstand their policy by recognised constitutional and parliamentary means." Lord Hartington, in other words, deliberately renounces such advantages as are to be obtained in the conduct of party warfare by denunciation, detraction, vituperation, or personal abuse in any form. Does he gain or lose by thus restricting his vocabulary, or by denuding his armoury of poisoned arrows? Nobody who knows the condition of public life in England, and Lord Hartington's place in public esteem, will be at a loss for an answer.

II.

AS GUEST AT THE CRYSTAL PALACE, AS STATESMAN, AS ORATOR, AND AS LORD HARTINGTON.

[LONDON, *May* 21, 1890.]

Short memories are best in public, and the ceremony of last Wednesday at the Crystal Palace was of a nature to make forgetfulness an act of virtue. Let us go back ten years, or a little more, and imagine the astonishment that would have followed upon the announcement of a banquet to Lord Hartington with Mr. Chamberlain in the chair. Mr. Chamberlain was then in good and regular standing as a radical member of the Liberal party. Mr. Gladstone was rehearsing at Hawarden the part of Achilles before Troy. Lord Hartington was in command, and the strident voice of Mr. Chamberlain was heard one evening in the House of Commons referring to him as "the late leader of the Liberal party." Come down six or seven years later, down to the period of "ransom" and of the "unauthorised programme," and the same voice is heard deriding his present hero as "Rip Van Winkle." But on Wednesday night matters have so far advanced that the "late leader" of 1878 and the "Rip Van Winkle" of 1885 is described by the same Mr. Chamberlain as holding "a unique and proud place in our political history."

It might be indiscreet to ask what has happened in the interval, or to let mere reminiscence lead us into comparisons or into comment. But this may be said, that the homage now offered by the member for Birmingham to Lord Hartington expresses the general opinion of the reasonable men of all parties and of no party. In spite of, and perhaps sometimes because of, the attacks upon him from whatever quarter, he has steadily advanced in position and in reputation. And it is now Mr. Chamberlain who says of him, and says truly, that no man has ever received in larger degree that national confidence which is reposed in sound judgment and true patriotism.

What is the secret of this all but universal confidence in Lord Hartington? There is no one secret, or none unless you are content to describe it as character; which does not bring us much nearer to a solution of the problem. But this also may be said: that Lord Hartington has been a little more than thirty-three years in public life, and never during that long period has been suspected of doing any public act from any but a public motive. His disinterestedness was recognised before his abilities were understood. It was known, indeed, that he had ability of the kind which enables a man to pursue a political career and to administer a great office. He was Secretary of War so long ago as 1866, and has been Postmaster-General, Irish Secretary, Secretary of State for India, and then at the head of the War Office. He has led the Liberal party—led it for five years while in opposition to Lord Beaconsfield, and led it extremely well. All this implies very considerable capacity, but all might have been done without more remarkable gifts than those possessed by many men in public life and by many men in great business enterprises.

Besides, he had none of the showy qualities which in these days lead so often to an overestimate of a man's real power in affairs. In the earlier part of his career he was a very bad speaker. He hated speaking, and only spoke because he must. It was very laborious to him, and to his audiences. He improved slowly, and not perhaps till within the last few years has been at his best. His speeches are now good examples of lucid statement, of good sense, of connected argument, of sincerity; and they have that elevation of tone which only comes from elevation of character. But the speeches are listened to and read because they are his; his place in the country is quite independent of his oratory. The English people have learned to think of him as a man whose integrity is beyond question; whose convictions are his own, and are not marketable nor to be abandoned because they are no longer somebody's else; who has clear views and sober judgment; and who has proved his unselfishness by acts which convince the dullest or the most critical. Not to many men has it been given twice to refuse to be Prime Minister. "The public," said a distinguished Englishman, "know very well that Lord Hartington is honest, but he has never yet had all the credit he deserves for ability or for political sagacity and power of leadership."

"There," said a very great Duke once to a very young lady to whom he was showing his house, "there is the room where I sit all day long and earn my living by writing cheques." It was both jest and earnest. A great nobleman, any great landowner, almost any of the men whom Mr. Chamberlain once—in the presence of one of them on the platform—described as men who toil not neither do they spin, is one of the hardest-worked men in the kingdom. Lord Hartington is still what he has been all his life, heir-apparent to the Dukedom of Devonshire. But his life has been burdened with duties hardly less imperative and hardly less wearisome than those which appertain to the actual possession of property and title.

What he cared for most at one time was perhaps Newmarket; a word which to the ear of those most accustomed to it means more than racing. There is a social life at Newmarket which, if not continuous, fills a considerable portion of the year, and fills it in a way far otherwise enjoyable than the crowded drawing-rooms and often still more crowded dining-rooms of Mayfair. Lord Hartington has owned racehorses, and has a house at Newmarket, and has been as constant in his attendance upon the functions of that fascinating spot as circumstances would permit. But circumstances have often forbidden, and many a time he has been slaving in the thick air of Downing Street when he would have liked to inhale the breezes that blow across the Cambridgeshire heath. Not a great hardship? Possibly not, and possibly it seems less to him who was born into the drudgery of a desk in Wall Street than to one of those "idlers" whom Mr. John Burns holds up to the execration of 100,000 English artisans, hard at work listening to speeches of a Sunday in Hyde Park. But it is to be said, and said seriously, that few men toil harder than those who earn their living like the Duke above referred to, or like Lord Hartington himself.

Early this year Lord Hartington was very ill, and when he was able to travel was sent abroad. It was on his return and his recovery that this dinner was given him, when some 1100 ladies and gentlemen sat at meat together. They belonged, no doubt, in great part to the Classes. There were Dukes and Duchesses, and many other ornamental personages whose place is among those privileged and titled sections of society on which, as we have all heard, no American can look without abhorrence. However, matters are so ordered in this country that rank does not in all cases deprive its possessor of the esteem and respect of his fellow-subjects. Rank or no rank, this was a company of men and women of whose goodwill any man might be proud. The compliment was a very high one. The gathering served a political end, no doubt, but the main object of it was personal. If eulogy was the thing wanted, there was other eulogy than Mr. Chamberlain's, though perhaps none better. If it be ungracious to recall earlier days when different relations between these two men existed, it is not ungracious to quote what Mr. Chamberlain so well said: that at such a crisis England is in need of statesmen who—

> Care not to be great,
> But as they save and serve the State.

What Lord Derby said of Lord Hartington is interesting, not only because Lord Derby is of his own order, and of great repute in public life, but because he is one of the coldest of men. If there be an individual without enthusiasm, Lord Derby is he. But even he warms a little when he has to speak of the Liberal-Unionist leader. Mr. Goschen is a man of finance and of affairs; not devoid of a certain dryness of mind; he, too, is among those whom the occasion inspires. So is Sir Henry James, a lawyer, another of the speakers, to whom, however, it fell to praise Mr. Chamberlain more especially, and most of all in his capacity of chairman and of favourite target for Gladstonian shafts. But the best that could be said was not so full of meaning as the mere presence of such an assemblage in Lord Hartington's honour.

LORD RANDOLPH CHURCHILL.

I.

[LONDON, *December* 18, 1888.]

I GIVE him the name by which he is most commonly referred to. In these busy times, people seldom say Lord Randolph Churchill. They say Lord Randolph; often, with a kind of affectionate brevity, Randolph. Affection, however, is not the feeling just now shown most freely to him by his party. It is a little startling to see him rise in the House of Commons without a solitary cheer from those about him. Those who frequent the House are used to this spectacle. I went down on Monday for the first time this year, and the incident had all the force of novelty. A Suakim debate was on. I cannot suppose that the American public takes a deep interest in Suakim, and it is not a subject upon which I am going to enter. But I apprehend we all have an interest in Lord Randolph; even those who think him the spoiled child of politics. There is only one more striking figure in the House to-day. Lord Randolph is sometimes reproached with having held different opinions on the same subject at different times. It may be so, but, if it be true of him, it is ten times truer of that other and older figure who sits surrounded by his shattered and divided legions.

Divided also from his former associates and colleagues is the still young leader of the Tory Democracy. He has renounced his central place on the Front Bench. He sits at the corner of the second bench; above the gangway, however, not below. The gangway is a Rubicon which he has yet to cross, though, after last night, there are people who hint that he may in time cross not only the gangway but the floor of the House. That is mere unprofitable guesswork. The future may take care of itself; to-day is quite interesting enough to those who care for the high lights of current politics. There at the corner of his bench sits Lord Randolph; his hat on, his head sunk, not much of him visible above the shoulders except the historical moustache, at which he is pulling in the historical fashion. Mr. Punch and Mr. Tenniel and Toby have made it historical if it were not so otherwise. The moustache, and its owner's restless habit of twirling it, are as familiar now to Mr. Punch's public as were the straw in Lord Palmerston's mouth, or the legs of Lord John Russell, seeking ever vainly for their resting-place on the floor they were too short to reach. And Mr. Punch's public is world-wide.

Lord Randolph is down on the paper for a question about Suakim, to which I will refer presently. But even in so simple a matter as putting a question he has a manner of his own. Many other men have their own manners in putting questions—not always good ones. It used to be the custom to read all the questions out. To save time, that has been stopped. They are numbered, and the member in search of useful or useless information has only to indicate his interrogatory. But some of them are so eager for momentary distinction as to rise at full length, pause a moment, then loudly and even pompously, "Mr. Speaker, sir, I beg leave to ask the Under Secretary of State for Foreign Affairs question No. 20, which stands in my name." When the Speaker calls out "Lord Randolph Churchill," the noble lord, as he is styled in House of Commons parlance, half rises from his seat, lifts his hat, says softly, "Question No. 3," and sinks back to give another tug at the light-brown moustache.

It is known he is going to speak on Suakim, and there is a strong muster of Tories, gloomily wondering "What Randolph will do next." The scene, if we had time to look at it, is striking for more reasons than one. No less a person than Mr. John Morley opens fire on the Government, crowded together in a thin black line on the Front Bench; then, and often during this eventful evening, hurriedly consulting among themselves; a group of clustering and agitated heads. Mr. John Morley is hardly at his best; has not yet, I think, learned to be ever at his best in the House of Commons. There is still something about him which suggests the student rather than the debater. When a man's mind has run for a quarter of a century in one channel, it is not so easy all at once to turn the full force of the stream into another. He is clear, forcible, fluent enough—master of himself and his ideas; not quite master of his audience.

The occasion is great enough to bring Mr. Gladstone down to the House, and to put him on his legs; but does not rouse him to a great effort. His voice is neither clear nor strong; many and many a sentence do not reach to the bench under the gallery where I sit. The Tories, who will believe anything and say anything of Mr. Gladstone, tell you that this indistinctness is calculated. He prefers they should suppose him incapable of rising to the old level; intending, for his part, when the right moment comes, to rise as high as ever, and be heard in the remotest recesses of the House and the country. Sir James Ferguson, who has replied to Mr. Morley, replied in an ineffective way. Mr. Stanhope, Secretary for War, on whom the answer to Mr. Gladstone devolves, is resonant, business-like, direct; capable of so stating his case as to be understanded of the people and of the House, and to produce an impression. As he nears the end you may see Lord Randolph take off his hat and put it under the seat, and you know that he means to follow the Secretary for War.

The House by this time is full, surprisingly full for the fag end of an autumn sitting. The Tory benches are well covered above and below the gangway, and they maintain a grim silence as Lord Randolph is seen to be on his feet, and

Mr. Courtney—for the House is in committee—calls on him. The Opposition cheer, and the cheer is a cordial one. Whatever may be their private sentiments about the orator, they more than guess that he is going to make himself disagreeable to the Government, and that is enough for them. The nervousness, if it be nervousness, which is denoted by the continuing movement of the forefinger to the upper lip, has ceased. If you have studied him in Mr. Tenniel's cartoons only, and have never seen him in the flesh, you may be surprised to note that this slender, carefully dressed figure is rather above the average height. There is not a trace of embarrassment; the stranger would never guess that he stood alone, surrounded by enemies, or at least by opponents; by men once his supporters, now angry, suspicious, resentful.

If he were still Leader of the House he could not be more at his ease, more sure of himself, more ready to meet all comers. The foes at his back seem to give him no concern, and if he has friends in front, their friendship is not of a kind which calls for expressions of gratitude. Slight as the figure is, the stamp of energy on it is as impressive as the stamp of elegance; and both are impressive. It is a Democratic age, but the story of all ages, or of many ages, is the same; the Democrat prefers the Patrician for leader. The voice has the ring of authority in it. The House is silent as death. The faces on the Treasury Bench are the faces of men who wonder what is coming, and are getting ready to meet it. The scene, like so many scenes in the House, is dramatic, and the yellow light that floods the Chamber from the ceiling adds to the illusion, and to the theatrical character of it. Mr. Gladstone looks eagerly across the table. Mr. Morley, Sir George Trevelyan, Sir William Harcourt, are all alert. The one unmoved personage in the Liberal phalanx is Lord Hartington.

Almost the first sentence that Lord Randolph utters is a debating sentence: "When I recall the language in which I attacked the Government of the right honourable gentleman opposite (Mr. Gladstone) for engaging British military forces in the Soudan, I cannot refrain from expressing regret and alarm at what appears to be a recommencement of a course which I then so strongly denounced, and still at the present moment denounce." I quote it not because I am going to follow the speaker in his argument, for I am not, but as a good specimen of the right way of saying things to the House of Commons. The truth is, the two men most unlike each other are the two men who have taken almost identical views on the Soudan business—Lord Randolph and Mr. John Morley. This single sentence is a reminder to the House of all the disasters that befell Mr. Gladstone's policy in Egypt, and a warning to the present Ministry that they are entering upon the same road. That is what I call a debating manner, and a House of Commons manner.

Still more striking is the passage in which he pays off part of his debt to Lord Salisbury. The question I mentioned above was a question as to Lord Salisbury's statement in the House of Lords that the retention of Suakim was of no advantage to Egypt. That was a private opinion, said Sir James Ferguson, who is Lord Salisbury's mouthpiece in the Commons. "Such an answer," now said Lord Randolph, "is flippant. To say that a declaration by the Prime Minister, made in a debate in the Lords, after full notice, is a mere private opinion, is a preposterous proposition. I should like to know what would have been the concentrated fury of honourable and right honourable gentlemen on this side of the House if the member for Midlothian had ever taken up such an attitude." The hit was palpable, but what followed went further home. Nothing has of late brought so much Radical criticism on Lord Salisbury as his calling Mr. Naoroji a black man. "I protest," proceeded Lord Randolph, "against the idea that Ministerial utterances, on Ministerial responsibility, are to be treated as private opinions when it is convenient. I can quite understand that the opinion of the Prime Minister the other day as to the colour of people in India is a private opinion which does not bind his colleagues, and which need not bind them, but is truly a private opinion —and perhaps a temporary opinion." The House, or rather the Opposition, received this with shouts of laughter and cheers. Tory faces grew blacker than Mr. Naoroji's. It was not a mere sally of wit, it was an illustration perfectly germane to the question at issue, and that was what made it so effective.

As he proceeds the speech becomes closer in argument, and more and more evidently hostile in purpose. I have heard him in the House, especially in earlier days, when his tone was one of mere banter, and when sincerity was not the thing that most impressed his hearers. He has more styles than one. To-day his style is serious enough to suit the dullest, yet point after point is made with a clearness and rhetorical force to which the dullest cannot be insensible. The voice, though not very various or deep, is what the French call a carrying voice; it penetrates everywhere without apparent effort. At times it is sibilant with passion; at all times there is meaning in every tone. He leans slightly forward, is sparing of gesture, cares little, apparently, for mere oratorical ornament. But the lips open and shut with an unusual degree of muscular energy, and the eyes have a light in them which burns. He watches the House as closely as the House watches him. He speaks for half an hour. When he sits down he is again cheered from the Liberal side, and again the silence of those about him is unbroken.

The English, said Montesquieu, like a man to be a man. There is in that phrase a hint of the source, or of one source, of Lord Randolph's power. He is without a party in the House, without any considerable following, but he is a man to be reckoned with from sheer force of character and courage, even more than from his extraordinary abilities. It is far too soon to sum up a career which, perhaps, has hardly more than begun. There is much, if you like, to be said against him, but what does it avail? Here is the one man among the English Tories who has shown capacity for leadership, in something more than a party sense. He it was who saw the meaning of the new suffrage; who perceived that if the Tory party had any hope of a future less sterile than the past, it lay in coming to terms with the new masters of this country. To struggle against the new Democracy was hopeless, but to win over the new Democracy was not hopeless. He it was who taught his party how they might become the popular party. He showed them the road. He set up the guide-post. It is hardly too much to say that he gave them power, and brought them into office with a fair prospect of a long tenure of office. They have shown their gratitude in the way we all know. Well, the day will come when the Tory Ministry will again be in difficulties, and must again appeal to the country. Then, if not before, they will bethink themselves of the discarded colleague who has the ear of the country.

II.

LORD RANDOLPH'S COLLECTED SPEECHES AND HIS ORATORY.

[LONDON, *April* 13, 1889.]

Mr. Jennings has edited, and Messrs. Longmans have published in two volumes, a selection of the speeches of Lord Randolph Churchill from 1880 to 1888. They are interesting from several points of view; most of all, perhaps, as an *Apologia pro vita sua*. Lord Randolph was born just forty years ago; his public career really began, it may be said, less than ten years ago. He had been member for Woodstock six years earlier, but of those six years little trace is to be found in Parliamentary annals, and none at all in these volumes. His active and continuing interest in practical politics is coincident with Mr. Gladstone's entry into office in 1880, and the specific mission which he then accepted was to make things uncomfortable for the Liberal Government. He laid down his platform in a sentence—would that all platforms were equally brief—it is the duty of an Opposition to oppose. Because his own chief would not oppose with sufficient energy, his mission gradually, and as it were by force of circumstances, enlarged itself. It became his duty to make things uncomfortable for those of his party leaders and friends who would not themselves make it uncomfortable for the enemy.

He first joined, then organised, then led the Fourth Party, and the regular people soon found that the Fourth Party under Lord Randolph had to be not merely counted but weighed and reckoned with. Probably no man ever sowed more political wild oats in a given space of time than did this young guerilla chief in the session of 1880. The crop has not been harvested for this book. Lord Randolph's views broadened; his convictions became more settled; his ideas of policy were enlarged; his aims began to lead him into fresh and ever more extensive fields. The Irish question attracted him. The first speech in the first of these two volumes is on Landlord and Tenant. Then comes Coercion and all the rest. Mr. Gladstone's amazing foreign policy was too tempting to the critic to be let alone, and frequently the critic makes Egypt a specialty. Financial Reform follows, though not till 1884. Tory Democracy had already made its appearance, and in the same year the bold inventor of it delivered his "Trust the People" speech at Birmingham. In the same year, in May, came the arraignment of Mr. Gladstone's Government for its declared resolve to desert General Gordon; a speech that, read now, reads like a fulfilled prophecy.

By this time Lord Randolph had become the most popular of Tory orators in the country, whatever he might be in the House of Commons, and among those to whom he ironically referred as his leaders. No speaker was in such demand. In 1884 alone, there are nine speeches to great popular audiences in such great towns as Birmingham, Leeds, Manchester, and others less great, but always important political centres. The attacks on Mr. Gladstone's Government are incessant. India is added to the young orator's repertory, and Russia in her relation to India—another gloomy page in the Liberal Prime Minister's Foreign Policy. So it goes on through 1885, till the general election and the Tory triumph.

Five years had passed since Lord Randolph had taken his seat on the front bench below the gangway. He had fought on his own line, if not for his own hand, yet so great was the place he had won, so formidable had he been found, so indispensable had he made himself, that when Lord Salisbury formed his Ministry he could not do less than offer Lord Randolph the Secretaryship of State for India, with a seat in the Cabinet. Office steadied him, as office usually does the most impetuous and gifted. His guns were turned, the whole broadside, against the enemy, with no reservations in favour of his friends. Then came the Tory defeat, so soon to be followed by the Tory, or, at any rate, Anti-Home Rule and Unionist triumph of 1886, and with it the Chancellorship of the Exchequer and Leadership of the House of Commons, to be followed more speedily still by his resignation. All the outlines of this exciting period will be found drawn with a firm hand in these speeches, and many of the incidents and episodes filled in with no lack of colour. The Dartford speech belongs to the official period; on the whole, the most famous of all the speeches; the official declaration and adoption of Tory Democracy, with its hardly less remarkable supplement delivered at Bradford three weeks later. From the time of his unlucky resignation down to the present, he appears more often than otherwise as the champion of retrenchment and reform, the pitiless censor of departmental mismanagement. The attacks on Mr. Gladstone do not cease. Ireland never disappears from his horizon, and his last word is a protest against the Tory policy in Egypt.

These volumes, it will be seen, are not meant, or not primarily meant, as an appeal for a verdict upon Lord Randolph as an orator. Their primary purpose is clearly political. Mr. Jennings's very interesting and spirited introduction deals almost wholly with politics; with Lord Randolph's relation to the public life of his country since 1880, and to his own party. That he has been consistent, that he has seen how things were going, that he, like Disraeli, has educated his party, that he has taken strong and coherent views on great questions, that he has steadfastly opposed a policy of mere coercion and nothing else for Ireland, a policy of meddle and muddle for Egypt, a policy of inefficient extravagance in the administration of great public departments,—these and such as these are the points on which Mr. Jennings lays stress. If not always convincing, he is always readable. He has told the story of Lord Randolph's resignation, not fully, for it cannot yet be told fully, but in such a way as challenges reply, if reply there be. There is an obvious suggestion all through this narrative that the mantle of Disraeli has fallen on Lord Randolph's shoulders. There is a very measured, sustained, suggestive, and most damaging attack on Lord Salisbury. The contrast between Lord Salisbury's conduct to his colleagues on his withdrawal from the Derby Ministry in 1867, and Lord Randolph's conduct on his withdrawal from the Salisbury Ministry at the end of 1886, is very skilfully drawn. The whole introduction, in fact, is a clever piece of political argumentation, and the reader cannot but infer from it that the main object of the republication of the speeches is the political and personal vindication of the author of the speeches.

There is no reason why it should not be. Lord Randolph has been assailed with a pertinacity that is anything but benevolent, and many of his assailants have been of his own party. It is one of the open secrets of current politics that Lord Salisbury dislikes and dreads him. There is at least one member of Lord Salisbury's family who dislikes and dreads him even more than its head. There are two or three of the Prime Minister's colleagues who share these animosities to the full. Lord Randolph has to face, moreover, hostilities which, though not personal, grow out of circumstances. It is probable enough that he resigned without reckoning on Mr. Goschen as his successor. But for Mr. Goschen, Lord Randolph's place as Chancellor of the Exchequer could hardly have been so filled as to satisfy public opinion. The more important post which he left vacant as Leader of the House of Commons was put in charge of Mr. W. H. Smith, who is too amiable to quarrel with anybody, but in no sense an ideal leader. Mr. Goschen and Mr. Smith cannot be supposed to be eager to see Lord Randolph resume the two places which they have divided between them. Then there is Mr. Balfour, long his associate in the Fourth Party; long regarded as too literary, too philosophical, too much the student to plunge bodily into this rushing stream of politics. Yet Mr. Balfour, thanks in no little measure to the retirement of Lord Randolph from the Ministry, has become the second — there are those who say the first — personage in the Government. Mr. Balfour is too loyal a character to engage in intrigues, but some of his friends are credited with taking part in this recent Birmingham business, expressly with the view of preventing Lord Randolph from re-entering the House with that powerful constituency behind him, and, at no distant date, resuming the leadership. What has happened at Birmingham might be cited as of itself a more than sufficient reason for offering to the public this brilliant record of a brilliant decade.

Orator is not a word to be used lightly, and it may be doubted whether Lord Randolph has applied his mind to the study of oratory in the sense that Fox did and that Burke did. Never to let a day pass without speaking was Fox's rule, and he, like most great orators, became what he was at the expense of his early audiences. Lord Randolph has very definite aims. His temperament lacks, possibly, the sympathetic and passionate quality necessary to eloquence of the very highest order; his intellect is not distinctly imaginative or poetic, and both poetry and imagination have to do with oratory. These volumes contain not many passages that will be quoted as perfect models. There is, in some of his very best moments, a note of impatience in the thought, sometimes a loose structure of the sentences; a want of finish and delicacy. He has not that large and easy movement which is one of Bright's most striking qualities. But why measure him by a standard which he does not set himself to reach? Disraeli, if Disraeli be his model, was not an orator either in this high manner. Lord Randolph has what he needs for his purpose. He is in the very front rank of platform speakers, and as a House of Commons debater he has, at most, but one living superior.

I will put it as a test of good platform speaking that the speech shall seem good to the audience, yet be a poor speech in fact. One such I have heard Lord Randolph deliver. It is not in the present collection, nor does it deserve to be. It was delivered in the summer of 1885 in the park at Canford Manor belonging to his brother-in-law, Lord Wimborne. There was a great Tory gathering, a festival, a pitched tent holding six or seven thousand people, filled full on that rainy afternoon. He had been ill the night before and all the morning. It was doubtful whether he could speak, and of preparation he had had much less than he wished, so that in substance and in thought the discourse was necessarily deficient. It was a thin speech, and fallacies were made to do duty for argument. Yet, from beginning to end, he held the rustic audience below him, under the dripping canvas, and the smart audience on the platform about him, including many of those who are generally thought by those who appeal to the public the severest critics of all, his own family.

I had never heard him before outside the House of Commons, and I studied him as closely as I could. His method was admirable; his lucidity would have delighted Matthew Arnold himself; the neatness of his points such as bursts of cheering would have rewarded in the House, as they did here. Never did he leave these bucolic hearers in the least doubt as to what he meant. Canford is in Dorsetshire, and than Dorsetshire there is no denser county in England, mentally speaking. It was an audience of clods. Every sentence which he addressed to them was simple, direct, intelligible to a child. He went from point to point, never coming to the second till the first had been mastered. Every phrase told, and I remember thinking, as he went on, that there was nothing they were not ready to believe when stated with that homely persuasiveness. Beyond doubt they believed they were doing their own thinking. No suspicion crossed their minds that the orator was leading them hither and thither at his will. It struck me as a wonderful forensic effort; any lawyer who could talk like that to a jury would rank as a consummate advocate. From beginning to end there was hardly a proposition which was entirely defensible, and there was not one which seemed in need of defence. I thought of the juror who disputed the greatness of Erskine. "It is no credit to him to win his cause, for he is always on the right side." By the time Lord Randolph sat down there was nobody in the tent who dreamed that there was any other side than his. To produce such an impression as that does not prove a man a great orator. It does prove him possessed of a very rare and admirable gift of speaking, and makes him a force in the State.

Pruned as these pages have been—the "Moloch of Midlothian," for instance, is gone—they still contain many sharp sayings about men of high political position, and about some who are less high. It has never been Lord Randolph's habit to mince his words. I do not know whether he acts or speaks on a theory, but it may be imagined that in his early years of political effervescence, with his reputation to make and wishing to make it rapidly, he felt the necessity of compelling attention. Personalities are sure to command attention if not approval.

A great American orator deliberately adopted that theory for the sake of the cause to which he gave up ambition and many other things—I mean Wendell Phillips. In the course of a public address he once spoke quite casually of Seward as a liar, and there came a protest from his audience. He declined to withdraw the word. "I meant it," he said, "and some day, when I can find time, I will tell you why I use personalities." I do not know that he ever found time in public, but I asked him afterward. "Well," answered Phillips, "in the early days of the Abolition movement we were a handful without position or authority, but we were determined to be heard. We might have talked till doomsday about the wickedness of slavery, and the country would have remained deaf. But when we denounced the wickedness of slaveholders, people pricked up their ears, and when I called Webster a scoundrel, Webster's friends began to protest, and so the controversy went on. If I had said that Seward did not tell the truth, who would have cared?"

Lord Randolph avoids "liar"; he has a taste for amplification, and he prefers to speak of "the inexhaustible, the inveterate, the innate capacity of the Liberal party for the falsification of truth." His invective loves a shining mark. Mr. Gladstone has been the object of it more often than anybody else; perhaps more often in published letters to the newspapers than in public speeches. But even from these reprinted speeches a whole anthology may be collected. The ills of this empire are due in no little measure, in Lord Randolph's opinion, to "the marvellous talents, the stupefying eloquence, and the illimitable ambition of this one man." He said in 1884—

"The Prime Minister is the greatest living master of the art of personal political advertisement. Holloway and Horniman are nothing compared with him. For the purpose of recreation he has selected the felling of trees; his amusements, like his politics, are essentially destructive. Every afternoon the whole world is invited to assist at the crashing fall of some beech or elm or oak. The forest laments in order that Mr. Gladstone may perspire."

Invective here, as often, turns to ridicule. Nothing could be more amusing than the passage in the Dartford speech in 1886, in which the leaders of the Liberal Opposition are likened to the Dutch generals who held command in turn, each for a day. "You have one day Mr. Parnell leading, and another day you have Mr. Labouchere, and another day you have Mr. Conybeare leading, and every now and then you have Sir William Harcourt leading, and occasionally, as a great treat, Mr. Gladstone drops in from Bavaria."

Very different from this are the sentences in the Gordon speech, in which he contrasts the courage, the perseverance, the eloquence of Mr. Gladstone in his desperate adherence to Mr. Bradlaugh, with his indifference to the fate of Gordon.

"If the hundredth part of those invaluable moral qualities bestowed upon Mr. Bradlaugh had been given to the support of a Christian hero, the success of General Gordon's mission would have been at this time assured. And this struck me as most remarkable when the Prime Minister sat down—that the finest speech he ever delivered in the House of Commons was in support of Mr. Bradlaugh, and the worst speech he ever delivered was, by common consent, in the cause of the Christian hero. That is an instructive historical contrast."

There is much to be said about Mr. Gladstone's relations to General Gordon, but now is not the time. I will but ask you to note that Mr. Gladstone is never so good as when he is advocating a cause with which he has little sympathy. Mr. Bradlaugh as an unbeliever was odious to him, and he put forth his full strength in his cause. Lord Beaconsfield was of all his opponents the one whom he found most antipathetic, and his eulogy upon Lord Beaconsfield is a far finer performance than his eulogy on Bright, who was his comrade and friend.

Mr. Chamberlain is not spared. "Mr. Chamberlain is a very clever man, who has succeeded in persuading his party that the tactics of a town council are identical with the science of government; but his time has been so occupied with developing the gas supply and the debt of Birmingham that he has never read English history." But Mr. Chamberlain need not now detain us, nor others on whom Lord Randolph's lash has fallen many a time heavily. Many of his perorations are carefully wrought out. That which winds up the Manchester speech of 1884 on the Government of

Failure is not the best, but a good average example of Lord Randolph's more elaborate manner.

"But seeing what I have seen to-day and hearing what I have heard elsewhere, I now feel confident and sure that the British Nation, having to decide between the House of Lords and its long centuries of great tradition on the one hand, and the faults and the follies and the failures of Mr. Gladstone's four years' government on the other—which they will abolish and which they will preserve—will, by their wisdom, by their knowledge, and by higher than earthly guidance, award the palm and the honour and the victory to those who, conscious of the immeasurable responsibilities attaching to an hereditary House, have dauntlessly defended against an arbitrary Minister the ancient liberties of our race."

Those sentences would bear revision, but redundancy is, in a young orator, one of those faults which presently ripen into virtues. He has the root of the matter in him, and though it is in the nature of things that flowers should come earlier than fruit, they are sometimes to be seen together on the same tree. For you cannot read one speech, still less can you go through this body of discourses on so many different subjects, without feeling that they are the work of a man who has mastered his subjects, who is no amateur, who shrinks from no labour with a definite purpose before him, who is capable of affairs, and capable of imparting his knowledge of them to other people; a man with something more than the courage of his opinions; with the strength of intellect and of will to impress them upon the public, and sooner or later to engraft them on the institutions of his country.

If an American who has not taken the trouble to follow English politics closely, reads these speeches, he will surely, I think, come to one clear conclusion. He will find some inconsistencies in them. He will not always approve Lord Randolph's attitude to men of longer service than himself in public life. He would like to strike out some of the adjectives. He might be puzzled to know exactly where the speaker stands on certain questions—the Irish question for one. Various other criticisms would occur to him, of more or less consequence. But he would, I apprehend, say to himself that though Lord Randolph is called a Tory Democrat, there is a great deal more of the Democrat than of the Tory about him. He would recognise in this young Englishman, aristocrat as he is by birth and position, a true champion of the people. He would see that he is disposed to seek for the foundations of things where they are to be sought in America, and that he had adopted for his own guidance Lincoln's memorable maxim—"Government of the people, by the people, and for the people." And he would be likely to conclude that Lord Randolph stands nearer to the English people than any other of his party, and that sooner or later the English people will prefer him before all others.

MR. BALFOUR.

[LONDON, *March* 16, 1887.]

MR. ARTHUR BALFOUR, the new Chief Secretary for Ireland, is an amiable figure in public life. With at least two of his predecessors in that ill-omened office he has a point of close contact. He is, like Sir George Trevelyan and Mr. John Morley, a man of books, though not, like them, eminent as a writer of books. He is a reader, a student, a man really remarkable in these days of superficial culture for the soundness of his acquisitions. Mr. Morley the other day in his wise and beautiful address on the study of literature, said: "There is a commission now at work on a very important and abstruse subject, and I am told that no one there displays so acute an intelligence of the difficulties that are to be met, and the important arguments that are brought, and the practical ends to be achieved, as the chairman of the committee, who is not what is called a practical man, but a man of study and thought and literature." The commission to which Mr. Morley referred is the Commission on Currency, and Mr. Balfour is its chairman. I believe Currency to be a subject which nobody ever really understood, but it is certain that Mr. Balfour, an amateur, surprised his colleagues and the men of business who came before him by the extent of his knowledge, and, as Mr. Morley notes, his acuteness of perception. Mr. Gladstone has been known to say that Mr. Balfour and Lord Rosebery were the only two young men he knew who bought books. Neither of them is so young as he was when Mr. Gladstone made this interesting observation, which continues true of Lord Rosebery, less true now perhaps of Mr. Balfour, whose houses are full of books. The new Irish Secretary's politics have never been what Mr. Gladstone's became in middle age, Liberal, but political differences did not keep the two men apart. The younger one shared with one or two others the privilege of being Mr. Gladstone's pet boys.

He is no longer a boy, pet or otherwise, but still a young man; very young, indeed, to have won the position he has in English politics. He was born in 1848. His mother was a sister of the present Lord Salisbury, his father a Scottish laird of the larger kind. Whittinghame—pronounced for some reason inscrutable to any but the Scotch mind, Whittingem—is a considerable estate in Haddingtonshire. Its present owner made it more considerable still some years since by a large purchase of adjacent land. Those were the days when land was at its highest, and when landed investments were still thought the surest of all. Everybody knows what has happened since. In London Mr. Balfour lives in Carlton Gardens, one of the fashionable streets of the West End, looking rearward on St. James's Park. He has been in Parliament since 1874, when he sat for Hertford. When Lord Randolph Churchill formed the Fourth Party, Mr. Balfour was one of his recruits, of whom there were three in all. But his connection with that gifted and wilful leader was always thought to be less close than that of Sir Henry Wolff or Sir John Gorst.

When in 1885 Lord Salisbury formed his Ministry, he made Mr. Balfour President of the Local Government Board. The people who know everything—they are the most numerous class of the community—then said that Mr. Balfour was left outside the Cabinet because he was Lord Salisbury's nephew. This did not mean that uncle and nephew were on bad terms, but that the Tory Prime Minister did not choose to be suspected of a job. The nephew did well in the Local Government Board. Then, having mastered the work of one difficult department, he was, in the usual

English fashion, pitchforked into another of which he had the alphabet to learn, and in 1886 became Secretary for Scotland. I do not think he need regret it. The Scotch Secretaryship is a post a shade less impossible than the Irish Secretaryship. To put him there was to give him an experience. It was roasting a man before a slow fire as a preliminary to roasting him before a hot one. Scotch methods are unlike Irish methods, but the Scotch power of being disagreeable to an official who does not give them their own way is very considerable. Then in Scotland there are generally two parties on every question, while Ireland, as we all know, is united and unanimous. Ulster and the million of Protestants do not count. A Scotch Secretary who takes sides is certain to displease the other side. If he be impartial and hold the balance true, he enrages both. This has been Mr. Balfour's fate, and that is why I telegraphed you the other day that he quitted the Scotch Secretaryship detested by Scotchmen. The statement without this explanation was, I fear, abrupt.

Politicians profess to consider Mr. Balfour too much of an idealist for the rough work he has now in hand. They speak of him as an academic personage. So did they of Mr. John Morley, who, nevertheless, proved himself a capable administrator and skilful in winning the regard of the Irish people. These forecasts are seldom good for much. Mr. Balfour was not thought to correspond to either of the two models men had in their minds for Irish Secretary. He was not a dragoon officer, and he was not a Home Ruler. Now in these days people are coming, perhaps slowly, but still coming, to consider that these are the only possible alternatives. There are men—many men, perhaps—who look to General Lord Wolseley as the proper person for governing Ireland. There are men who, as Mr. Dillon rather incautiously said at Tipperary on Monday, look to Mr. Parnell as the future ruler and master of that part of the United Kingdom. Between these two extremes lie the masses of thinking and unthinking voters, who are for anything that will end the trouble, or even that will mend it, and put it out of sight and mind for the time being.

Mr. Balfour is not Lord Wolseley and not Mr. Parnell. If he resembles either it is Lord Wolseley. He has already shown the iron hand beneath that velvet glove which the man of letters and of society has so long worn. He has nerve; so much is clear. Yesterday settled that. Sir Michael Hicks-Beach would have reflected long ere assuming frankly and fully the responsibility for Captain Plunkett's order to the Youghal police inspector: "Deal very summarily with organised resistance to lawful authority. If necessary, do not hesitate to shoot them." Mr. Balfour met the question put to him in the House of Commons with a courage which I doubt not the Irish themselves admired. He sustained Captain Plunkett and approved his order. "It appears to me," said the quiet young Minister with his quiet manner, "that Captain Plunkett acted not only according to his duty, but in the manner which is best calculated to support the authority of the law, and in the long run to prevent the injuries and loss of life which must ensue if it is supposed that the police, in the execution of their duty, may be attacked and maltreated with impunity." There is a ring about that which in New York and Chicago must seem familiar. If Mr. Balfour is going to administer his office in this spirit, Sir George Trevelyan may have to reconsider his recent dictum at the Devonshire Club that in Ireland the game of law and order is up. But "ifs" of that sort lead to unprofitable speculations.

It is an axiom of modern English politics that no man can succeed as Irish Secretary; a premise from which an argument for Home Rule might certainly be started. Mr. Balfour's friends wondered that he should accept the post. It is, in any case, a post which none would covet for ambition's sake. Any man would far rather keep to his books and to the society in which Mr. Balfour is known to delight, and which delights in him. The English press gave him but a doubtful welcome on his accession. The Irish press—I mean the Parnellite press—responded after its manner. Every new Secretary is to the Parnellites a new enemy to be met. In Parliament and in their papers they do their best at once to take stock of the new man. They search for his weak points. They experiment on him in the House with an ingenuity which is, in its way, very striking. They approach him in a spirit of inquiry which may be called scientific; it is a desire to give to themselves a complete account of the strange being with whom they are newly brought into relations. They detected in Mr. Forster a strong, firm love of justice, of peace, of goodwill to men; and they harassed him with accusations of tyranny, of provoking strife, of oppression and cruelty. Sir George Trevelyan, sensitive to a fault, proved an easy target. Mr. Campbell Bannerman was perhaps the only one of the series of whom they could make nothing. He had a tough skin and seemed careless of attacks. Sir Michael Hicks-Beach was bland, cool, difficult to rouse, dangerous when roused. Perhaps Mr. Balfour's critics will present him to us as illiterate and ill-mannered. But down to the present time his character and capacities have been of that amiable and large kind which I have tried to describe.

MR. CHAMBERLAIN.

I.

AS THE NEW SOCIALIST AND THE PROPHET OF A NEW JERUSALEM.

[LONDON, *January* 8, 1885.]

ANOTHER note has been sounded in that war of classes which it is the fashion with some men now to predict, and with others to promote. The note is not exactly new, nor does it come from a mouth hitherto silent. But it is more distinct than before, and more resonant of the base but glittering metal by which its volume is augmented. Mr. Chambĕrlain has been speaking at Birmingham—not a novel circumstance that, certainly, but he has been announcing a new era in public life and a new departure in politics, and this he has done in language of a very remarkable character.

I said long ago that Mr. Chamberlain seemed to be of opinion—though he hesitated to express it—that the politics of the future were to have a good deal to do with Socialism. From time to time he has let fall a sentence which showed a keen desire to conciliate in advance the new forces that, as he thought, were to be potent in government. I quoted some of these experimental deliverances recently. If I return to the subject it is not merely because Mr. Chamberlain has made another speech; he is always making speeches, and they are, whatever else may be said of them, very readable. But he plainly considers that the moment has come when he may himself be more plain-spoken than before. If a new era is dawning, a new departure to be taken, he means to be the herald of the one and the leader of the other. There is every probability that he will be,—always provided that his forecast of the future be not mistaken. The only competitor whom he seems to fear is Lord Salisbury, and he has accordingly done his best to disparage Lord Salisbury's claims to the authorship of the great concessions just made in respect to the franchise.

For the moment, and be the reason what it may, Mr. Chamberlain is the most conspicuous political personage among the Liberals next after Mr. Gladstone. He describes himself, rather cruelly ignoring his friend, as "the" Radical member of a Liberal Government. And he has done a good deal in this latest harangue to justify his claim to the monopoly. But in order to do this, he has put a new meaning to an old word. If Mr. Chamberlain is to be accepted as a guide, Radical is henceforth to mean something not very different from Socialist. It is his attempt to merge the two, or, at least, to get Radical and Socialist to work together, which makes this last speech so important.

If, says Mr. Chamberlain, you will go back to the origin of things, you will find that when our social arrangements first began to shape themselves, every man was born into the world with natural rights, with a right to a share in the great inheritance of the community; with a right to a part of the land of his birth. The date when these rights existed in the shape thus described Mr. Chamberlain omits to specify. Crude generalities of this sort may do no particular mischief, but graver matter follows at once. All these rights, it seems, have passed away. Apathy and ignorance on the one side, force and fraud on the other, have dispossessed the original and rightful owners. "Private ownership has taken the place of these communal rights, and this system has become so interwoven with our habits and usages, it has been so sanctioned by law and protected by custom, that it might be very difficult and perhaps impossible to reverse it." What is this but an intimation that Mr. Chamberlain would reverse it if he could? And what would this reversal be but the adoption of Mr. Henry George's profligate doctrine of the "nationalisation" of land?

Whether Mr. Chamberlain has really been bitten by the particular madness of that rhetorical enthusiast, I cannot say. But they have certain defects in common. Both Mr. Henry George and Mr. Chamberlain are men of imperfect education. The range of Mr. Chamberlain's acquired knowledge of what had been done in the world before he was born into it, is not in proportion to the energy of his natural abilities. His want of familiarity with the history of earlier social organisations, and of the very matters on which he discourses so positively, leads him to take false views. The sense of historical perspective is wanting. He and Mr. George are for ever making new discoveries of grievances and remedies, each as old as time. The fact that the remedy they propose has been tried and failed would discredit it with most men. But men who are unaware of the facts cannot be much impressed by them.

Then comes a passage to which nothing but a full quotation can do justice:—

"But then I ask what ransom will property pay for the security which it enjoys? What substitute will it find for the natural rights which have ceased to be recognised? Society is banded together in order to protect itself against the instincts of men who would make very short work of private ownership if they were left alone. That is all very well, but I maintain that society owes to these men something more than mere toleration in return for the restrictions which it places upon their liberty of action. There is a doctrine in many men's mouths and in few men's practice that property has obligations as well as rights. I think in the future we shall hear a great deal about the obligations of property, and we shall not hear quite so much about its rights."

It was Proudhon who first announced that Property is Robbery—*la propriété c'est le vol*. Mr. Chamberlain's new gospel is less epigrammatic; savours perhaps more of Rousseau and the *Contrat Social* than of the famous or infamous pamphlets, *Qu'est-ce que la Propriété*, with which Proudhon began his strange career. It is probable, moreover, that the property against which Mr. Chamberlain meditates an attack is landed property. He has before now shown signs of a singular hallucination on this point; as if confiscation which began with land would stop with land. His animosity against an aristocracy based on acreage has carried him great lengths, and seems likely to carry him much greater.

He would probably disclaim sympathy with Proudhon, and condemn his maxim, and deny that his own doctrines had much in common with those of the French Nihilist,—for Nihilist Proudhon was, though he lived and died before Turgenieff had invented the name. But the disclaimer and the denial would signify little. When Proudhon enunciated his dogma he was an almost unknown man. Mr. Chamberlain is a Cabinet Minister, with a numerous following in the country. He was speaking to an assembly of 600 Birmingham working men who had asked him to dine with them in the Town Hall—an honour without precedent in the history of that precedent-making city. He must be judged by his position and by the circumstances in which he spoke, and they are such as to fasten upon him the gravest responsibility.

Mr. Chamberlain's language, it must be said, is the language of a man at war with the existing organisation of society. To law he pays no reverence; he does not recognise legal rights as real rights. A law, to Mr. Chamberlain, is only something to be repealed. To speak of the "ransom" of property is to adopt the phraseology of the brigands of Macedonia. To say that society owes to men who want to make short work of private ownership something more than toleration in return for the restrictions it places upon their liberty of action, is to express with ceremonious circumlocution the sentiments which fill the breasts of the tenants of Newgate. Newgate is one of the restrictions which society has placed upon the liberty of action of those who want to make short work of private ownership. I do not employ these paraphrases or illustrations of Mr. Chamberlain's language from choice, still less from incivility. They are forced upon me, as they are forced upon everybody who undertakes to put the inevitable significance of Mr. Chamberlain's propositions into plain English. It may astonish him—I hope it does. Astonishment would be the best proof that he meant less than he said, and that he had no idea of the real scope of the monstrous statements to which he has committed himself.

Protests against this gospel of spoliation there have been, of course. The press has protested. Mr. Chamberlain's colleagues in the Cabinet, if all reports are true, have protested. A Council which, in Mr. Gladstone's absence, lasted over three hours is said to have devoted no small portion of its attention to the new attitude of its most radical member. The expressions in private life of the abhorrence such language has aroused, among men who are Mr. Chamberlain's political friends, are numerous, open, and energetic enough to surprise the Birmingham orator, if he heard them, or heard of them.

This one speech has done much to make moderate Liberals and moderate Radicals even—for such there are—look with distrust on the great measure of enfranchisement which has just become law. Is this a foretaste, ask they, of the benefits to accrue from giving the vote to those who have it not? The answer would afford a fresh surprise to the man who is so ready to believe the baser the stronger instincts of the people.

The answer is that the people will repudiate the robbery proposed to them. The six hundred of Birmingham may cheer their guest. They may not take the measure of his meaning all at once. But the men in public life who know their countrymen best are convinced that Mr. Chamberlain will presently discover that he has made a mistake in his estimate of the forces to which he appeals, and of the aims of the multitude with whom political power is henceforth to rest. The Franchise Act did not repeal the Ten Commandments. Morality has not expired, nor is that empire of Chaos, to which Mr. Chamberlain regretfully referred, likely just yet to be restored. The rôle of Anarch may suit him for the moment, but the reign of universal darkness, if ever it comes, is likely to put a very different man from Mr. Chamberlain on its sable throne.

II.

AT THE DATE OF HIS MISSION TO WASHINGTON.

[LONDON, *October* 26, 1887.]

Mr. Chamberlain has been so long a conspicuous figure in English public life that it may not be easy to say anything new about him. I send you, however, not a biography or any attempt at a complete account of this interesting person, but casual notes enough to fill the column you perhaps expect. He now goes among you as Her Majesty's Plenipotentiary, and that is, at any rate, a totally new character for the politician whom a great portion of the Liberal party have been wont to call "Our Joe." You have heard it said, very foolishly, that this mission was meant to take him out of politics. I daresay it will take him out of politics while he is in America; not longer. He does not go there to discuss Home Rule. The Irish, if a cable despatch may be believed, think he ought not to discuss the fisheries question because he is not a convert, like Mr. Gladstone, to Mr. Parnell's views about governing Ireland. That is a notion which has the merit of originality. When the contest is over they will do him the justice they deny him now. He was a friend to Ireland long before some of the noisiest she now has lifted their voices for her. He is not less her friend because he adheres to his own ideas, and has his own opinions about the policy that ought to govern her relations with England. America, I fancy, is liberal enough to accept

Mr. Chamberlain on his merits; and to hear what he has to say on mackerel, and welcome him for what he is without complaining of what he is not.

He is, in fact, one of the most American of Englishmen. Probably he would not admit it, but it is true, as you will soon find out for yourselves. The quality which differentiates Americans and English is open-mindedness, and that is what Mr. Chamberlain has. With most Englishmen the fact that a thing exists is a reason why it should continue to exist. "It is the custom"—that is the final answer to every criticism. Mr. Chamberlain is the foremost man of that small body of Englishmen who decline to be satisfied with this stereotyped reply. It matters not what his present differences may be with the Gladstonian wing of the Liberal party. He is one of the real leaders of the English Democracy. Mr. Gladstone? Certainly not. Mr. Gladstone has been going through a series of conversions to beliefs and principles which Mr. Chamberlain has held since he entered public life.

He is a Radical, and his Radicalism is what the word itself implies—it goes to the roots of things. On more questions than one Mr. Chamberlain has shown only too great a readiness to tear down the tree in order to see what the roots were like. He preached some pernicious doctrines, no doubt; pre-eminently pernicious was his doctrine of Ransom. He does not always seem to have thought out his subject. But he is penetrated, saturated with faith in the righteousness of the idea he has espoused. Enemies have accused him of ambition, of interested motives, of trying to supplant Mr. Gladstone, of I know not what. Well, I used to differ strongly from Mr. Chamberlain when I thought him drifting toward Socialism, but I never doubted his sincerity.

Perhaps, as has been said before now, his great fault as a leader is impatience. He has such a horror, not to say hatred, of abuses that he can tolerate no delay in remedying them. If you asked him, you might find he thinks the

Constitution of the United States itself a too conservative instrument. But what he has sought to give to his own country has been in great part such reforms as would bring it into line with America — universal suffrage, free schools, democratic local government, religious equality, and the like. And until these fundamental reforms have been achieved he wants to run the legislative machine at full speed. He Americanised English politics in one sense about which opinions may be divided. He introduced the caucus. If he did not introduce it he established it, and made it the power it has since become. They taunted him with it only the other day: the one-man power, somebody called it, and Mr. Chamberlain was the one man. He might be forgiven that and much else if he would but reconsider some of his notions about property, and persuade himself that a landlord has some rights which a tenant and society in general are bound to respect. It is an odd fate which makes him at this moment a bulwark of the landlord system in Ireland.

He has gained a reputation as an administrator and head of a great department. A single story will show what is thought of him. One of the permanent officials of a department of which Mr. Chamberlain has been the Parliamentary chief once told me this: "We used to think ourselves lucky if we got back a set of papers from our presidents in two or three weeks. Now everything is returned within twenty-four hours."

I strongly advise you to get a speech from Mr. Chamberlain if you can. He will not talk politics. He may talk something else. He is, however, at his best in a militant mood; best in a great debate in the House, or in presence of a great audience half hostile. Perhaps some of our Irish friends would supply the half. He never speaks in these days in the House except to an accompaniment of Irish interruptions, and nothing shows him to better advantage than this state of things. His cool readiness of repartee seldom fails him, nor his temper. Mr. Gladstone once said that in his time he had known three men in the House of

Commons who always said exactly what they meant and no more. The three were Lord Palmerston, Mr. Parnell, and Mr. Chamberlain. He can take blows as well as give them. Mr. Gladstone's attack on him in the closing speech of the Home Rule debate last year was borne with a stoicism that Mr. Gladstone himself might have envied, and perhaps did. You would never have guessed from his placid face and unruffled composure of manner that he was the object of all that elaborate invective. On the platform as in the House he meets a running fire of questions, taunts, objurgations, insults even, with a tranquillity which enables him to frame a retort before the storm is over. There are greater orators. There is no better debater—no man in England who surpasses him in the power of effective speaking. It is now many years since he passed out of the second rank into the front rank.

The American interviewer, whatever else he may say, will not be able to say of Mr. Chamberlain that he is a typical Englishman in appearance. I have touched on some of his mental unlikenesses to the typical Englishman. A bolder pen might describe physical points of difference, but I will say this: he does not spring from the class which for so many centuries was the ruling class in England. He has nothing to do with the aristocracy or with the Established Church. Birth gave him no privileges. Professor Huxley once said of himself that by birth he was a plebeian, and that he stood by his order. Mr. Chamberlain comes of that great middle class which is, in this country, a plebeian class, and is justly proud of being. He was born in it and married in it, and has said more than once that he is never so happy as when among his own friends and people at Birmingham.

The cockney would call him a provincial. He won his first celebrity as Mayor — thrice Mayor — of Birmingham, which he reformed and swept clean, and lighted and set in order throughout. And because he showed himself master of local administration, critics who were masters of nothing but adjectives sometimes called his politics parochial. He still lives at Birmingham, or rather near it, having a place with some acres of land about it, so that this land reformer is also a landowner. Mr. Chamberlain when forty years old save one retired from business. He has been able to devote himself since 1874 exclusively to public affairs. London gossip long since fixed the exact figure of his yearly income. If he desires it to be known in America, he will tell anybody who has the courage to ask him.

He has, beside his place in Warwickshire, a house in London and a place in London society. Mr. Gladstone not long since thought fit to jest at his social position. There was a sentence about cushioned ease, meant apparently to bring him into disrepute with the poorer members of the party of reform. Mr. Gladstone's known respect for rank might have kept him silent on such a topic, but since it did not there is this to be said: No man in England reaches Mr. Chamberlain's position, or anything like it, without becoming an object of attraction to society. But society sought him, not he society. His opinions have survived the contact, and society itself has laughed at the failure of one or two of its leaders who thought they could "lionise" the great Radical. His safeguard against that process was like that of the Dutchman who escaped drowning. He did not go in the boat. He stayed away from houses where he thought people wanted to make a show of him. Not even Royalty made an impression on his Radicalism; neither Marlborough House nor Windsor Castle has won him over from any one of his convictions. The officials of the royal household will tell you that Mr. Chamberlain came to Windsor an object of royal aversion, and left it almost a favourite. The Queen liked him. Like the sensible woman she is she can bear plain truths, when told in low tones. One promising courtier ruined his chances by a loud voice which he could not subdue to the conventional pitch. I might add something about one or two other personal traits, but it is quite time for these indiscretions to come to an end.

III.

ON HIS RETURN FROM AMERICA.

[LONDON, *April* 10, 1888.]

The dinner given last night to Mr. Chamberlain by the Devonshire Club was made a public dinner by the act of the Committee. They wished the speeches reported, and reported they were. One of the morning papers has three columns of them. With that vanishes all notion of the privacy which is supposed, and sometimes only supposed, to envelop all transactions in a club, and I hold myself at liberty to say what I have to say of this festival as freely as if it had taken place in the Guildhall.

Who first conceived the notion of such a dinner I do not know, but it presently came to be thought that it might turn out to be something more than a recognition of Mr. Chamberlain's American successes. The Devonshire Club, as is well known, was founded as a Liberal club. During the last two years it has experienced the fate of all Liberal clubs, and is discovered to contain members of both Liberal wings. It has Gladstonian members and Liberal-Unionist members. So has the National Liberal Club, which is now understood to be the most radical of all club organisations in the United Kingdom; the National League probably excepted, and the National League is not exactly a club in the London sense. Lord Hartington said last night: " We of the Devonshire Club had the honour of being the inventors of this kind of gathering, at which we have been enabled to listen to speeches from distinguished members of our party upon questions of great public interest and importance, and, at the same time, to maintain that kind of social charm which does not belong to the ordinary public dinner."

Many such entertainments have been given at the Devonshire under the name of house dinners; last night's certainly the most notable of all. With the split in the Liberal party arose difficult questions, as you can imagine, but they were cleverly solved. The invitation to Mr. Chamberlain was, no doubt, in some minds regarded as the best answer of all to these puzzling questions, and for two reasons. It was found possible to make the occasion non-political, in the sense that both sections of the Liberal party took part in it. And there was a hope that it might somehow, or to some undefined extent, tend to foster good feeling between the two opposing branches of a once united party, if not, indeed, to promote a reconciliation between them.

The dining-room, or, as it is called in England, the coffee-room, of the Devonshire Club will seat nearly 200 guests, and it was crowded. The group which sat in the middle of the chief table was a remarkable one—none like it can have been seen in London since the spring of 1886. In the centre was Lord Granville, the man whom you would have chosen out of the whole company to preside over a banquet of conciliation. The face is as kindly as it is shrewd, and its acuteness is not more marked than its distinction. He has been a Liberal leader for the better part of two generations; a Whig; one of that great aristocracy which has so skilfully managed to combine advocacy of popular rights and the support of great reforms, with loyalty to its own order. Of Liberal ex-Ministers who, when the dissolution of the Liberal party took place, stood by Mr. Gladstone, Lord Granville has the longest claims to political renown. He had held great offices and done great services. His name is a complete guarantee of the neutrality of the ground where he stands. No young Gladstonian need hesitate to be found in Mr. Chamberlain's company with Lord Granville there to answer for him. He has done honour to the occasion by putting on the star and blue ribbon of the Garter.

Mr. Chamberlain is on his right. He has been so recently among you and you know him so well that, though this feast is held in his honour, I need say little about him. I suppose he might, had he but said Yes instead of No the other day, have rivalled Lord Granville's splendour by appearing with the Grand Cross of the Bath, and have heard himself addressed as Sir Joseph. Good sense and sound judgment saved him from that. If you hunted England through, you could hardly find two distinguished men more unlike in some essential particulars than Lord Granville and Mr. Chamberlain, but there they are, side by side, and you will presently hear that, on the particular most essential and interesting to us in America, the two are in complete accord.

Next beyond Mr. Chamberlain is Lord Hartington. There are many people in the room in whose minds the spectacle must give rise to reflections. The ex-Mayor of Birmingham, the ex-partner in Nettlefolds, makers of wood screws, the Radical, the merciless critic of the nobility as men who toil not neither do they spin—in a word, Mr. Joseph Chamberlain, and on either side of him two nobles of whom one at least belongs to one of the greatest families and is heir to one of the greatest titles in the kingdom. The intimacy of Lord Hartington's relations with Mr. Chamberlain dates, as so many other things date, from the springing of the Home Rule Bill on the Liberal party by Mr. Gladstone, now more than two years ago. Their agreement in opposition to that scheme has brought them close together, spite of all differences—and they are many—on other points. You may find even external contrasts if you look for them. Mr. Chamberlain's smooth white face, with its curious likeness, often remarked, to portraits of Pitt, has not a point of resemblance with his neighbour, whose full beard and moustache, both brown, the brown hair beginning to have a touch of silver in it, set as in a frame the straight, high-coloured features, and the blue eyes looking out from beneath a high forehead. A hundred times has Lord Hartington been discussed by friends and foes, and his character remains to most of them, in some points, still a puzzle. It is the puzzle of simplicity.

For Lord Hartington is a man who dares to be himself. His face and his manner have both changed of late years, but there never was a time when you could doubt that they accurately reflected the entire genuineness of nature which is his characteristic. They have gained in power, for one thing. The habit of thinking on high subjects, the burden of responsibilities, the conscientious toil of State business, have left their print on these features and on the man himself. Circumstances have brought Lord Hartington and Mr. Chamberlain together, and are likely to keep them together. There is identity of opinion between them on the question which each thinks most vital to the Empire. Of real sympathy, outside of politics, there can be very little. They are two types, and no community of political conviction can make them one.

In the absence of Mr. Phelps, who is on the Atlantic, Mr. White, American Chargé d'Affaires for the next two months, sits on Lord Granville's left. *Sedet eternumque sedebit,* so far as this dinner is concerned. He will not be asked to rise in answer to any toast to his country or his absent chief. America has to get on to-night as best she can without recognition by the authorities of the Devonshire who have in hand the official ordering of this dinner. But since there was not the least intention of incivility, the matter may be left where it is. Mr. White is glad enough to escape from speaking, and knows that no slight to him or his country was meant. Mr. Colmer, next to him, is from Canada, and he too is relieved from the duty of speech. I began to think, as I reflected on these peculiar arrangements, that the United States and Canada could not have such great interests at stake in this Fisheries Treaty as we have all supposed. And perhaps they have not.

There are other notable personages. Sir Henry James is at Lord Hartington's right hand; one of the three or four first lawyers in England; ex-Attorney-General, with the distinction of having been offered by Mr. Gladstone in 1886 his choice between the Home Office and the Lord Chancellorship, and of having declined both in obedience to his convictions. He could not join a Home Rule Ministry, and did not; and has endured as best he may the parting with old colleagues. If you give a glance at the build of the lower part of his face, you will not doubt that he has sufficient force of character to bear whatever befalls him. The fulness of the brow is not more striking than the solidity and energy of the lines of all that is below. Mr. Childers is on the other side; a most substantial person, with capacities for business; can add up columns of figures with an expert accuracy for which the Chancellorship of the Exchequer was once thought none too high a reward. Mr. Fowler is next him; Fowler of Wolverhampton, a rising young Liberal of fifty-eight, with prospects of Cabinet rank in the next Home Rule Government; date not yet even approximately fixed. And there are many more who would interest you.

The speeches? Well, no doubt, the speeches are what most of us came to hear, and they were well worth hearing, and anybody who likes may read them in the three columns they fill. But I cannot ask you to find room for any paraphrase of all these admirable sentiments, and my comment on them must be, or shall be, of the briefest. You have all heard Mr. Chamberlain in America, or all read him, and know his brisk, incisive method; with that metallic note in it proper to an orator from Birmingham. If I say he was not quite at his best on this occasion, it does not follow that he did not deliver an excellent discourse. He did, and what he said of himself and of America, and what he omitted to say of his treaty, was all good. Ever since his return from what I fear he still calls "the States" he seems to have a kind of halo about his head; a beautiful halo in gold; an aureole such as encircles the heads of early Italian saints; an expression of all the beatitudes which fill his soul. He wore it at this dinner also; whether he listened, or whether others listened to him, there was ever the same radiance; the same electric glow which illuminated the place on which he had bestowed the brilliancy of his American successes.

It was from Lord Granville that the speeches of the evening came. He has long passed for the best, I think—certainly by universal consent one of the two or three best—after-dinner orators in England. When I have heard him in the House of Lords I have thought him not less admirable in that still more difficult atmosphere. He has what few of his countrymen have. He has lightness of touch; he has the easy method which comes from temperament and is perfected by immense pains and much practice. He has a sense of form, a turn of phrase which is French, a rare felicity in saying delightful nothings which, as you listen, you accept as vital, or at least of high concern, to the business of the moment. Sparkling sentences fall from his lips; the utterance of them so natural that you hardly do justice to the art and tact and delicacy which have contributed to their construction. .When he came to serious topics, Lord Granville was both serious and sincere. What he said of America and Americans was free from every tinge of patronage, or of that condescension which Mr. Lowell long ago remarked in the foreigner. He had a difficult thing to do in referring to the political differences between himself and Mr. Chamberlain. It was done as gently as if a woman's hand had been laid on the wound. He omitted no proper compliment to the guest of the evening, but you could listen to the whole without a thought of flattery. The word reminds me that I am myself perhaps expressing my admiration of Lord Granville without remembering a familiar apophthegm, and without paying him the best compliment of all by imitating his reserve.

MR. JOHN MORLEY.

[LONDON, *March* 3, 1888.]

MR. GOSCHEN's description of Mr. John Morley as the "St. Just of our Revolution" has elicited from the ex-Chief Secretary for Ireland an elaborate protest, which takes the form of an article in the March *Nineteenth Century* on French Revolutionary Models. The article is interesting from more points of view than one; most of all as Mr. Morley's first distinct effort to rub off the label of Jacobin which has, rightly or wrongly, stuck to him for some time past. Perhaps it first became conspicuous when he quitted the serene heights of literature and plunged into the quagmire of politics. Yet in literature it was, serene or otherwise, that he had first given to his critics a pretext for fastening upon him the name he now seeks to get rid of. If Mr. Morley had not written about Robespierre and Danton, about Voltaire and Rousseau—and written of these and others, let me add, in what must be called a sympathetic spirit—never would he have been called upon to distinguish between himself and the Jacobins. Never would he have been told that he found his models in the heroes of the French Revolution and looked for his methods in the Reign of Terror.

So long as these accusations were couched in the usual form, Mr. Morley seems to have thought they might be neglected. But he is himself an inventor of epigrams and nicknames, and he knows better than most people the value of a telling phrase. So when the Chancellor of the Exchequer summed up and condensed all these charges into the phrase quoted above, the most long-suffering and amiable of men thought it time to turn. Nobody will complain, for his defence is the occasion of a very characteristic piece of autobiography. As for St. Just, Mr. Morley meets the suggestion of a likeness between himself and that lurid revolutionary figure by quoting M. Taine's account of him. The hand of the practised dialectician is visible in this proceeding. M. Taine paints St. Just all black:—

A sort of precocious Sulla, who at five-and-twenty suddenly springs from the ranks and by force of atrocity wins his place.... Blood calcined by study, a colossal pride, a conscience completely unhinged, an imagination haunted by the bloody recollections of Rome and Sparta, an intelligence falsified and twisted until it found itself most at its ease in the practice of enormous paradox, barefaced sophism, and murderous lying—all these perilous ingredients, mixed in a furnace of concentrated ambition, boiled and fermented long and silently in his breast.

Can I be such a monster as this? queries Mr. John Morley with his most innocent air. You might as well have called me Nero, or Bluebeard, or Torquemada. No doubt, but the St. Just of M. Taine is one thing. The St. Just of the writers to whom Mr. Morley seems to have gone for some of his views about the French Revolution is another and very different man. What is Hamel's life of St. Just but one long eulogy upon a man whom the world ought, he declares, to bless without reserve? Louis Blanc's admiration of him is more cautiously expressed but is none the less profound. It is the St. Just of the triumvirate, the colleague of Robespierre and Couthon, whom most men have in mind when they speak of him, whether by way of comparison with Mr. Morley or not. He is a sufficiently appalling figure however you look at him, but neither Mr. Goschen nor anybody else ever dreamed of suggesting the faintest analogy between the private lives of Mr. John Morley and of the young robber and libertine whom M. Taine describes. Mr. Morley is himself so familiar with the literature of the French Revolution that he does not always appreciate other people's ignorance of it. If he had reflected he might have reminded his readers that M. Taine, who began his career as a radical, wrote his history as a partisan of the counter-revolution.

What Mr. Goschen had in mind was, possibly, a trait very remote from all these evil qualities of St. Just. With all his sweetness and sweet reasonableness, there is in Mr. Morley a note of implacable austerity. He is profoundly loyal to his own convictions; he holds to them with an apostolic fervour; he believes that thus and not otherwise is the world to be regenerated, if at all. He would go to the stake for them, or to the guillotine, and Mr. Goschen perhaps imagined he would expect others to do as much for theirs—nay, he might, in pressing circumstances, aid in conferring upon some of the more dangerous enemies of civilisation the glories of martyrdom. Torquemada? Well, possibly even Torquemada. Mr. Morley would revolt against the suggestion of cruelty; unaware, it may be, how far the cool asceticism of his political faith may carry him. The Torquemada I mean is not the hideous monster of the story books, but the more gentle yet not less awful figure whom Victor Hugo has drawn.

Against Mr. Morley's private life no one, so far as I know, has ever said a single word, nor is there to my knowledge a single word to be said. His character is stainless, and something more. Stainless, after all, is but a negative epithet, and Mr. John Morley's is one of those rare natures abounding in positive virtues, and sympathetic beside. No man in public life has so few enemies. I do not know whether he has one. Few have more friends; attached and affectionate friends; no one has more of charm and fascination of character and conversation. This may seem to you the strained panegyric of personal friendship, and wanting in reserve. But I will take leave to relate an anecdote, though to relate it may itself be a departure from that reserve which private life imposes. I once sat with half a dozen others at a dinner-table in a country house when some one started this question, "If you had to be shut up in a dungeon or on a desert island with but one man for company, whom would you choose?" Five out of the seven men—whose names I should like to give—answered, John Morley.

He has read everything, said one man. So have many others, in the sense in which the words were spoken. But the results of Mr. Morley's reading flow out to others with so much simplicity and natural ease, with such absence of all pretension, with such accuracy, and are at the same time so fused with his own thought, that his talk is all his own, whether in variety, or fulness, or delightfulness of manner. You must, I admit, get him to converse on some subject he cares for, and not merely on frivolities. Then his talk is an illumination. He is even agreeable in argument. Of how many men can that be said? A political opponent once paid him a singular compliment. "If all Radicals were like Morley we could at least discuss things, and to discuss them would be a pleasure." The man who said that—I suppose I must not name him—stands among the first three statesmen of England, and in character none of his rivals is above him. Mr. Morley does not, like Dr. Johnson, talk for victory. He is persuasive, patient, capable of listening with politeness to what he thinks in his heart hopeless nonsense.

With all this, he applies to politics the most pitiless logic. It is vain for him to deny it; his methods are often French, whether revolutionary or not. He abuses the historical method. He has read deeply, and deeply considered his reading, and sees what results flowed from what causes, and he discusses current affairs as if they belonged to the Middle Ages or the Reformation, and could be dealt with accordingly. Nothing is more plausible, nothing seems more solid, nothing is often more mischievous in practical politics. He has the credit of having converted Mr. Gladstone to Home Rule, and he is perhaps the only English Liberal whose adhesion to Mr. Gladstone on that great question did not involve a renunciation of principles. It is a coincidence that Mr. Gladstone should devote part of his current article in *The Contemporary* to dissertations upon autonomy in the United States, in Norway and Sweden, in Austria-Hungary, and elsewhere. Mr. Morley says, " Parallels from France, or anywhere else, may supply literary amusement; they may furnish a weapon in the play of controversy. They shed no light and do no service as we confront the solid facts of the business to be done. . . . The only history that furnishes a clue in Irish questions is the history of Ireland."

What Mr. Morley says of his intellectual training has that interest which always belongs to an account—best of all if it be his own account—of the growth of a man's mind. It was the historical chapters in Comte's *Positive Philosophy* that first led him to a true view of the literary and social history of Western Europe—the view, that is, which he expressed in his books on Voltaire and Rousseau. His essays were, he admits, reactionary against Carlyle, whose diatribes against the Bankrupt Century then held the field. In a general way, the masters to whom he went in early manhood, so far from being revolutionists and terrorists, belonged entirely to the opposite camp. "Austin's *Jurisprudence* and Mill's *Logic* and *Utilitarianism* were everything, and Rousseau's *Social Contract* was nothing." Mill was the chief influence for Mr. Morley as for most of his contemporaries in those days. Later came many modifications of Mill's doctrines, but for a while he was disciple and not critic. Turgot attracted him; Turgot was to him " a great and inspiring character." Burke is, of course, included in the list of formative teachers. Mr. Morley held Mill's doctrines about politics, that the test of practical, political, or social proposals is not their conformity to abstract ideals, but convenience, utility, expediency, and occasion. "If I were pressed," says he, "for an illustration of these principles at work, inspiring the minds and guiding the practice of responsible statesmen in great transactions of our own day and generation, I should point to the sage, the patient, the triumphant action of Abraham Lincoln in the emancipation of the negro slaves." Nothing could be more interesting than such a tribute to Lincoln from an English scholar. But is there any record of Lincoln's having studied Comte's *Positive Philosophy*, or even Mill's *Logic* and *Utilitarianism?* Again does Mr. Morley go to America for an ideal or hero, Washington. He quotes Jefferson's character of Washington as coming far nearer to the right pattern of a great ruler than can be found in any of Carlyle's splendid dithyrambs.

Such then were Mr. Morley's teachers, such are his models of great men in public life; remote enough, certainly, from the precursors of, or actors in, the French Revolution. Nobody could be less like Rousseau than Mill. Never had any ruler less of the Jacobin in him than Washington or Lincoln. The defence is complete as far as it goes. How comes it, then, that such a name as Jacobin was ever bestowed on Mr. Morley? The answer would take me too far, and no answer could be final. But I may say that it is not so much his line on the Irish question, as the arguments by which he enforces his Irish views, that cause him to be thought revolutionary. He would be the last to deny that the Irish battle has been fought on grounds that can only be called Socialistic, and that the issue whether Ireland shall have a Parliament of her own is made to turn on questions which disturb, or threaten to disturb, the whole existing fabric of social order.

LORD ROSEBERY.

A SPEECH AT BIRMINGHAM TOWN HALL.

[BIRMINGHAM, *April* 1, 1883.]

Lord Salisbury has been speaking here for two days, but of him I shall not have much to say because I did not hear him. I gather that he made a good impression on Birmingham as a platform speaker and a very bad one as a statesman; which might be expected in a place where Toryism has not much root. People talk of it as a bold thing on Lord Salisbury's part to attack the Liberal enemy in his chief English stronghold. This sort of metaphor, like metaphors in general, is misleading. It requires no courage for a Conservative to address a Birmingham audience. He is not pelted nor even hissed. The radicalism of the Midland metropolis is robust enough to endure with patience all that Lord Salisbury can say against it, to its face or behind its back. The presence of the Tory chief in Birmingham is less a proof of his own valour than a tribute to the central importance of Birmingham in politics. I do not know whether his many audiences, or any of them, were largely composed of opponents. What I heard was that the Midland counties had been ransacked to provide him with hearers enough to fill the Town Hall. On Thursday evening, said an American friend who had come from London to sit at Lord Salisbury's feet (and who had to stand instead of sitting), the platform was covered with white ties, and the body of the house was filled with men more accustomed to using ploughs than making them.

Most of my pilgrimages to Birmingham have been made to hear Mr. Bright. This one was to listen to a younger man, Lord Rosebery; one of that younger generation who are to have a hand in shaping English affairs for the next twenty years or more. Lord Rosebery is the man of to-day in Scotland; of to-morrow in England; on the threshold of the Cabinet, to which he is every day gazetted by the newspapers.

A Town Hall audience in Birmingham is of itself worth coming to see, especially if the comer be an American. Often as I have seen it, to see it again is always a fresh surprise, so unlike is it to every other audience in England. An American friend instantly described it as "so American"; and it is. American in keenness of feature, and still more American in its quickness of mind and rapid judgment on men, and on what men have to say. There is no great manufacturing town in England where so many working men are their own masters. Their habit of thinking for themselves on public affairs, which has given Birmingham its political fame, was acquired by thinking for themselves about their own business and about the business of their town; for the wise conduct of which latter they have also a deserved celebrity, to which Mr. Chamberlain has contributed. It is the most difficult and critical audience a public speaker in this country can be called on to face,—some five thousand men extremely wide-awake and well-informed, and taught by Mr. Bright to be exacting in the matter of oratory.

Lord Rosebery was to address them as president of the Junior Liberal Association of Birmingham. He said later in the evening that if this was the Junior Association he should be glad to know what the Senior was like. It was enough that it was a Liberal meeting—no need to glean for hearers in the agricultural outskirts of the town, or disturb the patrician repose of three counties. Lord Rosebery was a stranger to them,—this is his first appearance in Birmingham,—but whether from his reputation, or his face and manner, or for whatever reason, they gave him the sort of welcome commonly reserved for old friends. It was expected of him to answer Lord Salisbury, and to Lord Salisbury accordingly the greater part of his speech was devoted. The answer was minute and effective, but it had the disadvantage of being an answer. Lord Rosebery has a constructive power which may be put to better use than is to be found for it in controversy and retort. His talent for repartee may be employed on lesser occasions; here it would have been worth his while to state his own case from his own standpoint, and leave Lord Salisbury's sinister sarcasms to answer themselves; or to be answered by Mr. Chamberlain, since to him if to anybody the challenge from Hatfield was addressed. But when he had passed from Lord Salisbury and entered upon a peroration devoted to a definition of Liberalism, and the worth of Liberalism to the country, the speech reached a higher level; and its epigram became more glittering. It might be difficult to put more sense and wit into a phrase than are condensed in Lord Rosebery's summary of his own speech: "That the future of this country rests not with the wasps but the bees." His audience was swift to catch the point and to applaud; as they did this declaration, delivered with genial sincerity: "The difference between Liberalism and Conservatism is essential and eternal: the one can, and the other cannot trust the people. I cast in my lot with the party that can."

No quotation would convey a vivid notion of Lord Rosebery's method as a whole, or give any hint of that charm of manner which won upon his audience from the beginning and carried it captive to the end. I must content myself with saying that he offers a most interesting example of the orator whose purpose is persuasiveness. The final secret of his success with an audience is sympathy, not authority, or not yet authority. His definition of Liberalism, good as far as it goes, does not go far enough to account for his own influence over the thousands whom he addressed for the first time. There he stands, remote in more ways than one from the generality of his fellow-men; by distinctions each one of them too commonly a cause of separation between him who possesses them and him who does not. Once in a while it happens that instead of widening the gulf they narrow it; when, as in Lord Rosebery's case, this favourite of nature and fortune does really look upon men as his fellow-men; not with mere civility, or sterile good temper, but with a feeling of goodwill. The highest kind of oratory is not possible to any man deficient in this feeling. Nobody would undervalue the oratorical endowments Lord Rosebery possesses: voice, presence, power of clear thinking, and the rest. But an orator who is to move the people must be a man of the people at bottom—not a democrat in the political sense, not by any means necessarily a radical, but one who holds with Jefferson that men are born equal, or, at any rate, are born men. This conviction may in the long run make him irresistible.

LORD SPENCER.

I.

HIS SERVICES AS VICEROY OF IRELAND.—HIS REWARD.

[LONDON, *July* 10, 1885.]

No gratitude in politics, says the cynical observer. He has been saying it lately, with only too much appearance of truth, with reference to the return of Lord Spencer from Ireland. The policy of which the late Viceroy was the exponent is no longer the policy of the English Government. It was odious to a large part of the Irish people. Lord Spencer himself was fiercely attacked because he enforced this policy. All that may be admitted. Yet I apprehend that many of the very men who criticised him and his administration most bitterly admired him secretly, and respected him. In the conduct of the warfare they carried on against English rule, the Parnellites assailed every English ruler with about the same degree of energy. They wanted to break down the system, and to the Irish mind a man is always the impersonation of a system. These fervid Celts find no excitement in aiming at an abstraction. They prefer a target of flesh and blood. They have launched volleys of arrows at Lord Spencer. In Parliament they tried every means to discredit him. They toiled day and night to turn him out. They held him up to execration as a monster guilty of innocent blood. They taught the peasants of Ireland, whose political literature consists of nothing but Mr. Parnell's weekly organ, to believe that this Englishman delighted in oppression and in cruelty. But now that Lord Spencer is no longer Lord-Lieutenant of Ireland, I believe that even Mr. Parnell and Mr. O'Brien would acknowledge that much of their fury against him was feigned, under what they thought a political necessity. The generous instincts of Irishmen would compel them to admire a man who has shown so many of the qualities which they most value.

Whatever be the real opinion of the Irish, the English, at any rate, owe Lord Spencer much. He has ruled Ireland as England wanted it ruled. Nobody here disputes that he has filled his high station with rare courage, with great capacity, with complete devotion to what he thought his duty. The place had no temptation for him. The work has been very heavy. He has spent three years in hourly peril. He wanted neither money nor distinction. He had everything which in England is thought to make life desirable. He sacrificed much of it, and risked all, in obedience to the summons of the State. The task set him was perhaps an impossible task, but he wrought at it with just as much conscientious industry as if complete success lay within his reach. He has kept order and cut down the category of crime to one-fourth what it was. Whatever else be said of him, he has shown the qualities which belong to a ruler of men. England has seldom been better served.

Well, what is Lord Spencer's reward? How is he welcomed? What recognition does England offer him? None. He lays down his vice-regal power and comes home to a country which seems to have forgotten his existence. Newspaper eulogies are cheap, but there are few or none on the late Lord-Lieutenant. Honours and decorations fell in a shower as the Gladstone Ministry went out of office. Lawyers and Treasury clerks, artists, financiers, politicians, came in for their share, but Lord Spencer's share was nothing. Parliament votes him no thanks. Hardly a civil word for him is to be heard in either House. He is not discredited, he is not censured, he is simply neglected. It is left to the historian to do justice to him. The historian will find ample materials for praise in the record of Lord Spencer's services, and in the encomiums of journals and of Ministers uttered while he was still in power. The rest the historian will have to supply for himself.

There is, however, one exception to this rule of silence and forgetfulness. The Queen has conferred upon the Countess Spencer the order of Victoria and Albert of the second class. The distinction is one hitherto reserved for royalty. There are four classes. The fourth is bestowed rather freely. The third is more select. It was the third which was given to the Duchess of Marlborough on her husband's retirement from the Irish Viceroyalty in 1880. The second is conferred for the first time on a lady not of the royal blood or kinship. The Queen, in other words, has done what she could as Queen to mark her sense of Lady Spencer's services; for Lady Spencer has been, in the fullest sense, the consort of Lord Spencer in his Viceroyalty.

Lord Spencer left Dublin amid cheers and some hisses. The presence of Lady Spencer did not quiet these latter demonstrations; which, to be sure, were not very numerous. Chivalry, also, like gratitude, has little place in politics.

II.

HIS NEWCASTLE DECLARATION FOR HOME RULE.

[LONDON, *April* 23, 1886.]

Newcastle, though not possessing the political importance of Birmingham, is one of those half dozen great towns which have a great share in moulding the general opinion of the country on a great political issue. It has long had a rather peculiar reputation as the home of Mr. Joseph Cowen. That eloquent but impracticable politician has sat for Newcastle since 1874. Through good and through evil report, the Tynesiders have clung to their hero, read his newspaper, voted for him, tolerated, if not adopted, his not very coherent or even consistent scheme of political doctrine. Their fidelity to him has brought upon them a reputation for eccentricity which detracts a little from the value of their public protestations. On the other hand, they have steadied their ship by taking on board a second pilot in the person of Mr. John Morley. Mr. Morley, whatever else he may be, is a man whose mind works by orderly processes, and not by feminine impulses. He would confer distinction on any constituency in the kingdom, and he has done something to sober the judgment of Newcastle. He spoke there on Wednesday evening in company with Lord Spencer. A speech from either is a political event, but the crisis is one in which the late Viceroy's name has a significance with the country which makes his the most weighty declaration yet heard on the side of the Government.

There is no better man than Lord Spencer, said Mr. Gladstone the other day in the House of Commons. He acquired a knowledge of Ireland — of agrarian and political crime among other things—which no other man can pretend to. He occupied a unique position before the English public. When it became known that he saw his way to support Mr. Gladstone's Home Rule scheme, the mere fact of his adhesion was, I think, a better argument with many than the most elaborate argument from anybody else. For two years he had been the chief instrument of coercion. He had enforced the Crimes Act, detected and hanged the murderers of Burke and Lord Frederick Cavendish, and many murderers beside, suppressed in great part agrarian crime, restored social order throughout a great part of Ireland, ruled with a firm, just, masterful hand. His one mistake—which perhaps was not his—was his toleration of the National League which had sprung from the ashes of the Land League, and presently grown more powerful than its predecessor. But beyond doubt he had governed Ireland, and when his successor, Lord Carnarvon, took upon himself to reverse the Liberal Viceroy's policy and let Mr. Parnell govern it, the English sense of Lord Spencer's capacity and services became stronger than ever.

So it was a shock to the English public to be told that the Viceroy, who to their mind had proved the feasibility and the wisdom of English rule in Ireland, had declared for Irish rule in Ireland. When they had got over the first shock, they saw the force of his testimony. Many of them said to themselves: If Lord Spencer thinks Home Rule the sole remedy, whose opinion can be weighed against his? His speech at Newcastle will do something to strengthen this feeling.

There are topics on which his testimony is highly interesting. He takes throughout the most generous view. He gives the people of Ireland credit for honest intentions and good sense. He believes neither in the wish of a majority for complete separation from England, nor in their readiness for government by anarchy. The fanatics and rebels he sets down as a small section of the whole body of Irishmen. In any case, he pronounces separation impossible. He is generous to men who never were fair to him; whose political aims obliged them, as they thought, to heap calumnies on him. He volunteers to say that he has never heard or seen evidence of complicity in crime against any of the Irish representatives. Nor do I suppose that Englishmen generally believed that the connection between the Irish parliamentary party and the party of crime was of a kind likely to furnish evidence to the records of the Castle. Lord Spencer touches on these matters to strengthen his sanction to the bill. His speech abounds in interest, in weighty matter. There is something almost pathetic in his delivery of it at Newcastle in the company of Mr. John Morley, the most uncompromising English opponent of Lord Spencer while he was Viceroy. It is the humiliation of the captive in the Roman triumph, cry those who so long sustained him. These bitter things might be left unsaid. They will detract nothing from the general belief in his honesty, or from the value of his support to Home Rule.

LORD RIPON.

WITH A NOTE ON ENGLISH RULE IN INDIA.

[LONDON, *February* 27, 1885.]

Lord Ripon has had his public dinner from the National Liberal Club, and made his speech, and other men have made speeches in his honour. Five Cabinet Ministers were present, and many ladies, cries one enthusiastic advocate of that singular policy known as India for the Indians. The ladies were rightly there. Politics with them are a matter of sentiment, and Lord Ripon's policy in India has been described as a policy of sentiment; not on the whole unjustly. The late Viceroy is a man of many excellent qualities; with a fervent love of justice; with a deep desire to do justice to the natives of India; and with something of the spirit which leads a man to face hostility and hatred in defence of his beliefs. As Lord Ripon, he deserves much of the honour paid him as Viceroy of India. If you ask what he has done during his term of office, the answer becomes a little difficult. He has made himself beloved by the natives, and not beloved by the Anglo-Indians, but in both cases it is for what he wanted to accomplish rather than for what he has accomplished. Not much has been changed by his rule. India is governed to-day very much as it was governed the day Lord Ripon landed in Bombay. The Ilbert Bill, about which so fierce a controversy raged so long, was shorn of its most important provisions before it was allowed to become law. And Lord Ripon's administration will be remembered chiefly by the protracted and embittered struggle about that measure.

What Lord Ripon represented in India was that doctrinaire spirit which has got hold of some leading English Radicals, and is much heard of here in England. Possessed with a profound conviction of the utility of parliamentary government based on popular rights, they would people the world with Parliaments on the model of the House of Commons at Westminster. Persuaded that the franchise is a talisman, they would put it into every hand. Perceiving that in such countries as England and the United States power must rest with the people, they would give the people power in countries which have not one single point of resemblance to the United States or to England. Their dream is to apply the maxims of constitutional government to countries which, for more centuries than Europe can remember, have known no constitution but the will of the ruler for the time being. The Asiatic is to become a cockney. Mussulman and Hindoo, Brahmin and Buddhist, Bengalee and Sikh, the most submissive and the most warlike of races, the most fanatical and the most tolerant, the most ignorant and the most enlightened, the most loyal and the most hostile of British subjects in India are, to the Radical mind, of the same mould, fit for the same institutions, to be treated with the same panacea. They are to be educated, they are to be taught to govern, they are to govern. And when once this beneficent fancy has become fact, the British will have performed their mission in Hindostan, and may retire, although every man who knows India knows that their retirement would be the signal for a fresh outbreak of the strife which has desolated the peninsula from the beginning of time.

There is no great danger that the Radical will be allowed to carry his experiment very far, but it is for attempting to take one step in this direction that Lord Ripon is now a favourite toast with Radical orators. Lord Ripon's opponents agree with him that England holds India in trust for the people of India. The natives are entitled to good government, to justice, to education, and to many other things. But Lord Ripon and his opponents part company when they pass from principles to measures. "Take away the British sword from behind educated India," says the Anglo-Indian, "and in twelve months there would not be a glib Baboo who should dare to open his lips." Does Lord Ripon doubt it? Would he venture to try? Can he foresee a period when such an experiment can be made? The plain truth is, India has never been ruled otherwise than by the sword, and whether the sword be English or native, it will still be the sword. England won her great Oriental empire by force, and by force she will have to keep it, if she means to keep it at all. She is not loved by the people whom she governs, but those people are nevertheless more wisely and less oppressively governed than at any period of their past history, or than they would be if the British garrison should set sail to-morrow for its island home.

MR. LOWELL.

WHY THE ENGLISH LIKED HIM AND WHAT HIS INFLUENCE
HAS BEEN.

[LONDON, *March* 24, 1885.]

THE announcement of Mr. Lowell's recall gives rise to many expressions of regret and goodwill besides those which appear in the newspapers. Nor is the expression of goodwill a new thing. In discussing his address on Democracy last year *The Spectator* observed that Englishmen, whether they knew Mr. Lowell or not, looked on him as a personal friend. His writings, his speeches, and his public services had brought him so close to all English-speaking people that their feeling toward him was one of affection; in short, there were ninety millions who would rejoice in any good fortune that befell him and sympathise with him in trouble. The solicitude to know whether he was to remain Minister has been general. "Will President Cleveland keep Mr. Lowell in London?" is the question which every American in London has been asked over and over again since last November; perhaps twice a day on an average. And when the inquiring Briton was told that Mr. Lowell would have to go, the next question generally was, "What, then, did the President mean by Civil Service reform?"

The causes of Mr. Lowell's popularity in England are manifold. I may as well repeat, however, what I have said before, that it would be an entire mistake to suppose that conformity to English opinion or feeling is, or ever was, one of them. Never has an American Minister in London been more American than Mr. Lowell. It would be thought ridiculous here to accuse him of Anglomania, and not less ridiculous to defend him against such a charge. But there is nothing to be gained by blinking the fact that the accusation has been made in America. It will, I presume, die away of itself now that no political end is to be gained by reiterating it.

Be that as it may, it would provoke nothing but a smile from any Englishman who heard it. Mr. Lowell, like one of his predecessors, has always passed here for being not only intensely American but even aggressively American. The same sort of thing is said about him—though in less degree—that used to be said of Mr. Motley. He tolerated no criticism of his own country; not even the most harmless. In the slang of the period, you could always get a rise out of Lowell by touching on any American trait. "Hawthorne insulted us all," observed an English lady, "by saying all English women were fat, but I dare not say in Mr. Lowell's presence that an American woman is thin." That is but one of many similar anecdotes that might be told.

"At any rate," said Mr. Lowell a year ago, " I must allow that, considering how long we have been divided from you, you speak English remarkably well." This daring sentence he addressed to the Master and Fellows of Emmanuel College, Cambridge, who rightly thought they could not completely celebrate their Tercentenary without help from the American Minister. It is instantly picked out from its context and commented upon by the London press; not ill-naturedly, but with a certain surprise that any American, shielded from violence though he be by the sacredness of his diplomatic character, should venture upon a flight of humour so high as this. Yet never since Mr. Lowell has been in England has he ceased to assert the claim of his own language as spoken in his own country to equality with the English of England, if not to something more than equality. The Masters and Fellows of Emmanuel College, perhaps less jealous guardians of English fame than the English press, or less conscious of their mission to protect it against all comers, received Mr. Lowell's observation with laughter and cheers. That also is English. John Bull may think you a presumptuous person for standing up to him, and may sometimes intimate his dissent from your attitude by knocking you down. But whether he strikes or hears, he will certainly like you the better for taking the chance of either.

This very energy of Mr. Lowell's Americanism was, indeed, one of the secrets of the attachment English men and English women had for him. No doubt they thought it sometimes inopportune, but they would have liked him less, and respected him very much less, without it. The American who believes he can win English esteem by sinking his Americanism knows little of the English. If they themselves conform to nobody, they expect nobody to conform to them. Aping English manners, or paying court to English prejudices, is the last way in which a foreigner may expect to conciliate English goodwill. They like above all things, though they do not always know it, an exotic flavour. They value above all things genuineness of character. They expect a man to be himself, and not somebody else; an American if he is lucky enough to be born under the Stars and Stripes; or a Turk if he owns allegiance to the Crescent. The American accent, as they call it, is heard with pleasure in England. The most frivolous society is of one mind on this point with the most serious. What society wants above all things is to be interested, and the surest way to interest is to be novel. What has made American women who have married English husbands such favourites in London? Many of them are pretty, or clever, or both, but they have a position apart because they are pretty, or clever, or both, in a different way from English women who happen to be pretty and clever. They have naturalised in England a whole host of American phrases and American ways, and the English are quite aware that they are the gainers by all they have borrowed from their pretty American cousins.

One of the many services Mr. Lowell has done is the enabling Englishmen to understand America better than ever before. Here was a man who had everything the best Englishmen had in culture, and something beside which they had not, and that something was distinctively American. It was not humour alone, nor wit alone, nor quickness of mind. It might be called a capacity for taking new views, but that would not explain it completely. Perhaps flexibility is the word which comes nearest to expressing the quality which Englishmen so frequently lack and Americans for the most part possess. I will not try to define or describe; I wish only to indicate a differentiating trait, and I pass on, lest I find myself discussing personal matters too freely.

But I shall be safe in saying that Mr. Lowell has made for himself a reputation as a talker quite unlike any English talker, and certainly not inferior to any. In that form of conversation addressed to a larger number of persons than usual, and called an after-dinner speech, he has confessedly no rival in England. All the ease of friendly talk, all the finish of oratory, all the freshness of genius, all the kindly wisdom of the man of the world, are to be found in these unique performances, and they alone would have been enough to give him a foremost place in public life. Then, by way of showing that he could be serious and sparkling at the same time, Mr. Lowell delivered in Birmingham to the most critical audience in England that memorable address on Democracy, in which the American Idea was put before the Englishman with such force of statement and such enchanting persuasiveness as to make him, perhaps for the first time, admire a theory of political organisation which he had always been taught to dread.

Of Mr. Lowell's purely diplomatic work the time has not come to speak, nor is the history of it fully known outside the State Department in Washington. But everything I have said above is a testimony to his fitness for the post he held, and a proof that he did his duty as Minister well. An

Envoy's position is no longer what it was. The cases are now few in which he is anything more than the agent of a policy settled for him at home. His usefulness depends on his dexterity in presenting an argument, on his intimacy with the Ministers of the country to which he is accredited, on his bearing, on his power of seeing and seizing the points of a situation, and—to sum it all up—on his gift of doing what must often be a disagreeable act in an agreeable way. A Minister who is on good terms with Lord Granville will get his business transacted quickly; the matter will often be discussed in confidence; the kernel of wheat sifted out from all the diplomatic chaff; and they will know in Washington what can be done here and what cannot.

Most of the papers in which Mr. Lowell's departure is discussed hint at the possibility of his remaining in England after his official mission shall have passed into other hands. "It has always been difficult," says *The Times*, "to regard Mr. Lowell as a guest; it is still more difficult to think of him as a parting guest; and it is almost impossible to speed his parting. He came among us as an old friend; he has made himself a part of our life and literature; and we are still entitled to claim him by virtue of his citizenship in that wider literary nationality which includes both England and the United States." And this writer, who speaks the sense of all, concludes: "If he decides to make his permanent home in the country which has never treated him as a stranger, we must ask America to console herself for his loss by regarding him as still deputed to represent her highest culture in the republic of English literature." There is in this, as in the other expressions of regret in public and in private, a tone of almost affectionate friendship rarely heard from an Englishman in public, and not often in private.

The English hope that Mr. Lowell will remain in England has, however, but a slender basis to rest on. More definite and very flattering proposals have been made him, only to be rejected. He will go home when he has welcomed his successor and done what he can to make his new paths smooth. Whether he will return is probably a question yet to be settled. Certain it is that the loss of official position would make little difference to Mr. Lowell should he decide to live in England. Social relations depend hardly at all on official position. There have been many foreign Ministers in England whose knowledge of the real social life about them has been limited to such superficial impressions as they could collect from Ministerial parties and state dinners. An Englishman does not ask a man to visit him in the country, or to dine with him quietly in town, because he happens to be a plenipotentiary. He asks his guest because he likes him, and because he knows his other guests like him or admire him. Mr. Lowell will not be less liked or less admired because he lays down his diplomatic rank. He has had, and may continue to have, his choice of the most agreeable and cultivated society in England. But it by no means follows that he may not prefer the society which is to be found in his own country.

May 20.—The American Minister went yesterday afternoon to Windsor, and returned an hour or two later to London. On the down journey he bore the name of James Russell Lowell. When he travelled up to London he signed himself E. J. Phelps. The transformation scene was enacted in the presence of the Queen. Mr. Lowell, as the Court Circular in its large style tells us, was introduced to Her Majesty's presence by Earl Granville, K.G., and presented his letter of recall; and the Hon. Edward J. Phelps was likewise introduced, and presented his credentials as Minister for the United States of America. So ends one of the most striking chapters in the diplomatic history of the United States. I have given already a long, but by no means full, account of it, and I shall add but little out of the store of anecdote and opinion which remains. You know how general has been the expression of regret at Mr. Lowell's departure among all those classes whose relation to social or public life is a close one. You have heard of the tributes offered him by the working men. The story of the address from Worcester has been told. The other day at Westminster Abbey, among all the speakers who strove to do honour to the memory of Coleridge, not one omitted his sentence of farewell to Mr. Lowell, there present, and the chief orator of the occasion.

If I may testify to my own experience I will say that I have not for months met a friend or acquaintance who did not ask whether Mr. Lowell was really going, and whether, though he ceased to be Minister, he would not remain in England. The other night I met at supper a number of men eminent in a profession which seems more than most others to monopolise the attention of those who belong to it —the theatrical profession. No doubt it is the virtue of an artist to be absorbed in his art; and actors do certainly practise this virtue with admirable industry. But they joined one and all in the lament over the loss of Mr. Lowell. There was nothing conventional in what they said. It was the simple and sincere declaration of a genuine feeling. The relation between art and letters is a close one. My friends did not generalise on the matter, but they felt, I think, that in a country where personal merit often counts for less than inherited distinction, Mr. Lowell had done a service, and a great service, to those whose place in the world depends on themselves. No man has done so much here for democracy in a social sense as this really American Minister.

Mr. Lowell's visit to the Queen last week was a private visit and must be respected as such. It is a mere commonplace to say that he was cordially received, and that the Queen's regard for him, long known to be friendly, has been signified in a marked way. What Her Majesty said to Mr. Lowell was meant for Mr. Lowell only, but what she said of him to a third person may be repeated. The Queen said that no Ambassador or Minister during her reign had created so much interest in England as Mr. Lowell; no other had won so much regard.

MR. PHELPS.

I.

HIS DIPLOMATIC RANK IN GREAT BRITAIN.

[LONDON, *April* 28, 1885.]

It may be interesting to point out the precise place in the order of diplomatic precedence which Mr. Phelps will occupy on his arrival at the Court of St. James. As he is not an Ambassador he will rank, of course, after all the Ambassadors; of whom there are at this moment seven, Turkey having two. The senior member of the entire diplomatic body is a Turk, an unspeakable Turk, Musurus Pacha. Count Munster, whose quarrel with Prince Bismarck has led to neither his resignation nor removal, comes next; then Count Károlyi, the Austro-Hungarian, who is followed by Count Nigra, of Italy, who is one step before M. Waddington, the Ambassador of the French Republic, who immediately precedes M. de Staal, of Russia; to whom succeeds the special Ambassador of the Sublime Porte, Hassan Fehmi Pacha.

That closes the list of Ambassadors. The first in the list of Ministers is Count de Bylandt, the popular envoy of the Netherlands; the second is Baron Solvyns, the not less popular Belgian. For the third you must go all the way to Persia, long represented by Prince Malcolm Khan, and from Persia all the way to Brazil for the fourth—the well-known Baron de Peñedo, with a social reputation of his own. Portugal comes next but one to her ancient dependency, Spain intervening, and Sweden following. Then the list descends in order through the Ministers of Salvador, China, Guatemala, and the Argentine Republic to Mr. Lowell. But on Mr. Lowell's departure the United States loses its present proud position after Guatemala and the Argentine Republic. Denmark steps in, and after Denmark, Colombia (supposing Admiral Jouett not to have extinguished her meantime); then Roumania, Chili, Mexico, Siam. It is worth pausing in this downward scale to note that Siam is represented by His Royal Highness Krom Mun Nares Varariddhi, a name which I affectionately commend to the closest solicitude of the proof-reader. We resume with Costa Rica, proceed with Venezuela, and go on by way of Hayti, Servia, Japan, and Uruguay.

Last of all will come Mr. Phelps as Minister of the United States of America. He will be entitled to an uninterrupted view of the backs of twenty-three Ministers and seven Ambassadors at Court and elsewhere. When he calls upon Lord Granville, at the Foreign Office, seven Ambassadors and twenty-three Ministers will have the right to go in before him. The business of the United States cannot be transacted before the affairs of Guatemala, of Costa Rica, and of Hayti have been disposed of. Salvador is to be heard before her; she will wait upon the good pleasure of Siam; the world-wide interests of the kingdoms of Servia and Roumania may claim a full discussion before the ear of the British Secretary of State for Foreign Affairs is open to the trivial concerns of the petty Republic beyond the Atlantic, with its fifty or sixty millions of people.

It is, I hope, obvious that diplomatic precedence is not determined by such slight considerations as the relative importance of the Powers represented. It is determined first by rank. An Ambassador is a being superior to a Minister, and any Ambassador goes before any Minister, alike in matters of ceremony and matters of business. Seniority is the only other condition of precedence. The Ambassador who has been here longest takes precedence of all his colleagues, who follow according to the dates of their appointment; or,

I suppose, strictly speaking, their credentials. The rule is the same with Ministers. When Mr. Phelps arrives, the Vermont lawyer of sixty will be—for all official and social and ceremonial purposes—the youngest diplomatist at the Court of St. James; absolutely last on the official "List of the Foreign Ministers at this Court in the order of their Precedence in each class," as the Lord Chamberlain phrases it. As other Powers change their Ministers less frequently than we do, he will climb upward but slowly. It rests, nevertheless, with the United States to say whether he shall remain at the bottom of this long roll of inferior plenipotentiaries. The moment Congress chooses to enlarge the Legation into an Embassy, the American Ambassador will take his place with other Ambassadors. There are usually six; an American would therefore be one of seven who rank above all Ministers and other diplomatic agents. Failing this, he will remain for an indefinite period as bob to the diplomatic kite.

II.

HIS EXPERIENCES OF LONDON.—HIS DEPARTURE.

[*June* 8, 1885.]

Mr. Phelps has now been three weeks in London and has had some opportunity of seeing what his new position is like. London, on its part, has seen something of the man about whom curiosity was as keen as curiosity about anybody can be in a society hardened to every sensation. The place Mr. Phelps fills is one in which first impressions go for much; it may almost be said that they are decisive. In the world he now enters people are too busy to spare time for second thoughts. For better or worse, a new Minister has to present himself before an instantaneous camera; the photograph which is the work of a second is permanent. His actual acquaintance with London society is even more brief than it seems because the Whitsun holidays have to be deducted from the three weeks. A great part of London has been out of town for ten days or a fortnight. Most houses have been closed; social events are few during the Parliamentary recess. Mr. Phelps took possession of Mr. Lowell's house in Lowndes Square on Monday. It is, I think, without precedent that two successive American Ministers should occupy the same residence. It will presently go near to be thought that the Republic is able to afford its representative a permanent home in London; which, as we all know, it cannot.

During these three weeks Mr. Phelps has made two appearances which may be called public. He was present with Mrs. Phelps last Tuesday at the State Concert in Buckingham Palace. This is one of the few remaining ceremonials, drawing-rooms and levees excepted, by which English royalty now reminds the English world of its ornamental character. The State Concert is given by command of the Queen. The Queen herself is transacting the business of her realm in that central and convenient spot, just 600 miles from London, known as Balmoral. Her Majesty was represented on this occasion at Buckingham Palace by the Prince and Princess of Wales. The United States Minister figures last in the long list of Ministers which follows the short list of Ambassadors; Mrs. E. J. Phelps with him. It was their first appearance at any such function; it was also Mr. Lowell's last. What I hear from a sure witness there present is that the reception given to Mr. and Mrs. Phelps was of a friendly kind. The Princes and Princesses, said my friend, showed themselves eager to greet the new American Minister and his wife, and there was much shaking of hands and such talk as the circumstances permitted. Civility and even cordiality are the order of the day.

The part which Mr. Phelps had to play at Buckingham Palace was a passive one; to be exchanged next day for an active rôle. On Wednesday Mr. Lowell's successor had his first public dinner to eat, his first speech to make, and for the first time to face an audience composed for the evening of

Her Majesty's Judges at the Mansion House, and next morning of the whole reading public of England, not to mention America. The Lord Mayor proposed the health of the United States Minister; the audience cheered him, and the moment had come when Mr. Phelps had to show that he could or could not wear that many-coloured mantle which Mr. Lowell had put off. Englishmen seem never to grow tired of admiring our late Minister as a speaker, and they do not expect America to produce two Lowells in succession. It might be said that a notion had gained currency to the effect that not only was Mr. Lowell by general consent the best after-dinner speaker in England, but that he was the only one whom America had to boast of. Mr. Phelps has pleasantly undeceived them. Comparisons would be impertinent and I shall make none. It is enough to say that Mr. Phelps, if he surprised, certainly also delighted his audience. There are sentences in his short address worth, for the purposes of international comity, all the despatches ever exchanged between the two Governments. "The American representative who comes here finds that it is no foreign mission on which he has been sent. On both sides of the Atlantic he is equally at home. He has changed his skies but not the hearts by which he is surrounded." Again: "The fraternity and sympathy that exist between the two nations depend not on diplomacy or treaties, but on the personal sympathy and good feeling of the people of each country." And again—as an example of the rhetorical neatness which Englishmen admire in the good American speaker all the more because it is less common here—referring to Lord Coleridge, Mr. Phelps said: "He came as the guest of the American Bar; he remained as the guest of the American people." A few phrases of that sort are quite enough to give an orator in England an exceptional place.

There was but one feeling as Mr. Phelps spoke; there is but one judgment on his speech among those who either heard or have since read it. *The Times* expresses the general opinion in discriminating words, saying that he chose his topics with the utmost judgment and treated them with perfect taste. It was something of an ordeal at once for his audience and for himself, and both emerged from it with mutual satisfaction. "Mr. Phelps," continues this organ of the popular thought of England, "spoke with a grace of diction and an elevation of tone which prove him fitted to fill Mr. Lowell's place as well socially as in office." These are cordial words, and the best possible proof of their genuineness is supplied by what follows in the same journal on the much more important subject of the relations between the two countries:—

"A sympathetic American representative will understand that for Englishmen to wish to provoke American ill-will is inconceivable. He will comprehend their general disposition to friendliness, and something warmer. He will put to the true account the accidents of local manner and expression. He will feel himself accredited to the British people no less than to the Secretary for Foreign Affairs."

This will not suit those, if any there be, who think it the first duty of an American Minister to make himself disagreeable to England. But it will satisfy the immense majority of Americans at home and abroad, to whom a good understanding between the two countries seems desirable in the interest of both.

April 6, 1888.—Many reports have been set afloat about Mr. Phelps's journey. The truth is, he finds after three years' absence that there are private affairs at home requiring his attention. He has earned, if any Minister ever did, the right to look after his own business by long-continued and successful conduct of the business of his country in England. He has made himself in the highest official circles a reputation as a diplomatist second to none other. The English bench and bar have recognized in him a jurist worthy to rank with their most learned. He has delighted the public as an orator, maintaining and enlarging in England the fame of Americans as public speakers. He has won the general regard, and with it the sincere friendship of many of the best Englishmen, by his personal qualities. He has, with Mrs. Phelps, captivated the world of London, where they have made for themselves a place apart. He has been throughout the most patriotic of Ministers. He has, indeed, little inducement to be anything else. Thorough Americanism is—it cannot be said too often—whatever may be thought out West, one of the things the English most admire in an American Minister or any other American. And he has totally forgotten to be the representative of any party or section at home.

February 1, 1889.—Perhaps never on the departure of any Minister has such a scene been witnessed as that at Waterloo Station this morning. The crowd had become dense. All hats were raised as the train moved. Not a few ladies were crying, and even men looked grave. Friends and public alike sent cheers after the returning Minister and Mrs. Phelps as a last farewell. There have been indeed, since the date of Mr. Phelps's return became known, such a series of demonstrations in his honour as are entirely without precedent. The company at the Lord Mayor's dinner was the most distinguished ever collected in honour of any guest. Mr. Phelps's speech on that occasion will rank as a masterpiece of oratory; as Lord Rosebery said, dignified, eloquent, and pathetic. The press, with perhaps two exceptions, has joined heartily in these tributes. Feeling in private is even deeper than in public. The Century Club dinner to the Minister was a mark of affectionate respect, and there have been hundreds of others to which no public allusion can be made. The Queen's invitation to Mr. and Mrs. Phelps to spend Monday night at Osborne is reckoned by social experts a signal proof of her personal regard for both. It is not usual for the Queen to receive retiring Ministers as her own guests. Lord Salisbury and the official world may take what view they will of the Sackville incident; the people of Great Britain have not on that account abated one jot of their friendliness for their American kin beyond sea.

If, however, there be in America any who wish the people of the two countries to be enemies, they, and they only, have cause to reject and resent these manifestations of goodwill to the American Minister. They, and they only, are entitled to condemn Mr. Phelps's four years of honourable service abroad. He has, from beginning to end, done his country honour as well as service.

May 5, 1889.—Whether it is permissible to mention the Attorney-General except to anathematise him, I know not, but if it be there is a passage in his speech to the Bar which deserves notice in America. He said a few words to the Bar—as at Balaklava, there were six hundred—in answer to their demonstration in his honour on Saturday last. "It may be," remarked Sir Richard Webster, "it certainly must be, that I have made mistakes in this and every other position of importance that I have held. But I cannot help repeating that aphorism which has almost become of worldwide celebrity, uttered by a great man at a great representative meeting a few weeks ago, when he said that the man who did not make mistakes very seldom made anything." No saying, perhaps, ever had a more immediate and general celebrity than this of the late American Minister to England. It has been quoted and requoted and quoted again, in all companies, and at all times, ever since he announced it. If he had said or done nothing else during his four years in London, this alone would have made him famous. He has left it behind him as a kind of legacy; as a memento of his mission; as a portable and quotable proof of that excellent good sense and pure American humour which from the beginning made him popular.

JOHN STUART MILL.

[LONDON, *May* 10, 1873.]

MY acquaintance with Mr. Mill began at Avignon, where he was then living, in the summer of 1866. Mr. Hughes had given me a letter to him. Reaching Avignon about four in the morning, I sent a messenger from the hotel at eight to Mr. Mill's residence, outside of the town, with Mr. Hughes's letter of introduction, and a note inclosing it to say that I had made the journey from Geneva to see him but had only a few hours to stay, and asking him to send word whether it would be convenient for him to receive me. With a considerate kindness which I afterward found to be characteristic of him, he replied that he would not give me the trouble to drive out to his house but would come to the hotel immediately. He arrived almost as soon as the messenger who brought his note, and without sending up a servant announced himself merely by a knock at my door.

I can see as clearly as ever that dingy parlour of the Hotel de l'Europe at Avignon into whose narrow windows streamed a ray of sunlight that fell on the face and figure of Mr. Mill as he entered. A man close on six feet in height, spare in body and limbs, with the student's stoop of the shoulders, and a half uncertain walk, which presently appeared to be due to nervousness, not weakness, for he was of that tough fibre which packs great strength into a little space. Summer as it was, and in the south of France, he was dressed wholly in black. His face was narrow from want of flesh, but with sufficient breadth of jaw, and with a breadth between the eyes and under the forehead giving room for the brain that did not find room enough in the skull, which rose above and stretched so far back and on either side as to seem, spite of its complete baldness, less high than it really was. On the left side of the forehead, at the angle in front of the temple, was a sort of lump or wen nearly circular in shape. This was noticeable only, not in the least repulsive. His eyes were restless, the glance of them penetrating for an instant but quickly withdrawn or diverted, and they had this peculiarity, that they did not seem less frank on account of their great mobility. The nose was strongly aquiline, the lips drawn close, but flexible, the whole expression of the face denoting the incessant activity of the mind; a man who, you would say at once, must be a student, and a great one. Not only the nose was aquiline, the whole face was eagle-like, yet bore a kindly expression as of one who cared for something more than books or ideas, and whose philosophy was human, or, better still, whose life was a kindly one, and whose affections were not less strong than his purely intellectual qualities. In all points his appearance was singular yet manifestly without affectation. The inventory of his traits will convey a faint impression of them, and will convey none at all of the diffident charm of his manner, which somehow, contrary to the general rule, put you at ease, though apparently showing he was not so. It was, indeed, rather a want of restfulness than a want of ease. I have often noticed it since, when he was surrounded, or nearly so, by intimate friends with whom he could be under no constraint. It was consistent with the most perfect intellectual serenity. Yet it amounted undoubtedly to shyness.

He began by saying that he was glad to see a friend of Mr. Hughes, and always glad to see an American. "At this time," he added, "I am particularly so, for I have met nobody of late who could tell me how matters are going in your country." Of his interest in them there could be no doubt, and at the moment for my own sake I heartily wished it had been less. He was bent on questioning, and when I made one or two efforts to turn the conversation to topics on which he and not I should bear the burden of it, he brought it back almost immediately. When I said to him that he was making me talk, whereas I had come to hear him talk, he put aside my complaint; declaring that whether in his home at Avignon or at Blackheath in London he had scanty means of information respecting America, that there was no subject which interested him more, none, in fact, in contemporaneous politics which now and for years past had seemed to him so vital to the rest of the world, and that I really must allow him to get all he could out of me. There was no choice but to submit. One result is that I have very little to repeat now of the conversation.

His questions went back over many debatable fields of the war, especially over Emancipation, and notwithstanding his disclaimer indicated a minute and generally accurate knowledge of events which was most extraordinary in a man who, during the Rebellion, had had to take most of his facts in the shape in which it then suited the English and Continental press to present them. It is needless to say what his views were, or on which side his opinions and feelings were enlisted. We Americans have long known that Mr. Mill was one of the too few Englishmen who wanted to see the Republic hold together. In 1866 we were in the midst of embarrassments hardly less perplexing or less ominous of disaster than during the doubtful period of the war itself. President Johnson ruled over us, and it was a question whether the South was not going to recover by intrigue what it had lost in battle; and whether we were not about to hand over the Negro without civil rights to the unchecked jurisdiction of the States, and re-establish the supremacy of his old masters in everything but name. Mr. Mill's inquiries ranged over all this ground. He would not believe,—and happily his incredulity has been justified by events,—that we could or should either sacrifice our allies in the war, or again imperil the national sovereignty by a concession to the demand of subdued states for immediate readmission. Dear as the Anti-Slavery cause was to him, the cause of the Republic was not less so, and he held it for the interest of the world that the Republic should show itself as conscious of its rights as a Monarchy, and not less resolved to maintain them, whatever had to be sacrificed to do it. There was no nonsense about him, if I may be pardoned such an expression,—no desire to refine too nicely, no toleration for theories of any kind which stood in the way of national sovereignty; not the slightest indication of a liking for constitutional metaphysics, but a sound common sense and keen perception of practical necessities. I thought of this in later days when it became the fashion of fashionable persons in Parliament and out of it to sneer at what they thought Mr. Mill's inclination to speculative views in politics, forgetting that he had spent thirty years of his life in an office which required from him the most intimate acquaintance with the most difficult politics in the world, those of the British Empire in India, and that no man in England understood them better, and that few men had a training or a character which would have better fitted them for administrative duties.

When I add that this catechism about American affairs lasted from ten in the morning till nearly three in the afternoon you will be able to judge of the sincerity and extent of his interest in our fortunes. He did not confine himself to politics. His questions turned presently to the state of scientific inquiry, of education, including the success of our common school system and the non-success of our university system. He knew perfectly well how high the average of ordinary instruction is in America, and how low the average, or the best example, at that time, of university education. An improvement in the latter was, in his judgment, our most pressing need, and he thought we had reached the point where there was no longer an excuse for delaying it. He was specially solicitous to know whether the ignorant clamour against the higher education, against the most liberal culture, including classical as well as scientific branches, was likely to prevail. I never heard a more sincere contempt expressed for narrowness of that kind than by this chief of the Utilitarian philosophy which is sometimes appealed to as to its justification.

Presently he touched on Free Trade, and I asked him whether he still adhered to the well-known statement in his *Political Economy* which Protectionists are in the habit of quoting in their own defence; to the effect, namely, that Free Trade was not an absolute doctrine but a question of circumstances. "Certainly," was his answer. "I have never affirmed anything to the contrary. I do not presume to say that the United States may not find Protection expedient in their present state of development. I do not even say that if I were an American I should not be a Protectionist." He added that he quite believed the best of the Protectionists held that doctrine as a temporary one, ready to exchange or modify it when the country should have proved itself able to compete with European manufactures.

This was my first interview with Mr. Mill. My last was less than three weeks ago, at a dinner-party given by a common friend. The seven years intervening had passed lightly over him, filled though they had been with mental toil and with some harassing political anxieties. He looked very much as he looked in that hotel parlour at Avignon, but he talked with less vivacity than usual. His friends thought he had been during this last visit to London, if not unusually well, at any rate unusually social. He had gone about a good deal and received many friends at his new rooms in Albert Mansions. He had just parted with the house at Blackheath Park which had so long been his home during his visits to London. It was one of his plans to be able to see more people, Blackheath being so remote from the social centres of London as to be inconvenient both to himself and his friends. His friends rejoiced at the change, in the hope to see more of Mr. Mill.

London, however, was not the place which Mr. Mill preferred to call home. He did not like London, nor England, nor even the English over much. At least, he did not like them in the English way, nor were English influences those which chiefly bore sway over his mind. The Philistinism of English politics and of English society was repugnant to him. Avignon was his real home. It was the shrine which entombed the remains of his wife, but he loved it before she was buried there. After it became her resting-place he never cared to be elsewhere. The French climate suited him far better than the English; the south of France best of all, and his mind worked there more freely than under the pressure of the leaden atmosphere of London. It is easy to see how much he owed to French literature of the last and the preceding century especially. If he came to London as a duty, he escaped to his loved Avignon with an ever fresh delight. He was a botanist, and had made a study of the flora of the country about Avignon, and it was to see the spring glories of his plants and to pursue his work that he quitted London this year earlier than was expected. He enjoyed scenery in its most lovely and in its grandest forms alike, enjoyed it passionately, and had in him the genius of a descriptive poet, and the capacity to write poetry of that kind of which Wordsworth was the greatest master. Between his soul and that of Nature there were harmonies which he did not choose to put into verse, but which were tender and true.

His nature was, indeed, emotional, and even passionate. Considering what he wrote about his wife it is strange anybody should ever have doubted it. The conception of him which a political opponent vulgarly summed up in calling him a " book in breeches," was absurd. You could not hear him talk without seeing that he felt strongly, that he loved deeply, that the capacity of hating also was not wanting to him. It was, I suppose, his moderation in controversy as well as his addiction to philosophical pursuits which gave him with the general public the repute of coldness—especially with the public that had not read enough of him to discover the numerous passages that glow with enthusiasm or with indignation.

As a talker he had a manner of his own. Talker in the common dinner-table sense he was not. He seldom told a story for the sake of telling it, nor kept a store of anecdotes to be produced for the mere amusement of listeners. Nor would he talk to everybody. On subjects that interested him and to people whom he thought interested, he would pour out in easy profusion his stores of information. Among the men whom I have known in England I remember but two who were comparable to him in the variety and fluent accuracy of his knowledge. These two were extremely unlike him and unlike each other, Mr. Carlyle and Mr. Gladstone. But they had this quality in common. He would meet men on their own ground if they were worth meeting, and they sometimes found him stronger than they were themselves in their own specialty. The play of his mind was not less remarkable than the fulness of it.

It is common to speak of his parliamentary career as a failure. It was not a failure, or if there was a failure anywhere it was the House of Commons which failed and not Mr. Mill. The House of Commons contains many members of moderate culture and mental ability, and takes its tone from its own majority. A man of talent will succeed in that House. A man of genius will be less likely to. Beyond all other legislative assemblies the English House of Commons is impatient of ideas, and intolerant of them; intolerant also of men possessing them. It looked on Mr. Mill with suspicion. It was thought a good joke to call him a philosopher. Mr. Lowe, one of the men of talents, sneered at him as such, just as Mr. Disraeli sneers at Mr. Fawcett for being a professor. The Tories never forgave him for the name he applied to them, the stupid party, though it appeared he did not use the phrase in the way they supposed. The landowners held him in abhorrence for his views respecting property in land. His own party, so far as he had a party—I mean the Liberals—were afraid of being compromised by him, and on many of the questions which interested Mr. Mill the Liberals are no more liberal than the Tories —not as much so on some; the woman question, for instance, about which Mr. Mill was very much in earnest. I once heard one of the most eminent Liberal statesmen in England or the world say Mr. Mill was "crazy" on that subject. Yet almost against its own will the House listened to him. He was not a practised elocutionist, and certainly never took lessons, like his friend Grote, in public speaking. Nor was his voice strong, nor his delivery effective in the common way. The attention he compelled was due to the clearness of his statement, and the known weight of his opinion. He could discuss complicated administrative details as ably as Mr. Gladstone; and for that kind of discussion the House has a liking. In attention to business he was more exact than almost anybody. He was always in his place, be the subject what it might. He sat on the third bench at the end next the gangway, and of course below it. While he was in Parliament he was the member whom strangers were sure to inquire for, and they were almost sure of seeing him at any hour while the House was in session. The fatigue would have been insupportable if not mitigated by sleep. Mr. Mill slept sometimes, as everybody does, the leaders on the Treasury Bench included—everybody except Mr. Disraeli, who is said to be never so wide awake as when he seems sound asleep.

His election for Westminster was a very difficult one. He had but a halting support from the Liberal managers. The Grosvenor influence, which is very powerful in that borough, was only half given him. The Radicals and above all the working men carried him through triumphantly once; a second time proved too much for their strength. He was not an "available" candidate. His own committee complained of his independence. If Westminster has two characteristics more prominent than all others, it is a Whig constituency and a shop-keeping constituency; in other words, its liberalism is conservative and timid. Mr. Mill knew it as well as anybody, but nothing could prevent him from alienating one section of his supporters by his declaration in favour of Mr. Odger, and irritating another by his opposition to Mr. Bouverie, a Whig of the Whigs, and dear to the borough which still prides itself on having sent Fox to the House of Commons against all the efforts of the Court and the Government. In the last election I stood on the hustings in Trafalgar Square where Mr. Mill addressed, or attempted to address, the electors. There was the usual howling mob. It had been given out beforehand that Mr. Mill should not be heard. Mr. W. H. Smith's army of news agents were there to prevent him, nor could the best efforts of a body of resolute working men obtain silence. What they did insure him was immunity from the assaults a candidate has occasionally to endure. The scene at times was almost riotous. Mr. Mill stood through it all with head bared and with unshaken coolness, but he had to speak to the reporters. In some public meetings in St. James's Hall, on the other hand, his speeches proved a great success. He was popular with the working classes as he deserved to be, and they understood him far better than either the traders or the aristocracy understood him.

GEORGE ELIOT.

[LONDON, *December* 25, 1880.]

GEORGE ELIOT lived and died surrounded by two worlds; one composed of those who read and admired her books but had no knowledge of her personally; the second a select circle of intimate friends whose affectionate admiration of her and her work alike went much beyond that of the generality. I cannot give a better notion of my incompetence to write about her than by saying that I belonged to neither of these companies. Not that I did not, in the ordinary sense of the words, read George Eliot, and respect her rare genius and culture. But I was mostly content with reading her once, and was inclined to judge her novel-writing by the standards commonly used in weighing the merits of writers of fiction. This would by no means content the Eliot worshippers, or even the more devoted part of the public she had gathered about her. You were not deemed worthy to express an opinion on George Eliot's stories unless you considered them as something much more than stories—which undoubtedly they were—and debated (and admitted) her claims to high rank among philosophers, among social reformers, among the leaders of modern thought—nay, among poets; for it was no small number of persons who at one time convinced themselves that the author of the *Spanish Gypsy* was a poet. In the newspaper eulogies which have appeared since her death the same tone of adoration for an all but universal genius is discoverable. I never sought admittance to the famous Sunday afternoons at North Bank, being quite sure I should not come up to the accepted standard, and that I had not incense enough to burn on that particular altar. Many of those who made up that band are men whose judgment deserves respect. And now that George Eliot is gone, and the door is shut for ever, I regret that I never took advantage of the opportunities I had of knowing her better.

First and last I have met George Eliot perhaps a dozen times. For society, in the common sense, she did not care much. She was not often to be seen in the world. She preferred that the world, or some of the best of it, should come to her. To the last, and even after her marriage, there was some question about her actual position. Everybody knew that she had lived openly for years with the late George Henry Lewes, and that she was not married to him. There were many excuses for the irregularity of their relations. Mrs. Lewes was living, to be sure, but was hopelessly insane. Between Miss Evans and Mr. Lewes there were very strong intellectual ties and sympathies, independently of attachments of other sorts. He had that kind of influence over her which a merely clever and studious man of eager and strenuous temperament sometimes exercises on a very sensitive nature. For Miss Evans, though in some points firm and masculine, had the sensitiveness, the susceptibility to external impressions, which is one of the surest characteristics of genius. She was convinced—and she often said—that her obligations on the intellectual side to Lewes were very great. Others thought the obligation was the other way and that George Eliot, so far from owing anything to him or gaining anything from her long association with him, was distinctly a loser by the connection. It is certainly true that after Lewes had established his influence on her mind there was a marked change in the character of her work. She was aware of the change, and took pride in it, and thought her work had gained by it in quality and value. Not a few of her friends and admirers thought it had deteriorated; and that as Lewes's influence became more powerful the change in her method of writing became more pronounced and the deterioration more evident. He used to say, almost boastfully, that in order to write *Daniel Deronda* George Eliot had read, at his instance and under his guidance, a thousand books — books of Jewish history and literature, and vast quantities of Talmudic lore. No doubt; and it was precisely the attempt to digest this mass of learning which makes *Daniel Deronda*, as a novel, so inferior to the *Mill on the Floss*. She had built on similar lines in earlier books, and with a result the same in kind but less disastrous in degree.

From the very first she was defective in purely artistic qualities, in the sense of proportion and in regularity of construction, for example. Her mind was extraordinarily vigorous; her knowledge quite copious enough for her real work long before Lewes began his systematic cramming. If he had been the judicious critic and adviser he thought himself, he would have worked in a direction the very opposite to that which he followed. He was devotedly attached to Miss Evans; what he did he did loyally. But he was a man who valued himself highly, who probably overvalued his own work, which is multifarious and of various degrees of badness in its remarkable versatility; but who never had a misconception of his own place in the world so astounding as when he thought himself appointed by Providence to "form" the mind of George Eliot. What he really did was to lay upon her a burden greater than her mind could bear; he cramped the natural play of her genius, he overloaded her wit with his library learning. Before she wrote *Adam Bede* she had translated Strauss's *Life of Jesus*, and had shown the extent of her familiarity with a sort of erudition then much less common than now, to acquire which implied a natural force of character and courage, as well as a bent toward serious study of great subjects. Lewes fostered a taste he should have checked, for there are plenty of metaphysicians and few great novelists. He did more than foster it, he perverted it; turned it morbid, and instead of letting it work itself free in a natural direction diverted the whole force of the current into the one channel where it ought never to have been allowed to flow.

What society, however, considered and discussed was not the effect of Lewes's advice on Miss Evans's literary pursuits, but the effect of his living with her, and whether such an offence against conventionality ought to be condoned; and to what extent condoned. The excuses I referred to above never counted for much; at best they were secondary. What counted was the exceptional splendour of the woman's genius; her immense reputation; and perhaps her indifference to the opinion of society about the matter. It is, of course, to be understood that the relations between herself and Lewes lacked no element of regularity except the legal bond, which did not and for the reasons mentioned could not exist. Every now and then you heard a report that Mrs. Lewes was dead, and that the long-existing union between her husband and another woman had been solemnised with the usual forms of religion and law. But when Lewes died she was still Marian Evans; and now that Marian Evans, having in the interval become Mrs. Cross, is dead, Mrs. Lewes is still living. But the Evans-Lewes household was a perfectly decorous one. No sort of similarity could be found or was, so far as I know, ever suspected, between the life of lawless and various adventure led by the great French writer with whom she is rashly compared, Georges Sand, and the life of George Eliot herself. In the latter there was neither that swift succession of freely gratified caprices of passion, nor that ostentatious and reiterated defiance to the world which stained the career of the Frenchwoman. George Eliot was the faithful wife of one man who was not her husband. Had she been a nobody or a mediocrity, the world, if it had chanced to know the fact, would have frowned and passed by on the other side, and have kept its front door closed. But the curiosity to see so great a woman was very strong indeed. Respect for her was strong; regret that there should be any blemish in her life was keen; there was possibly some pity for her, which she would have rejected disdainfully; and there was a desire to know her which finally overleapt all barriers. If she had cared for lionising, or would have permitted it, she could have been lionised to her heart's content. But she never accepted much of the homage offered her. It was sometimes said that she remembered the peculiarity of her position when hosts and hostesses were willing to forget it. She went to a few houses freely; but was, naturally enough, somewhat exacting in the niceties of female diplomacy, and to the last there was the chance of rebuff against which neither she nor her hostess could always guard. I have known of at least one case in which a distinguished guest under the same roof publicly refused to be introduced to her, justifying himself by saying he would not make the acquaintance of a woman on whom he would not allow his wife to call. He was wrong, but while it was possible that such things might happen Miss Evans could not be blamed for her shyness about going into miscellaneous company.

Her passion for music was one of the strongest of her nature, and she was often to be met at houses where very good music was to be heard. At one such I saw her several times. It was one of the most beautiful houses in London, filled with fine pictures and rare books, and graced by a cordial hospitality which every one of its guests must remember pleasantly, where Mr. Browning and Lord Houghton, Sir Frederick Leighton and Mr. Millais, Herr Joachim and Herr Henschel, and many other famous artists and writers were to be met; with a throng of less renowned but not less charming people. The Leweses—as it used to be the fashion to call them—were as much at home there as anywhere, and the spacious rooms were sure to be rather more crowded than usual when they were expected. This house has been twice closed; once some years since by the death of its master, and then after a while was reopened to the more intimate friends of its mistress, whose death last year closed it for ever. The only fault one could find with these musical parties was that—as a celebrated London talker said of a continental intruder whose stories were fresher than his own—they spoilt conversation. Nobody dare utter a syllable while Joachim's violin was talking or Redeker's rich voice filled the room. I have known George Eliot less scrupulously silent at a dramatic entertainment. I chanced to sit next to her on the first night of Tennyson's "Queen Mary" at the Lyceum. The acting of the piece did not please her, and she favoured me with a running commentary on the performance, which was more brilliant than either the play or the acting. Her criticism disclosed a singular talent for sharp pleasantries. To me this was novel, but I believe most of her friends who saw much of her were aware that she had a gift of saying very bitter things in a melodious manner; which gift she, for the most part, charitably kept under control.

George Eliot's appearance has often been described, but the descriptions do not always harmonise. She has been called—I suppose most people called her—extremely plain. A noted wit and writer is reported to have said of her and Lewes that they were both so ugly it was impossible to believe any harm of them. This sharp-tongued person avers that he said it not only of, but to them. Let us hope his memory in that matter has played him false. About Lewes's ugliness there could be no two opinions. There was not a good feature in his face, yet his face as a whole was one which you would look twice at, and which had at any rate the merit of not being commonplace. George Eliot, when you saw her in repose, had a forbidding countenance. People who did not like her used to say she looked like a horse; a remark which has also been made about a celebrated living actor. It was true so far as this: that the portion of the face below the eyes was disproportionately long and narrow. She had that square fulness of brow over the eyes which Blake had, and which led Blake to affirm that the shape of his head made him a Republican. George Eliot's radicalism went much farther than mere republicanism. She never can have been a beautiful woman, either in face or figure.

She was tall, gaunt, angular, without any flowing ease of motion, though with a self-possession and firmness of muscle and fibre which saved her from the shambling awkwardness often the characteristic of long and loose-jointed people. There was no want of power in her movements nor in the expression of her elongated visage, to the lower part of which went plenty of jaw and decision of contour. She was altogether a personage whom at first sight the beholder must regard with respect, and whom, upon further acquaintance, it was perfectly possible to find attractive, not from her talk only, which was full, but from her mere external appearance and still more from her expression and the animation of her face. Her eyes were, when she talked, luminous and beautiful, dark in colour and of that unfathomable depth and swift changefulness which are seldom to be seen in the same orbs, except in persons whose force of character and force of intellect are both remarkable. They could be very soft, and she smiled with her eyes as well as with that large mouth of hers; and the smile was full of loveliness when it did not turn to mocking or mark that contemptuous mood which was not, I gather, very infrequent with her. In conversation which did not wake this demon of scornfulness, born of conscious intellectual superiority, the face was full of vivacity and light, whether illuminated by a smile or not. I have seen it, when she was talking on a subject that moved her, irradiated and suffused with deep feeling.

She had her humble moods too. Boldly controverting everybody else, leading the talk, often monopolising it, always confident, sometimes despotic, she bowed herself before Lewes in a humility that on occasions was positively distressing to her friends. Lewes's friends and hers, to be sure, were largely the same, but few of them were under any such delusion as she was about the relative superiority of that strangely-matched pair. Lewes attached some people to him and had sterling merits, but he was never popular, and of his many books hardly one can be called successful. Strange indeed would it be if the vast multitude of George

Eliot's readers who saw in her the greatest woman, and almost the greatest writer, of her time came to know that she fancied herself the intellectual debtor of George Henry Lewes. But so it was, and the fancy made both her domestic life and her later books very different from what they would have been otherwise.

THOMAS CARLYLE.

[LONDON, *February* 8, 1881.]

To Mr. Emerson, to whom I owe many other things, I owe my introduction to Mr. Carlyle. On my first visit to London, fourteen years ago, I left Mr. Emerson's letter at the door of the house in Cheyne Row, and the same evening brought me this note:—

5 GR'T CHEYNE ROW, CHELSEA, 28*th Aug't*, 1866.

DEAR SIR — If you will be so kind as come down to me to-morrow (Wedn'y), at 8 P.M., we will have a cup of tea together.— Yours sincerely, T. CARLYLE.

The little note is lying before me, the handwriting of it not less distinct and hardly less firm and even than another specimen of the same hand six-and-thirty years younger which is beside it, addressed to his brother. To know Mr. Carlyle was such an event that the least particulars imprinted themselves on my memory, such as that it rained in torrents, and that the cabman who was waiting at the hotel in Piccadilly grumbled at having to drive so far as Chelsea—a matter of twenty minutes. He protested he did not know where Great Cheyne Row was, and upon my explaining innocently—for I had not at that time had much experience of London cabmen—that Mr. Carlyle lived there, demanded scornfully who Mr. Carlyle might be. Cheyne Walk he admitted he knew. It led to Cremorne. As I had been to the house the day before I was able to assure him that Great Cheyne Row led out of Cheyne Walk. The street was, and still is, a very modest street. There is a chandler's shop on the corner, and a laundry next door but one to Mr. Carlyle's. So humble are the surroundings and the house itself that years afterward, when I took a German-American friend to call on Mr. Carlyle he looked about him in wonder as we stopped at the door, and asked half incredulously, "Does so great a man live in so little a house?" A similar remark had been made before in a still more sententious form by the Shah of Persia, who, when driven to Pembroke Lodge, in Richmond Park, to see the late Lord Russell, observed, "Great man, little house." The neighbourhood now is not much better or worse than it was in 1866. Cheyne Walk, indeed, is a much more splendid affair than then, the Embankment having since been completed, and all along the riverside imposing mansions built. But this stream of prosperity has not turned aside into quieter nooks. The house in which Mr. Carlyle lived then, and in which he died Saturday morning, is that which he chose on first settling in London in 1834. The name of the street has been modified within the last few years from Great Cheyne Row to Cheyne Row, and the spirit of modern improvement personified in the members of the Street Committee of the Metropolitan Board of Works has altered the number of the house from 5 to 24. But it is the same house; of three low stories, of the dingy yellow common to London. When my cabman pulled up before it on that rainy evening of August 28, 1866, he made it evident he had but a poor opinion of the society in which I moved.

A maid-servant answered the bell, and I was shown into a room on the left of the narrow passage on the ground-floor. The room was dimly lighted. A lady came forward, whom I afterward knew as Mr. Carlyle's niece, Miss Aitken, and said in a whisper that her uncle was still asleep but that he expected me and I was to wait. On the left of the door, against the wall, was a sofa, and on the sofa was Mr. Carlyle. He soon woke and I introduced myself, Miss Aitken having vanished. Now I had heard before coming to England an awkward story or two of the great writer's odd way of receiving strangers. Americans, it was said, were less welcome than others; and though I knew very well that Mr. Emerson's introduction was the best I could have, I was not over-confident of a cordial greeting. But I found that in this, as in some other points, the Carlyle of common report and the actual Carlyle were two different persons. His hearty way of saying, "Eh! and so you are a friend of Mr. Emerson," and his outstretched hand, were quite enough to put a shy man at his ease. Not even in America had I ever seen anybody to whom ordinary social usages were more obviously indifferent. It was the hour when London dines, and in order to dine arrays itself in swallow-tail and white tie. Mr. Carlyle had dined early, and the tall figure that rose from the sofa was clad in a dressing-gown of a red pattern reaching below his knees. He questioned me eagerly about Mr. Emerson; about his health, and whether he meant to come to England again and how soon; and whether his fame at home grew, and his books sold. His manner as he spoke of his American friend was gentle and affectionate. It was the same afterward when he went back to that topic, as he often did.

As soon as he had satisfied the first keenness of his curiosity for the latest news about Mr. Emerson, he said he usually took a walk at this hour, and would I go with him? I remembered the pouring rain and wondered if he would go out in it, but the weather was a thing to which, as I found later, he gave no thought. By the time he had put on a coat and hat and seized his big stick, it rained no longer. It was quite dark, and it had long been his habit to walk after the sun had gone down. He did not seem to care for the river and the fresh currents of air which blew freely along its banks. His steps were bent toward the quieter corners of quiet old Chelsea. Almost the whole of that neighbourhood was at that time quite unknown to me, and I had no idea where we went. Nor did I care; it was enough for me that I was walking with Mr. Carlyle. It was a pleasure to note his firm, swift stride. His pace was such as few men of past seventy would have cared to set; and he maintained it to the end. The stream of talk ran not less swiftly. I have no notes of what was said, and should not use them if I had, but I remember clearly the subject and scope of his strange outpourings. Kindly and friendly as he was to me, out of the depth of his regard for the friend whose letter I had brought, he was then, and often afterward when I saw him, in a despairing and hostile mood with reference to the world in general. He discoursed on London and on Londoners, storming against the sordid and hollow life by which he was surrounded; complaining of the very houses amid which he took his devious way. They were built, he said, to tumble down in ninety years. The tenant had only a ninety-nine years' lease from the landlord who owned the ground; he could not afford to build solidly and honestly; his architect had learned how to run up a wall which would stand just long enough not to become the property of the landlord; computing that the wall should fall down before the lease fell in. Yes, it was more the fault of the landlord than the tenant, but it was a devil's system all through, and the devil had a sure grip on tenant and landlord both. And what did it matter? "They are just a parcel of pigs rooting in the mire;" and so on. With all this were mingled flashes of kindly humour and human sympathy which lit up the gloom and almost savage hopelessness of his temper at the moment. This lasted for perhaps half an hour. It was past nine when we returned. The candles had been lighted. The fire—for though it was August a fire had been kindled —blazed cheerfully. The table was spread: the tea was made and keeping hot under its Scotch cosey; and by the time he had laid aside his wraps and reappeared in his ragged red dressing-gown, the stern, strong, sad face reflected the pleasant light which shone on it, and his mood changed with the changing circumstances.

Without any question or hint of mine he began to talk of America. "They think," he cried sharply,—"some of you think, I am no friend to America. But I love America,—

not everybody's America, but the true America; the country which has given birth to Emerson and to Emerson's friends; the country of honest toilers and brave thinkers. Never shall I forget," he went on with kindling eye and a deeper tone, " that the first money which ever came to me for a printed book came from America. When your people reprinted *Sartor Resartus* out of *Fraser* they sent me a good sum for it. They need not have sent it. I had no claim on it or on them; but they sent it, and I did and do thank them for that. By and by they republished my *French Revolution*. Do you know, I had not had a penny for that book from the English public till a good while after American friends remitted to me a pretty sum for it? Twice over, twice, my first money came to me from your country. And do they think I forget it, and am not grateful for it, and don't love the country which showed its love for me?" Then, breaking off suddenly with one of his explosions of wild laughter, half pathetic, half sneering, he exclaimed: " Yes, I angered you all with my *Ilias in Nuce*, but who shall say I was not right; or right *then ?* But you were the stronger at last; you conquered, and you know people will have it I have said might is right. Suppose I did say it? I knew what I meant by it—not what they think I meant,—there is a real, true meaning under it. A man is an atheist who believes that in the long run what God allows to triumph is not the right."

And again turning the talk not less suddenly, with a quite indescribable inflection of voice which masked an odd mixture of good-humour and contempt, which the phrase also masked, he said, " You went up and down the country, did you not, with your fighting parties?" He had clearly imbibed from some of his German friends a none too high idea of the military quality of our armies and commanders.

There was no detail of a life strange to him which had not some interest for him. He put all sorts of questions as he sat behind his teapot and took huge sips from his cup and munched his bread and butter and plum-cake. He asked about the law in the United States, the schools of law, and the practice of it, and whether it much differed from English law, and how; and had I got here soon enough to visit the English courts and compare them with the American courts, and in which did I think a man had the better chance of getting justice done him,—"supposing it was justice he wanted"; and at which the loud, bitter laugh broke out again.

Answering as well as I could this volley of questions, I sat watching the old man and trying to make the Carlyle of my guesses and fancy match the Carlyle in the flesh, on whom I looked for the first time. There is little need to describe a face so well known as his; known by countless photographs and many prints of every degree of merit. It is so marked a face that I never saw a likeness of him which had not some unmistakable look of the man himself. No sign of decay was there about him. The eye was full, the glance swift, sure, penetrating. The hollowness of the socket, the deep shadow beneath the eye, were the traces, not of illness, except such as was chronic, but of lifelong vigil and study. "Writer of books," as he described himself in his famous petition, was stamped on every feature. A sad, stern face I called it just now, and I know not whether it was more sad or stern, nor whether the sadness of it was not deepest when he laughed. He had still a florid complexion, and the ruddy hue stood out strongly against the iron-gray hair which fell in shaggy clumps about his forehead, while the eyes, naturally deep-set, seemed lost beneath the thicket of eyebrow which overshadowed them. The moustache and beard he wore full; wrinkled and gnarled rather than curled. When he laughed, the grim squareness of the jaw showed itself. It was a portentous laugh; open-mouthed and deep-lunged, and prolonged; ending mostly in a shout of triumph, and seldom quite glad or kindly. The bony hands clutched the table meanwhile with a muscular grip, and the laugh was likely to be followed by a torrent of speech that bore down everything before it.

Woe to the man who ventured to gainsay him when in that humour; as I more than once saw proof of afterward.

Tea and questions over, the strung fibres relaxed a little. He sat himself down by the fireside, on the floor, his back against the jamb of the chimney-piece, took a comb out of his pocket and combed down his tangled bushy hair till it hid his forehead altogether, and you could no longer see where the hair ended and the eyebrows began. This done, he filled and lighted his pipe; a long clay pipe quite new, known, I think, as a church-warden; quite two feet from bowl to mouthpiece. As the perfume of the tobacco filled the room and the clouds of smoke rolled about him, he began to talk again. It was no longer talk in the common sense of the word; there were no more questions, no pauses. It was a monologue, and no small part of it sounded strangely familiar, as if I had sat in that little parlour before and heard the same voice pouring out the same words and ideas. He had, in fact, by that time fallen into the habit of repeating orally what in days long gone he had written,—not consciously or purposely, but as if the same trains of thought came back to him; and he was content to have a listener while he thought over the old problems that had vexed him, and once more offered his solution of them. Page after page of *Sartor* did he repeat, not *verbatim*, but in substance, and of that deep study called *Characteristics*, diverging then into *Past and Present*, and again into one or another of the *Latter Day Pamphlets*. I was fresh from reading most of these; all of them were at that time pretty well known to me, and I never had a stranger sensation than in thus hearing from the mouth of the philosopher the oral repetition of his written and printed wisdom. With intervals of silence or conversation of a more familiar kind, he went on thus for quite two hours. When it seemed to have come to an end I rose to take leave, and upon my telling him I was going to Berlin he asked me to come again on my return and bring him all the news of the Prussian capital.

Before I next met him I did go to Berlin, and had seen among other notable persons Prince Bismarck, and General von Moltke, and the King, and the whole garrison of Berlin and Potsdam, 50,000 strong, returning from the seven weeks' campaign which had made Prussia head of Germany and revealed Prince Bismarck to the world as its greatest statesman. Of these astonishing results, most of which had been achieved when I first saw Carlyle, he had said something during that first evening; rejoicing with great joy over the victory of his Prussian friends. On my return he showed himself keen about every detail; about Prince Bismarck most of all, whose greatness he had recognised long before most people; as he had that of the Prussians generally. "I had long thought they had a fine silent talent in them; and it was sure some day at the right moment to be seen of all men." Prince Bismarck he summed up as "the one man now living whom God had appointed to be his vicegerent on earth, and who knew that he had been so appointed, and who went about to do the work given him to do." He had never seen, oddly enough, a portrait of his hero, and asked sharply if I had brought one. Pulling half a dozen out of my pocket together, I handed him first a photograph of General von Moltke—a singularly fine face— at which Carlyle looked with manifest disappointment; then suddenly crying out, "It is not Bismarck you have shown me." The right one satisfied him. He looked at it long, and finally asked if he might keep it. I gave him all I had. "Ah," said he, "that is right friendly." After a while he added, "You won't forget to take Emerson one." Mr. Emerson's name was never long unmentioned, and when I went to say good-bye to Carlyle on returning to America, he gave me not only messages but injunctions to see Mr. Emerson soon, and to tell him all I had heard and seen of Carlyle himself.

During some years I saw Carlyle at intervals in his own house, and once or twice met him elsewhere. He was not a recluse but he did not go into what is called society, and there were not, I think, many London houses which he entered at all. Lord Russell's was one which he used to visit, and Lady Stanley of Alderley's. In the street or in the park he was to be seen by those who knew his ways; or often enough in an omnibus. Everybody knew him in Chelsea, and latterly people used to lift their hats as they passed that gaunt form and looked into the sorrowful face, deep shadowed beneath the spreading brim of his soft hat. Among his intimate friends were Mr. Ruskin, Mr. Browning, Mr. Allingham, Dr. Tyndall, Mr. Lecky, and, above all, Mr. Froude. For years Mr. Froude has been with him daily; walking, driving, sitting with him; giving invaluable hours to his beloved master. Mr. Ruskin, who lived little in London, saw less of Carlyle, but to the last was among the most affectionate of his disciples. He could, if I may use such a phrase, take liberties with Carlyle which nobody else ventured upon. Everybody knows that at times the sage became vehement, and the conversation, if he were contradicted or argued against, was likely to be stormy. When Mrs. Carlyle was alive she used to break in upon these scenes with the parliamentary cry, "Divide, divide, divide"—the signal for the end of a debate. I have seen Mr. Ruskin in similar circumstances walk up to Carlyle, put his arm about his neck, and hush him tenderly to silence and calm.

Carlyle seldom troubled himself about conventionalities. What he felt, that he said; and as he felt it; and it did not matter whether he sat in his own room or in a public hall. At one of Dickens's readings he has been known to burst out in irrepressible, long-continued, stentorian laughter that amounted almost to a convulsion; swinging his hat in the air meanwhile. He had an unbounded admiration for Dickens. The most conspicuous books in his dining-room were a set of Dickens's in red cloth, which had grown dark with constant use. All his books had the same appearance of much handling. He had none of the dandyisms of the amateur or the collector. As Swift said in his ironical way of Bolingbroke, "He had an altogether mistaken notion of the true uses of books, which he thumbed and spoiled by reading, when he ought to have multiplied them on his shelves." I once asked him if he often read novels. "Not often," was the answer; "but when I do I have a debauch." It was one of his ways of seeking complete mental relaxation. At another time he told me that after he heard of the loss of the manuscript of the first volume of the *French Revolution* he did nothing but read novels for three weeks. The story of the loss is so well known in substance that I will not repeat it; though there are details which have not been quite accurately given. Mill was so horror-struck at the accident that he could not make up his mind to communicate it to Carlyle himself. Mrs. Taylor broke the news to him. But it was one of those calamities which no "breaking" could soften.

His *French Revolution* must have been known to the French mainly through Barrot's translation; a book of which I once owned a copy, and at times tried to read, but found unreadable by one who was able to read the original. A dull man once said—I think in *Blackwood*—in one of those flashes of false wit which sometimes come to dull men, that Carlyle's *French Revolution* would be a valuable book if it were translated into English. It is not translatable into French, or scarcely translatable. The life, the animation, the rapidity of movement, the picturesqueness, the dramatic quality, evaporate in translation. But there is at least one Frenchman who, so far as a knowledge of English can make a man competent to judge of that wonderful prose-poem, is a competent judge of it. I mean M. Louis Blanc; who knows, to say the least of it, as much English as you and I know. He, unhappily, no more approves of the book than his fellow-countrymen who have had to form their opinion of it on the vapid rendering of M. Barrot. "It is a history," I have heard M. Louis Blanc explain more than once, "written in the future tense;" which was his way of saying that it was not a history at all. But M. Louis Blanc, though one of the most sincere men who ever lived, a man wholly incapable of a consciously dishonest judgment or criticism or word of any kind, is, as all Frenchmen are on the subject of the Revolution, a partisan. He is a Robespierrist, and Carlyle's verdict upon Robespierre and upon Jacobinism, and upon the Revolution as a whole, is such as necessarily to put M. Louis Blanc into the ranks of his antagonists. Moreover, they are rival historians, and Carlyle is known to have expressed with characteristic emphasis, and in words I prefer not to repeat, his estimate of the value of M. Louis Blanc's history. Neither could judge the other justly. The public, which as a whole is capable of impartiality, has long since set the seal of its approval on both histories—on Carlyle's for one kind of merit, and on M. Louis Blanc's for another and very different kind. And yet both their theories of the Revolution cannot by any possibility be true. They mutually exclude each other.

But these reflections and memories are leading me too far. I must be content to add an anecdote or two and so bring this letter to an end. Dean Stanley, who was among Carlyle's friends, and who is one of several ecclesiastical pets of royalty, once arranged a meeting at the Deanery between Carlyle and the Queen, by the Queen's desire. It took place not long after he had declined the Grand Cross of the Bath —the acceptance of which would have made him Sir Thomas Carlyle, G.C.B. Perhaps the interview was meant to dispel the foolish notion that the Queen was vexed by his refusal. More probably it was because the Queen, who was little likely to concern herself about such reports, wanted to see the philosopher. Her Majesty is, after all, a woman, and has more than once shown that she has a woman's curiosity. They met at five o'clock tea; and a considerable number of persons were present. Carlyle was duly presented by the Dean and was graciously received. It is said that he at once took the lead in the conversation, and even gave voice to his loyal wishes for the Queen's health—two breaches of etiquette which made the hair of the assembled courtiers to stand on end. This I believe to be scandal, but what is certain is that Carlyle, upon the Queen's polite speeches to him coming to an end, forthwith looked about him for a seat and sat down, to the unspeakable horror of the company, every other member of which knew well that it was high treason to sit in the Queen's presence till Her Majesty had commanded them to be seated. But the Queen, less horror-struck than the rest, and with that good breeding of which she is mistress when she chooses, saved the situation by seating herself, and waving her royal hand to the rest to be seated also; enforcing her command with the voice, after a moment, upon one or two upright members of the group.

You remember, I daresay, the distress and difficulties into which Dean Stanley fell in consequence of his unlucky attempt at setting up a monument in the Abbey to the late Prince Louis Napoleon. Carlyle's opposition to that scheme did not, so far as I know, chill the friendship between him and the Dean; though in other cases the Dean took opposition hardly; and in Carlyle's case had to retract an accusation against an innocent third person of forging Carlyle's signature to the memorial against the plan. But it is said that this incident confirmed Carlyle in his dislike to being buried in the Abbey. "There must be a general jail delivery of scoundrels now lying there before any honest man's bones can rest peacefully in its walls," he has been known to say. There is a question whether he or another gave the Dean that almost savage nickname which society now laughingly applies to him; and which, referring too clearly to the Dean's eagerness to secure the bodies of departed heroes, is better fitted for talk than print. But I may quote without offence, I hope, his remark of an earlier date when Dean Stanley's adhesion to the Broad Church party exposed him to much High Church enmity: "There goes our friend the Dean, boring holes in the bottom of the good ship Church of England—*and doesn't know it!*"

Carlyle had very definite views about poetry, and was wont to express them in his usual definite way. It was a maxim with him, at one time, that a man who had anything to say could say it in prose; say it more freely and intelligibly, and that if he resorted to poetry it was from a want of clearness in his own mind as to what he meant. "If he have a message to the universe worth hearing, in God's name let him deliver his message in a manner all men can understand." For mere form he avowed his contempt; and this contempt for form is one of the things for which the French used to reproach him, and have reproached him since his death. One of the strongest expressions of it was in his early estimate of Mr. Tennyson. I don't remember that he has said in print what he used to say freely in private. Mr. Tennyson made what Mr. Arnold calls his decisive appearance in the world in 1842, when he published those two volumes which established his position and fame; the appearances in 1827, in 1830, and in 1833 having been tentative merely. It was then that Carlyle used to utter his protest against the new oracle; then that he denounced Mr. Tennyson's muse as the parent of "respectable" verses, and Mr. Tennyson himself as a man who wrote poetry because his mamma persuaded him to. In his more benign moods he would couple Mr. Tennyson's tutors with his mamma as the advisers of the young bard. But he long insisted on the poet's want of divine or prophetic, or as he called it, "seeing" power. By and by this hostility grew less. The truth is that Carlyle was never entirely insensible to the value and beauty of poetic form; witness, among many other proofs, the praise of Voltaire's *vers de société* in the *History of Frederick*. He and the poet became friends; and there was, and is, in Mr. Tennyson a quality of rugged sincerity which made him, when they came to know each other, a *persona grata* to Carlyle.

Exercise of one kind or another Carlyle took regularly. During many years of his life he rode; during the eight years especially which he devoted to the *History of Frederick*. That book, he declared, was nearly the death of him, and he computed that he had ridden on horseback full 20,000 miles while engaged upon it; and that otherwise he should never have finished it. His travels in Germany to visit the scenes he was busy upon were another relief, of a certain kind, but the pleasure of travel was marred by his want of an easy conversational knowledge of German. It was his visit to the great battlefields of Frederick which earned him the eulogium of a skilled military critic, that he had an eye for country which would have made him a great general. Neither then nor ever did he spare himself fatigue, nor would he take such care of his health—except in his own way—as his friends urged on him. He held to his walks and rides as sovereign against all ills; against dyspepsia, for one thing, which was his lifelong enemy. The most striking instance of his perseverance I can give you occurred on his eightieth birthday, a day celebrated by his friends here and in Germany and elsewhere with every loyal demonstration. It was in December. The day was one of the coldest ever known in London. There was a gale of wind and snow and the streets were so covered with ice that walking was not without danger. Making sure that the many calls on him, and telegrams and other evidences of friendliness that poured in, and, above all, the extreme severity of the weather, would keep him indoors, I went to see him at an hour when I knew he was usually out walking. But in spite of everything out he had gone.

Long as was his early struggle with poverty, the latter years of his life were passed in comfortable circumstances. He never, probably, was in any real pecuniary trouble. He was able to live on little, and had few wants but books. For more than twenty years, and I know not how much longer, his writings brought him a considerable income. In 1866 I was instructed to ask him to write something for this journal, and to offer whatever sum might be necessary to secure it. He took the proposal in a friendly way, saying how glad he should be to address his friends in America whom he well knew to be numerous. But he objected that at the moment he had no subject; that he had said what he had to say to the world, and that little or nothing more was to be expected from him, except, he added, some kind of autobiography, more or less complete, which would not be published in his lifetime. Upon my hinting that any subject and any terms he might like to name would be gladly accepted, he answered that no money that could be offered him was an inducement: "I have, in fact, more money than I know what to do with."

And with that I leave these reminiscences; adding only that I have a deeper feeling of gratitude to him than I am likely ever to express in any way.

THE CARLYLE MEMORIAL.

[LONDON, *October* 27, 1882.]

The unveiling of Mr. Boehm's statue of Carlyle which took place yesterday was a simple ceremony enough. Few invitations were sent except to subscribers; the general public was not asked nor expected to come. The plan usual on such occasions of sending invitations to peers and celebrities of all sorts had not been followed. This was to be a tribute to Carlyle from his friends. Two awnings had been raised for shelter in case of rain; a few chairs stood beneath them; a platform rose a foot high at the base of the pedestal for the speaker; and that was all. A local crowd, and not a very large one, had gathered about the gate of the inclosure in which, amid a few low trees and shrubs, the statue has been placed. The hour fixed was half-past two.

Professor Tyndall, the orator of the day, was among the first to arrive, with his wife and her mother, Lady Claud Hamilton. They were received by the Rector of Chelsea, the Rev. G. Blunt, and the Rev. Mr. Hoare, two of the committee. Mr. Browning appeared soon after, and Mr. Conway had been there from the first; both true to their early faith in Carlyle whoever else might fall off. Lord Houghton came all the way from Yorkshire to be present. Lord and Lady Arthur Russell arrived from their place in the country on the same errand. The Dowager Lady Stanley, the soul of the memorial, and her daughter, had not so far to journey. It was remarked of this venerable and admirable lady that she stood during the whole proceedings. Mr. Lecky, long among Carlyle's most frequent and valued associates, came with his wife. The number of ladies was considerable. Mr. Boehm, R.A., the sculptor of the statue, now by common consent at the head of his profession, was one of the group. Mr. Froude was not present, nor will his name be found among the subscribers to this memorial. The absence of the man who was Carlyle's biographer, and had for years been one of his most intimate friends, was commented upon but not explained. Probably Mr. Froude thinks it requires no explanation. I, at any rate, have none to offer. Mr. Ruskin's absence was presumably due to ill-health.

Dr. Tyndall stepped on the little open platform covered underfoot with red cloth at a little after half-past two, when perhaps a hundred people were gathered about the statue and some hundreds within hearing outside. The keen October wind that swept the shore did not prevent him from baring his head, the background of granite throwing into broad relief the strong, keen features and gray hair. He delivered his address from memory, in his usual lecture-room manner; lucid, expository, convincing. The audience listened in silence. Once or twice a murmur of approval went round, but there was not much cheering till the end. It was a happily conceived address, with just enough of personal reminiscence, dealing skilfully with some controverted points of Carlyle's character, dwelling with force on the human side of it, his pity and his love for his fellow-men, and condensing into an epigram the intellectual significance of his morality as "dynamic not didactic." His courage, the splendour of his imagination, his commanding qualities, the fearlessness of his beliefs and of his teaching, were all touched in swift sentences. It was hard to say which most impressed the extremely critical listeners, the glowing vindication of Carlyle's true nature against evanescent prejudice, or the wholly unlooked-for tribute to his American friend. There came a hush on the audience at the first words of the wish for a companion memorial to the man "who loved our hero and was by him beloved to the end— the loftiest, purest, and most penetrating spirit that has ever shone in American literature — Ralph Waldo Emerson" — and the name was followed by cordial applause. As the veil was drawn away every head was uncovered.

When Dr. Tyndall had concluded Lord Houghton came forward — quite unexpectedly to the committee — and moved a vote of thanks to the orator. This rather superfluous proposal led up to an elaborate and interesting speech about Carlyle. As the motion had been made, it had to be seconded, which Mr. Lecky was asked to do and did in a few words. Then Mr. Browning moved to thank Mr. Boehm, a motion which Mr. George Howard supported and everybody approved, and with that the proceedings came to an end.

Mr. Boehm's statue, in one material or another, has been seen by the London public before now, and admired. For the original marble Lord Rosebery gave Mr. Boehm a commission, and Lord Rosebery's consent had to be obtained for this reproduction in bronze, and was handsomely granted. The statue rests upon a square pedestal of polished red Aberdeen granite, lifting it to a height well above the railings, and clearly visible to every passer whether on foot or on horse. The inscription, sunk in gilt capitals, is: "Thomas Carlyle. Born December 4, 1795, at Ecclefechan, Dumfriesshire. Died February 5, 1881, at Great Cheyne Row, Chelsea."

Carlyle appears clad in dressing-gown and trousers and seated in an arm-chair, beneath which is a pile of books. The treatment throughout is realistic but simple and effective. The face is a likeness which everybody who knew Carlyle in his old age agrees in pronouncing excellent. The deep sadness of the eyes, the outward arch of the temples, which were singularly full and projecting, the stamp of life-long thinking set upon head and countenance alike; the power, the ruggedness, the pathos of this strange face are all there. The lines of the mouth indicate truly its too frequent habit of scornful laughter. Carlyle sits as I have often seen him, twisted a little to one side, the head leaning forward and to the right. There is dignity in the attitude and entire freedom from any attempt at posing. The one question about the statue was how it would bear the light of open day. Mr. Boehm has fashioned his bronze of a grayish green hue curiously well adapted to the prevailing tones of the spot, and the shadows are not too deep nor is the delicacy lost of the lines in the finely-modelled face. Altogether, as portrait and as work of art, a memorial Carlyle's friends may rejoice to see; one for which posterity will thank the artist and the other givers.

The site for the statue is well chosen. There runs along the Chelsea Embankment in this vicinity for some distance a semi-public inclosure planted with shrubbery and flowers, divided by gravelled walks. In front is the main roadway of the embankment; in the rear another road skirting the houses. In the inclosure and on a spot just opposite the end of Cheyne Row, which terminates in the rear road just mentioned, the statue has been set up, with a little open space about it. The back is turned to the street where Carlyle lived so long. The face looks through the gray mist out upon the river, and past the river to the park, the groups of houses, the factories and tall chimneys which are huddled together on the opposite side. Long before this stately embankment of carved stone was thought of, the great writer used to walk on this shore. The same river rolls by, the dull sky above it he has so often gazed on, and on both the sad, stern face of this pathetic sitting figure will henceforward gaze for ever.

That a memorial statue of Carlyle is now here to be seen is due largely to the resolute and affectionate energy of a woman, the Dowager Lady Stanley of Alderley. She was one of the first to promote it, she was one of the few who persevered to the end in the face of opposition and indifference that discouraged not a few of the original supporters. The appeal to the public for subscriptions was responded to at first with some liberality. Then the unhappy *Reminiscences* appeared and the flow of money stopped in a moment dead. For some time nothing could be done. The sum in hand or promised was not sufficient to warrant the committee in proceeding. But Lady Stanley was determined the statue should be set up. How she contrived to relight the quenched embers of enthusiasm I know not. Relighted they were, and by her hand, and from some source or another, from many sources certainly, there came heat and flame enough finally to melt and mould this bronze into the likeness of the grim Scotchman. Mr. Blunt's share in the work was also a large one, and one is glad that the Rector of Chelsea should be a clergyman of such openness and liberality of mind as to take a leading part in a memorial to a man whose creed was so widely different from his own.

The ceremony chanced to fall upon a busy week and the papers give but scant accounts of it, and only a few of them have leisure for any fresh comments on Carlyle's character or influence. Nor are the comments, in truth, particularly fresh. Once again we hear of his "miserable infirmities of temper," and of the indiscretion which brought them to light. Conversing yesterday with one of Carlyle's oldest and nearest and most distinguished friends, present at the ceremony, I heard a remark worth many columns of such comments. "If ever," said he, "a continuation of the biography appears, my turn, I suppose, will come. The last two volumes leave off where my relations with Carlyle began. Very likely he said hard things of me as of others, but I do not care what he said nor what is published. I always knew that in certain moods he would criticise harshly. But these surly outbreaks were only on the surface; the spirit which animated them, which seemed sour and angry enough at the moment, was no part of his real character. I loved him all through it. I shall never cease to love him."[1]

This loyal and friendly defence will not satisfy everybody. Nor will Professor Tyndall's fine image of the mountain peak shrouded in mist, "from which presently the cloud passes away, while the mountain in its solid grandeur

---

[1] It was Mr. Browning who said this.

remains, as by and by will stand out erect and clear the massive figure of Carlyle." Nor do people agree much better about the true value of Carlyle's teaching. The Conservatives say that in the political and social theories he proclaimed lie the principles of the only conservatism which can hope to make head against democracy. The Liberals evade that point; and think Carlyle will live as the writer who described the Revolt of Women and the Flight to Varennes. Yet the French, who are surely entitled to be heard about their own Revolution, have never accepted Carlyle as the historian of it. M. Louis Blanc attacks him again and again, and many other Frenchmen, from many different points of view, have attacked him. Michelet, who denounces Carlyle as careless about right and about ideas, has a most picturesque criticism of his method: "For Carlyle the Revolution is the churchyard in *Hamlet*. He picks up and weighs these skulls with a bitter smile in which gleams too often only a mocking pity. This is the skull of a madman, that of a fool. The word we miss is that cry from the heart, 'Alas! poor Yorick.'"

And yet Dr. Tyndall could say in entire sincerity that Carlyle's defects of feeling, if such there were, could only have reference to the distribution of his sympathy, not to its amount. Which of the two estimates is the right one must be left for another generation to decide.

MR. HAYWARD.

[LONDON, *February* 9, 1884.]

Not a few, I suspect, of those who read the headline of this letter will ask, "Who was Mr. Hayward?" The question is one I have heard from Americans in London when they were told they were to meet him at dinner. It is one no Londoner would have put, nor any foreigner on his second visit here. Mr. Hayward's fame and position are the most striking example that can be quoted of the extreme narrowness of purely social renown. Who in London was known so well? Out of London no one was known so little, though an exception may be made in favour of Paris where his acquaintance was very large. Nor was his celebrity of to-day. For a generation he has had no rival. For two generations he has been a figure. He was the contemporary of Sydney Smith, of Sam Rogers, of Macaulay, and held his own with the best of them. And he died only last Saturday. Nobody who ever met him will forget him; but I suppose among those who knew him not his memory may be only transient.

Abraham Hayward was born in 1802. He never had what is called in this country a start in life. He went to no public school and to neither University. He began life in a solicitor's office; thence, by a not very usual transition, he made his way to the Bar, to which, however, he was not called till he was nearly thirty years old. He made no effort for practice, though he edited a law journal and was ultimately made a Q.C. He had neither fortune nor family. One of his grandparents was a Jew, and thence he got his first name Abraham; by no means then a passport to society. He translated *Faust* into English prose, and it is still the best translation for those who wish to learn the exact meaning of the original. He wrote for *The Morning Chronicle*. From an early period he was a frequent contributor to *The Edinburgh* and *The Quarterly Review*, and his essays have been republished. But none nor all of these incidents in his personal history gives the least clue either to the origin of his social career or to his extraordinary ascendancy in the world amid which he lived. Nor do I know, nor can I find anybody who does know, how Hayward got his first step in the life he led so brilliantly. I always meant to ask him and he would have told without hesitation. But it is too late.

Three series of Hayward's Essays have been collected; a fourth and last appearing under the title, *Eminent Statesmen and Writers*. The first, issued in 1858, was so far from being successful that for years the two 8vo volumes could be bought for five shillings. Afterward the demand grew, they became scarce, and a copy in good condition is difficult to procure for five times five shillings. The subsequent series sold fairly well, but nothing Hayward has published can be called popular. Yet, in their kind, his Essays are among the best in the English language. They are excellent studies. They abound in anecdotes derived from his personal intercourse and experience. They abound equally in a kind of knowledge rare among English writers, a knowledge of the Continent and of Continental personages. On certain literary epochs or periods Hayward was an authority. He was saturated with the literature of the last century, French and English both, and he had at his finger ends everything that had happened during his own time. The details of the Junius controversy were as familiar to him as its generalities are to most men. The same may be said of the various questions raised about Byron. Nobody did so much as Hayward toward exposing and discrediting certain reckless calumnies on that great writer. Nor was he ever so overloaded with his facts as to be unable to handle them. His pace is never sluggish. Directness and lucidity are perhaps the chief merits of his style, to which there is wanting the indefinable something which constitutes charm. But he is always and eminently readable. Dulness was a goddess to whom he never offered the smallest homage. Mr. Matthew Arnold intimates somewhere that Hayward might have done a higher order of work in literature, and no doubt he might. But what he did was excellent of its kind, and you must go to his essays for a great deal of interesting and valuable and delightful knowledge not to be found elsewhere. This is not slight praise. The papers on the art of Dining, on Whist, and others, are classics. He edited the *Letters and Literary Remains of Mrs. Piozzi* and the *Diary of a Lady of Quality*, and later in life wrote a monograph on Goethe which is a sound piece of work. And he was for a quarter of a century a contributor to *The Times*. Mr. Delane was his intimate friend; and Mr. Hayward befriended the late Mr. Chenery, when he became editor, in many ways.

It is to be added that Hayward is the author of some of the most polished *vers de société* in the English language. They have never been published, and it must, I suppose, depend on the directions he left whether they ever will be. But they were printed for private distribution. He used to say he never gave a copy to a male friend. He made no exception in my favour, yet a copy lies before me which I did not buy nor borrow nor come by in any irregular way. And though it does not absolutely belong to me, I hope not to part with it wholly.

Hayward never entered Parliament or gave himself up to political life, but he was a born politician and knew every move on the board. Though a regular writer on literary topics in *The Quarterly*, which is Tory, he was a steadfast Liberal and the close personal friend of Mr. Gladstone, to whom he was equally devoted and useful. Their relations may be denoted by a single incident. When Mr. Gladstone was forming his present Ministry, Hayward was one of the two or three friends, not colleagues, whom the Prime Minister consulted. He was in Harley Street day and night, and was the means of communication between Mr. Gladstone and *The Times*. Nobody knew better than Hayward, or so well, what was said and thought in the world he lived in. It is the fashion now to disparage the political influence of London society; but it is none the less a force, a great force, which no Minister can afford to leave out of account. Until Mr. Chamberlain invented the caucus—I say invented, because the English machine is very different from what is supposed to be its American prototype, and a more formidable and dangerous weapon—no body of opinion could be brought to bear on a government so directly or so powerfully as that of London itself. The clubs, the dinner-tables, the drawing-rooms of the West End have made and unmade Ministries before now, and may again, spite of Mr. Chamberlain's elaborate precautions to counterwork the forces which to him were perhaps unmanageable.

What made Hayward famous beyond all other things was his genius for society. Genius is not too strong a word. A man who without any help but his own aptitudes and force of character makes his way into that jealously guarded company, and makes himself in the end a power there, can only be described by using words of wide range and rare application. It is to be remembered that he became famous in one of the most brilliant periods of English society. He had many competitors besides those I have named, the late Bernal Osborne, for example. He met on equal terms all the ablest men in public life. He was asked to almost every great house in town and country; asked not once or twice, but continually asked all his life long. He was the intimate friend and trusted adviser of great ladies as well as distinguished men. He became long since a sort of arbiter in the fashionable world. His influence and authority reached almost everywhere. If the mistress of a palace in Mayfair wanted to weed her visiting list, it was Hayward whom she consulted. If she wanted to form a visiting list, he again would be her adviser. Nor does that mean merely ladies of doubtful claim to social position. I knew of a case not many years ago where he was called in, the lady in question being of high rank, spotless reputation, with a good house, a popular husband, and plenty of money. She was, with all that, new to London, felt that she needed a pilot, and Hayward was the pilot she chose.

If you could get at the secret of Hayward's power it would be worth knowing. But the truth is, there was no secret. The freemasonry of society is a very complete organisation. The moment a man is known to one of the brotherhood as a desirable acquaintance, he quickly becomes known to a wide circle. The beginning of Hayward's success must date from his first introductions—however they came about. Here was a new talker, a man who could enliven a dinner-table, and he was welcome accordingly. His supremacy and authority came later. He took immense pains. He amassed facts. He knew everything about everybody. His memory was marvellous in its tenacity. Later in life, people who did not like him used to say he was asked everywhere because he was feared everywhere. No doubt he was feared. A man who knew enough to shatter, or at least to shake, half the reputations in the room might well be feared. But that is only an incident—by no means the foundation or essential support of his position.

The truth, or part of the truth, is that he cultivated conversation and every other element of social success as a fine art. He studied it and practised it as a painter studies and practises painting. It was the business of his life. He talked on a system, the first rule of which was never to seem to talk on a system. The rarest of all conversational powers is the power of relation or narrative. The least prolixity or confusion is fatal. Hayward went to the point of a story as an arrow goes to its mark; not less swift and direct and sure. He knew something on every subject, but he was never didactic and never pedantic. He had profoundly meditated on La Rochefoucauld's remark, that confidence supplies more than wit to the burden of talk. He would be heard, and he would be admired, and he was. It was never monologue. He detested monologue, and used to say that Macaulay was insupportable. He cared little for the reputation of mere wit, and drollery he despised.

Despotic, an enemy might say. Very likely he was. Certainly as age came upon him the dislike to interruption grew, and possibly it sometimes became intolerance. There is a story of a Sunday dinner at Strawberry Hill which I heard more than once. An eminent Frenchman was among the guests. He had a Frenchman's ideas about conversation, and perhaps a Frenchman's ambition to shine. He talked well and much. He cut into Hayward's best stories, and such was his own skill as a *raconteur*, helped, no doubt, by the freshness and novelty of his stories and his style, that he held the table and fairly talked the Englishman down. After dinner Hayward went up to his hostess and said to her, with that familiarity which was his habit, "Lady Waldegrave, you really must not have Count X—— here to dine again."—"But why, Mr. Hayward?"—"Because he spoils conversation." The anecdote was one which Lady Waldegrave herself told, with the friendly good-nature she invariably showed to Hayward. She was his friend to the last. When people talked of giving him up, she always answered, "Never. He has been my friend and he has amused you all for forty years." She might have added, save for politeness' sake, that Hayward was much more likely to give them up than they him. There were people who insisted they had heard all his stories, that he had grown tiresome, that they were going to drop him, and so on. But his social prestige survived to the last.

Hayward had antipathies, urged those who had an antipathy to him. Such things are likely enough to be reciprocal, but I do not think it was true of him in the sense in which it was meant. He hated things rather than people; qualities and defects of character. He could not endure a man to be slovenly of mind, inaccurate, loose in talk. When such a one came in his way, still more if he put himself in his way, Hayward was merciless. If a pretender undertook to contradict him, or set him right, or to tell a story wrongly, woe unto him. Hayward would break in on him, correct him, retell his story accurately in half the words, and leave him with a rankling sense of having made a fool of himself, which lasted long. That is the origin of half the enmities to Hayward, to be heard of in London right and left. It mattered not in what company the fool betrayed his folly. Hayward feared nobody. It was one secret of his success. He made his courage and his power felt by friends and by foes. He attacked Lord Beaconsfield (one man whom he really hated) just as freely as he attacked Lord Beaconsfield's latest parodist and parasite. He delivered his criticisms on Carlyle with as much liberty of speech as if he were gibbeting (which he often did) some new pretender whom Carlyle himself would have gleefully joined in dissecting. Probably he never wrote an article which gave him keener delight than the memorable paper in which he convicted Disraeli of appropriating without credit a passage from Thiers's eulogy on Marshal St. Cyr, and embodying it in his own speech on the Duke of Wellington. It added zest to his task that he was able to demonstrate that the passage had not been borrowed from Thiers, but was a bodily transfer of an incorrect translation which had appeared in *The Morning Chronicle*. As to Carlyle, Hayward thought, perhaps, that some of the praise bestowed on Carlyle for introducing Goethe and German literature in general to the English public belonged to himself, as it did; some also to Coleridge, he would equally insist. He denied to Carlyle the originality his disciples claimed for him. "The only original book Carlyle ever wrote," cried Hayward, " was *Sartor Resartus*, and the only original idea in that is borrowed from the *Tale of a Tub*." It would be difficult to deny that the substance of the Clothes-Philosophy of Herr Teufelsdröck had previously been expounded by Swift. I am sorry to say that Mill was one of the objects of Hayward's dislike and that his conduct to Mill will not admit of a complete defence.

Nobody knew better than Hayward, however intolerant he might be, what was due to the company or to his host. Staying not many years ago at a country house, I asked my hostess who were to be the Saturday to Monday party. She mentioned Hayward and two other well-known men, both of them in a way good talkers, and neither supposed to like the third, nor yet each other. She was troubled when she heard this, but it was too late to make any change and the three duly arrived. As they were all three men of the world and of good breeding, there was no particular reason for alarm except that the party might not "go off" well. In point of fact nothing could have gone off better. The three were civil to each other, of course, and the two whose meeting was most dreaded became almost friendly. Dinner passed off without a single collision between Hayward and either of the other two. So did the more perilous hours in the smoking-room after the ladies had gone to bed. It is a pleasure to recollect that the only point on which Hayward grew warm was in behalf of a great American. One of the party said something in disparagement of Franklin, about whom he evidently knew little. I answered what I could, and Hayward broke in with a cry of encouragement: "You are right, you are perfectly right. Franklin was right; no man who knows the facts can say he was not right." It was the Hutchinson letters we were discussing. Sunday passed also, and when I said good-bye to Hayward on Monday he was in the act of offering some books to one of the others; again a characteristic thing of him, for he was generous, and altogether devoid of anything like egotistic acquisitiveness.

I have known Hayward as long as I have known anybody in London, or almost as long. I owed my first meeting with him to a dear friend of his, himself one of the most delightful talkers then to be met. He had the kindness to ask me to dine with him at his club. Hayward was the only other guest. It was an evening never to forget. Hayward, perhaps not sorry to have a listener to whom all his stories were sure to be new, poured out from the fulness of his memory anecdote after anecdote in inexhaustible profusion. I have heard him a hundred times since in the midst of excellent company, with everybody to spur him on, and I have never heard him excel his performance of this first evening. Swift, sparkling, copious, equally wonderful for variety and for easy precision, his talk sped on hour after hour, checking itself to give room for others to talk, and resuming with the same untiring freshness and exuberant spirit; and always with an unexpected turn and some delightful novelty to offer.

London will look in vain for Hayward's successor. Until within a few weeks he was always to be met in St. James's Street or in Pall Mall in the afternoon; his slight bent form among the most noticeable and most noticed of the many well-known figures which throng those historical pavements. He had a strong face; forehead, nose, mouth, jaw alike denoting the power he possessed, the Hebrew blood in him growing more marked as he grew older. He might have passed in the eye of a stranger as a student more familiar with books than men. But the moment he met an acquaintance whom he liked, his eye filled with a friendly light—the thin small hand was put softly into yours and the first word told you his last thought. He never fell into the commonplaces of conventional greeting. He preferred to offer you a pungent comment on the uppermost topic of the day. A criticism, an apt anecdote, an epigram, and with a kindly nod he passed on again. He used to say he had outlived his time. The proof that he had not was the geniality which to the last underlay his most scornful words. Certain it is that he had not outlived the respect or admiration or regard of his own world.

LORD HOUGHTON.

[LONDON, *August* 16, 1885.]

DISRAELI said of him that he had dined with Louis Philippe and received Louis Blanc at dinner. It was true, though the antithesis may seem to an American less sharp than it was meant to be, for Louis Blanc remained a personage in France long after Louis Philippe and the sons of Louis Philippe had ceased to have serious pretensions to power. But Lord Houghton had known everybody, and he had the secret of making everybody with whom he came in contact give him of his best. Perhaps no man of any age was to be seen at so many London parties, or in so many different country-houses during the year. The confidence of demeanour which earned for him very early in life Sydney Smith's sobriquet, "The cool of the evening," remained with him, but it mellowed with age. He was not only admired, he was liked, and the liking was mingled with much affection. If latterly he had peculiarities which annoyed people, his more beautiful qualities never lost their attraction. I once heard him criticised by one or two young men who were impatient at some mark of increasing years which he had shown. There sat by another young man, himself one of the most critical of his species, with the right to be difficult which comes of character, position, fine gifts and early success. He listened to the tirade and when it was over remarked, "You may say what you like, I shall always keep a warm corner in my heart for Houghton." And he did, and whether in town or country this young patrician showed his senior that considerate friendship and unfailing courtesy which belong, perhaps, more to Houghton's time than to this.

He died at seventy-six, having got as much out of life during every year of that long period as it was possible to get. Few men had more various interests. Literature occupied him in early life; politics were one of the things to which he gave attention early and late. He had travelled widely; east as far as the Ganges, and west beyond the Mississippi. But during all this period what he really cared for was the company of his fellow-creatures and their applause. He collected books, some of them very curious, and many things beside books. Fryston Hall, his Yorkshire home, was in its way a museum, and the most interesting object in it was its owner. Among all the accumulations of his life the most entertaining to him, no doubt, and to us when we could get at them, was his store of personal recollections of men and women.

Thorough Englishman as he was, there is a sense in which Lord Houghton was not English at all; he was not insular. He came nearer than most of his countrymen to rating a Frenchman at his true value, and, I may add, to being rated at his true value by Frenchmen. He was at home in Paris; there were few European capitals where he was not at home. He wintered in Rome, in Florence, in Athens; wherever fancy or the pursuit of health took him, and was everywhere a citizen of that great republic of well-bred persons which is the most potent international league that has yet been organised. There are stories of his last sojourn in Rome which might imply that he even felt too much at home, and sometimes omitted to examine his engagement book carefully enough to impress on his mind the broad distinction between those houses to which he had been invited and those to which he had not. And as Roman society is not merely exclusive but sharply divided into black and white, or clerical and non-clerical in politics, this amiable readiness of Lord Houghton to visit in houses of both colours, and to carry his impressions from one to the other, was sometimes misunderstood. But his faculties were not then what they had once been, and a man who for fifty years has been used to being asked everywhere may be excused if he credited some of the Roman nobility with remembering claims to attention which they had for the moment forgotten. No importance belongs to such gossip, whether true or false.

Lord Houghton's freedom from mere insularity showed itself in his culture quite as much as in the range of his acquaintanceship. For the purposes of the man of the world what he knew was more than sufficient. He met scholars and statesmen, men of science and men of letters, artists and poets, on even terms. The diffuseness, the want of concentration, which were fatal to his hope of permanent fame as an author, were invaluable to him in the many worlds amid which he moved so easily. His independent fortune relieved him from all thought of money-making by his pen, and his ambition never ran decisively in any single channel along which he might have poured the full stream of those rare and delicate gifts which went meandering each its own way through flowering meadows and pastures ever fresh.

His literary work, it is true, stretched over a long period of his life. *Palm Leaves*, by Richard Monckton Milnes, was published in 1844. *Poems Legendary and Historical* belong to the same date. *Poems of Many Years* had preceded this in 1840, while the *Memorials of a Tour in Greece* goes back to 1834, and there were other volumes of poetry and prose between these dates—all by an author who all this last season was to be met wherever a candle was lighted in London. Since 1844 he has published various political pamphlets, an essay or two, and a volume of personal sketches under the title *Monographs*. He edited Keats and wrote a critical biography of him which remains classic. Of other miscellaneous work there is a good deal, but it is hard to believe that anything which bears Lord Houghton's name will live. Emerson in his *Parnassus* has not found room for a single line of Milnes's verse, and few Americans, or Englishmen either, if challenged, could readily supply a quotation from him. What he wrote had finish, grace, often feeling, but nothing supreme, nothing of such excellence as to keep its place amid the tremendous competition to which every new aspirant for fame in literature is subjected. If, in a word, Lord Houghton had been a man of letters, and that only, his death would have been mourned, not by the world of letters and other worlds as now, but by his personal friends only.

He wrote occasional verses, I may add, down to the very last. Stanzas by him but without his name appeared in one of the London papers this summer. I met him at dinner a few days later, and after dinner he asked me if I had read this production. When he heard I had not he offered to recite the verses, and upon some one sending for the paper he said, "No, I can repeat them." And so, pulling himself together, and amid a company of listeners that filled the drawing-room, he declaimed the little poem. Despite a certain imperfection of articulation he declaimed it very well, and he was not above showing that he was pleased with the compliments showered upon him.

The needy writers who concentrate upon London have long known Lord Houghton as friend, adviser, kindly critic, and, above all, an unfailing source of help when they wanted money. The anecdotes of his gifts are many; perhaps the best of them all is that in which Carlyle bestows on him a eulogy in terms strangely cordial for him. If Carlyle is rightly reported he hints at having himself had, or been offered, a £50 note in his days of poverty. It seems unlikely that he took it but he knew of many less scrupulous than himself who profited by Lord Houghton's bounty. This poet-peer, indeed, seems to have had an undying faith in the possibility of fresh genius and in his own power of discovering it. He lavished encouragement as freely as money; with, I fear, not much return for either. This hopefulness about other men, this belief that the sources of poetry were not dried up in this prosaic age, was one of the beautiful traits of his character. His expression of it in money is, perhaps, its most unusual form. Certainly if Lord Houghton had had a multitude of sins his charity would have covered them all.

Like most Americans I made Lord Houghton's acquaintance not long after I first came to London. I have seen him often since, and though of late years he was thought, naturally enough, to have lost some of the charm which used to be his, I never met him without hearing something fresh from his lips, something which nobody but Houghton would have been likely to say, or to say so well. He is one of the last of the last generation of talkers; men whose conversation had a solid basis of knowledge and good sense, with wit or humour or lightness of fancy above. Mr. Kinglake and Mr. Charles Villiers are his sole survivors. I do not include Mr. Browning because Mr. Browning, with all his seventy-three years, belongs as much to this generation as to the one which preceded it, with some of the finest qualities of both. But Lord Houghton had upon him the stamp of a time anterior to this, when life was more leisurely and more various, when men thought it possible to cultivate something beside the useful, when a certain ornate elaboration of phrase did not seem artificial, and when they had a breadth of manner which came from regarding social intercourse as a fine art. The last of the great talkers who went over to the majority before him was Hayward, and a comparison between Hayward and Houghton would be an interesting one if there were space for it in a letter. Houghton, however, who was long a rival to Hayward, had what Hayward had not—wit and felicity of speech and persuasiveness. Hayward used to say of him that he had finer mental powers than he often showed in talk, or even in books. He had, moreover, a singularly complete equipment. He had literature, anecdote, large acquaintance with the inner history of courts and of general society. He delighted in surprises and uttered with the most captivating carelessness an epigram which he had spent hours in polishing. You have seen and heard him in America, and if your impressions of Lord Houghton are as pleasant as his were of his American friends I need say nothing more. You must have heard him speak also, and have formed your own opinion on the justness of the applause which his English speeches have obtained. In Parliament he had no higher rank as orator or debater than he had with the country as politician. He continued to deliver neat little essays in the House of Lords, but there was always the note of the amateur in his political speeches. He owed his oratorical fame to his occasional addresses and to his after-dinner harangues. They were innumerable and many of them were admirable.

Lord Houghton's breakfasts have been talked of and written about so much that little which is fresh can now be said. Undoubtedly he studied, as few Englishmen study, the art of bringing people together who will go together. He liked celebrities; one might say he had a passion for them, and if one came in his way at the last moment he would add him to a chosen company of guests at the risk of some incongruity. But this was the exception. Nor do I think he ever made allowance for the roughness of manner which some of his own countrymen show at times to those who are not their countrymen, as well as to those who are. They mean no rudeness, they merely lack the polish which a Frenchman, for example, expects and concedes in every form of social relations. Lord Houghton once had to breakfast a foreigner of great distinction in literature but not then widely known in England. He happened to bear the same name as an Englishman whose eminence was of a different sort and adorned by a title. As titles are not always, nor even commonly, used among intimate friends, there was room for ambiguity when Lord Houghton named his guest to another, an Englishman, to whom he proposed to introduce him. "Delighted," said the Englishman; then, when the unhappy and untitled foreigner was brought up to him, so keen was his disappointment that he turned his back on him with an "Oh!" of unconcealed disgust. The mistake was one which Lord Houghton was not likely to repeat, nor did I ever hear of the Englishman being asked again by him to breakfast.

Incidents of that sort were rare, and the celebrity which Lord Houghton's entertainments long since won was deserved. Latterly he gave very few breakfasts. The fashion has somewhat gone out, perhaps because most of the men in London who are most wanted on such occasions are too busy to give up their mornings; or have been so busy the night before that they have no mornings. Yet Hayward, who was as fresh at ten in the forenoon as at ten in the evening, used to advise a friend to pay no attention to the set of the fashion in such matters. "People come to your breakfasts," said he, with a characteristic touch of his worldly shrewdness, "what does it matter whether others give breakfasts or not? The fewer there are, the more they will be liked."

The best of all the stories on this subject is one which I think has never been in print, and which Hayward delighted in telling. Carlyle was once storming away in his usual fashion against the decay of everything, and, in particular, of reverence for great men. And as he could never long discuss a subject without bringing in an illustration, he presently observed that if Jesus Christ were to return to the earth and come to London nobody would pay him the least attention. Then, interrupting himself, he added, "Yes, I think Lord Houghton would ask him to breakfast."

LORD SHAFTESBURY.

[DEESIDE, *October* 16, 1885.]

THOSE who had never met Lord Shaftesbury were wont to think of him as an austere man in private life. He was not that. He was genial, liked a good story, and was ready to tell one at his own expense. Even in England where the Peerage is profanely spoken of as the Daily Bible (which would have shocked Lord Shaftesbury beyond anything), there are people who do not follow changes of title, or recognize a son when he has succeeded to the name of his father. One of these individuals, said Lord Shaftesbury, once wrote him a letter in recent years, reproaching him for occupying so much of his life with devotional efforts. "It is all very well, your praying and speech-making at Exeter Hall and your professions of sympathy with the poor. You call yourself a philanthropist. Why don't you do something? Why don't you go to work like Lord Ashley who passed the Factory Acts?" This fervent person had no idea that the Lord Ashley who passed the Factory Acts, and the Lord Shaftesbury whom he was rebuking, were one and the same person. This and many other anecdotes I have heard Lord Shaftesbury relate, with as much real enjoyment as if he had been leading the exercises at an Evangelical prayer-meeting.

Lord Shaftesbury's face and whole appearance were striking; he was the sort of man that, once seen, you would never forget. There are excellent photographs of him, but if they are not to be bought in New York you have only to turn to any good likeness of the first Earl of Shaftesbury, and you will see the last. The distinguishing features have come down through seven generations; long lived ones they must have been, for the first Earl was born in 1621 (created Earl in 1672), and the eighth has but just come into his title, himself fifty-four years old. The late Lord Shaftesbury was born into this world in 1801; his father in 1768. The portraits of the intermediate earls I do not know; the third excepted, who wrote the *Characteristics*. The line, however, is direct, each earl from the first having been succeeded by his eldest or only son, all but the fifth, who died without male issue, the title devolving on his only brother; the only one of them all who was not named Anthony, and father to the late man.

The kinship of the seventh earl to the first is written large in his powerful face; resolute, perhaps a little severe; the features those which belong to a man of organising and ruling capacity; the eyes, as might be supposed, rather too near together. He was a man to narrow his creed and broaden his life; believed implicitly you were going straight to a real hell of actual brimstone and utter everlasting torment if you varied from his own religious doctrine, but would take much pains to make it comfortable to you on this side the gulf. He was deaf of late years but his faculties seemed otherwise as clear and keen as ever. I met him not seldom last winter near his house in Grosvenor Square, walking in the pitiless north-east wind with no better outer garment than a short cloak, cut rather like a policeman's cape and not much longer. As for his character and his lifelong efforts for the classes of people whom others left to themselves, they are part of the history of the past two generations. It is enough to say that there is no single individual who did so much practical good by intelligent, organised endeavour as did Lord Shaftesbury. His life is a standing answer to the sneers about the efficacy of Acts of Parliament.

He has left a successor to the title; successor to himself

there can be none except in a qualified sense. Much of his work has been done once for all; done so well and decisively that it needs no furtherance in the future. There is always, however, a place for a Peer of position, character, and wealth, to whom the religious side of life is more than all else.

MATTHEW ARNOLD.

[LONDON, *April* 17, 1888.]

I WISH to have done with the one point in my memories of Arnold which is a painful one, and I will begin with it though it belongs at the very end. I resented, perhaps more keenly than you did at home, his late—his last—article on America. It is the fashion now in New York—or it tries to be the fashion—to take foreign criticisms lightly, and it is a good fashion when not carried to extremes. But to an American living abroad, living where this attack on his own country appeared, it is less easy to take it lightly. America is, at best, none too well understood in England. You may say you do not care whether you are understood or not, but that is not quite a serious answer. You do care, and must care. In no conceivable event can the relations between the United States and England be a matter of indifference to the people of either country. They depend on the opinions the people of each nation form about the other. Arnold's paper on Civilisation in the United States had a direct tendency to diminish the respect of the English for the Americans, and therefore to lessen their goodwill, and so to make the feeling between the two countries less cordial than before. That is why I thought it so deplorable. The influence of it is more quickly perceptible here than with you. It was already to be seen in the rush of lesser and, in ordinary circumstances, quite unimportant persons into print, each with his little sheaf of anti-American prejudices which he was impatient to air. Arnold's death has enhanced the effect. His last article is sought for and read because it is his last. It is reproduced in part in the papers. The leading paper of Liverpool, to mention only one, discussed it editorially through a column and a half. The dead hand of the great writer lies heavily on us; more heavily than when it held the pen. True, the more cultivated and intelligent classes are incredulous. They do not think we can be quite what he painted us. But who does not know that the Masses and not the Classes now rule in England?

Arnold himself thought I was unfair to him, as I thought he was unfair to us. He saw for the first time the points he had made against us collected together, and the friction of each against the other sharpened them all. I sent him my despatch. He wrote me as follows:—

April 13.

My dear Smalley—I don't think the "nice" Americans ought to take to themselves what I say about shortcomings in the life of their nation, any more than the "nice" English what I say about shortcomings in the life of ours, but I was determined to say at some time what I thought of the newspapers over there and of the prevalent "greatest nation upon earth" strain, and I am not without hope that it may do good.

. . . .

I think you will end by judging this article of mine less unfavourably.

The sentence or two which I have omitted are even more kindly in their tone to me than the rest and I cannot print them. I must adhere to the substance of what I said, but if there were a word in it which pained him as coming from a friend I would give anything to recall it. If he had lived it might have been no great matter; a blow given or taken is soon forgotten. But never does the *irrevocabile verbum* seem so hopelessly beyond recall as when the shadow of death has fallen upon him of whom it was said.

As I look over Arnold's letters to me, I find many relating to his two American journeys. We had talked the first over together some time before he finally resolved to go.

Undoubtedly he went to America with hopes doomed in advance to disappointment. He wanted to make a large sum of money, and he referred again and again to the sum which Thackeray brought back with him, as if that were a kind of precedent. Thackeray's gains amounted to £10,000. If Arnold really expected that his lectures would return him that sum, or anything like it, his visit must have seemed to him a failure from the financial point of view. He soon became aware that lecturing is a business which requires experience and natural aptitudes. He had no experience and no special fitness for the platform. Nor was he a man to care for money for its own sake, or for his own sake. It happened to him at this time to desire the use of a considerable sum, not for himself, but for another. This need was what drove him to lecturing. Yet his mood was not in all respects an over-sanguine one. He wrote in April 1883: "I want to talk to you about America next January—though probably I shall be a horrid fiasco there."

The discussions and his negotiations with various agents went on for some months. It was not till August that his mind was made up. Here is the note announcing his decision:—

Fox How, AMBLESIDE, *August* 6.

MY DEAR SMALLEY—You have been so kind about my going to the States that I am bound to tell you the uncertainty about it is at last removed. I have got all the leave I want, and shall go in October—*jacta est alea*. Very likely I shall fail to draw; but I should not have been more likely to draw two years hence, when falling into dotage.

It is, I imagine, true of Arnold that whatever offended his taste offended his whole nature. He found much in America that offended his taste, and he said so with that keenness of phrase which nothing could blunt. He found much also to like, and like heartily, but a kind of reserve seemed to come over him when he sought to express in public his appreciation of what he most valued in America. He expressed it freely enough in private. If he had yielded to his feelings he would, I believe, have suppressed most of what he said against us. He said it because he thought it ought to be said. In private he was wont to speak of his visits in the pleasantest possible way, and of people he had met in the United States as very "attaching," a word he delighted in.

There is a passage in a letter on his return from America in 1885 which shows how he valued American opinion. After referring to something which had pleased him in *The Tribune*, he says:—

To be sure, I have had so long a stage of what Dr. Johnson calls "wholesome neglect" that perhaps notice and kindness in the end of my days will not spoil me.

Then he goes on:—

The American people is a great deal bigger and stronger than it was, but I cannot agree with those who think it less sensitive to foreign, at any rate to English opinion. It is natural it should be so, and, on the whole, though there are some inconveniences, useful.

I have dwelt long on these American experiences of Arnold's, and there is a great deal to be said on other points. But I wish to cite lastly a passage which I have just re-read from the preface to the *Discourses in America*. I took down the volume, a gift from him, to look again at the inscription in the beginning, which I trust he would still re-write; then I began to read and came upon this:—

I am glad of every opportunity of thanking my American audiences for the unfailing attention and kindness with which they listened to a speaker who did not flatter them, who would have flattered them ill, but who yet felt, and in fact expressed, more esteem and admiration than his words were sometimes, at a hasty first hearing, supposed to convey. I cannot think that what I have said of Emerson will finally be accounted scant praise, although praise universal and unmixed it certainly is not. What high esteem I feel for the suitableness and easy play of American institutions I have had occasion, since my return home, to say publicly and emphatically. But nothing in the discourse on "Numbers" was at variance with this high esteem, although a caution, certainly, was suggested. But then, some caution or other, to be drawn from the inexhaustibly fruitful truth that moral causes govern the standing and the falling of States, who is there that can be said not to need?

After all, Arnold's visits to America were but an episode of his career. What he said of America bears little proportion to what he said on other topics. The work of his life was done before he first crossed the Atlantic. He will be judged in America, as elsewhere, by his poetry, by his criticism, by the influence of his writing on other writing and thought of the time; and by what he was in actual life. I have known him for many years and it is on this last point more especially that I have still something to say.

It happens often enough that a man's death brings suddenly to light a much greater mass of regard and admiration for him than had been expressed during his life. This is what has happened in Arnold's death. The tributes to his character and genius are astonishing to one who has noted the currents of opinion about him in recent years. I should always have said that his fame, though of the highest, was not in England itself a wide or general renown. He himself did not believe it to be. It might have been likened to the reputation which a great physiologist or great chemist commonly has. He is a celebrity among physiologists and chemists; perhaps among men of science in general; but not with the public unless to his scientific attainments he adds, as so few do, the power of expression in writing. So it might have been said of Arnold that the sources of his reputation were to be sought among men of letters. His power of expression in writing was surpassed by that of no man of his time, yet not even this power brought him, or seemed to bring him, general popularity. His books were read, not indeed by one class, but by limited classes. I think it very possible that they were better known in America than here; a remark true, or true at first, of many of the best modern English authors in many different fields. It was true of Carlyle, and it was true of Mr. Herbert Spencer. I choose two examples as far apart as possible.

However that may be, the outburst of admiration which has followed upon Arnold's death proves that he had reached a much wider circle than was supposed, or than he himself had supposed. I wish he could have known the real truth. He used to say that his public was not and could not be a large one. Tuesday's newspapers would have convinced him to the contrary. The newspapers in this country do not devote columns to the death of men who are but the heroes of coteries. To a surprising degree he had acquired that reflex or secondary renown which, in the case of a really great writer, is often the most extensive. The number of people who had read about him was greater than of those who had read him; or who had read and mastered what he himself most valued in his work. The reviews and magazines in which he wrote of late so often had brought him into direct contact with an audience more numerous than that to which his books had introduced him. He had lived to see the ideas and phrases which he had coined pass into general circulation. So long ago had this come to pass that they had lived through that decisive yet not always pleasant period of popularity when the caricaturist and the buffoon fasten upon them. Who has not heard culture ridiculed? Who does not know the wretched impostors who have strutted about in Arnold's cast-off clothes, and presented themselves to a credulous public as the true prophets of a gospel which they knew only by its catchwords? Their profession of it tended to bring it into a contempt which nothing but a genuine inspiration could have survived.

Much has been said of Arnold's place in English literature and of his influence upon it, but the English themselves do not seem to be aware of one service he rendered them which may be ranked among the most useful of all. He

taught them to understand what the French mean by a
sense of form in prose literature. Lucidity first of all; the
word is one of those which he has added to the common
stock of commonplaces; but also something much more
than lucidity. He has defined the merits of French style as
the merits of regularity, uniformity, precision, balance. But
it is not style only which is here in question; it is the shaping and ordering of whatever literary work the writer has
to attempt; the recognition of the fact that there exist certain rules, arbitrary in part, in part springing from the
genius of the language, or from the natural love of symmetry and beauty which dwells in the human mind. He
affirmed certain principles. His criticism, indeed, was not
always an affirmation; it was often a suggestion; but
whichever it was, it was profoundly instructive. He acknowledged Sainte Beuve as his master; to some extent
Sainte Beuve was his spiritual father. He adopted and
practised the method of the Frenchman, whom he first
commended to the English public as the finest critical
intelligence of modern times. He imitated neither Sainte
Beuve nor any other writer. His style is of his own creation; or rather is a natural growth and the natural expression of his own mind; natural, but as a delicate fruit is
natural, by help of all that art and care can do toward the
perfecting of it. There are habits of expression to be found
in Arnold's prose to which a French critic would take serious exception, but that is not the point. No style is perfect,
and Arnold found himself in the position of being compelled
first to attract and then to hold public attention. He knew
the value of a phrase that fixes itself in the memory. He
knew the value of repetition; the dulness of the public is
such that to say a thing once is of little use. But he sacrificed no essential quality of style to this desire to fulfil his
mission.

This, however, is not the place to develop such considerations as these. I indicate them and pass on. Nor do I enter upon a discussion of Arnold's poetry, or of his religious and political work and influence. Those who care for his poetry care for it more than for any other, or almost any other, of his time. Those who do not cannot be coaxed into liking it. His religious or theological influence he himself thought conservative. I remember his astonishment when to some account of a late book on this subject— I think *God and the Bible*—you, or rather, as I said before, one of the wilder spirits in your office, prefixed the headline "British Unbelief." He saw how much there is in current theological dogmas which it has become impossible to preserve. All the more he wanted to preserve what had not become impossible. But the orthodox were furious, and, I suppose, may for some time yet continue to be furious. If they but knew it, Arnold was on their side, only wiser than they.

He had no better fate in his handling of political topics. He was not and could not be a partisan. He applied to current disputes the solvent of a clear intelligence to which nothing was entirely admirable. I am afraid, had he been an American, you would have called him, as you call a man of a very different order of mind, Mr. Lowell, a Mugwump. His treatment of the Irish question is an example of what I mean, but into that I will not venture. Of persons he wrote with a freedom that sometimes gave offence. *Friendship's Garland* had long since proved that he had no prudishness in saying what he thought ought to be said, even though it might give pain to individuals. There was an almost equal want of reverence in his allusions to Mr. Sala and to Mr. Gladstone. His epithets sometimes stung; sometimes he changed them lest they might sting. It once happened that he said to a statesman with whom he had been conversing, "By the bye, I have written an article which is coming out in the next *Nineteenth Century*, in which I have called you an extraordinary young man." Nothing more was said, but when the article appeared the adjective extraordinary, which was probably used in an equivocal sense, had been cancelled, and a laudatory one had been substituted. The talk had shown him how he had misjudged his man. He proved in one celebrated instance how little he really had of that selfish vanity which is supposed to be characteristic of authors. The attempt to explain the Trinity by a reference to "the three Lord Shaftesburys" was, whatever else may be thought of it, one of the wittiest things in modern literature. But it gave offence, and when he was convinced of that he expunged it and expressed his regret for having wounded the susceptibilities of the very people who had least spared his. Nor did he ever seem to care how much publicity he conferred upon persons of no importance. If they served his purpose he named them. His books are full of examples, and posterity will be in many cases not a little puzzled to identify these flies in amber.

His circumstances in life have been much commented on. He was never rich and never poor. His Inspectorship of Schools gave him a moderate income, his books brought him in something, he was paid high prices for those magazine articles which he wrote rather freely late in life. When he resigned his place in the Education Department he continued to receive, under the rules governing the English Civil Service, a yearly sum equal to two-thirds of his salary. He had a pension upon the civil list in addition. Twice in his life, however, he sacrificed brilliant opportunities. The first was when, upon his marriage, he resigned the place as private secretary to the late Lord Lansdowne which he held from 1847 to 1851. To be private secretary in those days to a nobleman like Lord Lansdowne was to be sure of preferment, unless something happened to displease the nobleman. It was not natural that Arnold should pass from such a post to a mere school inspectorship. The second opportunity was during Mr. Gladstone's Ministry of 1880. Arnold had then become recognised as the great writer he was. His services to education had gone far beyond the routine of his office, and his reports on continental systems had impressed even the bureaucratic mind. Many men, and among them some Ministers, had long felt that the failure to provide some better place for a man like Arnold was a discredit to the Government. A Charity Commissionership fell opportunely vacant, worth £1200 a year. It was not magnificent but it was reckoned a prize in the Civil Service; pay fairly good, a life berth, and the duties not too laborious. Arnold's friends bestirred themselves. Mr. Gladstone gave a promise. The appointment was as definitely settled as such a thing can be; the commission actually drawn up and waiting for signature. Just then came out in some review one of those articles in which Arnold assailed the Dissenters with that gentle and terrible ridicule which has so often infuriated its victims. They turned upon him. Mr. Chamberlain, I believe, became their mouthpiece; himself, of course, a Dissenter and a Philistine. It is impossible to know just what was said or done, or what influences were brought to bear on Mr. Gladstone, but Mr. Gladstone yielded—he, the Churchman of Churchmen, sacrificed the advocate and champion of his Church to the wrath of the Church's enemies. The Charity Commissionership was given to another. Arnold never complained. All through his educational work he did the duties imposed upon him with cheerful loyalty. It was drudgery, but useful drudgery. What he might have done had Fortune showered her favours on him, it is idle to guess. There is a theory that he abandoned poetry because he questioned whether his own sincerity and passion were sufficient, or were quite irrepressible in verse. But to one who once asked him why he wrote so little poetry in his later days, he answered, "Ah, if you knew how much harder it is than prose!"

Arnold's place in English society was not perhaps quite what his American friends may have supposed. It is natural to imagine that the company of a man so gifted would be sought everywhere, and so it would have been, everywhere but in England. In England it was sought, but not universally until a comparatively late period. He was, of course, known to and liked by many of the best people in the best circles of that huge whirlpool to which the name society is now given. Thirty or forty years ago he might not have been much regarded by the merely fashionable world. Things have moved rapidly since then, and most rapidly of all during the latter part of that eventful period. Yet Hayward, who knew, if any man knew, what London society was like, once selected Arnold as the type of distinguished man whom the fashionable did not care for. We were discussing one morning at breakfast—it was in the days when breakfasts were still given—the way in which society was made up. Hayward said that literary men had no real position there, and he related how he had lately been asked to compose a list for a lady of great rank, new to London, who wanted to give good parties and dinners. "She would not have thanked me," said Hayward, "if I had put Matthew Arnold's name down." Some of us dissented; especially one man whose house had a renown of its own for smart assemblies. Hayward turned on him sharply: "Lady —— gave a party last night to the Prince and Princess of Wales. Whom had you there among all the writers and journalists and painters you know?" The suddenness of the assault took him by surprise but he contrived, by good luck, to indicate two or three of the company then present who had been invited by his wife, or, more probably, by himself. "Well," growled Hayward, "you don't pretend you had Arnold?"

This little scene occurred some ten years ago, perhaps twelve. It remains true that among those two or three sets of fashionable and (sometimes) frivolous but generally charming women who contend among themselves for precedence in smartness, Arnold was not a very frequent guest. They would, if they had thought on the matter, have said when challenged, "Oh, he is not in our set." A lady who had met him said he frightened her, and on being further interrogated explained that it was his gravity of manner which caused this state of alarm.

A still more significant anecdote may be related. One of Arnold's friends was lunching on Monday with a lady of great social position, whose rank is as high, or nearly as high, as any subject of the Crown can hold, and who bears an illustrious name. The news of Arnold's death had just come and this guest mentioned it to his hostess. She received it with a blank face—blank but for the expression of that effort toward polite interest which good breeding induced. Arnold's name was clearly unknown to her. By an effort of memory she presently identified him as a man who had written books.

He had, of course, the society he cared most for. He was a favourite with many of the most cultivated and intellectual people who make part of the English aristocracy, and was to be met at dinners, and even parties, for which perhaps he did not greatly care, and in some of the most delightful country houses in England. It is needless to say that in the world of letters, and among the people to whom literature and art are more than fashion, he was something more than a favourite; he held the place awarded to a master. Anything he desired socially was easily within his reach. He had been staying this year at a house not far from London whose owner is one of the ornaments of the patrician order; one of those men of character and high capacities whom it is permissible to the most severe Republican to admire in spite of his rank. Arnold's talk had kept the men—there were but two others, Dr. Jowett one of them—at table by themselves after dinner till long past the hour when custom required that they should rejoin the ladies. The ladies complained, and at once the other men agreed in laying the responsibility on Arnold. "We forgot the time, we forgot you; we were listening to him." A friend told me yesterday a curious proof of devotion. "You know Arnold dined with me pretty often and liked his glass of port. I gave him of course my best and I drank it with him, always at the expense of a sharp attack of gout next day."

Both at Wilton and at Aston Clinton he had been a guest within the last few weeks, as often before, and at both houses was thought in great spirits; his talk was continuous, his health apparently good. But when a walk was proposed he said, "Yes, only you must go at my pace." And he spoke of so arranging his house in London as not to be obliged to go above the ground-floor. He had long known that he had disease of the heart, and his physician, Sir Andrew Clark, had imposed upon him certain rules of life. I heard from a Liverpool acquaintance whom I met at the funeral the medical secret of his death. The little leap over a low fence which he had taken the day before was fatal. There was no reason why, but for some such accident, he might not have lived for many years.

How charming he was amid a circle of people who suited him! With those who did not suit him, and perhaps also among strangers, he could be less charming, and there were people no doubt who thought his manner—what shall I say?—oppressive. I have heard it said that he had a schoolmastering manner. It may have been so at moments. He had been set for a great part of his life to examine little boys and girls in reading and arithmetic. He was an Inspector of Her Majesty's Schools—that was what the governing powers in this practical country thought the best use they could find for this rare and delicate genius. He was tall, and he had no choice but to look down on these poor little atoms of humanity with whom he came into these inspectorial relations. So, perhaps, other larger atoms of humanity conceived the notion that he carried his head high. Let it be admitted that his mental attitude was sometimes that of the superior person. It could not be otherwise. His function, one of his chief functions in life, was criticism, and the critic is by necessity superior to the person criticised, if only for the time being. He is judge over him, and so long as he is judge sits in a higher seat. Nor was Arnold's superiority temporary or accidental. He was, moreover, the most convinced of men. His very moderation of statement proves it. He had no occasion to reassure himself by violence of language. Few men used fewer superlatives. His talk was less remarkable than his writing for brilliancy of phrase-making but it was admirable talk, and with all his autocratic ideas he had the art, the indispensable art, of catching the note of the company he was in.

I add for my own sake an acknowledgment of my obligations to Arnold. His friendship was a possession impossible to value too highly, but to the influence of his writings I owe more than to almost any of his time—in some very practical ways certainly more than to any other. This debt I share with others—with at least a whole generation. What his place may be in coming times it is useless to foretell. His influence, it has been well said, was so potent, the effect of it so thorough, that much of his work may be said to be done, and much of it lives in the writings and thoughts of other men. Thus, if not otherwise, has Arnold left a mark on English literature never to be effaced. So long as men admire purity, delicacy, distinction, sanity, so long will he in whom these qualities were supreme be a venerated and beloved figure.

MRS. PROCTER.

[LONDON, *March* 9, 1888.]

I HAVE in Mrs. Procter's handwriting a list, which she described as very imperfect, of famous men and women whom she had known. It fills two closely covered sheets of notepaper in double columns. The handwriting is wonderful—clear, firm, elaborate, every letter perfectly formed. If I should send it you, which I have not the least notion of doing, it would demoralise your composing office. She was eighty-six when she wrote it. She had an orderly mind, perhaps rather precise, and she has classified her celebrities into artists, dancers, musicians, actors and actresses, literary men; and has included no living person. I select a few, though as a rule nothing is less interesting than catalogues of names. Among the artists are Sir Thomas Lawrence, Turner, Landseer, Rossetti, Cruikshank, the unhappy Haydon, and De Wint. Fanny Ellsler and Taglioni are the two dancers. The musicians include Mendelssohn, Chopin, Liszt—not an English name among them. It is startling enough to see the actresses headed by Mrs. Siddons, who was born in 1755. In her august company are John and Charles Kemble, Edmund Kean, Macready, and Rachel. Not less startling is it to find among Mrs. Procter's literary acquaintances and friends Coleridge, Southey, Wordsworth, Landor. She names neither Byron nor Shelley, though I am sure I have heard her speak of Byron as if she had known him, and there is a story of her telling which fixes it, if correct. A party was going to Eton for the 4th June. "I have not been to Eton," said Mrs. Procter, "for some years. The last time I went I drove down with Dr. Parr and Byron!" Dr. Parr is on her list; so are Sydney Smith, Cooper — she is careful to label him "American"—Motley, who is unlabelled; Hazlitt, Leigh Hunt, Charles Lamb, De Quincey, Longfellow, Emerson, Dickens, Lord Jeffrey, Count D'Orsay, whose literary claims are not of the highest, Hood, and Thackeray.

I have known Mrs. Procter for many years and met her in many different circumstances. She was a lady whom it was impossible not to admire, and she had qualities that you could not but like. About her gathered a certain number of devotees, and a certain other number of persons with whom devotion was a matter of duty, or perhaps of obedience. She had regal notions of what was due to her, and there was occasionally something imperious in her way of expressing her wishes. Mr. Browning was one of the most regular attendants at her Sunday afternoon levee, yet Mr. Browning, I somehow fancied, had been more her husband's friend than hers, and kept up this exact intercourse out of regard to Barry Cornwall's memory, and deference to Mrs. Procter's expectations. Mr. Lowell was one of her most favoured friends, and Mr. Henry James another, and both showed her the most unremitting loyalty and friendship. Photographs and letters of and from each used to stand framed on the little table in her fireside corner. Mr. Kinglake was another of her court, and I could mention many more. Nobody came empty-handed; nobody went empty away. Not only was her memory faithful to the last but it was of that extraordinary kind which enabled her to avoid, for the most part, telling the same story twice to the same people.

I have named some of her friends. There is one who has perhaps a better right than all of them to be named, though whether I ought to mention him is another question. However, I will. I mean Mr. George Smith, whose friendship was of the most practical, helpful kind, and of a loyalty proof against every trial, if trials there were. To him she gave, I think some time before her death, the letters Thackeray had written her, but I fear it is understood that they are never to see the light. They are, or some of them are, of an interest much greater than those to Mrs. Brookfield, now in print.

When Mr. Froude published, not wisely, Carlyle's rough comments on the Basil Montagu household, Mrs. Procter, who was Basil Montagu's stepdaughter, took a characteristic revenge on the ungrateful Scot. She printed some of the letters he had written Montagu and Mrs. Montagu—letters acknowledging their kindness and services to him in terms not often employed by a person who feels himself on an equality with his correspondent. She never forgave either Carlyle or Mr. Froude. Hers, indeed, was not a forgiving nature; her idea of human nature was perhaps a little cynical. Carlyle had ill-requited the kindness shown him, and she forthwith appointed herself to do justice upon him and upon his biographer. "Our Lady of Bitterness" one friend called her. However, she uttered her bitter sayings with a felicity of speech which entitled some of them to pardon. Her skill in the use of the knife was surgical. I believe I dwell too much on these traits, but you would have no just idea of this extraordinary woman if I left them all out of the picture. She had masculine qualities, too; energy, decision, abruptness, clear ideas of what she wanted and how to get it. I meant to say much more, but I leave the best side of Mrs. Procter's nature to your friendly imagination.

LAURENCE OLIPHANT.

[LONDON, *December* 29, 1889.]

LAURENCE OLIPHANT, whose death we are all regretting, may or may not have secured a permanent place in literature. His books were undeniably clever and those which dealt with religious or abstruse subjects had the stamp of sincerity and of individual thought. It is for posterity to say whether they will read them or not. But he has, at any rate, a permanent place in the memories of those who knew him. He had what a man so seldom has—he had attractiveness. He was an accomplished man of the world who could, and did over and over again, renounce the world at a moment's notice. He was in Mayfair to-day, the celebrity and life of a smart dinner-party; to-morrow he was off for Southern Russia to look after suffering Jews, or to Palestine to meditate in his lonely hut on the deepest problems of life and of thought.

Nobody had led a more various life. Nobody had seen the world on more sides. Nobody could tell you more curious and amazing experiences than Oliphant, if he would. But I often thought that one of the most striking things about him was his perfect simplicity of manner. If you did not know him, and know about him, you would not guess that this quiet, gray-bearded gentleman, who conformed scrupulously to the nicest code of social behaviour, was the hero of a hundred strange adventures. If there was anything not quiet about him, it was his eyes. In them burned the consuming fire which would never let him rest. He talked readily about anything but himself, and talked racily and well. But what was more delightful than his talk was Oliphant himself. Very likely he had been round the world since you saw him six months ago, but he walked into the room as if he had come from the next street. He was a favourite in London society so long as he chose to stay. He might be absent for years but he resumed his place whenever he chose, and was as great a favourite as ever. In soul he was a crusader — disinterested, devoted, chivalrous, and ever ready to abandon anything he most cared for at the summons of what he deemed duty, or authority higher than his own.

Oliphant is responsible for one act which is known to journalists, but little known, probably, outside the profession. He is the inventor of M. de Blowitz, the Paris correspondent of *The Times*. He was himself for a while the representative of that journal in France, and M. de Blowitz was his secretary, or perhaps employed at first in some humbler capacity. I have heard a story which sounds as if the latter suggestion may be true. A friend was dining with Oliphant. A servant came in with a message. Said Oliphant to his guest, "One of my staff is here on business. Do you mind his coming in?" The guest did not mind and he of the staff was summoned to enter. Oliphant spoke to him as he stood by the table, gave him his orders and a glass of wine, and sent him about his business. It was M. de Blowitz. Whether he was then called by his present name, or M. Oppert, or M. Oppert de Blowitz, or had finally blossomed into M. de Blowitz, I cannot say. M. Oppert he certainly was in the beginning. There is, or was, a distinguished Frenchman named Oppert, who used to find himself confounded with his Bohemian namesake, and did not like it. It was he who told me of the confusion. I use the word Bohemian in its geographical or ethnographical sense. Oliphant—the story is well known—quitted *The Times* one day very suddenly, on a summons from his spiritual chief, Harris, or for some similar reason. He telegraphed the manager in London that he was obliged to sail at once for America, and could make no arrangement for a substitute, nor had any successor to propose, but that there was a sharp fellow in the Paris office who could look after things for a day or two, till they could send somebody over. The sharp fellow was M. de Blowitz, and he has looked after things in Paris ever since.

ROBERT BROWNING.

I.

NOTES ON SOME PERSONAL ASPECTS OF HIS CHARACTER.

[LONDON, *December* 18, 1889.]

MR. LOWELL says that the characteristic of Browning's poetry is strength. It was characteristic of the man, too, and not less characteristic of him was his cheeriness. His entrance into a room filled it with sunshine. He had more manner than is usual with Englishmen; long residence abroad had left its mark upon him, and he had adopted some habits from his beloved Italians. He had a way of his own of greeting his friends. The right hand was raised and half-extended sideways and came down into yours with a kind of swing, the other hand sometimes supporting yours against the shock. The voice was loud, at times almost harsh, or rather strident, and by no means always subdued to the conventional tone of the drawing-room; still less often of the dining-room, where he liked to sit, as it were, on a throne, which others were always ready to build for him.

He would talk admirably in any circumstances but he preferred a gallery, and the most successful dinners were those in which Browning himself bore sway. He could hold his own against competition, if need were—his voice, when he chose, filling the room; and he struck fearlessly into the current of talk, and was far too much a man of the world to expect always to have things his own way and every company to consist of idolaters. There were, however, certain houses where only the faithful were asked to meet him—personal friends, at least, if not devotees of his poetry; and there it was that he spoke most freely and on the subjects for which he cared most. I will not repeat what I have said before about his talk. It was various, full, and full of illumination at times; at other times, if he thought his fellow-guests commonplace he allowed his talk to sink to their level. Not that he ever suffered this to be seen; he had no arrogance and no airs of superiority; but if the people among whom he found himself preferred, like the Englishman in California, the weather as a topic, there was no one more ready than Browning to lend himself to this caprice.

Browning drank port wine by preference, and he has been known to say that claret was a drink for women, port for men. His robustness of nature expressed itself sometimes in an intolerance of whatever he thought less robust than his own. What he liked when dining out was to find a decanter of port at his plate, and in houses where he dined often and his tastes were known the decanter was always there. He used to protest against it but he drank the wine, moderately, and drank no other when he could get port. He was not a very good judge of the wine he loved so well. One of his oldest friends supplied him for many years with '34 port. I should think Browning, first and last, drank his full share of that famous vintage. The nectar passed his lips without remark. When it was all gone his host had to fall back on '51, a wine in the opinion of connoisseurs inferior to '34, not only in age but in those qualities on which the perfection of port depends. Browning then, for the first time, praised his drink. The taste is one he shared with Mr. Gladstone, and their appreciation of the wine was perhaps about equal.

He was quite free from all the little vanities and irritabilities in which lesser authors indulge themselves, but he set a just value on his position and on the various recognitions of it which came to him. He was delighted when Cambridge made him an honorary Master of Arts, a distinction almost unique. His Oxford degree pleased him, and his Honorary Fellowship of Balliol. When Lord Rosebery gave his state dinner to the Shah—a representative function and guests were expected to come in uniform or court dress—Browning wrote to his host that, being asked as a man of letters, he thought it might be proper if he wore his gown as Doctor of Civil Law. It struck everybody as a happy thought, and Browning's appearance in the flowing scarlet robes of the University was one of the events of the evening— pleased his host and the Shah and Mr. Gladstone and everybody else.

He was in all essential things perfectly simple and genuine — transparently so, sometimes. The beginning of the Browning societies was an instance. Shortly before, Mr. Furnivall had driven out of the new Shakespeare Society a great part of its best members by the extreme violence, and even brutality, of his attack on Mr. Swinburne, and on the late Mr. Halliwell Phillips. The Society was asked to disown Mr. Furnivall but the machinery was in his hands and nothing was done, so the secession took place. Browning and some of the seceders met at dinner, and there was a discussion from which he, though a member and, I think, vice-president, held aloof. He was pressed for an opinion but would give none, and when asked if he intended to remain member of a society responsible for Mr. Furnivall said, rather shortly, that he did. A few days later it came out that Mr. Furnivall was about to start a Browning Society.

The formation of these Browning societies undoubtedly pleased Browning. He had lived more than half his poetic life in neglect and under a cloud of critical hostility and obloquy, all which he had borne stoutly and for the most part silently, adhering through evil report and through good to the faith that was in him. His fame grew very slowly. "My publishers," he once said, "know just how many copies of a new poem they can sell; they print so many—no more and no less." But never was a more striking example of the truth of Emerson's remark that the influence of any writing is in mathematical proportion to its depth of thought. Whatever else there might be, or might not be, in Browning's books there was plenty of hard thinking, and some of it was so hard that these societies were formed to make it easier. It was an act of homage to which he would have been more or less than human not to be sensible.

It came at a critical period, and he was a more important figure in literature by reason of the existence of these societies. He was quite aware of the ludicrous side of the business, and the effusive enthusiasms of his least wise admirers annoyed him more than he chose to own. One or two American societies seemed to have been founded and worked with little regard to that American sense of humour which so often saves people from ridicule. He was patient with them, accepted their tributes of admiration, took the will for the deed when the expression of it was absurd, and rejoiced to know that, beneath all the nonsense on the surface, there was a basis of real appreciation for what he himself most valued in his own writings. When appealed to, he no more professed always to know what he had meant than Rufus Choate to decipher his own handwriting after a lapse of time.

Before the time of the societies and their practical proofs of the difficulties that beset his verse, he used to be rather impatient of any suggestion that he was difficult, or more difficult than a thinker ought to be, and must be. This he expressed with startling simplicity. "They talk," said Browning one night to a dozen people, " of my being obscure. Do they consider that the commentators have been at work on Shakespeare for 200 years and have not made him out yet?" What answer could be given to that? He has been heard to assert that there is not a sentence in his poems which cannot be parsed. Carlyle said the same thing of his own prose.

Sometimes he burst out against the critics, much in the manner of Lord Beaconsfield's celebrated explosion: "Men who cannot write a sentence of English complain that I do not write English. They don't know whether I do or not." And there was one critic, himself a writer of verse, of whom Browning never could speak with patience. The man had misquoted him, and based his censure on the misquotation. "Yet I suppose he could read," said the indignant poet. The offender shall remain nameless.

There certainly was a time when Browning and Matthew Arnold were not very cordial. No two men could be more unlike in their conceptions of literature, and Arnold had expressed his in his usual fearless way with reference to some one of Browning's more inscrutable performances—the *Hohenstiel-Schwangau*, I think. When Arnold walked into the room Browning all but turned his back on him. The mood did not last, happily. The man of the world resumed his accustomed sway over the poet, and before dinner was over Browning had swallowed down his wrath and found himself able to converse with Arnold with good humour, though still stiffly. No one need blame either of the two nor is any stone to be cast at Browning because he was impatient of criticism which stood between him and the general appreciation he thought his due. He had spent his life in loyalty to an ideal, and whatever may be thought of the ideal, the loyalty and sincerity of the man are beyond praise. He used to say that he welcomed foreign opinion as the opinion of posterity. "You get proofs enough of it from America."—"Oh no," he answered, "I don't consider American opinion foreign opinion." It is a remark commonly enough heard in these days from English lips, but it came from Browning with a meaning which the American man of letters may well consider deeply.

II.

HIS POETRY AND HIS STYLE TESTED BY THE OPINIONS OF FOUR GREAT MASTERS OF STYLE.

[LONDON, *December* 24, 1889.]

"I wish," said Coleridge, "our clever young poets would remember my homely definitions of prose and poetry; that is, Prose—Words in their best order; Poetry—The best words in the best order." It would be difficult to find anywhere in literature a simpler definition of poetry. Coleridge is speaking of poetry with reference to poetic form, to style, and that is his requirement—merely the best words in the best order. He was himself a poet of a very high order, and a penetrating critic, with a great knowledge of books and with a habit of thinking things out. What he says on literary questions is never said flippantly; he is an authority. You may not accept his opinion but you know that it is of weight and must be put aside, if at all, otherwise than by mere impatience.

If then you take Coleridge's law and apply it to Browning, it condemns nine-tenths at least of all he has ever written. Even if it were possible to admit that Browning's words were the best there lives not the critic, I suppose, bold enough to say that these best words are in the best order. But it is not possible to admit that the words are the best. They are often forcible, picturesque, chosen with a singular power of fitting them to the fact he wishes to describe or the idea he wishes to express. But they are often without elevation, and of Browning's diction as a whole it has to be said that the prevailing note is not distinction.

The manner in which he has flung his words upon the page is equally without dignity. Nothing is more instructive than to note how the dignity of the thought is impaired by the want of it in the expression; by familiarity, by colloquialism, by—I regret to use the word—vulgarity. It was not in Browning's nature to be vulgar; there was nothing of vulgarity in the man himself. When he descended to it in print he did it wilfully; he wanted to get a certain effect; as Turner said, he would use mud from the gutter to get the effect he wanted for his painting. Turner injured many a noble picture by such caprices, and Browning has injured his poetry. He has lowered the tone, and he has sometimes sacrificed the thought or the idea itself. One of the greatest masters of style—the greatest in French literature, Pascal, whose few pages on eloquence and style are all of gold—says, "The sense changes as the words which express it change; the thought derives its dignity from the words instead of imparting its own to the words." I do not quote examples from Browning. His poems are examples throughout; hardly a page can be opened on which striking instances of this want of dignity in the use of words do not occur. I am writing for those who know him and appeal to their memory of what is constant and characteristic in him.

That Browning was a great poetic force not many now doubt or deny. But it is to be remembered how recent is the date when even this began to be commonly seen and acknowledged. He has been writing for more than fifty years. *Pauline* was published in 1833. Allibone's *Dictionary of English Literature* appeared a quarter of a century later and he allows Browning half a column—half as much as to the author of *The Columbiad*, and one twenty-eighth part of the space he devotes to Longfellow. Allibone was the least critical of human beings but he had, in a rough sort of way, a feeling for what was popular, and knew what people would want to read about and how much they would read. I quote him exactly as I should quote the figures from Browning's publishers' books, to indicate the vogue and circulation of his poems. His popularity is not twenty years old.

Nay, when he died, the most fashionable of the London daily papers wrote of him in a tone of supercilious patronage, with a sort of apology to its readers for asking their attention to a writer so remote from their world as Browning. That is behind the time and foolish, yet I suspect that Browning's poetry was far less known to the world of London than Browning himself. So far as he was read in society—which reads little—he was read by the younger generation of fashionable people; to the older he was, I might almost say, unknown. He was literally unknown to some. I have heard the mention of his name followed by the remark, "Browning? Is he not an American novelist?" The lady who put that question is a personage in society, full of every kind of social intelligence, and it was not many years ago. I doubt whether he has ever been the poet of the classes. The masses, or some of them, were probably those who read him most. The critics have praised him with very large reservations. But there was a class of readers neither literary nor smart who found in Browning something they wanted and who, for the sake of the kernel, were willing to prick their fingers with the husk or bruise their joints over the shell. They are the people to whom the problems of life are everything, and what drew them to Browning was his penetration and power in handling these problems. They would equally have been drawn to him had he written avowedly in prose. To them the substance was everything, the form nothing.

It avails nothing to quote Coleridge or quote anybody else to readers of this class. Bright was the type, the incarnation, of this middle-class—and generally non-conformist—audience from which the Browning recruits were drawn. Not that Bright read Browning, or cared for him as a poet; he did not. But what Bright valued in poetry was the expression of some feeling, religious first, then political, which he himself held strongly, or the effort toward the clearing up of some spiritual mystery. In literature of other kinds and of earlier periods, Bright had high ideals; Milton was his master, and had taught him much. But in what was of to-day he was practical, not to say prosaic; he cared too much for causes to be concerned with pure literature. Whittier was a Quaker, and wrote against slavery; all honour to him. Had there but been an English poet of equal calibre whose muse had sung the repeal of the Corn Laws, him too would Bright have honoured before all others. Well, there has always been a theological leaven in that great class among whom Bright was the greatest. There are hundreds who brood over the mysteries which Browning brooded over. It was a surprise to them to find that here was one who dared say in print, without reserve, what they hardly dared think in the secrecy of their closets. They devoured him, and it was out of their ranks that the Browning societies were recruited in England, with the astonishing Mr. Furnivall at their head. He, however, stands in a different relation to the Master. Browning interested Mr. Furnivall because Mr. Furnivall is a student of words; he is that, and not much more; a man to whom the idea of beauty is alien.

"The idea of beauty," says Matthew Arnold—"the idea of beauty and of a human nature perfect on all sides is the dominant idea of poetry." If Browning is to be tried by this law he will be condemned just as certainly as under Coleridge's. He had indeed a sense, and a very fine sense, of beauty; keen perceptions of it, and sympathies with what is beautiful, and a passionate love for it even. But will any one who reads him, who struggles with his abrupt, harsh, confused sentences, say that the idea of beauty is the dominant one with him? Nor does it help him if we add with Arnold, "the idea of a human nature perfect on all sides," as the other element of true poetry, for beauty is one of those sides, unless you conceive it as, for poetic purposes, enveloping the whole. When Browning sat down to write, the idea of beauty in spirit was still with him but the beauty of form, which is vital to poetry, he deliberately trampled under foot.

It may be put still more simply. Browning, as between himself and his reader, never did his fair share of the work. He gave processes, not results. He would not—he must have had a theory on the subject—complete his thought, or the expression of it. As it comes into his mind so it goes down on the written and printed page. He defies the known laws of syntax and disregards the known laws of literary form. He gives us, not a poem, but the materials of a poem; often in the rawest state. He has discovered, deep down in his own soul, a mine of gems and precious stones. He digs them up and brings them to the surface. He will not cut or polish them; he flings them before you all rough and shapeless. He writes a kind of poetical shorthand, or, as it were, poetry by cable. He gives you the key-words, hardly more; and we who have to decipher him, at the other end of the wire, are expected to supply the missing links and parts of speech essential to convert the whole into English. His sixteen printed volumes are chips from a poet's workshop.

But when you reflect that the writer of whom this can be affirmed, and of whom it is literally and strictly true, appeals to the public as a poet, what else can be said unless it be, in Johnson's phrase, that here was the potentiality of a poet, and of a very great poet; but of one who, unhappily, wrought on a theory or under impulses which made true poetry—"the tender charm of poetry"—impossible? Browning has the most splendid and admirable qualities. He has passion, he has sincerity, he has wide sympathies, he has a power of thinking deeply on some of the deepest subjects, he has a profound spiritual insight and spiritual energy, he has imagination, he has invention, he has reading, he has manliness and nobleness of nature, he has studied the human soul as hardly anybody else has studied it, and the mistake of his life was when he resolved that the expression of these gifts and qualities should be metrical, and that the world should accept Browning the thinker, the metaphysician, the man, as Browning the poet. "The man," said Emerson, "is only half himself; the other half is his expression." The expression, in Browning's case, is deplorable. Let any student ask himself what is the influence of this author upon his own writing. Let him read Browning, saturate his mind with him, and then sit down and try to write simply and clearly. The struggle will be a lesson to him. Here, unhappily, is a poet who has not distinction of style, and who has not urbanity of style, and who has not lucidity. They are the three qualities in which English literature is most wanting, the three qualities by which two or three great writers, in these modern days, have conferred the greatest benefit upon English literature. It is the want of them which makes Browning's influence as a writer mischievous; which, were his influence on English style to be permanent or widespread, would make it a disaster.

THE MASTER OF BALLIOL.

[LONDON, *October* 11, 1882.]

THE appointment of Dr. Jowett to the Vice-Chancellorship of the University of Oxford is recognised by everybody as a shining illustration of the new liberalism in the University. And not in the University only, but throughout England. The fact that Dr. Jowett was entitled by custom to the post does not lessen the significance of the event. The Vice-Chancellor goes out of office every four years and the then oldest Head of a college has a claim to succeed him. Dr. Jowett as Master of Balliol had this claim. None the less the nomination is in the hands of the Chancellor of the University, and the Chancellor of the University is Lord Salisbury. If he had chosen to pass over Dr. Jowett and select the next in turn, I apprehend no legal authority could have compelled him to respect precedent. Twenty years ago the Lord Salisbury of that day would surely have done it. Now, there is hardly a hint that Lord Salisbury thought of deviating from routine, and hardly a criticism upon him for installing as his vicegerent a man who is correctly and triumphantly described as an unrepentant heretic.

For heretic Dr. Jowett surely was in the eye of the great body of the Church twenty years ago. If he was not heretic in the technical sense he was something in their eyes much worse. He was not then Master of Balliol but the Regius Professor of Greek. Lord Palmerston's influence had got him that place in 1855. In 1860 he appeared as one of the authors of *Essays and Reviews,* and the storm broke on his head as on other heads which were concerned in the writing of that famous volume. He had made himself known by other means, and the country parsons of England, then a not too enlightened body, sought a characteristic revenge. Those of them who were graduates of Oxford had a right of voting in certain University matters. They tried to expel Dr. Jowett from his Professorship, and when they failed in that, voted to withhold his salary. This piece of clerical ill-temper did as much as any one thing to make the Professor popular. Presently he became Master of Balliol—some eight years later—and his reputation as a dangerous man did not prevent him from making his college foremost in the University. To be a Balliol man is of itself almost a distinction, and in academic distinctions—in the winning of university prizes and honours—it is some years since any other college has had a chance of rivalling Balliol. As a teacher, as a college head, as a leader of youth, Dr. Jowett may be likened to a very different man, the late Dr. Arnold. Their methods were not the same but their hold on the young men of their day is equally remarkable.

It is worth noting that of the five clerical authors out of the seven who contributed to *Essays and Reviews*, three were afterward promoted either in the Church or the University. The Rev. Mark Pattison was made Rector of Lincoln College the very next year. Dr. Temple, the Head-master of Rugby, was appointed in 1869 by Mr. Gladstone Bishop of Exeter. Few people can have forgotten the excitement and agitation which followed. An attempt was instantly set on foot to induce the Dean and Chapter to refuse to elect in pursuance of the *congé d'élire*. The Church Union naturally led the way. Dr. Pusey denounced the appointment as a horrible scandal. Though the capitular election is only a form there were six votes against to thirteen for Dr. Temple, and when the ceremony of confirmation took place twenty policemen were required to keep the peace in the church. Against his consecration eight bishops protested, formally or informally. The Bishop of London himself, who performed the ceremony, made a speech regretting that Dr. Temple had not published some declaration or recantation, and regretfully avowing that he had no alternative but to obey the royal mandate. I suppose Dr. Temple lived long enough to regret the apology he did subsequently make, and his withdrawal of his essay from the book. Contrast all this with the acquiescence and approval which thirteen years later greet Dr. Jowett's appointment to a place of administrative authority in the University of Oxford.

Meantime Dr. Jowett has gone on extending his fame as a scholar by the translations of Plato and of Thucydides. He has renounced none of his heresies. It is understood that the antipathy which Lord Salisbury as Defender of the Faith may feel to him is softened by some degree of political sympathy. Dr. Jowett is an example of the conservative influence in politics of humane studies, as M. Renan and M. Taine are in France. In truth, he never was an unbeliever in religion; at most a sceptic on some points; and polite scepticism about the beneficence of modern reform is at the bottom of his political conservatism. There is some point in the remark of a Liberal critic: "The most superfine moralising in the lecture-room did not prevent Balliol from being the home of a sort of cherubic Jingoism."

It can do no harm to take down once more from its shelf the dusty volume which two-and-twenty years ago convulsed the ecclesiastical world in England. The first edition—it went through many—has long been a scarce book; a well-shaped and well-printed octavo with the respectable imprint of orthodox publishers, Messrs. Parker and Son. Appearing to-day for the first time, it would convulse nothing; its radicalism has long since become the creed of church conservatives; there is nothing new in it, though something that is true. It can be read, in parts, if without great profit still without weariness, but almost with a sense that its interest is historical. The men who figure in it have grown old; two of the best known are dead; the contest in which they were engaged is going on but is fought in new fields. The militant clergy have abandoned the intrenchments they then defended, and what this volume really marks is the site of the victory then won for free thought and free inquiry.

Essays and Reviews was published in 1860, and Dr. Jowett's was not the least notable of the contributions to it. At that time the Church still held out for the Mosaic cosmogony. The efforts to reconcile the legend of Genesis with the facts of geology had not been abandoned. The doctrine of the verbal inspiration of the Scriptures was maintained with vehemence, and the charge of infidelity was one which the students of physical science and of philology both had to meet. It is hard to believe that it is less than a quarter of a century since this state of things existed, but so it is, and the outcry against Dr. Jowett can only be understood by reference to it.

Dr. Jowett's subject was the Interpretation of Scripture, and if I may use a familiar term he "gave away" his fellow-professors and clergymen. A sentence or two will show why they resented his defection so keenly. "Almost all intelligent persons," said he "are agreed that the earth has existed for myriads of ages; the best informed are of opinion that the history of nations extends back some thousand years before the Mosaic chronology; recent discoveries in geology may perhaps open a further vista of existence for the human species, while it is possible, and may one day be known, that mankind spread not from one but from many centres over the globe; or, as others say, that the supply of links which are at present wanting in the chain of animal life may lead to new conclusions respecting the origin of man."

To judge of the effect of such a passage as that, one has but to bear in mind that Darwin's *Origin of Species* had been published only the year before. The controversy which that book roused was then in the full vigour and virulence of its earliest period, and here from the bosom of the Church and from the monastic recesses of the University of Oxford itself came a voice on the side of the apes.

Hardly less offensive—certainly not less so to that great body of well-meaning persons who were sticklers for the plenary inspiration of the Bible—was Dr. Jowett's calm statement of the laws of interpretation of the Scriptural text:—

"But, however different the subject, although the interpretation of Scripture requires 'a vision and faculty divine,' or at least a moral and religious interest which is not needed in the study of a Greek poet or philosopher, yet in what may be termed the externals of interpretation, that is to say, the meaning of words, the connection of sentences, the settlement of the text, the evidence of facts, the same rules apply to the Old and New Testament as to other books."

This he sums up later in a single italicised sentence: "*Interpret the Scripture like any other book.*" There are other equally striking passages in this essay; equally striking then, equally commonplace now; but this is not the place to quote them. I may cite a line or two which does touch on a question now more burning than it was then:—

"It has not been sufficiently considered that the difficulties of the New Testament are for the most part common to the Greek and the English. The noblest translation in the world has a few great errors, more than half of them in the text; but 'we do it violence' to haggle over the words. Minute corrections of tenses or particles are no good; they spoil the English without being nearer the Greek. Apparent mistranslations are often due to a better knowledge of English rather than a worse knowledge of Greek."

That might have been written yesterday as a criticism on the Revised Version of the New Testament; to which it applies with singular closeness and force.

The great popularity of Dr. Jowett has come to him in spite of some defects of manner which are obvious and leave at times a wrong impression on the casual acquaintance. People who insist on animal resemblances in the human countenance would liken the Master of Balliol to some bird; especially to one which does not exist. He has the beak of a young eagle and the eyes of an owl not young. An acute benignancy is the predominant expression of his face. If you did not look close enough you might describe him as childlike and bland. A second glance will reveal the shrewdness and alertness of the features and the amplitude of the head, of which the lines are scarcely at all hid by a little snowy hair that sets off a softly rubicund complexion. His ways with his pupils are the subject of many a story—some hardly compatible with the dignity of his favourite historian. But he is none the less honoured in his own country, his own town, his own university, his own college, and his own circle of friends.

LORD LYTTON.

[LONDON, *November* 2, 1887.]

An idea has gone forth that Lord Lytton is sent to Paris in order to make the English Embassy once more a social centre. Lord Lyons has, perhaps, during his long tenure of office, undervalued social influences, or perhaps overestimated the social difficulties which the very complicated life of Paris offers. He did little more than he was obliged to do. The stately rooms of the great mansion in the Rue Faubourg St. Honoré have remained almost empty for the last twenty years. The English Ambassador was not a personage in French society except as Ambassador, nor was he, in truth, well fitted to take the lead in enterprises which require social initiative, frankness of address, cordiality of manner, and other the like gifts on which Frenchmen set a higher value than any other people in the world. He never tried to do what the late American Minister and Mrs. Morton accomplished. There was no Lady Lyons, and no man, however gifted, could have created such a salon as Mrs. Morton's. The American Legation, for the first time in its history, then became a real social centre. If anybody thinks that a slight matter or a thing easily managed, let him or her go to Paris and try.

Lord Lytton, however, is about to try, and Lady Lytton may be compared with Mrs. Morton as a hostess whose accomplishments command success. She was a Villiers, daughter to the Hon. Edward Villiers, and niece to that well-known fourth Earl of Clarendon who was twice Minister of Foreign

Affairs and before that had been Her Britannic Majesty's Plenipotentiary at the Court of Madrid, where occurred that event which had, much later, so grave an influence on the destinies of the late Emperor Napoleon and of France. If the French were as well up in genealogy as in gossip, something might be said of Lord Clarendon. The Villiers family has had more than one fascinating representative, and Lady Lytton's surviving uncle, Mr. Charles Villiers, one of the heroes of the Corn Law agitation, is to-day one of the most interesting men in London.

The English Embassy, moreover, offers advantages such as no American Legation could pretend to. It is a palace, and it has all the prestige which belongs to a palace and to a permanent diplomatic home. The American Legation in Paris, as in London, is here to-day and gone to-morrow. Mr. Morton arranged his diplomatic life handsomely. He occupied a large hotel, to use the French word, on the Place des États Unis, which the civil Parisians presently renamed in honour of the country he represented. But when Mr. Morton ceased to be Minister the hotel at the top of the Place des États Unis ceased to be the United States Legation. A salon may go to pieces much more rapidly than it is formed.

Perhaps an Embassy or Legation is now the only house in Paris where the various sections of Parisian society can meet. Political divisions are carried into society. There is, it may be said, no society. There are only social cliques. The Faubourg St. Germain long since closed its doors on outsiders, and even on itself. The watchword of the Legitimist faction is seclusion, so long as the Republic lasts. It is not thought good form to give balls and great parties while the king is kept from his own and while the princes are in exile. The La Rochefoucaulds and De Broglies are resolved that the Republic shall be dull, shall borrow no reflected splendour from the gaieties of a royalist aristocracy. While the Legitimists and Orleanists were divided into two camps they visited each other but little. Now they may fraternise, but at none of the great houses are great entertainments habitually given. The *haute bourgeoisie*, the great bankers, the *haute finance* of Paris, the Boulevard Haussmann and the Faubourg St. Honoré are divided from the Faubourg St. Germain as by a great gulf, and by a narrower one from each other. It was an event when the Duc de la Rochefoucauld-Bisaccia went on from his own house with the Prince of Wales and a few other friends to the great banker's whose new hotel in the Boulevard Haussmann was one of the wonders of Paris. As for the Élysée and the ministerial residences, their receptions are purely official. If you ask a true Parisienne why she does not go to these festivities, she will shrug her pretty shoulders still further out of her gown and tell you that the Republican women are impossible — a phrase of which the responsibility and also the explanation must be left to her.

Well, this is the social chaos out of which Lord Lytton has to create a new social life in the English Embassy. His enemies dwell bitterly on his political mistakes. They do not deny to him rare social qualities and gifts, or a graceful genius for verse. The French are such a singular people that Lord Lytton's literary reputation will be of as much help to him in Paris as his title. They will never be able to distinguish between the one he inherited from his father and the one which he earned for himself. The chances are that the French papers will call him Lord Owen or Sir Meredith, and at intervals, in respectful memory of the late novelist, Sir Bulwer. He is a "milord," and one kind of a lord is almost as good as another to a nation which, although fond of decorations, cares more for equality than for almost anything else. The distinction which literature confers in France is certainly of a higher kind than in England, and Lord Lytton may reap the benefit of his own and of his father's.

It may be thought curious that Englishmen should lay so much emphasis on the fact that he can speak French fluently and elegantly. They have always had a certain surly pride in their incapacity to sustain a conversation in foreign languages. They repeat to you with evident pleasure Prince Bismarck's observation that the late Lord Ampthill (better known as Lord Odo Russell) was the only Englishman he ever knew who was fluent in French and yet could be trusted. Lord Lytton was Secretary to the Paris Embassy from 1872 to 1874, and he may be forgiven his proficiency in the French tongue. The French themselves, be it observed, are sensitive to the compliment, as they think it, paid them by a foreigner who talks to them freely in their own language. They seldom return it.

What the French value not less is that flexibility of character which enables a man to adopt the tone of a world different from his own. It might not be easy to say what is, or was, Lord Lytton's world. He has lived abroad in the diplomatic service of his country almost all his life, beginning with America where he was attaché to his uncle, Sir Henry Bulwer, in 1849, and ending with Portugal, where he was Minister when Lord Beaconsfield startled England and India at once by making him Viceroy of the latter. He has lived in Florence, in the Netherlands, in Russia, in Turkey, in Austria, in Denmark, in Greece, in Spain, and in France. If ever an Englishman gets his English insularity rubbed off him, Lord Lytton has got rid of his; supposing he had any to begin with. You cannot meet him without seeing that he is an accomplished man of the world, and of many worlds. In no company would you pass him without asking who he is. His stature is not excessive, but the whole appearance of the man is striking. The square high forehead is set in a mass of dark curling hair. Blue eyes look from under it, half-dreamily. The features are strong and well cut, where visible, but all the lower part of the face is enveloped by a beard, dark curling like the hair, which a fanciful person might call Assyrian. Refinement, thoughtfulness, reflectiveness, acuteness, under a well-worn mask of unconcern— these are its characteristics. London society is well aware of his unlikeness to the average man of London society. You somehow get at once the impression that here is a personage for whom the world has no surprises in reserve. He has an imperturbable politeness which, in a country where people are expected to be demonstrative, might pass for indifference.

When Lord Lytton does talk he talks exceedingly well. He is full, various, novel; it is the talk of a man who has seen many sides of life, of a man who has read and written, of a poet, sometimes of a man of letters and of affairs. There is a flavour in it which is exotic. India has left a mark on him. The eyes are those of one who does not mean to be taken at an advantage; the whole demeanour as of one accustomed to his own place and to maintain it without an effort. He is, I believe, a favourite at Marlborough House, where very various reasons may be given for whatever favouritism is in vogue at the moment. Americans may remember Lord Lytton's appearance at the Lyceum on one memorable evening in the royal box. Miss Mary Anderson was the magnet who drew the princely party thither, and Lord Lytton's elaborate panegyric on Miss Anderson in *The Nineteenth Century* was perhaps the result of this visit. Rarely indeed has any dramatic criticism seen the light which was so minute in its record of gestures and expressions and fleeting glances and hidden purposes of the actress which, to an observer less skilled or less enthusiastic, would have remained hidden.

But like his friend Lord Beaconsfield, Lord Lytton is capable of much silence. In uncongenial company he carries taciturnity to its last permissible limit. In public he practises it as a virtue. There is a story of his final interview with Lord Beaconsfield before setting out for that Viceroyalty which was to bring so much censure on his head. The two men talked long together, and had said good-bye, and Lord Lytton was already on his way down-stairs when Lord Beaconsfield leaned over the rail and said, "One thing more, Lytton. You are going to India to carry out a great policy which a strong party in this country will oppose. You will be much attacked in the papers. Never answer them. Whatever you do, remember that I shall stand by you." The pledge was fulfilled. The injunction was obeyed. The two men were loyal to each other. Whatever Lord Lytton did in India or in Afghanistan, Lord Beaconsfield defended in Parliament. When Lord Beaconsfield resigned his Viceroy resigned with him. The Prime Minister put his own and Lord Lytton's resignation into the Queen's hands at the same moment. The storm that raged about the Viceroy and his Afghan policy fell with its full force on his chief at home, but he never flinched and never forsook his friend and servant, and he made him an earl as his last act. The discredited ruler of India—for in current public opinion he certainly was discredited—came home, and for the first time undertook to defend himself. There was a dress debate in the House of Lords. The ex-Viceroy delivered a speech; The Duke of Argyll answered him, and from that day to this Lord Lytton cannot be said to have taken part in public life. But he once more has before him a career splendid enough and serious enough to stimulate any man's ambition.

M. RENAN AND MARCUS AURELIUS.

[LONDON, *November* 16, 1881.]

ONE of the most crowded assemblies ever seen in a place which has seen many was present in the lecture-room of the Royal Institution on Friday evening, April 16, 1880. The lecturer was M. Renan, his subject Marcus Aurelius. Nobody who heard M. Renan that night will forget the beauty of his manner. The impression he left was a durable one; singularly so for London, where life hurries at a pace unknown elsewhere and the topic of to-day succeeds that of yesterday with pitiless rapidity. Marcus Aurelius became, for at least a week, the fashion in circles where a tincture of literature is permitted. M. Renan himself was a lion of no mean celebrity. Before the Royal Institution welcomed him, he had been giving a course of Hibbert Lectures, and as the Hibbert Lectures are, or are supposed to be, religious in their character, the invitation to the author of the *Vie de Jésus* had disturbed some pious souls and provoked some rather sharp comment from ecclesiastical dignitaries. A slight scandal of that sort inflicts no social injury; adds, it may be, a piquancy to the popularity of its object.

There could be no doubt about M. Renan's popularity. Nobody quite like him had ever been seen in a London drawing-room. People looked with some wonder and some incredulity on the short man with short thin legs and vast body, broad in the shoulders and still more capacious in the abdominal regions, who was pointed out as M. Renan. The ample but rapidly receding dome of the head, thinly covered with white locks, surmounted features of which none were fine. The eyes were small and restless, the nose long and rather bulbous, the chin square, and seeming more square than it was from the masses of pendulous flesh which hung about and below it; the flesh of a lifelong student to whom all rules of health were matters of indifference; sedentary, indefatigable, capable alike of the patient, half-mechanical toil which is a condition of mastering any great subject, and of hard thinking not less patient. There were good lines in the face when you came to study it, but in the general contour of the man was visible nothing whatever of the ascetic quality which an Englishman associates with the idea of scholarship. Between the grossness of the physical frame and the refinement of M. Renan's conversation and manner, the contrast was violent; and that also added to the attraction he exercised on all who came in contact with him. What he endured from being left to stand for hours in crowded rooms, besieged by admirers, will never be known. He bore it with that polite stoicism which is supposed to be characteristic of the French in general, but which recalls in his case what he said of his latest hero, *Comme les gens qui ont été très bien élevés, Marc-Aurèle se gênait sans cesse.* Altogether, people found him charming. He was received by his brilliant audience at the Royal Institution with enthusiasm. He acknowledged it with grace and returned it with warmth; going so far as to identify himself in a sort with his English hosts by virtue of his Breton origin. It was said of him that, with the exception of M. Louis Blanc, no Frenchman had ever been known to speak French so easily intelligible to the English ear. The truth was, M. Renan never forgot that he was addressing an audience to whom French, though more or less familiar for certain purposes, was a foreign tongue. He spoke slowly, articulated each word clearly, and when he came to a colloquial phrase pronounced at least two-thirds of the syllables composing it.

These and many other memories of M. Renan are revived by the publication of the elaborate work on Marcus

Aurelius,[1] of which he gave us that night a foretaste. The discourse as delivered, omitting a few words, was soon after published with the Hibbert Lectures in a small volume entitled *Conférences d'Angleterre*. There is certainly no sketch in existence from which so vivid a notion of the author of the *Thoughts* can be got. That which Mr. George Long prefixed to his translation of the Emperor's immortal legacy exhibits Mr. Long's usual diligence in the collection of facts, and that is the best that can be said of it. It is an inventory of matters relating to Marcus Aurelius. M. Renan's is a portrait, and a portrait in which the most subtle traits of character and the inmost secrets of the soul are made visible.

This is not a work separate and complete in itself but the seventh and concluding volume of the *Histoire des Origines du Christianisme*. M. Renan modestly refers to these volumes as a series of essays. No one of them has made so deep mark as the first, the *Vie de Jésus*, but the European public long since accepted M. Renan as an authority and his work as the most serious contribution of the time to the immense subject he dealt with. The Preface to this volume contains a most interesting account of the spirit in which its author has wrought, of his object, and of what he proposes in the future. "I have sought," he says, "without any other passion than a very keen curiosity, to apply methods of criticism which in these delicate matters are of recognised authority in our days, to the most important religious apparition which has a place in history. Ever since my youth I have been busy at this work. The preparation of the seven volumes of which it consists has taken me twenty years."

M. Renan adds: "I thank *la bonté infinie* for having given me the time and zeal necessary for carrying out this difficult programme." *La bonté infinie* can only mean infinite goodness, but the way in which the phrase is used, and the non-employment of capital letters, leave it open to con-

---

[1] *Marc-Aurèle et la Fin du Monde Antique:* par Ernest Renan, Paris. C. Lévy, 1881.

jecture whether the deity to whom M. Renan expresses his gratitude be or be not a personal deity. It is still more interesting to know that M. Renan does not even now consider his task complete. He began, so to speak, in the middle; he is about to begin again with the beginning. He began with Jesus, but Christianity in his view really dates its origin from the eighth century before Christ. The prophets, and among the prophets Isaiah especially, were the true founders of Christianity. "All Jesus really did was to repeat, in popular and charming language, what had been said seven hundred and fifty years before him in classical Hebrew." This was M. Renan's opinion when he wrote his first book; it is his opinion still. It is stated in language too precise and remarkable to be abridged. The whole passage is as follows:—

Inasmuch as some years of labour may still be left to me, I shall devote them to working out completely and in another direction the subject about which my thoughts have grouped themselves. To be strictly logical I ought to have begun a History of the Sources of Christianity by a history of the Jewish people. Christianity begins in the eighth century before Jesus Christ, at the moment when the great prophets, establishing their authority over the people of Israel, made of them the people of God, with the behest to set up pure religion in the world. Down to that time the worship of Israel had not differed in essence from the egotistic, self-seeking worship which was common to all the neighbouring tribes, as revealed, for example, by the inscription of King Mesa. A revolution was accomplished the day when a man inspired, but not belonging to the priesthood, dared to say, "Can you believe that God is pleased with the smoke of your victims, the fat of your goats? Away with all these sacrifices which only excite disgust; do good." Isaiah is in that sense the first founder of Christianity; all that Jesus has done is to repeat, in popular and charming language, what had been said seven hundred and fifty years before him in classical Hebrew. To show how the religion of Israel, which in its origin had perhaps no superiority over the worship of Ammon or of Moab, became a moral religion, and how the religious history of the Jewish people has been a constant progress toward "worshipping in spirit and in truth"—that, assuredly, is what ought to have been shown before introducing Jesus upon the scene of action. But life is short and its duration uncertain. I went about that which was most urgent: I plunged into the middle of the subject, and I began with the life of Jesus, assuming the earlier revolutions of the Jewish religion to be known. Now that it has been vouchsafed to me to treat the part which I thought most important with all the care I wished, I must take up the history at an earlier period, and devote to it what still remains to me of force and activity.

If M. Renan's opinion of the true date of the origin of Christianity prove a surprise to many, so will his reason for stopping where he does his inquiry into its development. He fixes in the second century after Christ the definitive foundation of Christianity. Its embryo period ends about the time of the death of Marcus Aurelius. "At that date the child has all its organs; it is separated from its mother; it will live henceforward by its own vitality." The history of the following periods is more strictly ecclesiastical history; a history of the growth, not of Christianity proper, but of the Church; and that has been fairly well done by others. Simultaneously with the decisive establishment of Christianity, grew up "the most admirable effort of the lay school of virtue which the world has yet known." The two did not work together, one was hostile to the other, "but the triumph of Christianity is only explicable after a careful statement of both the strength and the weakness of the purely philosophical attempt." Hence the importance of Marcus Aurelius. He is the epitome and brief abstract of all there was good in the old civilisation, and his *Thoughts* are a record of which neither the authenticity nor sincerity can be questioned. This volume accordingly, or the greater part of it, is for those who are students of a great religious system. Those who consult it for a different reason will find in it all that needs to be said, and said with every grace of style and fulness of learning, about one of the noblest figures in the world's history. Marcus Aurelius was not a Christian, indeed. He even had something to do with persecuting Christians; that is, he did not prevent the persecutions which were the consequence of the fundamental principles of the Empire. He softened the rigour of the laws; he did not repeal or annul them. But Christianity may still say of him, as the French Academy said of Molière—

Rien ne manque à sa gloire, il manquait à la nôtre.

It is too soon, I suppose, to set up the bust of the great Emperor and Philosopher in a Christian church, and carve that line on it. Meanwhile those who think such a suggestion audacious might profitably meditate on M. Renan's remark, that the *Thoughts* of Marcus Aurelius will never become antiquated because they embody no dogma.

GUSTAVE DORÉ.

[LONDON, *January* 24, 1883.]

M. GUSTAVE DORÉ's death is lamented by the English press in terms somewhat out of proportion to his real place and importance in the world of art. It may help to define his position if we say that he was a French artist whose fame as a painter was chiefly English and American. As the standard both of art and art criticism is considerably higher in France than in England (for prudential reasons I omit America), this is equivalent to saying that Doré's reputation was highest where it was exposed to least competition, and to the most lenient method of judgment. A Doré Gallery has been open in Bond Street for I know not how many years past, and has been constantly filled, and proved extremely profitable to Doré and his business partners. It is difficult to imagine such an exhibition permanently open in Paris, although this Bond Street gallery has been indebted to American support for no small part of its success. The English say he did not understand England, and cite his illustrations to Blanchard Jerrold's book about London in proof. But he understood one side of England very well. He early found out that a great number of people care more for the subject of a picture than for the technical merit of it. If it is religious and has some dramatic quality, that is enough. The Doré Gallery, accordingly, was filled in great part with Biblical subjects, such as "The Triumph of Christianity over Paganism," "The Entry into Jerusalem," "Christian Martyrs," "The Flight into Egypt," and the astonishing work which I once heard described as Christ leaving the Criterion. Pictures of this sort, painted in Doré's plausible, superficial style, inharmonious in colour and always deficient in that searching *technique* and sound learning on which the French insist, could never have made him in France the sort of idol he was here. Nor did they. He has never stood high as a painter in his own country. His vast canvases attracted attention in the Salon because they were vast and because they were Doré's. Certainly they were not without merit of some sort, or they would not have been hung, but no French critic dreamed of ranking Gustave Doré among the great painters of the day.

He was better known by his illustrations to famous books than by his paintings. Yet it must be said that the earliest of his illustrations remained his best. He has probably never done anything so good, so really illustrative, so sympathetic with his author, so genuinely powerful and original, as the designs for a cheap popular edition of Rabelais published in a single small folio volume in Paris, 1854. The book, oddly enough, is both illustrated by Doré and dedicated to him by the publisher, Bry. Next to this may be put the designs for the *Contes Drolatiques* of Balzac. These, like the preceding, were engraved on wood and often coarsely enough rendered, but are admirable in spirit and conception. The collector may be warned that only the early impressions of either are worth having. The *Contes Drolatiques* appeared in 1855, and copies (in French) of that date are of the original issue, though the book is described in its title as the fifth edition—meaning the fifth edition of the book, not of this illustrated edition. The English translation has worn impressions and is of little interest, nor is Balzac's powerful work one that can, in any form, be recommended for indiscriminate reading. For what was grotesque and ghastly and repulsive Doré had a natural gift, yet his illustrations to Dante are only moderately successful. The imaginative power and austere splendour of the great Florentine's genius were not in Doré's way. With Cervantes he succeeded better. His Milton is confessedly a failure, and many others are failures, the Bible most of all. These books were published in luxurious form, mostly in large folios, with much ostentation. They have never been sought after by the fastidious collector.

Possibly Doré did not care much more for the fastidious collector than did the fastidious collector for him. He liked the admiration of the multitude and knew how to secure it, in England if not in France. In his own genius there was much of the vulgar. Mere bigness pleased him. When he became able to dictate to publishers he insisted on big books. He never seemed to care to paint a small picture—the poverty of his method would have been too apparent, say the connoisseurs of his own country. Exaggeration was an element of his art. Yet in his own way he was sincerely devoted to it; loved it for its own sake more than for the money it brought him. Of money he always had enough, and more than enough, except perhaps at one or two moments of his life when he had formed expensive connections with people for whom no treasury was too full to empty. His rapidity was prodigious, and probably that fatal facility both of conception and execution did as much as anything to prevent his becoming a great artist. There was something positively marvellous in his quickness and comprehensiveness of sight. I once saw him look through a large volume of elaborate architectural drawings filled with minute details, in search of some ornamentation for a picture of his own. He turned the leaves almost as quickly as his fingers could move, closed the book, and remarked there was nothing he wanted. "But you cannot have really examined the plates?"—"Ask me about any of them," was his answer; and he described drawing after drawing, the mouldings of doorways, the figures of saints, the exact number of columns and corbels, the leafage of the capitals, and I am not sure he had not counted the spirals and the panes of glass. His eye took in these details at a glance, as Macaulay is said to have taken in a whole page at a glance instead of a word or a sentence, like ordinary mortals.

But his life and his art may be divided into two periods.

He began with illustrations, and various as these were in merit they won great fame, in France as elsewhere. By and by he took up the notion that he was formed for greater things than supplying pictures of other men's thoughts, and he devoted the last twenty years of his life chiefly to painting, and in this he failed. He had an ambition to descend to posterity as a historical painter. But he would not begin over again his artistic education. The faults which appeared on a small scale in his designs appeared over again on a large scale in his pictures. He was never a sound draughtsman, and bad drawing is more conspicuous and perhaps more offensive when displayed on half an acre of canvas than when seen opposite a printed page. Add to this that he had no sense of colour and it is easy to see how and why the labour and some really great faculties bestowed on his paintings were of slight avail. I don't think he ever had a real success at the Salon in Paris. Not one picture did he paint about which the French public gathered, or which French writers extolled. He had friends in the press, and friendship counts for much with a certain class of Parisian journalists, but nobody dared praise Doré without qualifications which made notice more bitter to him than neglect. Nor did these pictures sell. Some of them perhaps passed into the London gallery for further exhibition, but the majority repose to-day in the studio of the Rue Bayard. Nobody would buy them, so presently Doré himself came to understand that the highest hopes of his life, and his really lofty and worthy ambition, were doomed to disappointment. It will not do to suppose that the homage paid him in England and elsewhere consoled him for the want of it at home. Doré was a true Frenchman, and would eagerly have exchanged all his celebrity abroad for one column of cordial panegyric in any journal of the Boulevards. In more than one point he was the Haydon of France, though he never knew what Haydon was never allowed to forget — the meaning of the word poverty.

Doré lived in London a good deal and was to be met here

in the season, though he professed a dislike for dinners and society in general. Whatever people might think of his pictures they liked the man. He was liked in Paris also, where his house in the Rue St. Dominique, and later his enormous studio in the Rue Bayard, was a rendezvous for artists and men of letters and men of no letters. English he could speak after a fashion, but long as he lived here he never came to converse with ease, still less with accuracy, in the English tongue. He has been described as singularly animated and energetic—un-English, in short, in manner. He had more than one manner, as artists have by right. I never knew him in his earlier and happier days, nor saw much of him in Paris where lay his closest friendships and intimacies. There are stories of Sunday evening parties of which Doré was the life; where he was as exuberant in spirits as he was with his pencil. Most people, I fancy, whose acquaintance with him was formed in London drawing-rooms, would describe him as conventional, possibly timid; which he certainly was not. He talked volubly on his own subject and all others, but preferably on his own; and more about his own art than art in general. I have met him in houses where he knew he was asked because he was liked and not because he was a celebrity. In such circumstances he talked extremely well, with animation, ease, and manifest enjoyment of his own conversation. If you saw him at his rooms in a hotel on Piccadilly it was a chance whether he opened his mouth at all, no matter how numerous might be his visitors. The litter of the place was indescribable. He liked being surrounded by splendour but order was not his first nor his second law.

Two summers ago I met him in Switzerland. We were staying at the same hotel in Zermatt. The end of the season was near and the house almost empty, but Doré filled it with his voice and presence. He had more love of adventure and fatigue than is common to the French. There was a question one morning about ascending the Riffel and Gornergrat. The guides pronounced against it—sure to rain, if not snow; you will see nothing, perhaps you will lose your way,—and so on, as the manner of those gentry is when they are not in the mood for earning money. Doré listened, summoned his friends, and set out, as he said, for a stroll. When he appeared at dinner in the evening he was radiant. He had been to the top of the Gornergrat and the view had been perfect. He further announced that he was quite certain Zermatt had nothing else to offer equally fine, and he should be off next day; and so he was. He cared a good deal about scenery; not much, I thought, about the glory and danger of mere climbing. For this, to be sure, his physique was hardly adapted. Doré was short and rather fat, and perhaps, like Hamlet, scant of breath. He was active enough in his movements but never gave you the notion of being in condition, or, as the English have it briefly, fit. Yet he was an early riser and abstemious; got through much work with the brush before other people were down to breakfast, and much afterward. The physicians say he died from angina pectoris. That is as good a name as another for the chagrin and the destroying melancholy which settled upon a man conscious of great powers and conscious of defeat in the great object of his life.

CARLO PELLEGRINI.

[LONDON, *January* 23, 1889.]

CARLO PELLEGRINI was before all things an artist, and it was his singular talent as an artist that first made him known in London. He will always be remembered as a caricaturist. He had the gift—not a common one—of caricature; an eye to perceive the points in a man's face and figure which best lent themselves to ridicule, and a hand and pencil to put them on paper. His secret consisted in exaggeration. He took what was most characteristic in his victim and dwelt on it; enlarged it perhaps, though not always, but in any case brought it out and forced it on your attention. It might be only a detail which most people would overlook, or think unimportant, but in Pellegrini's hands it became essential and denoted the man.

He had the advantage of being a foreigner and of altogether alien race, so that what escaped the native observer seldom escaped him. He made his sketches more English than the Englishman could, because he was himself not English and what was distinctively English struck him at once. The comic or grotesque or eccentric features in the English character, and in English personalities, struck him most of all. His first appearance was decisive. He has never done anything more masterly than the caricature of Disraeli which opened that long series of masterly performances in *Vanity Fair*. He made the fortune of that journal, or helped make it, for Mr. Bowles, its editor, is too able a man to have owed his success mainly to any other than himself. The signature which Pellegrini adopted, "Ape," was not ill-chosen. He had the imitative power of his namesake, and much more than merely imitative power, for in his best work there is imaginative power also, and not of a low order.

To him, as to so many true artists, regular work was distasteful. His genius would not be commanded, and he did not always care to get between the shafts. The place which he from time to time left vacant was taken, and sometimes filled, by others. M. Tissot was one of those who took it. M. Tissot might have been a good caricaturist had he not been a caricaturist when he did not mean to be. His serious art, or what he desires should be accepted as serious, has so many elements of caricature that not much can be added by intention. Mr. Leslie Ward is perhaps the best known of those who keep the lamp of caricature alight in Mr. Bowles's paper; under the signature "Spy." He, too, understands in what caricature consists and where the essence of it is to be sought, and many of his drawings are excellent studies of his subjects and as good examples of genuine caricature as this generation can now supply. But Pellegrini, it may be said, stood alone; he had the indefinable something which the others have not. He trained his successors, but training is not temperament. His Neapolitan birth and blood counted for much. They counted for something also in his extraordinary popularity.

Nobody was better liked than the Pelican, if I may give him in print the name by which he was familiarly known to his friends. To say that he had not an enemy would be no compliment. It is only weak men who have no enemies. But he had fewer than most strong men, and it is the more remarkable because he was always engaged in work likely to make him enemies. It is not everybody who desires to be caricatured; even when the caricature is not malicious.

There was no malice, properly speaking, in Pellegrini's treatment of his topics, but there was a fidelity to facts and a keenness of perception into character which the patient might sometimes think meant mischief. If the patients had grievances, however, they kept them to themselves, or the sensible ones did, and the men of the world who really live in the world. I have met Pellegrini in various companies and never saw him greeted with a black look. His geniality was delightful, his talk was all his own. He spoke the most extraordinary English ever heard; with the accent of a man whose mouth is full of macaroni. It added flavour to his wit, as Artemus Ward's spelling did to his stories.

He brought into England some of the sunlight of his own Neapolitan sky. In his latter years he has been an invalid and the haunts that used to know him have known him more seldom. Yet his gaiety of mind never forsook him in public, nor was any evening dull with Pellegrini to enliven it. The stories he told, albeit sometimes realistic, the racy idioms he invented on the spur of the moment, his brilliant compromises between Italian and English grammar, his flowing manner, which was something between the street urchin of Naples and the dweller in Mayfair, the large gesture which, when you met him abroad, reached clear across the street, the childlike kindliness and sweetness—who is to give us all these now that Pellegrini is gone?

MR. WATTS.

[LONDON, *August* 12, 1884.]

IN another month the pictures lent by Mr. G. F. Watts, R.A., to the Metropolitan Museum will be on their way to New York. Mr. Watts has acted in this matter with a generosity characteristic of him. Mr. Frank Millett, who has conducted the negotiations for the Museum, gave him to understand that a section of the art world in America was no longer content to live under the almost exclusive influence of modern French art. There were young men who longed to see what the art of England had to say for itself, and this is the kind of appeal to which Mr. Watts has yielded.

It is no light thing for an artist to give his consent to a request for the loan of all his most precious work for exhibition three thousand miles away, and for an absence lasting all through the winter. The risks cannot be covered by insurance, though the pictures are of course insured. The money value of them is but a part of their value, and, in Mr. Watts's case, not the largest part, as I will show you in a moment. If they go to the bottom of the Atlantic they will be paid for, but how are the injuries due to mere locomotion to be estimated, and who will pay for these? It is no unheard-of thing for a great picture to be destroyed on its travels. One of Mr. Millais's met such a fate; so did one of Mr. Burne Jones's more recently. But there is a process of more subtle deterioration to be feared. It is known that the long-continued shaking and jar of a journey by rail first loosens and then detaches the paint from the canvas. There is less chance of this when the picture is on board ship, say the experts, though in the long run the ceaseless vibration of a steamer must do much the same mischief as the more violent agitation of a train. Greater or less, there it is; the picture will not return from a long voyage quite the same thing it was at the start. Of other accidents by flood and field there is no need to speak. Climate, in any case, is not without its influence, and all these chances of ill together are enough to make any artist not filled with public spirit hesitate before acceding to such a proposal. Mr. Watts's act is proof enough of genuine goodwill to America, and of paramount devotion to the interest of art.

Of the pictures you will see, not a few are destined by Mr. Watts ultimately for some public collection in England. The portraits will be likely to go to the National Portrait Gallery in South Kensington. The pictures of imagination may go to the National Gallery. The best of what Mr. Watts leaves behind him will, it has long been understood by his friends, be bequeathed as the artist's gift to his fellow-countrymen. That beyond all things else is the source of his anxiety about their safety.

The Metropolitan Museum addresses itself to Mr. Watts as to a representative of what is best in the art of England. The directors have been well advised in doing so; not less well because Mr. Watts holds a place apart. His work is in no sense typical; it is exceptional. If the Museum wanted merely an average specimen of average academical production, it is not Mr. Watts to whom they would have applied. In an age when painting has become largely commercial, Mr. Watts has deliberately sacrificed his pecuniary interests to principle and to pure ambition. I mean to an ambition pure in its nature and not vulgar. He has received, it is true, large sums for his pictures, and it would be altogether a mistake to think of him as in any way resembling those unappreciated and miserably unsuccessful geniuses — some of them slightly tragi-comic — of whom Haydon was a conspicuous example. His pictures have had a ready sale enough during the last forty years, whenever he has cared to sell them. His portraits have always been in demand. He has earned a good income, built himself a beautiful house to replace the old one which was pulled down, and the new mansion, to which the old name, Little Holland House, is still fondly attached, is one of the attractions of that famous street of art-palaces to which every foreigner of distinction makes a pilgrimage. It is not at all, therefore, an appeal for sympathy springing from insufficient means that is to be made for Mr. Watts.

But what he has done, and what is meant by sacrifice, is this. He has given during this long career about one-third of his time to the painting of pictures which were either commissions or of such a character as to be sold at once at the artist's price. The other two-thirds of each year he has devoted to the practice of the art he himself cared for. I remember once standing before the magnificent " Love and Death," and saying something about the energy and impressiveness of the chief figure. " Yes," answered Mr. Watts, "that is the only really popular picture I ever painted." Nobody else would have thought of making so wild a statement as that, for many of his best pictures, not to speak of his art as a whole, have long been admired, and long since attained a rank which can only be called classical. But this pathetic speech does after all indicate, though with an artist's picturesqueness and with great exaggeration, the remoteness of Mr. Watts from the Philistinism of the day. The aim of his life has been the ennobling of English art. You will recollect, perhaps, that extraordinary harangue of the late Lord Beaconsfield, delivered at one of the annual Royal Academy dinners, in which he declared that the leading characteristic of English painting was imagination. The weary old man had gone the rounds of the gallery that afternoon, gazing blankly on canvases still more blank, and having seen that in a great number of these productions poverty of conception was even more conspicuous than ignorant technique, had amused himself by propounding the most startling paradox he could think of, and so described the art before him as imaginative art. If any great picture by Mr. Watts had then hung on the walls, it might have justified the adjective and turned the sarcasm into serious truth. But it is given to few men to see the influence of their best work show itself on a great number of their contemporaries, and Mr. Watts is not one of the few. He has lived a life of poetic beauty. He has filled his mind with original conceptions and striven to record them on canvas. He has acted on the view which Mr. Ruskin first made in some slight degree acceptable to the British public, that art has just as high and serious a place in life as literature or science, or perhaps religion. He has ever maintained that it had a function to perform, and that, within certain clear limitations, it was quite as competent to express what is best intellectually and spiritually as any of its rivals. I can imagine that to Mr. Watts it has always seemed that England, the intellectual peer of any other country in the world in any age of the world, was the inferior of many in art. School of art she has had none. She has had Reynolds, whose gentle and pleasing gifts have endeared him to his own countrymen in one branch of art. She has had Turner, and is still debating whether she will accept him at Mr. Ruskin's estimate. She has had Constable, who alone of English painters has made English influence largely felt abroad. But she has not impressed the world either by the genius of any one painter or by the combined excellence of any one group, whether contemporary or scattered through the centuries. To a painter like Watts such a state of things appeared a reproach. It may not be that he ever said to himself that he would redeem this reproach, or turn it into a glory, but I am certain that he very early resolved he would try and that he has ever since been faithful to that purpose of his youth.

That is why he is, of all living Englishmen, the one whose work is most likely to be an inspiration to the young artists of America. The young artist of America may learn draughtsmanship and perspective and touch in many a different school, and when he has learned them may practise his trade with more or less success, and paint more or less clever and telling pictures. But what he will learn from Mr. Watts is loftiness of purpose, and perhaps a new ideal in art. He will see in the portraits which will hang next winter in the Metropolitan Museum how faithfully and patiently an artist of genius is content to record the features of the famous men who have sat to him. He will see accurate likeness and poetic insight into character in the same canvas. He will learn with interest that most of them have been painted by Mr. Watts for himself—painted because the men interested him and he wanted to stereotype his impressions of them and live among them, as he does. He will turn from picture to picture admiring the flexibility of the mind of the artist who has wrought them all, and the range of an art which can deal learnedly with so many topics. At last, he will find himself in the presence of those works which it is common to speak of as allegorical, which denote the high-water mark of the artist's ambition, and which he chooses to suppose the general public regards with a certain indifference. If he cares to profit to the full by what Mr. Watts has to teach him, let him surrender his soul to these. Here, if anywhere, has the artist's own soul put itself into closest communion with those who have any kinship with his. Many of them are well known; and the one I mentioned above, "Love and Death," is sure of that popularity in America which even England did not deny to it. There is another yet unfinished which is full of character and curiously illustrative of the artist's endeavours. Time and Death, two colossal figures, are in the foreground. Time has his scythe and is striding on with clearly marked steps. The Death by his side, a figure of a woman, advances with him, but by a gliding movement strangely contrasted with that of her companion. She holds in her gathered robe a sheaf of flowers—they are her harvest. The conception is novel and true, and one to which nobody could refuse the quality of poetic. Behind is the rushing form which one may call Nemesis; revengeful, irresistible, more formidable even than the two in front, which are, perhaps, after all, but servants to the other. You may say you do not care for this sort of art if you like. But you cannot say it is not art of a noble kind, and in these days all but solitary.

Whatever may have been Mr. Watts's relations to the public—and he is a great favourite with the best part of the public here—he has always been pre-eminently the admiration of his fellow-artists. Not long ago I heard the most spiritual and accomplished of the younger generation declare that he owed a great deal of what merit he had to Mr. Watts. Of his technical power as well as of his delicate feeling he expressed the highest opinion. To an eye trained in the modern French school the Englishman's method may be a surprise. His object is very unlike theirs. The best of the naturalists—for that is their proper name in art as well as in literature—are content when they have successfully and truthfully reproduced certain facts of light and shade, of relief, of roundness, or whatever else. They care nothing about surface. Mr. Watts has a tenderness of perception to which roughness of finish gives positive distress. He will take any pains to refine it away, yet he never becomes insipid, nor offers you the waxen smoothness in which one distinguished Academician delights. About whatever he does there is a real gracefulness. Said an artist to me once, "If you can think of a picture by Watts as torn to bits, and you chanced to pick up one of the bits, it might be a bit of a dress or flesh, or no matter what, you could not but feel that you held in your hand a beautiful fragment of a beautiful work." At times his sense of colour abandons him. He is not always at his full strength, nor perhaps always quite successful in making his picture instructive at first sight. But you will judge for yourselves what is the actual position which Mr. Watts holds to the art of his time.

TWO MIDLOTHIAN CAMPAIGNS.

MR. GLADSTONE IN 1879.

I.

WHAT HAPPENED BETWEEN LIVERPOOL AND EDINBURGH.

[EDINBURGH, *November* 25, 1879.]

FEW people can have had any notion of the sort of reception which Scotland has been preparing — almost secretly preparing—for Mr. Gladstone, at the beginning of his Midlothian campaign. Fewer still understood that his approach to the frontier of the country was to be the signal for an outburst of enthusiasm rare in the history of any country or any statesman. For myself I may say that I had no conception of what I was to see. I meant to come down and hear the speeches. My views did not go beyond that, but the other day—being then in Paris—I got a letter containing some hints as to what might happen on Mr. Gladstone's journey; hints which led me to cut short my stay in that American Capua, and hurry northward to Liverpool. "The Scot's blood is up," said my friend; "if you want to see the border on fire you must make the journey with Mr. Gladstone." He had left Hawarden Castle on Saturday, spent Sunday with his nephew at Court Hey, near Liverpool, and was to start from the Edge Hill Station, two miles out of town, by the 9.20 A.M. train on Monday, the 24th. But Liverpool certainly was in no state of excitement. When I asked the guard at Lime Street to put me into the carriage next to Mr. Gladstone's it appeared that the guard knew nothing of Mr. Gladstone's movements, and that nothing had been reserved for anybody going by that train save one compartment of the usual first-class carriage. The inspector knew no more than the guard, but on being told that Mr. Gladstone was waiting for the train at Edge Hill, bestirred himself and put on a saloon carriage. I used the word preparations just now, and it will be said by Tory critics that great pains were taken to insure as much state and ceremony as possible for Mr. Gladstone's journey. This incident about the carriage does not look like it; and I mention it because it shows how little there was of forethought in the matter.

There was, in fact, a singular absence of preparation in the usual sense. The machinery which every great organisation, such as the Liberal Associations of Scotland, possess, was not put in motion on Monday; certainly not for the purpose of organising enthusiasm. In certain Scotch and English boroughs addresses of welcome had been drawn up, but addresses are pretty much matter of form. Their presentation is not a thing to rouse the country or bring people in great numbers to see them delivered. If ever there was a spontaneous outburst of popular feeling in honour of a distinguished public servant, that of yesterday was spontaneous. The splendour of Mr. Gladstone's reception consisted wholly in its popular character. We shall see by and by that there were preparations on a great scale, but they were preparations to confine the popular demonstration within safe limits; not to promote them. Mr. Gladstone himself well said later in the day that the people of Scotland do not love to meddle in political demonstrations except when there is a strong cause, and the leading Scottish journal remarks with equal truth that there is not, as a rule, much shouting here for shouting's sake. But there is one thing that has stirred the slow Scot these last few days. Something of his old chivalry is left in him yet, and he admires the courage of Mr. Gladstone in storming such a Tory stronghold as Midlothian—the county for which Lord Dalkeith, the son of the great Duke of Buccleuch, now sits, and which Mr. Gladstone is to contest whenever the general election is held.

But this is a digression and Mr. Gladstone is waiting on the Edge Hill platform. As the train stopped I caught my first glimpse of him, surrounded by a group of friends to whom he was saying good-bye. A moment later, as he stepped into the carriage and a cheer saluted him, he raised his hat, and the strong features and sweeping lines of the forehead stood out in the gray morning. He looked in capital condition but I have seen him look as fresh when he rose to speak at one in the morning in the House after an eight hours' session, and it is hard to say what amount of toil or what burden of responsibility will overtask his physical powers. With a week of appalling work before him, he starts off as blithely as if taking a holiday; which, in the common sense of the word, I believe he never takes. The cheer at Edge Hill was a signal gun. It was taken up and echoed forward from station to station as the train sped northward. Between Edge Hill and Carlisle, where the first formal reception was to occur, the trains stopped at six towns, large and small. At all of them crowds had gathered on the chance of seeing Mr. Gladstone's face for an instant. There was a rush to his carriage, a cry of "There he is," a cheer, and then Mr. Gladstone put his head out of the window and bowed, then a few of the nearest seized his hand, sometimes with a "God bless you, sir," and then the train steamed slowly away, the people following as far as they could keep up. They were mostly working men.

It was not till we reached Preston that there was any sign that his arrival had been generally expected or counted on. The Preston station is rebuilding and the temporary station is nothing but a long and narrow shed. Into this some two or three thousand people had wedged themselves, and as the train passed along the serried file the cheers went off like volleys when the firing is by platoons. Here, I think, some local magnates captained the crowd, and there were peremptory demands for a speech. Mr. Gladstone complied, saying he could utter but two sentences; one to thank them for their unexpected welcome, the other to beg them to get out of harm's way before the train moved. His wife, he added, was much distressed lest some accident should happen; whereupon the people cheered for Mr. Gladstone and crowded closer than ever. By some clever manœuvring of the railway guards the edge of the platform was finally cleared, and the train got away without mishap; a rush accompanying and following till stopped by a barricade improvised out of luggage trucks and gallantly defended by a dozen big porters.

At Lancaster, at Carnforth, at Penrith, and other places, similar scenes occurred, but when Carlisle was reached the first formality of the day took place. The Liberals of the North did not care to let Mr. Gladstone quit English soil without a word from them. Deputations had come all the way from Newcastle on the other side of the island, and from Gateshead, as well as from Langholme and from Carlisle itself; each with a long address. For the whole reception not more than fifteen minutes were allowed and the proceedings took place in a hotel, but six or seven thousand people had collected in the station. Barriers stretched in every direction, and scores of policemen did their best to keep the throng outside of them. Their efforts were not very successful. I will not detain you a single moment with the official part of the proceedings. The addresses were cordial, the speeches both cordial and brief, and there was a presentation from the working men of Langholme of a parcel of tweed cloth, the work of their own hands, which gave Mr. Gladstone an opportunity to remark that if he were to have it made up at once, and wear it daily, the probability was that before the clothes were worn out the Government under which we now live would be worn out.

And here at Carlisle it was that Mr. Gladstone first indicated his own view of the enterprise upon which he had embarked. It is a crisis, he said, of an extraordinary character, and no other would have induced him at his time of life, when every sentiment would dictate a desire for rest, to undertake what may be called an arduous contest. Whenever the election might come it would be one of unequalled interest and importance. In eleven former dissolutions and elections it had been his fortune to take an active part; but in no one of those eleven, although they extended over nearly half a century, had he known the interests of the country to be so deeply and vitally at stake as they are upon the dissolution now approaching. What he said here, and later at Galashiels, tended to the same point. He had come down expressly to raise effectually before the people of this country the great question in what manner they wish to be governed. As Liberals or as Englishmen, they might disapprove many particular measures of the Government — and bad enough many of those measures were — but to his mind the question was not of the merit of this or that measure, or act or line of policy. It is a great deal more than that. It is a system and method of government to be upheld or to be overthrown; and what he now undertakes is to persuade the country that the whole scheme upon which the affairs of the country are conducted is a bad scheme, and that it is their business to place anew the fortunes of this nation in hands more competent to guide them with honour and safety than those to which they are now intrusted.

The thousands gathered in the Carlisle station could not have heard a word of this statement, but they knew perfectly well what they were there for. They wanted to welcome Mr. Gladstone; and welcome him they did. It was a rough crowd — rough in dress, in looks, in demeanour, but in no sense was it a crowd of roughs. They were artisans and other decent labouring folk, who had quitted their work in their working dress, not staying to wash the grime off their faces nor to hunt up their Sunday clothes. They were most eager to see their hero, whom most of them had never seen, and they paid little heed to the remonstrances of the police and porters when these came in their way. But they had a fine sense of politeness of their own. They never pressed upon Mr. Gladstone. The multitude surged all about him but left a clear space for him to stand or move in.

They took care of his wife and daughter in the same way. I saw the three arrive one after the other at the door of their carriage after the hotel business was done. First came Mr. Gladstone with two policemen preceding him to clear the path, which was already perfectly clear. A self-constituted bodyguard of some 500 men followed, having good-naturedly tossed a policeman or two out of their way as they came. A little later the cry was heard that Mrs. Gladstone was arriving. The wedged mass of humanity parted asunder at once, and she walked comfortably along the lane, followed, like her husband, by a tumultuous escort solicitous for her safety. A third detachment not less numerous had charge of the daughter. And so, amid cheers that ever broke out afresh, and along the line of rails encumbered for a long distance beyond the station with eager spectators who took up the cheer as Mr. Gladstone passed, we got happily away from Carlisle and were soon over the border.

At Galashiels, the men in the cloth mills had set their hearts on offering Mr. and Mrs. Gladstone a specimen from their looms. The Langholme gift was a borrowed idea from them, they say. But out of this idea had grown a demonstration of considerable magnitude. The train was to stop ten minutes. For the sake of those ten minutes people had flocked in from all the towns and stretch of country hereabout, so that when we came in sight of Galashiels it looked like a place of 40,000 inhabitants. Half that number, certainly, of men, women, and children, were in sight, and masses of them were packed together in spots whence they could by no possibility see or hear the orator. All the cheering we had heard before was a faint murmur to that which poured up from the streets as we neared the platform. The place was well suited for a spectacle and the arrangements were ingenious. A temporary bridge had been built, on one end of which Mr. Gladstone stepped from the door of his saloon, and when he had reached the other he stood at the angle of the road just below, so that to right and left, and well within hearing, the multitude stretched away on either hand. It was not a sea but a stream of faces. A church is at the corner around which the stream flowed; factories, all silent, for all their hands were out to have their part in the reception, were grouped about; and a purple-gray hill, its summit shrouded with firs, rose dark against the sky. There were flags, and music, and there was a multitude with one thought in their hearts; and there on the parapet above, the central figure of the scene, bareheaded, stood the man whom all these fellow-beings had assembled to welcome.

Uncovered he listened to the address offered him, and uncovered he replied to it. I thought it a piece of wilful imprudence in a man of seventy with such a week's task before him thus to risk taking cold, or worse, on that bleak November afternoon in a northern latitude. Nor was it prudent to speak at all in the open air; but Mr. Gladstone wears his seventy years as lightly as another man his fifty, and he faced his work gallantly. His voice, if one may judge from the expression of faces, reached the farthest edge of what he rightly described as a vast assemblage. He spoke for quite ten minutes, an exertion equal to half an hour under a roof, for the voice here had no walls to break against, and the waves of sound flowed out into space with nothing to check them. Two or three times he picked up his bundle of cloth and laid it down again; presently remarking that he had meant to address them holding their gift in his hands but that he found the weight affected his powers of speech so that he was less able to make them hear. Before he had ended, the engine-driver, being out of hearing, signified his impatience by a sharp whistle. The worthy man knew that his train was already a quarter of an hour behind time and that a fine impended over him. I hope they did not make him pay it, but the quarter of an hour was never recovered. It had grown to twenty minutes before Mr. Gladstone had got back to his seat and freed his hand from the last grasp of his too-enthusiastic admirers.

The train reached Edinburgh at twenty minutes past five. It was quite dark. The Waverley station is nothing more than the prolongation of a tunnel, confused and gloomy beyond the generality of such places. The public, as I afterward learned, had been excluded and only a favoured few —say five or six thousand—admitted by ticket. But here again there had been no official arrangement for receiving Mr. Gladstone, and the only people who acted in the matter were the railway authorities, and their action was limited to excluding people from the station. The people were quite ready to constitute themselves masters of ceremonies had they been permitted. They collected about the station and along the streets through which Mr. Gladstone was to drive by tens of thousands. We heard the roar of this multitude outside as the train rolled slowly beneath the great castle and along the wonderful natural ravine now degraded to railway uses. Once inside, the confusion was complete. The throng paid no more heed to the police than at Carlisle, and the turmoil was all the greater because of sundry constables mounted on steeds they could not manage. Lord Rosebery's carriage-and-four, with two outriders and a small army of liveried footmen, was standing at the edge of the platform, and Mr. Gladstone's saloon-car was stopped just opposite this equipage. Waiting to receive him were Lord Rosebery, with whom Mr. Gladstone stays during this week, Mr. Adam, and a number of local celebrities, together with officers of various Liberal Associations to whom the railway company had been good enough to concede tickets of admission. As the train stopped and Mr. Gladstone was seen at the door, the cheers rose louder than ever. It was not cheering, it was a prolonged outburst of inarticulate sound that filled this subterranean dungeon for some minutes without cessation. The ladies—for ladies there were in the midst of the surging mob—kept their handkerchiefs fluttering in the air, and the men had their hats off. I am told that somebody then and there handed Mr. Gladstone an address, but if this ceremony were really performed I saw nothing of it and the address in any case was not read. It would have been as easy to read an address at the mouth of a volcano. What I saw was an unchecked and irresistible rush of the people from all quarters to the spot where Mr. Gladstone was; a rush which bore down before it the masses of police in military array, and upset one of those cavaliers who were every minute putting lives in peril. Rider and horse fell just at Mr. Gladstone's feet but were speedily got out of the way unhurt. Then Lord Rosebery gave his arm to Mrs. Gladstone and led her to the carriage. Mr. Adam took Miss Gladstone, and Mr. Gladstone followed, nimbly avoiding a gray-haired lunatic who rushed toward him with a rug on which was inscribed the mystic word, "Welcome." Mr. Gladstone got in with Lord Rosebery and stood for a moment erect to return the salutes which poured in upon him. The roar redoubled. I saw the coachman look nervously at his horses. They were as nervous as he was but what weighed upon the mind of this personage was the rumour that the horses were to be taken out and the carriage to be drawn through the streets by the people. The coachman in those circumstances would have been a superfluous ornament and he plainly trembled for the loss of dignity that might befall him. But there was no time given for that sort of thing. The scene passed with a delirious rapidity. It could not have been five minutes after the train came to a stand that Lord Rosebery's carriage-and-four and outriders vanished under the archway; his guest still standing and bowing. And a noble thing to look upon was the grand gray head as it whirled past the lights.

Of what happened afterward I saw nothing; or rather, I saw only the dissolving and dispersing multitude which for hours had clung about the station and the bridge and clustered in thousands along Princes Street. But to complete my story I add that the welcome to Mr. Gladstone lasted all the way from Waverley Bridge to the gates of Dalmeny Park, Lord Rosebery's residence, five miles distant. For the whole length of that magnificent street of the New Town which looks across to the Castle—a street in some points without a rival in Europe—he continued standing bareheaded and gravely bowing his acknowledgments. The crowd was immense, and even in the station we heard its shouting. All day long the fervour of the reception had been growing; the volume and mass of the popular zeal augmenting from hour to hour. The wave rolled on from station to station, and only at Edinburgh reached its full height, and broke. It is commonplace to speak of the journey as a triumphal progress, but that is the phrase which most aptly describes the history of this day.

II.

THE MEETINGS IN THE MUSIC HALL, IN DALKEITH, AND IN WEST CALDER.

[EDINBURGH, *November* 28, 1879.]

THE last great Englishman is low, sang Tennyson, when the Duke of Wellington was laid in St. Paul's amid the mourning of a mighty nation. When Lord Palmerston died, Carlyle, in his turn, described Palmerston also as the last of the Englishmen. But great men are of many types, and those who have been happy enough to spend this last week in Midlothian may be permitted to think that there are giants still in the land, and that when Mr. Gladstone—distant be the day—follows his former chief to his chamber in the silent halls of Westminster Abbey, some surviving poet or heroic moralist will be found to say that he, too, stood high on the roll of England's worthies. There is not much profit to be got out of comparisons between this man and that and I shall attempt none between Mr. Gladstone and any of his predecessors. An amateur of historical parallels might produce a striking one if he would take Canning and Peel together, and see how many of the distinctive features in those two characters were reproduced in Mr. Gladstone. But this I will say, that if intellectual and physical power combined have anything to do with claims to greatness, it is idle to dispute Mr. Gladstone's right to a place among the highest. What he has done this week must extort the admiration, unwilling though it be, of those who like him least. The exhausting journey of Monday which I have described in a former letter with its perpetual succession of popular greetings, of official addresses, of crowds pressing about him, with his repeated speeches in the open air, and the demands of friends and inconsiderate strangers for personal recognition, and the thousands of hands grasping his—all this was enough, and more than enough, to task the strength of a strong man who looked forward to a period of rest afterward. But Mr. Gladstone's rest has consisted in delivering three elaborate orations on three succeeding days, each of great length, each a distinct and well-considered execution of a separate part in an elaborate programme; a programme which, as a whole, aims at nothing less than the overthrow of a powerful government by an appeal to a sovereign people. To make these speeches he has traversed and retraversed a spreading country, and at every step of his way has had to confront an enthusiasm that would not be denied; expressed, it may be said, in every possible form, but never without some drain upon the resources of him who was its object. He has been a guest, meanwhile, in a country house where the thick-coming social requirements of each day are enough to keep most men's minds occupied; calls, dinners, receptions following close upon each other with a rapidity that leaves the guest few hours to himself, that makes little division between day and night, and allows few moments for repose. It is in the midst of these distractions that Mr. Gladstone has done his work. Any one of his three great speeches would establish the fame of a lesser man as an orator, or as a party leader. And the three are to be followed by two more on Saturday and by a fresh series in remote districts of Scotland next week.

I have heard all the speeches and looked on during the incessant popular demonstrations in Mr. Gladstone's honour, and I may say that I am beginning first to conceive their magnitude as I sit down to describe them. I shall be thankful if within any reasonable compass I can touch in the briefest way on some of the more striking incidents of the week, and note, in this or a following letter, one or two of the most essential points in the speeches. The proceedings of the last three days, as reported in their full dimensions, fill twenty-seven closely-printed columns; and this does not include the two or three leading articles a day devoted to them. The three speeches by themselves occupy eighteen columns of solid type and are very accurately given.

Of all the meetings, those in Edinburgh and those at the extremities of the county, one thing may be said, that the eagerness to be present at them outruns all previous experience. The three which have already been held came within the jurisdiction of the Midlothian Liberal Association. They were, in theory, simply meetings of the county electorate convened, as the fashion is in Great Britain, to hear a profession of faith from their candidate for Parliament. They were, in fact, assemblies both of electors and non-electors, and from the latter there was a pressure for admission which nothing but brick and mortar could stand against. One of the Liberal managers, to whose kindness I am much indebted, told me that for every seat in the disposal of the committee there were at least ten applications; a great proportion of them such as in no ordinary circumstances would it have been politic or possible to refuse. But the Music Hall, the largest available building for Tuesday, holds scarcely more than 2000 persons, and the body of the hall was assigned to the electors as of right. Nobody was admissible without a ticket but tickets were sent to every elector without distinction of party, and extra pains were taken that no Conservative elector should be forgotten; a fact worth noting when you remember that hardly a discordant voice has been heard amid the general applause. A gallery was assigned to ladies; the standing space beneath it to non-voters, and the platform held some hundreds of more or less distinguished persons. Three o'clock was the hour; at two the doors were open. To see how things were going I strolled up George Street at half-past one. The street was already blocked up with people. Barricades of timber stretching into the roadway defended the hall, and these were held by an army of policemen—who even thus early had their hands full. Going round to the rear which looked upon a different street I found the door indicated on my ticket open, and went in. The hall was two-thirds full. In another ten minutes not a vacant seat could be seen from the platform, and it was not yet two o'clock. But people continued to stream in. When the doors for the non-electors were opened, there came a rush which left the police out of it altogether. The standing space was swallowed up at once. A great many people entered without tickets; a great many who had tickets were left struggling hopelessly outside and never got in at all. A lady told me in the evening that she had taken her footman with her to see her through the crowd. She quitted him at the entrance, but on going away found him waiting on the stairs. He had a soul above buttons and a taste for oratory; and—as he confided to the lady's maid and she in turn to her mistress—had watched his chance, gone in with the rush, and heard every word of the speech.

Not the least singular feature of the scene was the presence of a number of persons about the hall bearing each a white wand as long as himself. These Ushers of the White Rod may be familiar to the Scottish mind, but I never saw them before. With the help of a sixteenth century tailor they might have passed for surviving representatives of the court pageantry at Holyrood. But I doubt whether the gentlemen-ushers of Mary's day went about tapping spectators on the shoulder, or on the head, or in the eye, or wherever they could most conveniently reach their victims. Those who were thus admonished—for no reason that I could see —took it in such good-humour that I soon grew to think that the shortness of the Scotch temper had been overstated. An English usher who should take half the liberties these functionaries did with their fellow-subjects would be roughly handled. And they had a kind of chief set over them whose movements kept one fully amused during the long hour of waiting.

I first saw him erect on the platform surveying the scene. In a moment he darted off to one end of the hall. Then he walked rapidly up a side aisle and back again; returning presently to the platform and then repeating his promenade on the opposite side of the hall. Next he charged a line of innocent-looking men standing against a wall, and forced them to go and stand against another wall. By and by he ordered them back again. The windows that were open he required to be shut, and those that were shut to be opened. He severely rebuked a meek attendant on the platform in a white tie for some fault in arranging the chairs, and when they were altered caused them to be replaced as before. Exactly at half-past two, as the non-electors came pouring in, he was perched on the brink of the platform watching their incoming like a hawk. When the place allotted them was half full he clapped his hands thrice, and the doors were closed. After a pause he repeated the signal and they were reopened. And so on, with many other ingenious manœuvres, until three o'clock struck when he disappeared—I think through a trap-door—and I saw him not again. Nobody could say who he was or why he went through these performances. The Ushers of the White Rod reappeared at Dalkeith and at West Calder, but in the absence of their captain their efforts lacked the originality and vigour which marked them here in Edinburgh.

The painful discipline the audience had undergone diminished in no degree their impatience or their enthusiasm. Mr. Gladstone came ten minutes late; by no fault of his nor yet of Lord Rosebery's horses but because the 10,000 or 15,000 people in the streets could not all at once make room for his carriage. We heard their cheers as we sat waiting, and as these died away Mr. Gladstone was seen advancing from the back of the platform. The ladies in the upper gallery were the first to catch sight of him and they gave the signal to the rest with their handkerchiefs. The packed masses of human beings below struggled to their feet and cheered; cheered at first wildly, but after a minute or two settled down to their work and cheered with a persistent, unbroken, unintermitting roar. The Scotch are pre-eminently a business people. If they had taken a contract to cheer —a contract at high rates and executed under the continuous fear of competition, they could not have done better. It was such an explosion of pent-up enthusiasm as only those are capable of who habitually repress their emotions. Mr. Gladstone is pretty well used to these manifestations, but by this he was visibly touched. His face flushed all at once, and he stood, not bowing, but with bent head and a strange luminous softness in his eyes, till the storm beneath him had spent its force. For aught one could see, the people would have cheered till now had they not bethought themselves after awhile that they had come to hear Mr. Gladstone as well as make themselves heard in his honour. When that idea at last got possession of their minds they stopped cheering, and Mr. Gladstone began to speak.

It is idle, I see, to attempt to deal with the substance of this speech. I will finish once for all with the external aspects of the meetings at Dalkeith and West Calder.

Dalkeith is the town from which Mr. Gladstone's opponent, the Earl of Dalkeith, takes his title. It is a straggling, sleepy, dirty village seven miles or so southeast from Edinburgh, with the usual long street of gray stone houses. The Duke of Buccleuch owns, I suppose, every foot of the ground on which it stands. He owns the Corn Exchange in which Mr. Gladstone spoke on Wednesday; or will own it when the lease falls in. Meanwhile, he had no power to close its doors. There was the same pressure for admission here as in Edinburgh albeit the 3000 people who got in had, most of them, to come from considerable distances. I went by train from Edinburgh, being indebted once more to Scotch good-nature for permission to occupy one undivided eleventh part of a carriage designed by its builders to carry six. Extra trains were running but the stations had been crowded since noon, streams of Dalkeith passengers flowing steadily through. In Dalkeith the streets were in the same state; and were also covered with a fine adhesive mud which much prolonged the walk to the hall; elbowed as you were at every step whether you chose the pavement or the middle of the road.

Here, too, an hour or more before the appointed time, not of beginning but of opening, the long barnlike building was crowded. It had been besieged for hours before. A gallery spanned the farther end; two side galleries started from its angles with the best intentions but stopped short before they had got half way to the opposite extremity. The occupants of all three had a curious appearance of being suspended in the air, or perhaps hung up against the white walls, but the contrivance is an admirable one for exhibiting a mass of people to spectators on the platform, the floor below being flat from end to end; and I commend it to the next American architect who has to put up a political wigwam. The utmost good-humour prevailed; chastened by that stern sense of decorum which the Scot is so seldom without. They sat for the most part as patiently as if the Rev. Haggai Muckletongue were dispensing his views of damnation in the world to come. A band—perhaps I should say an orchestra for it played on stringed instruments—occupied the front of the platform and from time to time indulged the fine natural taste for discords which possessed its members each and all. Where they twanged away was the spot from which Mr. Gladstone was to speak, and it was a moment of vindictive joy when on a false alarm of his approach they were pulled up in the middle of what they called a tune, bundled ignominiously off their stage, and suppressed utterly for the rest of the day.

Not many minutes later Mr. Gladstone did actually arrive. I cannot go on describing the cheering and other forms of welcome bestowed on the orator, here and wherever he is seen or heard. But this was more effective than that of the day before because more compact in form. The Music Hall in Edinburgh has alcoves and wings. This Corn Exchange was like the tube of some huge piece of artillery, and the cheers came rolling along its bore in one irresistible mass straight to the mark—no scattering of grapeshot but the smooth course of a single ball which knew its way and tore through the air. And once more the profound, intense, sincere heartiness and admiring friendliness of the greeting given him went evidently to the heart of this veteran of the platform. All his life long Mr. Gladstone has been acclaimed in the House of Commons and by audiences of the people, but custom has not hardened his heart nor familiarity bred contempt for popular favour. It is true, I suppose, that never before had it come to him at a more welcome moment, or in a form more grateful to the finer feelings of the man; never with an overflowing fulness better fitted to stir his most generous susceptibilities.

If in Dalkeith there was little likeness to Edinburgh, the scene at West Calder on the following day was still stranger; more picturesque, more novel, set in a more rugged frame, and played out with a company that sought many odd means of reaching its end. West Calder is hardly even a village. In the dull light of a late November afternoon it looked a mere hedge of houses clinging to a hillside, wandering aimlessly away from the station and losing themselves amid the ridges and bare undulations round about. We found ourselves in full country, and began to see what wooing a constituency might mean among the wilder parts of Scotland—in the Highlands, away from railways and away even from roads. Yet this is only the south-western extremity of a populous, fertile, and perfectly-farmed metropolitan county. It was chosen no doubt as a convenient rendezvous, central to those electors for whom neither Edinburgh nor Dalkeith offered a near rallying point. Hall or other place of meeting there was none—no permanent building I saw that would have held 300 people. For the purpose of hearing Mr. Gladstone a pavilion had been erected;

for that is the smart name awarded to the roofed shed of unpainted deal in which the third of this series of orations was to be delivered. It held 3000 persons and was in all respects well designed and built, and even decorated inside with bands of gaily-coloured, printed cloth and wreaths of fir and pine.

All the way from the station, or from where the first cottage bordered the road, the simple folk who live here had decked their house-fronts as best they could, much as the interior of the pavilion was decked. Evergreens were strung together, masts were raised for flags, arches had been run up for the display of mottoes; flowers, and fancy work in cut paper that would have been tawdry enough elsewhere, relieved the sombre monotony of the stone, and the candles and Chinese lanterns at every window betokened an illumination for the evening. It was all honest and quaint, perfectly unpretentious and effective from its transparent simplicity and homeliness. I have seen nothing like it since I drove through the Rue Mouffetard, in the oldest quarter of Paris, on the day of the second Exhibition festival of last year. That was far more rich in device and various in effect than this and French taste had transformed plain materials into artistic ornament as only French taste can. But for all that, there is something in the feeling which entered into both that was curiously akin and appealed to very similar sympathies. And I may add that this is not the first time, nor the fiftieth, that I have chanced upon striking resemblances of one kind and another between the Gaul and the Scot—relics of their long historical intimacy.

Withal, a certain effort at ceremonious observance prevailed. The villagers were in their Sunday dress; the farmers who had come many miles, afoot or driving their own carts, wore raiment of a severe and antique cut which had done duty at kirk and at tenant dinners of dead landlords for some generations back. The women who stood about the doors kept smoothing the creases out of gowns from which came a faint odour of lavender, denoting their recent extraction from press and cupboard where these treasures are scrupulously hoarded. The windows of the ale-houses—so-called because of the whiskey they sell—were freshly scrubbed. I have it on the authority of a friend whom, in serious matters, I have commonly found trustworthy, that he saw several children with combed hair and faces that bore marks of water recently though ineffectually applied. More than that, the visitors who came by rail—those of us at least to whom privileged seats had been allotted—had to pay the penalty that attaches to this distinction.

Eager to see the collection of people in the pavilion I went straight to the rear entrance, but only to find it closed and to be told—as indeed we had been solemnly warned before by advertisement—that we must all repair to the committee-room, to "receive Mr. Gladstone." The committee-room was in the schoolhouse; guarded by the police and beset by reporters, note-book in hand, and keen for the name on your ticket; less keen when they had read it and found it a name unknown. A hundred or two men loitered in the schoolhouse and hung about the door. A brass band occupied a strong strategical position at the entrance to the lane and a second was held in reserve at the door of the committee-room. The musicians fumbled nervously with the mouth-pieces of their trumpets while the gathered dignitaries of West Calder looked furtively at their watches. Neither had to wait long. Before the clock had struck four the familiar sound of cheers came faintly out of the distance. Mr. Gladstone had driven, it appeared, all the way from Dalmeny Park, encountering by the road a steady fire of salutes from every hamlet and almost every house on his route. He was in an open carriage-and-four and he must have had his hat off quite half the time: through a country where the snow lay on the uplands and the pools were skimmed with ice freshly crystallising. And at seventy years of age, with a two hours' speech to make!

He had left the carriage I know not where and walked toward us as we stood in double line to receive him, his hat, as usual, anywhere but on his head. I felt like begging him to put it on. The colour of his hair—and there is none too much of it—was too near in hue to the snow that lay ghastly white about us. The band that was out on picket at the head of the lane struck up; the other, fifty yards off, entered instantly into competition with its rival with a wholly different and hostile air. One of the dignitaries whom I shall always remember gratefully and whose name I would immortalise for twenty-four hours if I knew it, silenced the nearest offenders. The ceremony was over, we were free to make the best of our way to the position; with the front seats reserved for the fleetest of foot.

Mr. Gladstone with a bodyguard of the most venerable among the conscript fathers of West Calder followed at his leisure. His seat, at any rate, was safe; none the less did he need defenders for the too overflowing zeal of his friends lining the road—the road which, for the reasons of state above mentioned, it was thought needful he should travel twice on foot, with the mud ankle-deep all the way. When he entered the house rose to him as it had risen on Tuesday in Edinburgh and on Wednesday in the home of Buccleuch. This is more purely than either of the others an audience of tenant-farmers; the veritable constituency of the county; the actual cultivators of the soil; the men who plough the land and do the voting; hard, shrewd Scotchmen; skilled in agriculture and dogmatic theology; whose life is one long struggle with the elements on week days and with the Prince of Darkness on Sundays. Not much rapturous enthusiasm to be got out of them, surely. Well, not much more, nor much less, than would take the roof off this pavilion had it lasted another five minutes. The cheers rose and fell only to rise again louder than before. It is astonishing how a man can cheer who has heretofore for the most part kept his breath to cool his porridge; astonishing in what lava-torrents a long pent volcanic fire pours on when once it has broken loose. Well might Mr. Gladstone in his opening sentence say it warmed him. The greeting these stern men gave him was not merely enthusiastic—it glowed with the fervour of deep affection. Now if ever was it seen how dark and true and tender is the North.

When the speech was ended it was past six o'clock, and night had set in, and the cold had strengthened. But there outside were the patient thousands to whom it had not been permitted to hear a word of that magnificent discourse but who had waited for another glimpse of their idol. Mr. Gladstone found it no easy matter to make his way to his carriage. Once in the carriage, it was impossible to move without trampling on the men and women who thronged the roadway. When after long waiting a start was made, they drove at a footpace all the way to the station. An electric light burned from the corner of the pavilion. A vanguard of two score men with torches led the procession. The windows were all lighted up, some with gay lanterns, some with only a rush-light or two; here and there you saw the lonely glimmer of a candle in a wretched garret. Presently the horizon to the east grew ruddy and the heavens were speedily filled with the flame of a huge bonfire set perilously near the houses, but which happily burnt itself out doing no mischief. It was a weird scene altogether; but for one night the poverty and pinched life of this little town had a glory of its own. And certain I am that he to whom it was offered must remember it as among the most precious of many tributes to his fame.

III.

THE CORN EXCHANGE AND THE WAVERLEY MARKET.

[EDINBURGH, *November* 30, 1879.]

I must appeal once more to the patience of my readers and beg them to accompany me to the Gladstone meetings held yesterday, first in the Corn Exchange and afterward in the Waverley Market. These assemblies were the fitting close and crown to the earlier demonstration of the same week, and they had at the same time each a distinct character of its own. During the whole week the interest and enthusiasm about Mr. Gladstone have been increasing. If you want the most practical evidence of the solidity and extent of the general feeling you will find scores of advertisements offering tickets to Saturday's meetings for sale or containing offers to buy. The price of a reserved seat in the Corn Exchange ruled as high as £4. That is only a detail though a significant one. You must have been here in order to get anything like an adequate notion of the excitement prevailing in a great city and possessing a whole people on this one topic.

I have seen great public displays of many different sorts in many parts of the world. I recollect none, certainly none which was purely political in character, which has risen to the height of this. I never heard, I doubt whether anybody ever heard, such a succession of speeches in a single week, so extraordinary as sustained efforts of oratory, and so extraordinary in their effect upon the audiences who heard them and upon the people in the midst of whom they have been delivered. But I will say this in mitigation of the censure which may be the penalty of a susceptibility I admit to be unprofessional. I do not plead that it is shared by all Scotland. But I do urge that the most veteran and practised expert in such matters now living shares it. Mr. Gladstone himself said yesterday, privately, that he had never seen anything like it in his life.

The purely electoral business of the week came to an end with the gathering on Thursday at West Calder. The meetings of yesterday were convened by the Liberal Association of the East and North of Scotland, and in one the working men of Scotland also took part. The Corn Exchange in which the first was held is an edifice well enough adapted for dealing in breadstuffs. As a public hall its one merit is its capacity. It will contain, and did yesterday contain, nearly 4500 persons seated. It is the building where ten years ago Mr. Disraeli proclaimed to an astonished world that he had been engaged in educating his party, and commemorated his satisfaction with the success of his efforts. The echo which that announcement produced has not died away, unhappily. It lingers in the building, and the frequent repetition of Mr. Gladstone's sentences from a distant corner of the hall marred their effect at the spot where I sat; but was less mischievous in other parts of the crowded room.

The singularly fine-looking body of men who filled the great area was no ordinary audience. There were delegates from every part of Scotland. Members of different Liberal associations had come from the most remote districts in the Highlands, and in still greater numbers from the central and southern counties. Glasgow alone had sent 800 to this and the other meeting. For some reason or other, it suits the Scotch to open their halls a couple of hours before the proceedings are to begin, and the eagerness to hear Mr. Gladstone—perhaps also the doubt whether late comers would be sure of admission—is such that the Exchange was crowded before two o'clock for a speech to begin at three. Part of the interval was improved as a season for meditation. During another part a band of university students in the rear sang a number of stanzas adapted to the tune of John Brown, and very odd and striking it was to hear a Scotch audience joining, as they did with great heartiness, in the chorus to which Northern regiments had kept time as they marched through the South. They were orderly and patient withal, nor did the strong passions that possessed them interfere with the preservation of an almost religious solemnity of demeanour. I never thought the time wasted during which I could study the bearing of the people among whom I have spent the week. Often as I have seen great assemblages in England this is my first experience of Scotchmen in the mass, and I think it must be said that the Scotch audience, with all its austerity and hardness, offers to the impartial spectator a more striking collection of faces than can be seen in most English meetings. I was constantly reminded of a remark I heard last summer from a distinguished English Liberal, to whom I was dilating upon the singular aptitude for political affairs I had observed in the men who took part in the Morayshire election in August. He said it did not surprise him at all; that the leaven of British politics was to be found in Scotland, and that England was continually indebted to Scotch Liberalism for such progress as was made in the direction of political reform.

I said something in previous letters of the audiences I had then seen, and of their more marked peculiarities. But this was the best of all; nor even in America have I remarked a higher average of intelligence in any gathering of equal numbers. On almost every face was set the seal of that conscientious thoughtfulness, that power of continuous application of mind, that sincerity of intellectual effort, which have done so much to make Scotland what she is. The note of indifferentism which distinguishes the superior classes in England, and above all in London, is not to be found here. These men are not ashamed to be in earnest nor to let it be seen that they are in earnest. Such a degree of seriousness would be voted slow in the clubs of St. James's Street and spread dismay among the polished triflers who are the ornaments of Belgravian dinner-tables. But it is probable that their weightier qualities are as valuable for the purposes of political life as the elaborate contemptuousness of that more elegant society which has decreed everything to be wearisome that is not flippant, and can tolerate no conversation in which frivolity has not the greater share. This is no time for disquisitions upon such matters, but I must avow that during this visit I have acquired a new sense of respect for the Scottish character and a better knowledge of the elements which compose its greatness.

Mr. Gladstone had driven from Dalmeny Park amid the demonstrations of popular respect which have saluted him at every step, and which yesterday were renewed on a greater scale than ever. I hear that long before he approached Edinburgh he had been surrounded by a troop of horsemen, and by crowds of carriages which went out to meet him and turned to accompany him into the city, driving three and four abreast. They were so numerous that the road became almost impassable and the police had to interfere. In the Grassmarket—a name which has figured often in Edinburgh history—and down the steep streets by which it is entered, and even on the slopes of the mighty rock crowned by the Castle, the usual multitude of spectators had collected. Their cheers gave us the first notice of his arrival, and when he entered the tumultuous outbursts of previous days were heard once more. The extreme respectability of this audience had no effect in diminishing the enthusiasm of the reception. A competent authority speaks of the gathering in the Corn Exchange as the most influential, representative, and significant political assemblage ever held beneath its roof. Great names certainly were not wanting among those who figured on the platform.

Lord Rosebery is exceedingly popular. Amid the tributes offered to Mr. Gladstone the audience found time to applaud their chairman with untiring energy. I do not know whether Lord Rosebery ever made you a speech in America but he is known here as one of the rising orators in the House of Lords. His speech for the Greeks, at Willis's Rooms last summer, was far beyond the usual range of English platform oratory. It was polished, vigorous, original. So to-day he performed the duty of introducing Mr. Gladstone in a manner quite unlike the conventional exercises on such occasions. His sentences were uttered with the clearness of a practised speaker, and they all told. There was not a sign of impatience as he pronounced a somewhat elaborate panegyric on Mr. Gladstone; prefaced by an apology for detaining his hearers from the accents of "that silver voice which during the past week has enchanted Scotland and enchained the world"; and followed by a just delineation of the popular tribute to the statesman: "These have been no prepared ebullitions of sympathy; these have been no calculated demonstrations. The heart of the nation has been touched." Lord Rosebery is young, not over thirty, I think, and it is safe to say that a man who has shown his abilities and won his position at that age—due though it be in part to his rank—and who is capable of turning out phrases of that degree of rhetorical neatness, has every prospect of a distinguished public career.

Mr. Gladstone's speech was wholly devoted to finance—a subject which passes for dry. It abounded in figures, in minute criticism of the financial mistakes of the Government, in painstaking analysis, and in elaborate exposition of financial principles. And it was one of the most interesting speeches ever delivered. It was not only interesting, it was amusing. It kept the attention of a delighted audience from the first sentence to the last. Never once did he lose his hold; not in the midst of the most formidable statistics, nor at any point in the labyrinthine evolution of his longest sentences. Mr. Gladstone's sentences, indeed, long as they are, are constructed on principles which permit any moderately attentive hearer to follow them without too much difficulty. His exuberance of diction does not always obscure; it sometimes even illuminates his meaning. He asked nothing of his hearers except their attention. They are not required to do any thinking for themselves; the thinking he had done for them. He left nothing to inference or computation. You were not put to the fatigue of adding two and two together. If he wished it to be understood that the sum of those factors was four, he said so. There is not an ellipsis in all the speech; not even such an one as is common in ordinary conversation. Every mental process was gone through with by the orator himself, not by his audience. It is this unexampled clearness and patient lucidity which is one secret of Mr. Gladstone's power in dealing with finance. I can only add, for I ought to be already in Waverley Market, that it abounded in humour beyond any speech I ever heard from Mr. Gladstone; humour of language, of voice, of manner, of gesture, which sent the audience repeatedly into roars of delight. But I imagine that when the Chancellor of the Exchequer read it delight was not his uppermost sensation. Sir Stafford Northcote had mentioned finance in his speech at the Lord Mayor's dinner as the point of all others on which he should prefer to see the Government attacked, because there they were strong. Sir Stafford will have plenty of time for repenting of his imprudence; an imprudence the more surprising because it was nothing less than a direct challenge to Mr. Gladstone, and Mr. Gladstone, by the confession of opponents as well as friends, both as a financier and a financial orator is without a rival.

I pass from this meeting, about which so much remains to be said, with reluctance, and I approach Waverley Market with still greater reluctance for I must condense into a few paragraphs an account for which as many columns would hardly suffice. I must not say a word of the glorious scene that was about us as we drove hurriedly from the Corn Exchange to the Waverley Market, nor of the unmatched loveliness of Edinburgh on that evening; with the full orb of the moon looking down on the countless multitudes that filled the street; on the Castle; on the towering twelve-storied houses of the old town; on the turreted roofs and pinnacles and spires and quaint gables and jutting windows from which sparkled innumerable lights; or on any other of the myriad beauties which together make Edinburgh the most picturesque of European cities, even in its everyday dress. While we had been hearing Mr. Gladstone—4000 of us—in the Exchange, a throng at least ten times as numerous was raging about Waverley Market. The speech in the Exchange was fixed for three o'clock; the proceedings in the Market for five, and the doors of the latter were to be open at three. Long before three the pressure of people about the barricades had become so serious that the police notified the committee they could not be responsible for the consequences if the doors were not thrown open. There was no rioting but there was a popular movement of a kind too energetic and emotional to be resisted. Many accidents occurred outside; not a few also as people rushed in through narrow gates; and when they were once in the matter became still more serious.

Arriving at half-past five—for the Exchange meeting lasted longer than was meant—what I saw was this: A covered space computed to hold 20,000 people, all standing except those in the galleries, densely packed together over every part of this immense space, the galleries not less crowded than the floor, and the mass of human beings surging hither and thither in a way that instantly struck you as most dangerous. Barriers had been put up but there were not enough of them, and the crowd was uncontrollable. There was no more tendency to rioting here than out of doors, but 20,000 men cannot stand still for three hours, and it was full three hours that they had been waiting for Mr. Gladstone with absolutely nothing to do. They had borne the delay, by all accounts, with wonderful good-nature, but it is certain they could not have borne it much longer. At every movement in one direction or another, one of those currents which begin no one knows how, which are like the movement of a tide and just as irresistible, passed through and along the hall. Men went down under the pressure and were picked up breathless. At every moment somebody with a white face and rigid body was handed over the heads of his comrades and deposited in some protected inclosure. Water was eagerly called for. Men who had not suffered from the movement fainted from the heat and long fatigue. The roof was so low that the heat of the gas was overpowering; and the light was ghastly enough as it fell on faces haggard with exhaustion. It was throughout an audience of working men; men of strong frame and much power of endurance; but their strength had been cruelly tried. It was nobody's fault. The arrangements were well conceived and carried out but the experiment was too full of peril to be tried often.

The peril was at its height when Mr. Gladstone came and it vanished with his coming. There were cases of fainting afterward, and all through the proceedings Mrs. Gladstone and Lady Rosebery were handing down vinaigrettes and tumblers, but the worst was over. Pain and weariness were forgotten in the joy of the people at the sight of their hero. It is useless to attempt to describe the explosion of delight with which he was greeted. It was a prolonged, hoarse cry taken up again and again, immense vibrations of sound sweeping through the air, broken, inarticulate, but full of an eloquence which surpassed the eloquence of the orator who had set this hurricane in motion. It certainly lasted five minutes and it was much more than that before anything like quiet fell upon the assembly. Mr. Gladstone stood as you may fancy him standing at the first sight of Niagara or the Alps; with the attitude and expression that come to a man upon the revelation of Nature's greatest marvels or of her most prodigious forces stirred suddenly to action. He was profoundly moved, and did not care to conceal that he was profoundly moved. So enormous was the audience that it lost almost its human character in the farthest parts of the hall. You could not distinguish faces; you could not tell whether the dim rounded substances which reflected the light from the outer edges of this mass were the heads of men, or whether they were not heaps of potatoes.

There was a tedious ceremony of address-offering; judiciously and mercifully abridged by Lord Rosebery's firm refusal to allow these documents to be read; and then Mr. Gladstone spoke. All the speaking theretofore had been dumb-show to most of us. Even Lord Rosebery's voice was hardly audible on the platform or for more than a few feet beyond the reporters — of whom, here as elsewhere, there were not less than eighty present from all parts of the kingdom. It was only when Mr. Gladstone rose, and had stood silent for some minutes, that silence finally fell upon the multitude. The first note of that marvellous voice rose like the peal of an organ. For the first time he spoke with visible effort; sending his slow syllables and deep tones to the uttermost end of the building; using his utmost power. He was everywhere heard over the spreading surface of what he so well described as an ocean of human life. It is probably the greatest feat he ever performed. To have kept up such a strain long would have been impossible. He spoke for perhaps twenty minutes. I know nothing more characteristic of the determined courage of the man than the fact that, after this, he once more met his mob of admirers outside and drove away through Princes Street, uncovered and in an open carriage as before. It was not till long past the range of houses that the lines began to grow thin and I know not where it was that the people of Edinburgh may be said to have uttered their last farewell.

MR. GLADSTONE IN 1884.

I.

THE ARRIVAL IN MIDLOTHIAN.

[EDINBURGH, *August* 28, 1884.]

THERE have been Tories who found it amusing to go about saying that Mr. Gladstone would never dare visit Midlothian again. His popularity was gone, his prestige wasted, his hold on the allegiance of Scotsmen to whom principles are more than party and party-leaders, shaken. Only yesterday, an hour before he entered Edinburgh, I was told by the landlord of my hotel, a Tory of intelligence, that the people of Midlothian were tired of Mr. Gladstone, disappointed in him, disgusted with his foreign policy, and would never again give him the cordial receptions of 1879 and 1880. These predictions, whether English or Scottish, have not deterred him from coming, nor reflected great credit on the prophetic gifts of their authors. The Prime Minister has not paid much heed to the sonorous warnings of the metropolitan Tory press, nor have the people of Edinburgh quite justified the forebodings of their hotel-keeper. Mr. Gladstone is actually in Midlothian, the guest of Lord Rosebery at Dalmeny, after a welcome from five-and-twenty thousand people who managed to pack themselves into the few yards of the streets of Edinburgh through which he had to pass.

The journey from Hawarden was less fruitful in incident than the memorable one he made in November 1879. He caused it to be known that he wished for no receptions at railway stations and had no speeches to make by the way. The reason is obvious enough. In 1879 Mr. Gladstone came to Scotland with a message *urbi et orbi*. He came to pull down a Government. He was not Member for Midlothian, but candidate. He had, as he said himself with one of his rare touches of humour, more things to say than he could find places to say them in. Now he is Prime Minister, and has a Government to uphold instead of a Government to overthrow. He is the representative of a great constituency, coming to render a long-deferred account to his constituents. He thinks it more respectful to them that his first words in public should be to their ears; the more so as he had to disappoint them when they expected a visit from him last year. He could not well have repeated the succession of animated little speeches which he made in 1879, without discounting the effect of the disclosures expected here on Saturday and Monday, or without baffling the curiosity he had encouraged. So the word was passed along the line by which he was to travel that there were to be no demonstrations. This did not prevent people from gathering in numbers wherever they might hope to have a look at their hero, but it permitted him to escape from their embraces with only here and there a sentence, not meant to be very significant.

My inn-keeping friend had asked me to take note of the fact that the streets leading to the station where Mr. Gladstone was to arrive were not very full. Princes Street itself had not much more than the usual throng in front of this hotel, but nearer the station the crowd was increasing and by four o'clock—ten minutes before the time appointed for the arrival—it was not easy to get near the place. The approaches to the departure platform were left free to the public; on the other side there were barriers and police. The street here branches into several streets and broadens into a sort of square, and there is plenty of space for a multitude. Opposite the entrance is the Liberal Club and this was decorated with much bunting while its windows and balconies were filled with spectators. But there was no great attempt at spectacle. I thought it a pity that Mr. Gladstone should have elected to arrive at the Caledonian Railway Station, at one end of Edinburgh. In 1879 he came to the Waverley Station, which is central, and drove thence along that magnificent street which may well be called princely, so that all Edinburgh had a chance to greet him. The difference is that Edinburgh now had to take a little more trouble and go a little more out of its way to see and cheer the man whom she really seems, spite of the Tories, still to honour. But perhaps no salute is quite so impressive as one which comes first from a mass of people, and is then taken up and repeated by other masses of people along the streets.

Lord Rosebery came to meet Mr. Gladstone, arriving from Dalmeny Park in an open carriage-and-four with postilions and outriders. As he drove past the Liberal Club, and through the crowd in the square, and into the yard of the station, he was cheered warmly. This young nobleman has a way of acknowledging such greetings which is perhaps peculiar to himself. He sits upright in his carriage, his hat lifted, looking straight before him, and with an air of being extremely bored. These outward expressions of enthusiasm do perhaps bore him, and, although he must be deeply sensible of the good-will they express, his face may indicate his state of mind for the moment. But if he had calculated the exact effect of countenance and bearing which would most delight his Scottish admirers, he could not have hit on anything better. With him were Lord Carrington, and Mr. Hamilton the chief of Mr. Gladstone's four private secretaries. A crowd had found its way to the arrival platform; a crowd composed of the elect of Edinburgh; her Lord Provost, her two members, her Liberal managers, a few favoured ladies, and various representatives of municipal and political bodies. Not the least attempt had been made to decorate the place. Edinburgh, the most beautiful city in the north of Europe, delights to keep down the expectations of the arriving traveller, and prepares his mind for the splendours of her architecture and natural scenery by an approach through stations unsurpassed for meanness and discomfort and dirt. No doubt contrast is a good thing, and the arriving traveller enjoys it in perfection as he emerges from these squalid dens into the splendour of the outer world. But it may be carried too far.

The train which brought Mr. Gladstone reached Princes Street Station with that punctuality which distinguishes Scotch railways, forty minutes after the hour fixed. It was five o'clock. The crowd of respectabilities catching sight of the engine wreathed with evergreens and flowers, made its usual effort to get under the wheels, but were reminded by the few policemen present that Juggernaut is not an English fashion and so with gentle violence were persuaded to stand back. A semicircular breathing space was left for Lord Rosebery, the Lord Provost, and other dignitaries. The train stopped cleverly with the door of Mr. Gladstone's saloon carriage just opposite this little group. Mr. Gladstone stepped out and the cheering broke loose. By the time Lord Rosebery's hand was in his, the greeting had been taken up outside, and the first notes of the multitude were mingling with the hurrahs of the interior.

The sight that met us at the doorway was striking, the sound was more striking still. The Prime Minister was deep in the midst of the densely packed crowd. The police had kept a road for him, an outrider went on before, the postilions knew their business, and the smart equipage was moving pretty quickly but every moment seemed to be caught and checked by the tempest that filled the square. Mr. Gladstone was bareheaded and bowing. Right above him was the castle-crowned crag which is the glory of Edinburgh, but for the moment people were of opinion that the glory of Edinburgh was Mr. Gladstone. The scene was magnificent; and the central figure of it was magnificent. It is almost five years since Edinburgh has looked on that face. Certainly it has not grown younger in the interval. There is another shade of white in the thin, ashen-gray hair and perhaps a more ashen hue on the cheek, a darker circle beneath the eye, sharper lines here and there. But the eye is just as luminous and deep-glowing, the mouth not less firm and a whit sterner, the effect of immense vigour and unquenchable energy just as tremendous—there is no other word for it—as in earlier days. He is moved by the overwhelming outburst of these thousands and tens of thousands of friends about him. He bows and bows again. From the station it is impossible to see the face, but I have seen it often under similar circumstances and I know very well how those almost stern features are softening to the touch of that affectionate welcome. The cheers seem as if they would never stop. As the carriage recedes a fresh burst from some more distant point comes back to us, nor does the throng disperse all at once. Driving along the same route a few minutes later I came in for the ground-swell of the storm that had spent its force. Knots of people were talking it over; the younger people were renewing the cheers. The balconies of the Liberal Club were still garnished with ladies. The police kept their station. Far out on the road to Dalmeny these guardians of order were to be met; like thrifty Scots as they were, the white gloves donned for the occasion already taken off and carefully tucked into their belts. Not the least interesting things to be seen were the modest decorations, the toy flags, even rugs and bedquilts hanging from the windows of the cottages of one or two hamlets on the road. One thatched hut had a fringe of flowers all along the edges of the roof. "Was that done for the Prince of Wales?" I asked the coachman, the Prince's visit to Dalmeny having ended only two days ago. "Oh no, sir," he answered; "they had flowers for the Prince and Princess but these are quite fresh." Which it might have pleased Mr. Gladstone to know. He knows well enough, for that matter, that among his staunchest friends in all this country are those poorer classes whose welfare he has long sought to promote, and to whom he is now offering the franchise which the Lords are striving to withhold from them.

II.

A DRIVE FROM DALMENY AND A MUNICIPAL RECEPTION.

[DALMENY PARK, *September* 1, 1884.]

Mr. Gladstone was to make his first speech to his constituents of Midlothian on Saturday, August 30, at five o'clock in the afternoon, and to start from Dalmeny at half-past three. The orators of America may be interested to know that he spent the morning—after getting through the little official work that had to be done—in reading a novel. There had been a rumour that he was behindhand in his preparations. Be that as it may, he had thoroughly considered what he should say by the time breakfast was over, and thenceforward devoted himself to the complete relaxation of his mind till the moment to speak came. He might well have found something to occupy him in the beauty of the scene and the preparations for the start. The faultlessly turned-out equipages which were to take the house-party at Dalmeny into Edinburgh drove on to the hard gravel carriage-sweep a few minutes before the half-hour. There were two open carriages-and-four with postilions and outriders, a landau and pair, a brake, and a Victoria. Staying at Dalmeny are one or two young men whose authority in such matters is very complete. They agree that there is not much the matter with this display, and when a young Englishman of the superior classes uses that phrase it may be understood as embodying the highest form of eulogy. Altogether, the front of Dalmeny at the moment was a scene of brilliant animation near by, and of perfect loveliness as the eye looked farther afield over lawn, hedge, and shrubbery, past clumps of venerable trees, through a glade of oaks whose foliage almost overhangs the blue waters of the Forth, then pauses an instant on the great island in mid-channel, and rests contentedly on the noble hills of Fifeshire which inclose the northern shore of this admirable stretch of sea.

The start for the seven miles' drive into Edinburgh was punctual. From the door of the house to the lodge the distance is two miles. It is one of the charms of Dalmeny Park that nature has not been turned out of it. There are delightful parks where every blade of grass looks as if it had been combed early that morning, and pomatumed, and every tree planted on a plan; as if the water in the lakes came through an aqueduct, and the very deer are domestic. Dalmeny with its 2500 acres is an example of the other method of treatment. Enough has been done but not too much. The natural forest comes close up to the house on two sides. It abounds in steep hills. From the top of any one of them which you climb you have enchanting views of a varied landscape glowing with delicate colour and soft tints. The long undulating avenue passes for most of the distance through dense woodland, but ever and anon the woodland breaks into spreading acres of corn, broad spaces of turf, and broader grazing fields. Wherever the forest opens there is a fresh surprise for you. At one turn the house you have just left reappears, the gray stone and stiff pinnacles of semi-Tudor fabric standing well out against the dark green of sycamore and fir. The castle of Barnbougle, rebuilt by Lord Rosebery in a curiously effective simplicity of style which will be more effective still when time shall have stained and darkened the freshness of the new stone, rises from a point of land reaching so far into the Forth that the rush of the tide from the North German Ocean washes two flanks of this once ancient and feudal keep. The union-jack floats from the tower. Ships are passing; the opposite shores two miles away are enlivened by villages, and here and there a massive country mansion is visible on the hillside; the more distant smoke and possibly the masts of Granton may come in view as you drive, and the next minute you are deep again in a labyrinth of branches that brush your hat for you the wrong way. Mr. Gladstone's admiration for this park is known. He has often been Lord Rosebery's guest at Dalmeny; nay, he has left his mark on the place where a little railing incloses a stump, level with the ground, bearing the pathetic inscription, "W. E. Gladstone cut me down, April 3, 1880."

The day was not quite all one could wish; there were only fitful gleams of sunshine, and once or twice the rain came down,—rain of that quiet sort which goes by the name of a Scotch mist. Before we were out of the park the sky had cleared, and the weather, though it could hardly be called fine, gave no more trouble. The popular greeting to Mr. Gladstone began at the very gates which open on the Queensferry road to Edinburgh.

Here were little groups of people on foot and in vehicles who had come thus far—it is five miles from Edinburgh—to be the first to greet Mr. Gladstone; or, possibly enough, they came from the country side. There they were, at any rate; and they raised the first cheer we heard, women adding their cries to the men's. One wagonette held two detectives and there were half a dozen conveyances filled with reporters. All these fell into the rear of the procession and followed to Edinburgh. Along these five miles of road there are few visible houses. Great fields of yellow wheat and oats border it, intermingled with park and forest. There is a village or two but, on the whole, the spectators must have travelled some distance. They increase in number as we drive on. Carriages are drawn up along the roadside and try to cut in. This sort of zeal is strictly repressed by the detectives and the intruders are forced to stay where they are or take up places far behind. Men on bicycles appear as if out of the ground and go skimming past with as much freedom of movement as the birds. Presently, as we approach Blackhall, the chief hamlet we pass, men are to be seen running along by the side of the carriages in front. The detectives look anxious. Not a uniformed policeman is yet visible and the detectives in their four-wheeled, one-horsed wagonette are powerless to interfere with this sort of thing, mischievous as it might prove to be. Just in the outskirts of Blackhall one perfervid Scot, a heavily built, well-to-do sort of man, suddenly abandons his wife and child, rushes after Mr. Gladstone's carriage, puts his hand on the panel, and keeps his place for a hundred yards. He means no harm but it is a relief to everybody when six well mounted policemen appear. One of them rides ahead, two on either side of Mr. Gladstone, one in the rear. As on Wednesday, the humblest people were among the most enthusiastic. The children had taken up the parable of the parents and lifted their little voices in welcome; a baby in arms was waving a handkerchief with the best strength of its fat little arms and a broad smile on its rosy face. Flags hung from some houses, a few banners with inscriptions are on the outer walls, but there was not much basis for decoration till the close-built streets of Edinburgh were reached, nor very much to attract attention even there, except the Liberal Club which kept on its smart dress of Wednesday and filled its balconies with the few members and their wives who were not at the meeting.

The crowds in the streets of Edinburgh were great, but I thought not so great as I remembered them in 1879. Such comparisons are really idle because the circumstances are different and no such piece of history as that of 1879 could by any possibility repeat itself. There is quite enough in the appearance of the multitudes of to-day to wonder at. There is cheering at every step as the carriages whirl past. Lord Rosebery has no idea of moderating the pace to gratify the curiosity of those who stand there to gaze, and the pace is something like ten miles an hour. To the disappointment of many spectators waiting in Princes Street, the procession turned off into Lothian Road and made for the Council Chamber by Castle Terrace, High Street, and George IV Bridge. Barricades had been put up and the middle of the street was kept clear. Police everywhere, and not much for them to do. From the windows of the grim, not to say grimy, houses of High Street, countless people looked down, in every stage of unwashed raggedness. This quarter of the Old Town is interesting, but squalid. Dirt, however, does not depress the spirits of the populace, and a pillow-case in holes produces quite as much effect, when waved with energy from a sixth-story garret window, as if it were a lace pocket-handkerchief. Lord Rosebery came in for his share of the popular greeting. His name was to be heard every moment above the din, but he chose to hear nothing and to assume that all this enthusiasm was aimed at Mr. Gladstone, and sat motionless on the front seat, his hat solidly planted on his forehead, with the air of an interested spectator.

This council chamber expedition, being only a prelude to the chief business of the day, was briefly despatched. Mr. Gladstone and the whole party descended with agility, marched across the courtyard of the building as rapidly as dignity would permit, mounted to the first story, tarried a moment in the room of Lord Provost Harrison who received his guests with his usual smiling face, made their way into the Council Chamber, sat down amid a company of scarlet-robed bailies, listened to an address of welcome to Edinburgh, not too long, and then Mr. Gladstone made his reply in that tone of easy conversation which one so often hears from him in the House of Commons. The colloquial tone deepens now and then as he touches some topic which stirs him, and he is never long without doing that. He was not to talk politics but he adroitly connected the Franchise Bill with the history of Edinburgh as one of the Scotch cities which had profited by the Reform Act of 1832. He talked of her university, of her ancient fame, of her share in the history of Scotland, "much of whose destiny has been determined in other days within her walls"; and he pronounced such a eulogy on Edinburgh and Scotland together as sent every Scotsman's blood rushing along his veins. Then, with scant ceremony of leave-taking, for the hour of the great meeting was already at hand, off he went; the carriages were again filled, raced down the hill we had just climbed, and up the same hill farther to the south by Lower Castle Terrace to the Grassmarket, and reached the Corn Exchange, where the speech of the day was to be made. Here, outside, the greatest throng of the day was collected behind barriers of solid timber guarded by policemen not less solid, and the lofty walls that flank the street called Grassmarket echoed again with Scottish shouts as the crowd caught sight of the uncovered gray head of the Prime Minister, whom every dweller in Midlothian delights to describe as "our Member." It was quarter past five. Within the long, low building was to be heard plainly enough the murmur and movement of the great audience, most of whom for the last two hours had been in their places, waiting more or less patiently for the arrival of the hour and the man.

III.

A SHORT STUDY OF MR. GLADSTONE'S ORATORY.

[DALMENY PARK, *September* 3, 1884.]

Descending from his carriage amid the shouts of the friendly mob in the Grassmarket, Mr. Gladstone walked rapidly (I hardly ever saw him walk slowly) up the passage and into the Corn Exchange. The long waiting audience inside had heard the roars without, and Scot answered unto Scot with that steady cheer which expresses so well the businesslike determination of this people to make their approval understood. The whole party passed into a large anteroom where half the notabilities of Scotland were waiting to receive their leader. An address or two was presented in dumb show. It is not possible for the Prime Minister to stir anywhere out of doors without having an address fired off at him. His present collection of these interesting but perhaps monotonous tributes numbers, I believe, over four hundred. Then at last the Member for Midlothian passed into the presence of his constituents.

His constituents—not all, but about half—had gathered themselves together in a building devoted on ordinary days to transactions in cereals. They had spent the afternoon in this cheerful spot and prepared their minds for the coming speech by a season of patient and, for aught I know, prayerful meditation. No doubt in the days of John Knox some minister would have "improved" this interval by some exercise of a religious kind; but whether any such function was performed on this occasion I forgot to ask. There are plenty of political reminiscences in connection with this market-place. Lord Beaconsfield made one of his best-known speeches here. Lord Salisbury's voice has been heard from the same platform on which Mr. Gladstone is to stand in a moment, and Mr. Gladstone himself delivered here in 1879 a speech of an hour and a half on finance. It is not a fine building; no degree of patriotism would enable Scotsmen of taste to describe it as otherwise than contemptible if considered as a public hall. It was not built for oratorical purposes. It has no dignity of proportion nor any structural features or scheme of ornamentation which can possibly be called architectural. An oblong, low, glass-roofed shed whose one merit is its capacity of holding 5000 people—that is the Corn Exchange of Edinburgh. The energetic committee who have these meetings in charge, and who have wrought miracles, have done their best to hide the bareness of walls and roof and to coax their guest into the conviction that this is not a railway station nor a warehouse. Draperies, flowers, evergreens, shields of strange device and every variety of legend, and a liberal use of colour are the chief decorative features. A high broad platform runs across the whole of one end, there are galleries on the other three sides, which may or may not have been improvised for the occasion, and all the disposition of aisles, entrances, and exits is convenient.

None of all this does any human being observe as we enter. The only thing it is possible to be aware of is the multitude of other human beings on their feet, on the benches, waving hats and handkerchiefs and sticks and umbrellas, and cheering steadily. The occupants of the platform, hundreds in number, half of them ladies, stand up to receive Mr. Gladstone. The whole audience cheers him before he is seen, cheers him more loudly still as they get their first glimpse of him, and the cheers grow in volume and intensity as he and his party make their way along a well-guarded passage, up a flight of steps, along the front of the platform, and so to the seats they are to occupy. Mr. Gladstone is not made of stone and this greeting touches him; there is a tremulous movement of the lines of his mouth to be seen if you look for it. Mrs. Gladstone may have heard her name proposed in hoarse tones from the centre of the throng as an incentive to fresh outbursts. The staunchest Tory could not but feel the genuineness of all this enthusiasm. The loyalty of Midlothian to Mr. Gladstone, so often questioned in recent years, is not likely to be doubted again so far as it depends on the purely popular voice. I say nothing of electoral prospects —it is too soon to discuss them. It would not be easy to believe that any chill of dissatisfaction—and dissatisfaction there probably is with parts of Mr. Gladstone's policy— would not dissolve in this fervent heat. But taunts about the probability of a hostile reception must come to an end in presence of the events of this week.

Silence obtained, Mr. Gladstone, after a word or two from Mr. Cowan, began his speech. The subject-matter and substance of this and his other addresses I will try to deal with in a final letter. For present purposes I may as well drop at this point the historical method and disregard the order of time, with a view to saying once for all what has to be said about Mr. Gladstone's oratory as a whole during this present visit. The first sound of his voice was listened for with something like anxiety. Is it possible that after five years that wonderful organ should be still in its full perfection of flexible strength? The curious in such details may note that a bottle of yellow fluid, from which a tumbler has been half-filled, stands on the table. The yellow fluid is egg-flip, gently compounded of the yolk of two or three eggs and two glasses of sherry. This is to keep throat and voice in order, and before the orator has made an end he has sipped a tumbler full. But the first note of the voice and the first half-dozen sentences of the first day were reassuring. There is no longer any fear that Mr. Gladstone may be overtaxing his energies. His friends say that he himself can take an accurate measure of his capacities and of the precise demands a particular hall and audience will make upon them. He feels, as the rest of us feel, that the voice is all right. Yet he does not once try its full compass. This speech is didactic, expository, argumentative, anything you like but passionate or pathetic, and you never know the full resources of this all but unequalled voice till you have heard it used in anger, in pity, in ridicule —above all, in one of those appeals to principle and to religious conviction which so often close some of his greatest speeches.

A stranger hearing Mr. Gladstone on Saturday for the first and only time might go away with a certain sense of incompleteness in his experience. He would have heard a speech which nobody else could have made, but he would by no means have heard the orator at his best. What I have said about the little call he made on his voice may be applied to the speech itself. He has not asked himself to do all he can. It is a speech with a definite purpose, and he has sacrificed everything else to the one great end of impressing on the country the vital importance of the Franchise Bill, and on the Lords the advisability of yielding without force to the will of the people. But let the stranger come again on Monday. The place is the same, the scene is the same, the same orator stands on the same platform. But he is no longer in the same mood of sweet reasonableness and nothing else. The very face has changed. On Saturday it wore a look of resolute placidity. On Monday the features are allowed their natural play, and if you sit near enough to look into those onyx-hued eyes you will vainly try to sound their varying depths. Anybody who has seen Mr. Gladstone often will discover that for this second address he feels himself—to use again his own expression—unmuzzled. There is no longer the dread of rousing popular passion against an institution which, in his heart of hearts, the Prime Minister is more anxious to support than to assail. The inexorable necessity of caution weighs him down no longer. He approaches this new task with a buoyant delight in the easy triumph he is about to win. The five years have rolled off his brow. Erect, elastic, exultant, he can hardly wait till the five thousand in front have done cheering — indeed, but for his obvious impatience to begin they might be cheering till now. In the first sentence on Monday you really hear his voice for the first time. No trace of fatigue from the prolonged effort of Saturday. None of the hardness of tone which was to be heard then. The compass, range, and quality of it are all better.

His task now is to retort upon his opponents the charges they have been heaping up against him. For five years the Tories have gone about insisting with vague but emphatic assertion and reassertion that the Prime Minister had falsified the pledges which Mr. Gladstone had given in the first Midlothian speeches. Three-fourths of his speech on Monday are one triumphant cry, "Prove it!" or rather, "You have tried to prove it; you have had the text, you have piled accusation upon accusation, you have had years to get up your case. I challenge you to put your finger on one count of this long indictment which you have supported by one syllable of evidence." He goes over the record. He reviews the situation. He passes from topic to topic, perhaps too rapidly, perhaps with a too comprehensive ambition, and with too much eagerness to survey in one single statement the whole course of his administration, and to condense into this hour and a half a complete epitome of all he said in a week in 1879, and all that his enemies have said in five years since, and to set in a halo of light all the contradictions and the inventions of his critics, and the perfect and absolute harmony between his own pledges and the accomplished facts of his subsequent career. But what a scope such a programme gives him! How he revels in it, how he heaps irony upon sarcasm, and how his defence rises to white heat, and the steel you thought he was shaping into a shield suddenly flashes before you a two-edged sword and cleaves asunder the foe in one blinding stroke.

Yes, this indeed is oratory, and in the two hours less ten minutes during which it lasts you may find examples of nearly every charm which it is possible for an orator to work upon his hearers. The effect he produces does not owe much to gesture. There is gesture, but it often lacks expressiveness. The arms are used pretty constantly but the same movement of the same muscles is made to signify, or meant to signify, very different things. It wants what on the French stage is called largeness or amplitude, and it is sometimes violent, sometimes deficient in the grace and suavity which the admirable smoothness of voice leads you to expect. The shoulders rise and fall at times abruptly, and at such moments the voice sometimes loses its purity, and harsh notes are heard. The rather frequent passage of the right forefinger across the lips, and the curious touch of the thumb on a particular spot at the summit of the broad arch of the forehead, are peculiarities which I mention for the sake of fidelity. So of the quick bending and straightening of the knees. If there be any blemishes of this sort you will hardly observe them unless after long familiarity with the speaker. It is the face which will rivet your gaze; the play of features, alike flexible and powerful, and the ever-restless, far-searching glance. Never was such a telltale countenance. Expression after expression sweeps across it, the thought pictures itself to you almost before it is uttered. Nor do the little blemishes really matter. What matters, what impresses you, and what you will carry away with you as a permanent memory, is above all other things the nobleness of presence, the dignity, the sincerity which are visible to the eyes of the most careless spectator, and which fill the hall with their influence.

I have been asked often enough by my own countrymen if any American was like Mr. Gladstone. I know of none, nor of any European. In appearance the late Mr. Daniel Webster was slightly, very slightly, like Mr. Gladstone, but the massive features and form had an addition of robustness of which in Mr. Gladstone there is none. I once saw and heard Webster in Worcester, when he spoke from the step to the gate leading into the front door-yard of the late Governor Lincoln of Massachusetts, beneath a lantern the rays from which fell straight on his face. He almost exactly realised what Emerson had in mind when he said that if Webster were first revealed to him by a flash of lightning, he should not be sure whether an angel or a demon were standing before him. Well, it is no compliment to Mr. Gladstone to say that nobody would take him for a demon, beneath a flash of lightning or otherwise. But Webster was of the earth. Mr. Gladstone has a light on his face that seems to come from the upper air. Webster was a speaker of extraordinary powers of mind. As Theodore Parker said of him, he could state a case better than any man in America. He was occasionally an orator. It is but seldom that Mr. Gladstone is not. I should like to draw a much more minute comparison between Mr. Gladstone and Wendell Phillips, for it would, I think, be much more illustrative, though I should begin by saying that neither Mr. Gladstone nor anybody else had that Apollo-like beauty of presence, or that voice of gold, or that genius for conciliating or controlling a hostile audience, which were among Phillips's many incomparable gifts. But I cannot do that. I have heard Castelar address 6000 Spaniards at Price's Circus in Madrid in his all too copious Castilian; supple, sympathetic, sinuous, and orator to the tips of his fingers. I have heard Bismarck, when in the white uniform of the cuirassiers of whom he was major, and booted to the knee, he gave his orders with military directness to the Parliament of Prussia. I heard Gambetta in a critical moment of his life, when in 1877 he closed a four days' debate in the Chamber at Versailles with what I think the greatest single effort of oratory I ever listened to in Europe,—and he, too, had a great deal in common with Mr. Gladstone. Both had the same miraculous suppleness of mind and inexhaustible abundance of various diction. Mr. Bright, the one Englishman living whose greatest speeches might be profitably studied side by side with Mr. Gladstone's, would be more profitable for contrast than for comparison. The lucid flow of Mr. Bright's simply constructed sentences, always direct, always the best word in the best place, always effective out of all proportion to any machinery of rhetoric evident to the eye scanning them in print—nothing could be more unlike the method of Mr. Gladstone, and nothing could be more instructive than a full statement of the secret of each. But on the whole, not much is to be gained by these brief reminiscences of great contemporaries, for the most part so essentially unlike Mr. Gladstone, and it is time to get back to the matter in hand, and, above all, time to have done with it.

What needs to be added for the information of the distant reader is this: that, with very rare exceptions, Mr. Gladstone is only to be seen at his very best in the House of Commons. He is not by natural gifts or character, and not pre-eminently by habit or practice, a platform orator. The stump is not his true pedestal. In these later years this is truer than ever, and it remains true in spite of his three excellent discourses here in Edinburgh before vast audiences. He can, when he chooses, be brief, but he prefers to be abundant. A Scotch audience gives him extraordinary advantages and assistance. They are apprehensive and responsive, quick to perceive and eager to applaud beyond any English audience whatever outside of the House of Commons, unless Birmingham, whose people are the pupils of Mr. Bright, be the one exception. And, like every true orator of his stamp, Mr. Gladstone is largely dependent on his audience. Midlothian realises his own description and gives him back in vapour (with incense mingled) what he pours on them in a flood. And yet he is not at his best,—not so good as when he persuaded an astonished

House of Commons in 1882 to pass censure by a majority of 130 on the Upper Chamber; not so good as when he coerced himself and put violence on every prepossession and sympathy of nature and his lifelong ecclesiastical passions, to entreat an intolerant majority to do bare justice to their atheistic and hated colleague from Northampton.

Admirable as he has been in these three speeches, he has not once risen to his very highest level in any one of them. It is enough to say that, as a whole, they are speeches which nobody else would have attempted to make. I should commend that of Monday to any student of Mr. Gladstone as an excellent specimen of his most discursive style. It is idle to go on describing it. There is the speech. Read that. And as you read it try to imagine yourself one of an audience where almost every upturned face bears the stamp of intelligence, and where—although Tories are mixed with Liberals—almost every heart is for the moment beating with deep enthusiasm for the speaker. Imagine the orator surrounded on the platform by almost everything that is most distinguished in Scotland: the flower of her peerage, the best of her politicians, the ornaments of her bar, the greater ornaments of her best society; all that Edinburgh and the country far round Edinburgh has to boast of in beauty and accomplishment and character. Listen to these cheers; listen to the murmur of kindled sympathies, often so much more telling than cheers; give yourself up for the hour, as they do, to the enchantment of this irresistible eloquence; this force of conviction; this tremendous energy of purpose and passion. You may get some faint impression of the scene, you may yield to the spell even of the printed phrase, and thrill to the touch of the spirit which audience and orator have in common. But you will deceive yourself if you think you have any real conception of Mr. Gladstone's genius till you sit beneath him or beside him, till that voice speaks to you, till you look into the face of the orator, till you feel the influence of a personality as persuasive as it is powerful; till, in one word, you are in his presence and subject to his sway.

IV.

THE HOUSE OF LORDS.—LORD ROSEBERY.

[DALMENY PARK, *September* 3, 1884.]

When Mr. Gladstone had finished his first speech in the Corn Exchange of Edinburgh and sat down, two things occurred. The newspapers in these circumstances always tell you that the right honourable gentleman resumed his seat amid loud and prolonged cheering; which is perfectly true. The applause was of a less frantic kind on Saturday than I have known it to be on more exciting occasions, but it lasted for a minute or two, and there was a ring of cordiality about it, due in part to the liking of the people for Mr. Gladstone himself; in part, no doubt, to the fact that they really do care more about the Franchise Bill, to which he had devoted his whole address, than about any other question but one. The strength and suddenness of the applause which broke out all over the hall whenever during this hour and forty minutes Mr. Gladstone uttered a word of remonstrance or warning to the Lords, showed that their anger with the Tory majority of the Peers was at least as hot as their enthusiasm for the Franchise Bill. Of this, let us hope, Mr. Gladstone took note, but it never, or hardly ever, induced him to depart from the limit of strict reserve he had imposed on himself with reference to this side of the agitation pervading the country.

Had he but chosen to put himself at the head of that great majority of his followers who are keen for a contest with Lord Salisbury's forces, the story I should have had to tell would be a very different one. As I sat and looked into the faces of the five thousand on Saturday, and saw the reflection of the orator's words in this multitudinous mirror, I thought I detected at many moments an unsatisfied expectation of something that did not come. Mr. Gladstone had only to utter a word that should have sounded like a word of doom to the Upper House, and the audience would have risen at him. Very early in his speech he chilled these heated hopes and, with a gravity that came near to being sternness, told his constituents that he did not conceive it to be the duty of a Minister of the Crown to lead an agitation having for its object an organic change in the Constitution of the realm. Yet, whenever a sentence was heard that seemed to embody a menace, or to hint at the possibility of peril to the Lords should they persevere beyond a certain point, the house welcomed it so warmly as to leave one in doubt whether, after all, they were not convinced that Mr. Gladstone foresaw a duty that might ultimately be laid on him. They gave him, at any rate, the benefit of the doubt, and if they were chagrined by what they thought his too great caution they smothered it in cheers.

The second incident was the contest between the audience and Lord Rosebery. The cheering for Mr. Gladstone never quite came to a natural end, but while the hall still resounded with applause the cheers were mingled with many cries, and presently hundreds of men were on their feet and shouting Rosebery with such energy—and it was much—as they had left. But Lord Rosebery sat still, hardening his heart to the appeals that poured in on him. Not a line in his face betokened a spirit of concession; he looked exactly as if he were the only man in the Corn Exchange who had missed the meaning of the audience, or had resolved they should be balked. The chairman, and then two other gentlemen on whom devolved certain routine duties, went through them with brevity. A resolution of thanks to the speaker—without which no meeting in this country is ever dissolved—was duly adopted, or declared adopted, for by this time the tumult was such that these proceedings passed in something very like dumb show. Then the roar grew louder, the cries redoubled, it was obvious to everybody that the audience would not be denied, and Lord Rosebery, still with an expression on his face of anything but delight with this demand, rose. The house rose with him. You saw men everywhere fairly spring to their feet, and blended with their joy in greeting Lord Rosebery was a note of triumph at having forced him to speak when he had clearly made up his mind to be silent.

The terms on which Lord Rosebery stands with his Scottish audiences are of the most singular kind. This is far from being the first time I have heard him speak in Edinburgh, or seen him surrounded by his admirers. Certainly he has not earned their homage by flattery. Plain speaking and high thinking are the usual characteristics of his oratory, but there is a secret deeper than that,—the deep sympathy he has with those about him, and not only has, but conveys to them. He identifies himself with his hearers, and his hearers with him. As he speaks, his thoughts and feelings are on a level with those before him. He begins as nobody else in this country does: "My friends and neighbours"; and I am not sure that the phrase he used three days later—of which in its order—was not even more significant. As for this present speech it is, as you have seen, one he had fully determined not to make and it was made with no forethought or preparation of any kind. He explained, and perhaps was not sorry to explain, that he meant to hold aloof from this and the other meetings of this series. Lord Salisbury had called him the patron of Midlothian. It was time, he declared, to put an end to this nonsense, and let better men take the chair. This expression of praiseworthy modesty was rather spoiled, to be sure, by Midlothian itself. Midlothian on all three occasions contrived to make it understood that whoever might be chairman, or whatever might be the programme, it regarded no meeting as complete till it had wrung some sort of a speech from Lord Rosebery.

What they got from him now was a declaration about the House of Lords which may give Lord Salisbury something to think of. With a reference (capable of more than one interpretation) to the conservative moderation of Mr. Gladstone as perhaps greater than he himself could have adopted, Lord Rosebery went on to say that the contest—the contest on which "we" have entered—is not a contest between the

House of Lords and the House of Commons, not a contest between the Government and the House of Lords; "it is a contest between the great mass of the nation that inhabits these islands and the majority of fifty-nine peers, and that, I warned them before that division was taken, was no weapon to use in a struggle with the people of this country." That sentence defined Lord Rosebery's attitude on this question, and we shall presently hear him define it with still more courageous precision before 15,000 working men at the Waverley Market. For the rest, this brief speech, thought out as it proceeded, touched two or three distinct keys, ranging from the humour of the first sentences in which resentment and recognition were oddly blended, to the firm statement of his own position, and winding up with a tribute to Mr. Gladstone in which each word fell readily into its place and the phrases of elaborate eulogy came forth as finished as if midnight oil had been burnt over them.

It was nearly eight o'clock when the proceedings ended. A great portion of those present had been in their places four or five hours, but they strictly obeyed the request of the chairman and kept them for some minutes longer while Mr. Gladstone and the Dalmeny party made their way off the platform and through the long, intricate passage kept open for them (hemmed in but not surrounded, as Mr. Gladstone might explain), which led to the doorway. The Scot is to be admired almost as much for his docility and considerateness amid all this excitement as for the energy of his enthusiasm—the more so as the people inside were longing to join those outside in saying good-bye. The departure was a more picturesque business than the arrival. Evening had long since fallen, and the stars looked down into the street between the tall, ugly houses. Lamps were blazing on the pavement, candles lighted dimly the uppermost windows of every dwelling, the throng seemed almost menacing in the sombre spaces, and the reverberations of the cheering came back to us out of dark courts and closes, darker with the half invisible crowds that swarmed inside.

The Grassmarket is not the most attractive or striking part of Edinburgh, but wherever you find yourself in this strange old town you are surrounded by sights not elsewhere to be seen, and by puzzling contrasts of Rembrandt-like light and shade, gloom deepening into the sheer blackness of receding streets, and the flare of gas falling on human faces with a ghastly radiance. There was light enough to show Mr. Gladstone to the people as he stepped out from under the canopy at the entrance, and all at once the confused murmur of a restless multitude swelled into a roar of welcome. He got into the carriage, and for one moment stood erect with his head bent to the company about him. The horses were too fresh and too much excited by the noise—to which, nevertheless, they ought to be well used—to make this upright posture agreeable, and Mr. Gladstone sat down as the others joined him and they were driving quickly down the street before everybody was aware they had appeared. Down the steep hill, under the arched bridge, racing past Castle Terrace beneath the solid shadow of the huge rock and out again into the air and light, then plunging once more into the narrow lane bordered by masses of men who had been waiting in Lothian Road, and so on by the Caledonian Station and the Liberal Club into Queensferry Street and away out on the road to Dalmeny, the five carriages swept on in close order, policemen riding in front and on either side and in the rear; a wave of cheers following. It was long before all sights and sounds of farewell salutation were left behind. Craigleith had a word to say, and Blackhall, which looks as if it usually put out its candles at seven, had put them in the window with a sincere intention of illuminating the village. As we passed the last house the escort of police wheeled aside, and the carriages drove on without any further protection or any further sign of greeting till at half-past eight the lights of Dalmeny and an open door became visible.

V.

THE GREAT MEETING IN WAVERLEY MARKET.

[DALMENY PARK, *September* 4, 1884.]

It was on Monday, September 1, at six in the afternoon, that Mr. Gladstone delivered his second address to his constituents of Midlothian (the second half of them) in the Corn Exchange of Edinburgh. The drive from Dalmeny, the reception in Edinburgh, the reception and scene in the Corn Exchange itself, do not differ materially from those I described in previous letters, and I need not do more than note one or two points of difference. The Liberal committee, for whose general arrangements no praise can be too high, contrived to pack some 500 more people than on Saturday into the same space; among them delegates from 128 Scottish Liberal associations. Taught by the experience of Saturday, when the heat was great and the air so poisonous that, while Mr. Gladstone was speaking, people were seen asleep, they had opened more windows and taken off part of the roof. The audience, and the orator too, were grateful for the change.

The committee did still better in getting the Earl of Stair to preside. Two years ago I heard Lord Stair make a speech five minutes long, three out of the five being taken up with the applause and laughter of his audience. Ever since that, I have been hoping to hear him again. On Monday he certainly did not exceed five minutes, and there are not many speakers to whom a Midlothian audience assembled to hear Mr. Gladstone would have listened even thus long in patience. But Lord Stair is born for the platform, though he has waited till he is near seventy and till the thick hair which overhangs his genial, ruddy face is altogether gray, before discovering his true vocation in life. The frank manner and hearty tones of voice and the simplicity and sincerity of the man win his hearers at once. He had not spoken two sentences before they settled themselves down to the enjoyment of a novel and delightful sensation, and, for the moment, forgot all about Mr. Gladstone. The secret of the success is precisely what Pascal says: You expected to hear a mere speech; you are astonished and delighted to find yourself listening to a man. Nor could the most practised artist in phrases have suited his matter better to the people before him. The diction is singularly direct; if it is not literary it is forcible; every sentence has a point to it; every word is unmistakably the utterance of Lord Stair's inmost convictions and feelings. The straightforwardness is admirable all through; never an arrow misses its mark; applause follows every period, and when Lord Stair sits down it is amid cries of Go on—and Mr. Gladstone there ready to rise. Mr. Gladstone is not the man to miss such a chance. His first words are an expression of thanks to Lord Stair for his hearty and heart-stirring speech. For the rest, the meeting followed its usual course: rapt attention for close on two hours to Mr. Gladstone; an irresistible demand for something from Lord Rosebery; a reluctant concession; a string of pungent sentences from him; and from one amiable old gentleman an attempt, good-natured, obstinate, and totally unsuccessful, to support some motion by a speech of which not five words could be heard above the din.

On Tuesday there is a complete change of scene. The Corn Exchange is abandoned. The Liberal committees have fulfilled their duties and laid down their wands. The message to the electors and non-electors of Midlothian has been delivered. The whole of the original programme has been accomplished. But the working men of Edinburgh had conceived the idea of holding a meeting of their own, with different aims and on a totally different scale. Mr. Gladstone consented to address them. The Waverley Market was selected, not without much reluctance and resistance from the Lord Provost and other authorities of Edinburgh, who well remembered the hours of distress and even peril which pent-up masses of men had to endure there in 1879. After negotiation it was agreed that the number of admissions to the meeting should be rigidly limited; that the city architect should put up such barriers throughout the interior as he thought sufficient to prevent dangerous pressure, and that the dispositions for approach and admission and the preservation of order within and without should be subject to police control. On these terms the working men were permitted to have their meeting.

I described the Corn Exchange as a shed. The Waverley Market is a combination of sheds, covering I have no idea how many acres; a parallelogram in shape, the roof a continuing series of steep-pitched triangles of iron and glass; galleries running round the sides and ends; a platform large enough for near a thousand people, all sitting, established in the centre of the south side, a sounding board of great dimensions over it. The area railed off, or rather built off, in front of the platform for reporters was as large as an ordinary hall. No covered space could be less fitted for a public meeting; its one merit is its bigness. It will hold at least 20,000 people. The limit on Tuesday is 12,000; which does not prevent 15,000 from crowding in, with or without tickets. There was the usual disorder at the entrances. Barricades protected them but the artisan amused himself by leaping over these obstacles. The 300 police, though well handled, were nowhere in presence of three times 3000 big fellows resolved to get in. And so, with all the precautions, there were ugly rushes and stampedes and people poured in wherever they could. But I saw nothing of all that and I have more than I can do to describe what I saw, distressed as I am by the fear that my readers will not give me due credit for my deep desire to be brief.

No such sights as those of Tuesday have been witnessed during this present Midlothian campaign. It is the first time Mr. Gladstone has really shown himself in that part of Edinburgh where his reception could be most impressive. On Saturday and Monday he turned away from Princes Street. On Tuesday he drove in state through nearly the whole length of it, spectators filling its countless balconies and windows, filling the sidewalks, disputing the roadway with carriages and street-cars, and letting loose the pent-up emotions of three days during which they had waited. The approaches to the Waverley Market were the most densely thronged of all. The police kept a passage open for the carriages, and the entrance to the market was reached easily enough. Lord Reay, chairman of the meeting, Lord Provost Harrison, Mr. James Thom, chairman of the committee of arrangements, and Mr. C. H. Yorston, the secretary, were there to receive Mr. Gladstone. The patient waiters outside had but slender reward for their long attendance. There was hardly a minute's delay—just long enough to allow all the carriages to set down, and then the whole party entered the building.

Nothing could have been better than the device for getting Mr. Gladstone comfortably into and out of the market. In order to do it, the whole of the western gallery and half the southern had been kept vacant. This sacrifice of space gave Mr. Gladstone a clear road and a clear view of the whole meeting, in whose view, and not far above whose heads, he walked for two or three hundred yards. Just underneath the gallery the floor was bare; beyond and on either side it was full. The gas was blazing, twilight still gleaming faintly through the glass roof. The glare fell full on the faces of full fifteen thousand men, all turning to Mr. Gladstone, all cheering. There was a rush toward him across the vacant floor; happily he was high above it. To say that this mass of people began cheering as they saw him, expresses nothing. The air was rent with the explosion of sound; the glass roof shook; I saw two or three ladies of the party actually put their hands to their ears; in the most literal sense of the word the noise was deafening. It silenced every other noise; you could not hear what the man walking next you in the gallery said. Nor did this hurricane blow itself out. During all that long promenade it beat pitilessly against the gallery; it was scarcely stilled when Mr. Gladstone vanished for a moment from sight; it burst forth afresh as he emerged once more to the general view and took his place on the platform. The faces and uncovered heads, near you and far in the distance, were the faces of men under such a stress of emotion as you seldom see in one, and almost never in many. There were the wildest gesticulations of uncontrolled enthusiasm. You cannot look into these faces at all without seeing that the vast majority are working men of the most genuine kind.

They have come here to offer their homage to Mr. Gladstone, and the measure of proud devotion they yield him is without stint; the expression of it is as various as the units who make up this great assembly; the sum and immeasurable accumulation of these individual loyalties such a tribute as no English Minister or English Sovereign has often received. As the cheers subside they are taken up again, and by the time you are persuaded that the countless thousands before you have no voice nor breath left among them they are cheering Lord Rosebery as they cheered Mr. Gladstone; cheering as if they simply could not help it,—it is merely the readiest safety-valve for the energy of passionate affection which their hearts cannot contain. I defy you to sit an unmoved spectator of this scene. It is nothing that women are crying—among them two or three of that fair company on the front seats of the platform, whose lives have been one long lesson in restraint and repression of feeling and the practice of stringent reserve in every social relation. They are crying with the most touching simplicity and openness. But look at the veterans of the platform all about; men to whom every demonstration of public life is hackneyed; long familiar with the caucus and all the machinery of politics, secret and public. They are shaken like reeds by this tempest. Look at Mr. Gladstone. He has bent to the storm.

Lord Reay rose to speak. It is a nervous business to face such an audience but Lord Reay, though hitherto more used to the library and the lecture-room than to great popular assemblies, secures the attention of his hearers and holds it to the end of his brief and effective speech. A very difficult task extremely well done. Then comes the usual written address to Mr. Gladstone of which the meeting firmly declines to allow one single word to be read. Then Mr. Gladstone rose, and for some further minutes it seemed doubtful whether they meant to allow him also to be heard. It is curious how an audience, nominally gathered to listen to a particular speaker, delights in the continuing sound of its own voice. Mr. Gladstone waited till he thought his turn had come, but had to begin in competition with some of the more remote of his friends. Once again he makes a supreme effort to send his voice to the confines of this concourse. It is all but impossible to discern the expression of the farthest faces or to make sure whether they reflect the thought of the speaker—whether, in a word, he is really heard on the edges of the crowd. But the greater part certainly hear easily at the beginning. It is a marvellous voice; more marvellous still when you think of the speaker's seventy-five years; still unequalled in England when at its best, but not quite at its best to-day. By the end of ten minutes it has grown a little less sonorous than at first; the effort to maintain the tone is obvious but to the end it is made to do its duty, and if the freshness and force of the mere voice are impaired the undaunted resolution with which it is used is all the more admirable.

He speaks for exactly twenty minutes. Most of this time he devotes to a close argument on the Franchise Bill, some of it very like what he had said on the same subject the Saturday before. The points are made clearly; there is little which goes over the heads of his artisan audience, and very little which goes straight to their hearts. It is as if the Prime Minister, because he is Prime Minister, disdained to use the rhetorical arts of which Mr. Gladstone is master. There was hardly a sentence which was addressed to the working men because they were working men. There was a want, not of sympathy but of the assertion of sympathy. Plenty of recognition of the welcome he received; but the return Mr. Gladstone made for it would have been equally acceptable to other classes of men. Yet there was nothing in the applause this speech elicited to hint at any sense of disappointment among those to whom it was delivered. Neither in its course nor after its conclusion could you perceive any falling off in the ardour of the audience.

Then came a call for Lord Rosebery and another tumult of applause as he left his chair. This is the third of the present series of meetings in Midlothian. The first two were strictly political; the audiences agricultural, suburban, and urban. This is a meeting of working men, called by working men, composed of working men, with little or no regard to party. It would be difficult to say in which of the three Lord Rosebery's popularity was greatest; it is, certainly, a very striking thing to see him greeted in the same spirit by three widely-different classes of people. "Such a reception." said a great political authority, "is a great political fact." Lord Rosebery's oratory is also a very considerable fact, worth studying at greater leisure than any of us have now. As he leans in an attitude of composure on the railing and looks about him, you might say he was the one man in this whole throng who was insensible to the excitement. With near a score of thousands of men proclaiming their devotion to him, he preserves his air of disinterested spectator, and when he begins to speak it is in a tone as remote as possible from the passion of those about him. But you will note two things. There is an absolute hush before he speaks, and when the voice is heard it is evidently heard to the uttermost ends of the building.

He is addressing such an audience as this for the first time but he knows exactly what to do with them. The carrying power of his voice is extraordinary; it rings out and reaches into far corners and fills the air, round, resonant, slightly hard in the middle register, but one of the most efficient and effective organs of speech ever given to a young man of thirty-five. He begins with a phrase familiar to American ears, strange to English or Scotch: "Fellow-citizens." I cannot remember to have heard it before. The sentences are short, and every sentence has a point. Yet somehow the impression is almost conversational and the speaker gets at once into relations of familiarity and personal friendship with those he is addressing. Nothing could be more odd than to see Lord Rosebery resting one elbow on the bar in front of him and engaging 15,000 people in easy talk. "Why do you ask our Member for Midlothian to come here?" queries he, and straightway a ready-tongued Scot cries back to Mr. Gladstone, "It's because we like ye."—"Well, but if I were you," retorts the speaker, "I would have done just the reverse." Who could resist that? An audience taken into the confidence of an orator and holdng a parley with him, roaring at his jokes, putting cheers for commas to his sentences; thinking with him, feeling with him—really I do not know whether audience or orator be the more astonishing novelty.

The quaintness of view is what strikes everybody. The reverse of the plan which Lord Rosebery says he would have adopted is nothing less than to have asked Sir Stafford Northcote instead of Mr. Gladstone. Sir Stafford is coming to Scotland. "He will not get fat on what he gets here," observes Lord Rosebery, in an aside audible half a mile away. "But if you want to do him good why not ask him to a meeting like this, and let him tell you what his version of the constitutional crisis may be, and then let him know what your version is; and if you will give him this party, and if you will ask me to come too, I will bring him here, and will tell him, 'There is the real Conservative party.'" That is humourous, no doubt, but it is a sample of the political penetration which the possession of real humour sometimes confers on a man. The sentence on the House of Lords is graver, and of the very gravest significance if you bear in mind that the speaker is himself a leading member of that House. The Tory majority, he bids them note, is not all the House. "I call you to witness, and I think you know, that there are in that House not one, nor two, nor a score, but many who will be prepared to march with the people,—abreast with the people, certainly, but if necessary in front of the people, in this just, this necessary, and, in the highest sense, this truly conservative campaign for the maintenance of the rights of the nation and of the true balance of the Constitution of this country." A declaration which, in a very possible turn of events, may be called momentous.

I must pass over much on which I should like to dwell and ask you to return with me into the open street again. We have been only an hour in the Waverley Market, but there is electricity enough in this heated air to convulse not Midlothian only but Scotland itself. Flash after flash burst out, the detonation which followed Mr. Gladstone as he left the building was incessant, the fervour fiercer even than when he entered. Again he took his way along the gallery, and again stood in the doorway, and in the presence of a multitude certainly more numerous than the one he had just left. Again the greeting of twenty or thirty thousand men rang in his ears. If they could have got at him I do not know what they would not have done—drawn him in triumph along Princes Street, I daresay, and left horses and postilions and outriders to go home by themselves. But that was not to be. The police and the stout timber barricades did their duty. Mr. Gladstone, with a brief word of farewell to his host who was bound for London, stepped into the carriage, and for the last time the procession, which for three days Edinburgh has followed and applauded, started homeward.

And now, at last, we are to have a scene which equals or eclipses the most brilliant of those of 1879. It is half-past eight; Princes Street is a mass of Scotsmen. The dozen mounted police have all they can do to clear a road at first, but, as they hear the tread of the horses and see the gleam of carriage lamps in motion, the serried ranks break up of themselves, and before we have reached the Scott Monument the pace is quite fast enough for the safety of the crowd. The crowd is thinking of anything but its own safety; its one object in life is to cheer Mr. Gladstone and everybody who is with him,—Mrs. Gladstone, Lady Rosebery, and the rest.

The evening is surpassingly beautiful. The full moon rides high in the cloudless, pale azure sky. The houses of the Old Town, climbing one above another on the swift slope beyond the ravine, their fronts untouched by the moonlight, gaze across at the scene with eyes of fire. Every window is ablaze. The picturesque irregularity of that steep mass breaks in its restless outline against the delicate blue beyond. Steeples and domes rise out of the solid blackness. The very chimneys arrange themselves in fantastic groups; so do the flying buttresses, or whatever they are, to the nondescript cathedral tower. Far below, the eye falls on the Doric colonnades and faultless proportions of that classic Edinburgh which Mr. Ruskin wants to pull down. Away to the west the Castle, steadfast on its noble base of rock, admirable in its battlements and spite of its paltry barracks, thrusts its huge bulk into view. Princes Street opens for its whole length on the left to the gardens and the glen over against which the Old Town rises. Its single row of buildings, all hotels and stores and clubs, is so brilliant with light, its sleek shopkeeping prosperity so animated, its windows are so full of cheering spectators, that for once it almost rivals the incomparably finer and older city to the south. And Princes Street to-night has something more to show you. As the four carriages advance, the people advance too. The crowd is still bent on one single thing: it will not let Mr. Gladstone out of its sight. It pours along the roadway. So dense is it, so innumerable are people and cars and cabs and every sort of vehicle, that there is danger at every step, but the danger does not stop them. They surge along the pavement; for the five minutes we are in it Princes Street is a rushing river of human beings.

Such was Midlothian's farewell to Mr. Gladstone. The last notes of it did not die away till we were far out on the road to Dalmeny. The echoes of it and of the stirring events of the week have been heard all over the kingdom. What Mr. Gladstone has said and left unsaid, what Midlothian for its part has done and means hereafter to do, in honour of its

Member, what the political results were to be,—all these are
matters which nobody interested in the near future of this
country can afford to neglect. But I imagine that, on this
last night of his stay at Dalmeny, neither Mr. Gladstone nor
those with him are troubling themselves about all that. The
spectacle of the day and evening has done its work; perhaps not much is said, but everybody feels that it is a brilliant and impressive ending to a brilliant campaign.

VI.

THE LIBERAL HEADQUARTERS IN MIDLOTHIAN.

[DALMENY PARK, *September* 6, 1884.]

This house has thrice been the headquarters of a Midlothian campaign; using campaign in the American sense. It
is in fact the one great Liberal house of this part of the
world. Midlothian has proved itself Liberal, but Liberalism
is by no means the prevailing creed of the landed gentry
hereabouts. When Mr. Gladstone came here in 1879 to begin his contest for the county, the Tories laughed in their
sleeves and in his face. Lord Dalkeith, son and heir to the
then Duke of Buccleuch, now himself Duke of Buccleuch,
held the seat, and meant to continue to hold it. The Duke's
friends looked upon Mr. Gladstone as a presumptuous intruder, and foretold his failure with absolute confidence.
The Duke was a magnate whose word there had been none
to dispute. When it was announced publicly that Mr. Gladstone meant to hold a meeting in Dalkeith itself, almost at
the gates of Dalkeith Palace, a shudder ran through the
community. Still, the meetings were held. In Edinburgh,
while the majority of the citizens were Liberals, there was,
and is, a Tory leaven which pervades the highest social circles—the county people, in a word, were Tories, and echoed
the murmurs of the Duke and of the Duke's family. If you
go into the New Club in Edinburgh, which is the chief club

of the place, where the most select and aristocratic society of Midlothian is to be met, you will find ten Tories to one Liberal. It is not that a Liberal is excluded because he is a Liberal. The club is not political. But in the world out of which this lesser club world is recruited, the proportion is about what I have stated.

Well, in this condition of things it was that Lord Rosebery invited Mr. Gladstone to Dalmeny. Against the overwhelming opinion of all his own social set; against the judgment, I believe, of the managers, or some of the leading managers, of his own party; against the enormous influence—territorial, personal, political, social, and pecuniary—of the late Duke of Buccleuch, this adventurous young nobleman entered upon this campaign. The day when he hoisted his flag on Dalmeny —I use the expression literally; it is the custom to denote by the flag the presence of the owner of a country mansion who is also lord-lieutenant of the county—was a memorable day in the history of Scotland, and of Great Britain. He assumed a vast responsibility, and the way to measure it is to think of what would have happened had Mr. Gladstone failed, first to carry the country with him by his first Midlothian speeches, and secondly to win Midlothian itself. I am not going over that story. It has never been told fully, but now is not the time to tell it. All I wish to point out is that Dalmeny has become a historical house. There are many Americans for whom it would have an interest because they know Lord Rosebery. There are few to whom its connection with the fortunes of the Prime Minister and of the Empire he governs can be wholly a matter of indifference.

In itself, or as an example of architecture, Dalmeny is not very remarkable. It was built in the early part of this century; a time when architecture was, if not one of the lost arts, certainly an art very different in principle and feeling from what it was a hundred years before, or is now. The author of this fabric was one Wilkins, an architect of repute in his day, not without some knowledge of what had been done before his time. The building he constructed is semi-

Tudor in design, of pale gray stone, with pointed doors, mullioned windows square at top, adorned with those bracket-shaped mouldings which Mr. Ruskin disrespectfully likened to the brass handles on old-fashioned chests of drawers; chimneys and turrets of great elevation with reference to the height of the building, and with a certain hardness of outline. Altogether, a house comfortable to look at; picturesque as you get your first glimpse of it through an opening in the thickly shaded drive from the east lodge; standing on a broad terrace, but as the fashion then was, on a lower site than would now be chosen among the many admirable ones which this park offers. From the front windows you look to the sea, a quarter of a mile away, and through the well planted trees comes the gleam of white surf breaking on a long strip of sand. The ground rises sharply behind the house; shrubbery surrounds it on two sides; on the third lies a stretch of turf and the path which takes you along the base of a steep hill and leads you gently to the platform where the restored Barnbougle Castle looks out from two sides on the sparkling waters of the Firth of Forth. Here it is that you may see Mr. Gladstone of an afternoon pacing up and down.

Since Mr. Gladstone arrived on Wednesday he has lived in a glass house. Every one of his movements has been chronicled with minute exactitude by the corps of reporters representing the very enterprising press of Edinburgh, and copious accounts appear daily in *The Scotsman* and other papers. The fact that he walked in the park (which the Scotch choose to call "policies") after tea on Wednesday was duly set forth. The list of guests at dinner is given. The visit next day to the Forth Bridge has a column to itself. The visit to the Forestry Exhibition on Friday is described at much greater length. In most points, the good taste and good manners of these narratives are as remarkable as their fulness. There is this to be said for the Scotch, they do not seem to require that decency should be sacrificed to gratify their curiosity. They read eagerly whatever is published about Mr. Gladstone or Lord Rosebery, not neglecting details which in ordinary times might be called trivial, but not demanding to know the unknowable. I must write a great deal more briefly than my friends on the Scotch papers do, but I shall be glad if, while using perhaps more freedom on some points, I keep within their limits of decorum.

For more than one reason, these days and the swift succession of events that mark them are historical. Mr. Gladstone is the chief figure but others cross the stage. Lord Northbrook has been here yesterday and to-day. He came to take leave of the Prime Minister and to receive his last counsels and instructions, if a Cabinet Minister can be said to receive instructions from anybody. It is really from Dalmeny that the new High Commissioner starts on his mission to Egypt. The situation seems almost pathetic. Here is a man who has everything in the world—rank, wealth, high office, honour, troops of friends—and who puts much of it all at risk in accepting a new post of difficulty, only because he thinks it a duty to accept. He even risks his health, for he has to go to Cairo in September. It is obvious he is quite sensible of all he takes upon himself; not the least obvious that he has an idea how much those about him admire his public spirit and his courage. It is but a single day that he spends here,—long enough, however, to make one of the group who are photographed in front of the house; a group including Mr. Gladstone, his host and hostess, and their guests. Then Lord Northbrook departs—says good-bye to everybody in that quiet way which is a curiously marked characteristic of the Englishman in moments when he feels deeply; steps into his carriage, and drives off. A knot of people in the distance are looking on. They have little idea that the man who speeds past them is going to found a new empire on the banks of the Nile. Yet that, if anything, is likely to be the result of Lord Northbrook's mission; and in presence of such an enterprise as that, questions of franchise—questions, that is, whether the franchise shall be conferred this year or next—look very secondary indeed.

BEYOND MIDLOTHIAN.

I.

MR. GLADSTONE AT HADDO HOUSE.

[ABERDEENSHIRE, *September* 16, 1884.]

SINCE Mr. Gladstone quitted Dalmeny, rather less than a fortnight since, he has been the guest of Colonel Farquharson at Invercauld and of the Earl of Fife at Mar Lodge. He journeyed to Invercauld amid outbursts of popular enthusiasm. He spent his time, alike under Colonel Farquharson's roof and Lord Fife's, amid companies of celebrities invited to meet him, and in a whirl of excursions, visits to the Queen at Balmoral, continual publicity at every moment of the day, and a quick succession of festivities arranged in his honour. The Scotch papers have reported his least movements with microscopic minuteness; the interest of their readers growing, it would seem, by what it feeds on, and the passion of popular loyalty to their leader rising daily higher and higher. By the time he was ready to leave Mar Lodge for Haddo House, all Deeside and all Aberdeenshire were in a glow of expectation. He had been looked for at Haddo on Saturday. Some complications, I believe, with royalty, including visits not only to Balmoral but to Birkhall, postponed his departure, and it was finally settled he should begin what may be called his return journey on Monday.

The day's engagements for Mr. Gladstone were sufficiently numerous. To leave Mar Lodge in the early morning; to drive to Birkhall and lunch with the Duchess of Edinburgh; to drive from Birkhall to Ballater; to journey by rail from

Ballater to Aberdeen, with popular receptions and in some cases brief speeches at each way-station; to face a multitude at Aberdeen, receive an address from the Corporation and make a speech; to journey again by rail to Old Meldrum,—more receptions, more addresses, and more speeches by the way, and at Old Meldrum itself—and then to drive with Lord Aberdeen to Haddo House;—such was the programme arranged for Mr. Gladstone, and such is the Scottish conception of the capacities of a Prime Minister of seventy-five for what they call repose.

Haddo House is a place remarkable in more ways than one. There is a story that when the Lord Aberdeen known to history as Prime Minister of England, grandfather to the Lord Aberdeen of to-day, first came into the property, he stood at the door of the house and gazed out upon the scene before him in a kind of despair. If you know this part of Aberdeenshire you know that Nature has done nothing for it except arrange the ground in undulations and occasionally lift it into a hill of good proportions. She quite forgot to provide trees. The Prime Minister that was to be beheld the nakedness of the land before him, and considered within himself whether he should abandon the home of his fathers, and go abroad to live, or whether he should try to improve it and make the place into something more attractive. He resolved on the latter. He called into council a painter, some of whose landscapes may still be seen with pleasure, Mr. Giles; not a landscape gardener by profession, but one of those men to whom it has been given to enter the inmost councils of Nature and discern what she would have done had she been in the right mood. He and Lord Aberdeen together planted and laid out this park with the most admirable perception of its potentialities. There is, perhaps, no place in Scotland or England which owes so little to Nature and so much to Art. The house looks no longer on the dreary slopes and waste stretches of rolling ground which, as so much of Aberdeenshire still does, Haddo once offered to the view. In front, the trees on two sides and a hillside where sheep are feeding, shut in the prospect. From the other façade the eye is carried past gardens skilfully cultivated, by a long straight avenue to the deer park, entered by a gate half a mile away, and still on by the same narrow avenue to the summit of this long hill, crowned by a statue set against a mass of forest and embosomed in foliage amid which the eye rests in content. Out from this central path lead others which you discover as you advance, into glades and depths of forest and grassy drives. Wherever you walk you come upon fresh beauties. Anything like the stiff symmetry of tree-planting which the French were then and before then practising has been wholly avoided. Nature has been conciliated, to parody Bacon's phrase, by obeying her. Every tree has been planted, and they all seem to have sprung up of themselves. Three lakes cover some of the 3000 acres included in the "policies,"—and there are drives and walks of infinite variety in every direction, and as delightful as they are various.

The house bears an inscription, cut into the reddish-gray granite of which it is built, which dates it in 1732. There existed then, I believe, only the central pavilion, a substantial three-story fabric of no great architectural pretensions but excellent in proportion, with mouldings and here and there a whole window-casing which suggest Italian influence. A balcony runs across the entire front, approaching from the ground at either end by broad stairways, half-spiral, the curve a true conic section; a broader balcony and porch in the middle. The impression is one—simple as the structure is—of dignity. On either side are two-story wings at right angles to the front and connected with the centre by intermediate buildings which make the transition by curves. These wings are covered with ivy. It is from the central balcony that Mr. Gladstone will by and by speak, while the kind of court inclosed on three sides by the central portion and the two wings, and open on the fourth, is the arena to be occupied by his escort; the multitude on foot being arranged on the lawn beyond the drive leading from both sides to the house.

It was known that Mr. Gladstone could not reach Haddo before half-past six but people began to arrive by noon. That may be taken as one more measure of Scottish enthusiasm. They came from long distances and most of them in dogcarts or small wagonettes. A field had been set apart for their vehicles and there they camped out for luncheon, and after luncheon devoted themselves to seeing everything that was to be seen of these beautiful grounds. It is not quite clear that there is anybody in Aberdeenshire so poorly off as to be obliged to travel on foot. A farmer who rents sixty acres and has a capital of £1000 is a man who seldom does a stroke of work with his own hands, but is always to be met driving about in a gig on his way to or from some near or distant market. Many of the people now arriving are not farmers. They live in Methlick, or much farther off. Many of them are labourers on the estate. Not a shopkeeper in a village for ten miles round who does not put in an appearance. It is their one chance in life to see and hear the foremost Englishman of his time whom they delight to call, and continually do call, even to his face, the Grand Old Man. Lord Aberdeen opened the grounds and gardens about the house to all comers, and all the afternoon in ever-increasing numbers they were to be seen on the terrace and in the shrubberies and walks. Their behaviour reminded one of that of the people at the East End of London when the Prince and Princess of Wales made an evening visit to Bethnal Green Museum and walked about among the company of working men, and classes much poorer than the working men. The royalties were never once "mobbed," as they are by well-to-do and fashionable crowds at the West End.

These Scotch men and women had the same good manners. Not a flower was plucked nor a branch broken. Nobody stared in at the windows. They would hardly walk on the turf but kept to the gravel. They were conscious of no merit, but conducted themselves with the good sense and good taste which are obviously natural to them and not assumed for this occasion. As the afternoon drew on the scores became hundreds, and by five o'clock they had taken position on the lawn in front of the house beyond the wings, and there they waited. Long before the hour they were drawn up in close order, stretching across the whole space from which a view of the balcony could be had. There they stood; a body of men and women to most of whom a day's work is an important matter, without a sign of restlessness or the least disorder; talking together, obedient to the least hint of the three policemen who constituted the whole visible force for keeping the peace among a thousand or two thousand persons little accustomed to restraint. A tea-table was set out where perhaps a hundred might be served at the same time by the smartly dressed damsels in charge of the urns and cake.

At half-past six a courier rode up with a message not audible from the balcony, but interesting enough to the throng below to straighten them all up and stretch their necks all in one direction. Five minutes later Lord Aberdeen arrived alone on a black horse, having quitted the party on the road in order to receive his guests at his own front door. Another minute and a cheer came from the invisible distance and grew louder and nearer, and then, where the road touches the angle of the left wing, an open landau-and-four with postilions flashed into sight. Mr. Gladstone sat on the back seat at the right; Mrs. and Miss Helen Gladstone with him. The cheers for Lord Aberdeen had hardly died away when they broke out afresh for his guest, who drove on to the entrance heralded by this roar and followed by a cloud of horsemen. The cloud of horsemen were the tenantry of Lord Aberdeen, near 300 in number, who had met Mr. Gladstone on the outer boundaries—the march, as the Scots have it—of the estate, some four miles away, and lined the road as he approached, welcomed him as he came, formed behind him as he passed, and so rode on with him beneath arches and shadowed by waving flags, to Haddo. As the carriage drew up, there was Lord Aberdeen to receive his guest;

there were a band of workmen with the inevitable address; there were groups of the servants appertaining to Haddo. It took Mr. Gladstone some minutes to run the gauntlet of all these. He does it all with graciousness of manner. Mrs. and Miss Gladstone are not forgotten; two bouquets are waiting for them and two ladies to offer them—daughter and grand-daughter of Mr. Marr, the oldest tenant on the estate.

Then Mr. Gladstone comes up on the broad balcony, where long since the party of guests at Haddo have been assembled, and shows himself to the company below. The cheers roll out once more, and the mounted tenantry as if waiting for the signal rode smartly into the open space of gravel, and were marshalled by Captain Duthie into some semblance of military array. Some drilling must have gone to the making of so good a squadron out of this purely agricultural material. The tenants rode their own horses; useful cattle, with now and then an animal that showed signs of the owner's pride in horse-flesh. They were not in condition for the work they had been asked to do—to keep pace for four miles with Lord Aberdeen's half-thoroughbreds—and most of them were steaming. The arrangements had been well thought out and carried out. There had not been a mistake from the time Lord Aberdeen took charge of his guest in Aberdeen itself;—so many minutes for each portion of the journey, so many for each address and speech, so many on the road, and here at the hour named were this fine body of fine-looking men on horseback and on foot. There before them on the balcony, the centre of a group with Lady Aberdeen at his side, stood Mr. Gladstone, his head bared to the gloom and chill of the evening, and the hills sending us back the echoes of the thousands of voices raised to salute him. Of the many welcomes he has received this is the most novel and the most picturesque. We seem curiously remote, as we stand there, from the nineteenth century. The keenest ear could not hear a railway whistle seven miles off, nor the tick of a telegraph instrument two miles distant. This courtyard crowded with mounted men, this Earl of Aberdeen who receives this Minister of England in this *grand seigneur* style, this loneliness all at once peopled as if by the summons of a chieftain, this figure of a ruler here to accept homage,—all these together are more a scene of ancient than of modern life; of feudal days than of these prosaic times; of muster for war than for the purposes of peace.

Mr. Marr as oldest tenant uttered his few simple sentences, full of good feeling, and Mr. Gladstone replied in a ten minutes' speech. For the first time I heard him suggest an excuse for the state of his voice. He has done more than enough to exhaust it, and it is rough, but still strong enough to reach the farthest listener. What he says has all the freshness which his voice lacks. Oddly enough, Mr. Gladstone had supposed he was to make the speech of the day at Old Meldrum, and it was there instead of here, its fitting place, that he had pronounced his meditated eulogy on the Lord Aberdeen in whose Cabine the had sat. Mr. Gladstone never stints his good words, but his admiration for Lord Aberdeen is expressed in terms beyond which even he could not go. He described the grandfather of his host as the dearest and most revered of all the political friends with whom it has ever been his happiness to act. He pays him another tribute now, as landlord, host, friend, and Minister, — words to which everybody listens with pleasure. That Lord Aberdeen has left an honoured memory which this Lord Aberdeen keeps green among all those who stand to him in the relation which their ancestors held to his.

With Mr. Gladstone's address this ceremony came to an end, except that the stirrup cup went round among the horsemen, and the tea-table was again beset, and the guests on the balcony lingered to see the assembly below disperse. The tenants and spectators of every degree who took their way slowly over those bare hills to their distant homes carried with them memories which will not die with them nor with their sons. If the day is impressive to those of us who have witnessed many a demontsration of public delight, far more impressive must it be to the dwellers on these Haddo farms who see Mr. Gladstone for the first time; and also for the last.

II.

AT HADDO, AT ABERDEEN, AND AT BRECHIN.

[BRECHIN CASTLE, *September* 18, 1884.]

During the two days which Mr. Gladstone spent with Lord and Lady Aberdeen at Haddo House, he was allowed to be comparatively quiet. A deputation came to call on him to whom he made a speech in the library; a speech of such interest that one can only regret that it was meant for their ears only. There was a drive on Tuesday afternoon to Gight, a spot with which Byron's name is associated, and to which might be applied in part Coleridge's lines—

> That deep romantic chasm which slanted
> Down the green hill athwart a cedarn cover,

—save that the cover is not cedarn. On his way to Gight he passed through Methlick, the little village which serves as telegraph office to Haddo. Lady Aberdeen has established there an institute and coffee-room for working men and an orphanage. Mr. Gladstone visited the first and opened the second. The villagers knew of his coming; he cannot move a step in any direction privately. They had decked their cottages and turned out in full strength to see him; so many children among them that Methlick did not seem capable of holding parents enough for them all, and the need of Lady Aberdeen's orphanage became evident.

Ceremony there was none. Mr. Gladstone and his party walked through the rooms, beautifully clean and well arranged. The Hon. and Rev. Edward Glyn, one of the party at Haddo, began with a prayer in the little room on the right of the entrance. Down went Mr. Gladstone on his knees in the middle of the room on the bare floor,—or perhaps there was an oil floor-cloth. Others knelt also, but not all. When Mr. Glyn had finished his prayer Mr. Gladstone said that was the best dedication and opening of the building, and he would only add his good wishes; with a word of tribute to the kindness of Lady Aberdeen.

Before leaving Haddo on Wednesday, Mr. Gladstone performed the usual ceremony—it has now become usual—of tree-planting. The hour was noon, the place a bit of lawn on the left of the gardens, the thing planted a fir—Scotch fir, I presume, for I see that an Aberdeen paper describes the little shrub, which may have been three feet high, as a noble tree. A group of people had collected; guests, labourers, and others. The day was hot, the sun blazing. Mr. Gladstone took off his soft gray felt hat. He bares his head with equal indifference to the bitter east wind and the fiercest rays of the sun — drives through Edinburgh in the cold of the evening or speaks from a bridge or railway platform, always uncovered. "Put on your hat," cried a man from some crowd the other day—as men often cry. "Never mind about the hat," answered Mr. Gladstone, undaunted by the caution, and on he went with his speech. And on he went with his tree-planting, plying his spade with an energy at which the professionals looked amazed.

This is not politics, I know, and it is time to be off. There is a hard day's work ahead for Mr. Gladstone, if not for the rest. Lord Aberdeen drives him to Aberdeen, nineteen miles, by a lonely road—not so lonely that people do not here and there collect to see him pass. Not so lonely, neither, that you may not see flags flying from tall poles, each by itself crowning a hill in the distance. They float amid solitudes. One of them was an American flag; alone and lofty, not a sign of other life to be seen,—as if an American had just landed and annexed the country. Nearer Aberdeen, but still miles out, the groups became greater, and long before the city was reached they were to be counted by thousands. The streets of Aberdeen were lined with people; the yard of the railway station was a mass. A policeman of a superior kind told me there were 6000 at least within the walls. I saw the station stormed. Men broke in where they could; poured in through the windows, and performed feats of gymnastics over barricades. I fear the dignitaries of Aberdeen suffered a little in their dignity. The crowd was no respecter of any person but Mr. Gladstone. When his carriage drew up close to the platform it was the centre of a mob; a mob of well-dressed admirers, dignitaries included, but still a mob. Mr. Gladstone himself was so struck by the reception given him in Aberdeen as to say that, of all the exhibitions of public and national feeling that had ever met his eyes in the course of a very long life, he had witnessed none more remarkable than that which had greeted him on their progress into Aberdeen to-day. He spoke from the seat of the carriage; hoarsely but strongly. Mrs. and Miss Gladstone sat, as usual, half buried beneath bouquets.

The railway journey to Brechin was a matter of more than two hours, thanks to the obstructive enthusiasm of people at the way stations. What I saw during this journey and have heard of elsewhere leads me to modify what I said about the state of mind of the Scotch people. When I saw them in Edinburgh I was always comparing them with the same people five years ago, and did not and could not think the scenes of delirium equal now to what they were then. But then it was only Edinburgh, or rather only Midlothian. Now it is all Scotland. The whole east coast and all Deeside are up in arms, and it is plain that the same thing would be true were Mr. Gladstone to visit the west. The scene in Aberdeen is magnificent, and so it is in this much lesser place, Brechin, as we shall see in a moment. But the incidents at the little stopping places are almost more significant. We stop perhaps half a dozen times before coming to Bridge of Dun. There is not one station so inconsiderable as not to turn out its group to see Mr. Gladstone. The groups are all in a state of the most curious excitement.

The deep Scotch nature is stirred; thoroughly, profoundly, and permanently. At none of these wayside stations till Bridge of Dun is reached is there any address or solemnity of any kind—not so much, apparently, as the least expectation of a word from Mr. Gladstone. The people are quite satisfied if he puts his head out of the window and allows himself to be stared at and cheered. The Montrose people seize their chance at Bridge of Dun, which is a junction, and make an address, and to this Mr. Gladstone replies. Here it is that the meaning of these local demonstrations seems, probably not for the first time, to impress him, and he says for the first time how much they impress him. " Put your finger down on the land where you will, and the popular sentiment I find to be pretty much one and the same. I rejoice in these local manifestations because what Ministers desire to know is whether they are acting in conformity with the will of the country;"—and so on. At Brechin he touched a not less expressive note: "These gatherings are local. They are not the accumulations of men swept from vast distances into one spot to make a show of public opinion. What I see is the fruit of the soil upon which I stand."

It behooves me humbly to confess that I did not wait for the arrival of the Town Council and Liberal Association of Montrose at Bridge of Dun, but went on by train at once to Brechin. The place is one I know very well, and I had no sort of conception of what they were preparing for Mr. Gladstone. The population, not of a town but of a county, seemed to be in the streets. I drove from the station, not without difficulty, along the route which Mr. Gladstone was to take a few minutes later. The decorations and arrangements would have been thought handsome anywhere. Reading of the emptiness of the Edinburgh streets while Sir Stafford Northcote passed through, I wondered what he would have thought of a turn-out like this in a town of perhaps 10,000 inhabitants. It would not be very rash to affirm that there were 10,000 people in St. Ninian's Square alone.

This was the central point. A platform had been erected, the freedom of the city was to be given Mr. Gladstone, people from the country for miles about had poured in to have their part in the proceedings. When Mr. Gladstone had been received at the station by the Earl of Dalhousie, whose guest he now is, and his host undertook to drive him in his carriage to the place of meeting, they were hardly allowed to get to the square, so beset were they by the multitude. The cheering, the pressure, the eagerness of each man to have some personal share in the greeting to Mr. Gladstone,— these and the other manifestations have by this time become so familiar that I dwell on them no longer. But here at Brechin we have Mr. Gladstone's testimony to the effect they have had on him and his plans. He came to Scotland, he says, solely to speak to his constituents in Midlothian. He refused addresses, and refused to speak elsewhere. Silence elsewhere than in Midlothian was his fixed and sincere intention, "but it has been conquered and broken down by the irresistible and general movement of every community at every point and every place through which I have passed on my journey northward." This energetic sentence is but a very moderate and baldly literal account of the matter. Scotland, like the Edinburgh audiences, has risen at him, and the voice of Scotland, when it is heard on a political question of the first magnitude, is one that even Lord Salisbury and his majority would do well to heed.

III.

A THREE DAYS' VISIT TO BRECHIN.

[BRECHIN CASTLE, *September* 20, 1884.]

Tory critics, who at times seem to find criticism difficult, have discovered what they call an incongruity in the circumstances of Mr. Gladstone's present tour in Scotland. He has gone there, they say, to attack the House of Lords, and most of the time he has been the guest of one or another of these very lords. This is just half true. He has not come to Scotland to attack the House of Lords, but there is no denying that he has been staying with Scottish Peers. The Earl of Rosebery at Dalmeny Park, the Earl of Fife at Mar Lodge, the Earl of Aberdeen at Haddo House, and now the Earl of Dalhousie at Brechin Castle, have successively entertained him. He goes hence to Glamis, which is the seat of the Earl of Strathmore, and will pass the last two nights of his stay in Scotland again at Dalmeny. As all these Peers except one are heartily supporting Mr. Gladstone in his domestic policy, there would not in any case be much incongruity in his spending his time under their roofs. There may be people whose notions about Peers are such that they hear with surprise of Liberalism as a great force in the Scottish Peerage. But it is. Beside those I have named there are the Earl of Breadalbane, the Earl of Elgin, the Earl of Camperdown, and others—all young men and all staunch Liberals.

Mr. Gladstone had an answer ready for the critics in his speech on the platform in St. Ninian's Square in Brechin, where we left him standing on Wednesday afternoon at half-past six. In the effort to pass the Franchise Bill, he said, Ministers, members of the House of Commons, and the people are doing their part. "Many members, I rejoice to say, of the House of Lords have done and will do their part, and among them all not one more loyally or with a more enlightened intelligence than Lord Dalhousie, whose guest I have the privilege of being, and whose name is equally dear to the political friends among whom he moves in the South and to the community in the midst of which he lives in the North." And the answering cheers of the people of Brechin showed that they were of Mr. Gladstone's mind. Lord Dalhousie, it is true, belongs to that wicked class which Mr. Henry George is for ever holding up to the execration of mankind. He is a landowner. But if Mr. Henry George, in some sane moment, would come to Scotland and go over the estates which this landlord possesses and manages, and hear what his tenants have to say, he would surely enlarge his conception of the relations that may exist between landlord and tenant. He might even discover that they were equally profitable to the tenant and honourable to the landlord.

The drive from St. Ninian's Square to Brechin Castle is a short one, through the chief street of the town to the new lodge at the entrance of the park, whence it is but a few hundred yards to Lord Dalhousie's front door. In old times the entrance was more distant, and a straight avenue of noble trees, half a mile long, led from lodge to castle. The noble trees were laid low long since. The road exists but is not used. The present drive is still charming; the whole park is charming, and charmingly planted; trees enough and well grown. The castle, as you see it to-day, is of the first half of the last century. The old castle was of I know not how early a period, but very early, and parts of this ancient fabric are still extant on the south side. There are quarries somewhere in this part of the world of red sandstone, brownish-red, not very unlike the material used for the palaces of merchant princes in New York, and of this not only the castle but all Brechin, and Brechin Cathedral, and the famed Round Tower of Brechin, are built. It occurs rarely in Scotland or England, or is used rarely. The Aberdeen quarries supply a red granite which would be not much inferior to this in warmth of colour, but the Aberdeen people have got it into their heads that cold gray is the right thing, and they have built their whole city in cold gray; so cold and so gray that Aberdeen is perhaps to the stranger the most depressing place in Scotland. The weight of all that mass of inexorable gray stone burdens the memory, and the cheerful hue of Brechin is a contrast and a relief.

Like many another castle of feudal times and illustrating feudal habits, Brechin has a cluster of houses at its gates— in this case at its back gate, happily, since the town of Brechin devotes itself a good deal to the making of linen, and there are bleaching grounds and factories and tall chimneys with unceasing plumes of black smoke not far off. The story goes that a certain Earl of this family gave a broad space of ground to the village, as it then was, on condition it should be used solely for recreation. As generations went by, the condition was neglected and the town sold the land. The sale happened in the time of that Earl who, not liking his next heir, cut down the avenue, and looked on in grim content while the land was sold and while factories sprang up. The factories are not visible in front but they are visible where, but for them, the castle would look its best. The South Esk sweeps past in curves of beauty beneath noble hills; comes rushing down in rapids, and then grows still before it reaches the lawn; flows smoothly under a bridge; turns sharply away from the sheer wall of rock on which the castle stands; slumbers in a deep pool below, into which a good diver might take a plunge from the brink fifty feet above the black stillness of the tired flood. Shrubs cling to the rock wherever they can get a foothold; the whole place for a hundred yards is a tangle of trees and vines. Then the river with another bend takes a plunge of its own over a dam, parts company with castle and the castle's lord, and is put in harness and made to toil six days out of seven in the service of Brechin millowners; disappears finally from view beneath another bridge whose lofty arches themselves are lost on the farther bank in forest. If the park has nothing to boast of in extent, it has in beauty. The gardens, which, as is the rule in Scotland, are at a distance from the house, are among the most pleasant in the kingdom. The ground has every natural advantage and everything has been done for it by art. It is so broken, lies about in such confusion of hill and dale, of wood and lawn, of rushing stream and glade and overhanging foliage and spreading field, that its five hundred acres broaden to the eye into twice five hundred or more. The Brechin estate is not what passes in this country for large; the bulk of Lord Dalhousie's property is about Panmure House; a vast mansion, twice as big as

Brechin; not twice as interesting. You may drive without, I think, quitting the estate, seventeen miles in one direction to Panmure, which looks on the sea, or three-and-twenty in another at Invermark, one of the finest glens and best deer forests in Scotland.

Mr. Gladstone was taken the former drive by Lord Dalhousie, but not the more attractive one, to Invermark, which he doubtless knows. One of his three days here was devoted to a sort of pilgrimage to family possessions: to Fasque and Glen Dye. All the country for many miles around is known to him. In the excursions he has made he has not quite evaded the usual demonstrations, but, on the whole, the three days have been quiet. To-day, which is the last of his visit to Brechin, he planted another tree. The pleasantries, now getting stale, about Mr. Gladstone's passion for cutting down trees can take a fresh start, and we shall hear of his trying to repair the mischief he has wrought. The truth is, Mr. Gladstone understands trees and woodcraft as a good forester does, and he will tell you that he never yet laid axe to a tree that ought not to have been cut down. He has been going over the park with Lord Dalhousie's forester. Not a tree that is not known to him, and he discusses them and their various merits in the tone of deep interest with which a man whose passion is horses dilates to you on the points of his thoroughbreds. When he comes to plant the vigorous young oak selected for him, he strips to his work, throws off coat and hat, and for the next five minutes the only thing of real concern to the Prime Minister of England is the right planting of this tree. The knot of labourers who are there to help have nothing to do but look on while this young man of seventy-five handles his heavy spade with the skill of long practice, till finally Lord Dalhousie interposes and orders the men to do the rest. One of the few ladies who were spectators presently observed what a pity it was that Mr. Gladstone should not have put a shovelful of mould in himself. She had believed the man in shirt-sleeves and gray trousers to be one of the forester's men—a compliment with which Mr. Gladstone was not displeased. Then Mrs. Gladstone planted a tree, and then Miss Helen Gladstone a third, and then the tree-planting ceremonies came to an end.

It is time this long narrative of these memorable visits should also come to an end. Mr. Gladstone has yet three visits to make, and his homeward journey to complete, and no doubt will deliver other speeches, and see other multitudes of admiring and devoted Scotsmen surrounding him at railway stations, and wherever else he may show himself. But the work he came to do is done, and so well done that nothing he has yet to say in Scotland will much add to the sum of his present political achievement. He returns to England to continue his struggle for the enfranchisement of two millions of labourers, and behind him is the unbroken force of the whole volume of Scottish opinion and Scottish purpose.

MR. GLADSTONE'S POLITICS.

I.

HOW HE DEALT IN SCOTLAND WITH FOREIGN AFFAIRS, AND
ESPECIALLY WITH EGYPT.

[DEESIDE, *October* 4, 1884.]

WHY did Mr. Gladstone come to Scotland? What has been the result of his visit, and what will be its probable effect on the course of public affairs? Such, I imagine, are two among many questions which Americans who have followed his journeyings are asking themselves. It is impossible not to put such questions; impossible not to frame some reply for one's self. The opinion I have about the matter is not, I fear, in all points orthodox from a purely Liberal point of view. I have a sympathy with English Liberalism and an admiration for Mr. Gladstone. But my point of view is, after all, that of an interested outsider. A foreigner owes no allegiance to English parties or to English leaders. The only thing he is bound to be loyal to is his own conviction, and that I will try to make plain.

That Mr. Gladstone is the first of living parliamentary tacticians has long been agreed. He has now shown that he can manage a nation not less adroitly than he manages the House of Commons. The whole effect — I doubt not the chief aim also — of his speeches here in Scotland has been to convince people that the Franchise Bill is the one thing now worth thinking about, or speaking about, or working for. The whole of his first long speech at the Corn Exchange in

Edinburgh was devoted to the Franchise Bill. When he spoke to the working men in Waverley Market he reverted to the same topic. It was only in his intermediate address that he handled other matters, and he did it avowedly on the ground that it was his duty to render an account to his constituents. The way in which he handled them, the degree of importance he seemed to attach to each separate subject, are characteristic of the man and singularly illustrative of his gift of making people see things as he wants them to be seen.

During the four years of Mr. Gladstone's administration two questions have been paramount, Ireland and Egypt. Other questions there have been, and on these he has much to say which is most forcibly said. He justly claims credit for the measure of justice done to Montenegro and to Greece. He has a good case in Afghanistan. He has perhaps a plausible one in South Africa. Every word about Ireland is apt, and his arraignment of the great conspiracy in Ireland against social order lacked nothing but an explicit assertion of Mr. Parnell's political responsibility for the crimes by which that conspiracy was carried on. But even on Ireland Mr. Gladstone is brief. In the pamphlet reprint of his speeches the second fills twenty-four pages. Ireland occupies less than three of the twenty-four. Egypt occupies less than three. The two greatest topics of the four years are dismissed in not quite one-fourth of the whole speech. Ireland, however, at the moment is not a burning question. Egypt is, and to Egypt Mr. Gladstone devotes less than one-eighth of his whole discourse. He has since delivered over the length and breadth of Scotland some scores of speeches; many of which I heard, all of which I have read. I cannot recollect that he so much as alluded again to Egypt. I am certain he nowhere dwelt on it. He has deliberately belittled this enormous subject. Alike by speech and by silence he has done what he could conscientiously to obscure its real significance, to extenuate its importance, to persuade the people of Scotland, and the people of England to whom he addresses himself just as closely, that Egypt after all is not a subject that deserves more than casual and occasional attention.

The suppression is the more surprising because during all the latter months of the session he never made a complete statement on Egypt. He answered many questions and disclosed nothing. He promised to find time for a full debate on Egypt, and unavoidable circumstances continually delayed and finally prevented the fulfilment of his promise. To this hour the country knows not the secret springs of the perplexing purposes which have prevailed—each in its turn and each conflicting with the other—in the Cabinet over which Mr. Gladstone presides. I do not doubt that, in his present silence as in other things, Mr. Gladstone is sincere. Before he seeks to convince others, he convinces himself. It is not his sincerity which is in question. Apart from the cleverness of his tactics, which we all admire, it is his statesmanship in great affairs abroad which is in question. What we all hoped to hear was a vindication of his proceedings in Egypt, from his own point of view. He deliberately suppressed it. I am sure he thinks he could vindicate them. If he did not choose to try, it was for the reason above given. He put the Franchise above Egypt, and he was determined to write Franchise so large all over the land that no Egyptian hieroglyphics should anywhere be visible. He knows that as to Egypt there is a case against him, and a tremendous case. I admit he could not argue it, could not defend his policy on the Nile, except at great length and in painful detail. I admit that with reference to his immediate purpose, and having regard solely to the politics of to-day, he acted prudently in slurring the subject. But Mr. Gladstone knows as well as anybody that history will not deal with it in that way.

If you look at what he actually said you will find the same shrewdness of treatment. He approaches Egypt from a totally unexpected side. With an irresistible air of taking his hearers into his confidence, and in a tone of delightful humility, he said, "I pass now, gentlemen, to the question of Egypt, and I think there is an inquiry that you have a right to put to me, 'What took you to Egypt?' You have a right to ask that." That is a masterpiece in its way. It shifts the debate from ground where every step would be dangerous, to ground where he can walk with a sure tread. Only, it is ground where now nobody cares to follow him. He preferred the safe past, which has but an academic interest, to the perilous present with a pitfall at every pace. Nobody wants to know what took him to Egypt, or doubts that he went there because he could not help it. The question of to-day—the question put by Englishmen and to Englishmen—is not, What took you to Egypt, but, How came you to make such a muddle of it when you got there? Upon that, Mr. Gladstone is discreetly silent. In vain will you search for one word of explanation of any of the acts or omissions by which Egypt has been brought to its present condition. There is a declaration of principles. The principle on which he applied his principles, as occasion arose, is left as mysterious as ever.

Well, in this matter too, Scotland has followed Mr. Gladstone's lead; followed it with a childlike submissiveness which would be touching if it were not carried too far; if this submissiveness did not sometimes manifest itself in a way discreditable to people who ought to cling to their own convictions; sometimes dishonourable. The word is a strong one, but I will justify it in a moment. The remarks which Mr. Gladstone made about Egypt were made to one of the most intelligent audiences that could be collected in the kingdom. Meagre as they were, misleading as I think they were, incredibly inadequate and insufficient as they were, his audience cheered them. Nay, they cheered before he had made them. They cheered the mere word Egypt. They cheered when he said, "I pass now to Egypt," as if he were coming to the most brilliant page in the history of his Government. They were prepared to acquit him without hearing a word of his defence; to award him absolution for the whole past, and *carte blanche* for the future. I verily believe they would have cheered him if he had declared he was right in opposing the purchase of the Suez Canal shares, or right in suffering an Egyptian army under an English general to march to an inevitable doom in the deserts of the Soudan. They cheered him even when he produced that astonishing certificate of British benefits to Egypt from Mr. Egerton,—that a certain germ of independence is being developed among the peasantry. Germ is a word which would come more naturally from Dr. Koch than from Mr. Egerton. Whatever he meant by it, a germ of independence which is only being developed seems a slight return for all these years of English effort in Egypt. They even cheered his cold reference to General Gordon. The press of Scotland, the Liberal press, *The Scotsman* itself with all its power of independent and courageous thinking, accepted and applauded his method of discussing Egypt.

In private, it is true, I heard some strong criticisms on Mr. Gladstone's Egyptian paragraphs. It is not everybody, not even all his personal friends, who surrender their judgment and conscience into Mr. Gladstone's keeping. But I heard, I am bound to say, far more assenting than dissenting opinions, and the uniform tone of the press on such a question as this must be accepted as a safe index to the body of opinion among its readers. I cannot refrain from quoting what seems to me a very painful proof of the state of feeling about the heroic and generous and loyal soldier who keeps guard over British honour at Khartoum. When his last message to the Government, and last report of his plans and wishes, reached this country, a Scotch Liberal paper of ability and position published it with the head-line, "More of General Gordon's Freaks." That is what I had in mind when I used the word dishonourable. It is not honourable to a nation to mock at the leader of its forlorn hope when bullets have been whistling about his ears day and night for four long months.

I should say this just as strongly if I took what I may

call the Gladstonian view of Egypt. Egypt is the gravest question of the day. My criticism on Mr. Gladstone is that he has deliberately put it aside, and withdrawn from the consideration of the people of England and Scotland issues tenfold more vital than those on which he makes his appeal to them. Whether an Englishman wishes to plant an empire on the Nile, or whether his main idea about Egypt is, like Mr. Gladstone's, to get out of it, he cannot but regard the decision between those two alternatives as momentous to the future of Great Britain. The question ought, therefore, to be faced and not evaded. To put it aside for the Franchise Bill is not an act of high statesmanship. It cannot greatly matter whether the Franchise Bill is passed this year, or next, or the year after. The class which is to get the vote has waited eight hundred years for it. Unquestionable as the rights of the two millions of non-voters are, they are not, in a broad view, urgent. Time is not of the essence of the franchise question. It is certain that the franchise will be granted, and granted soon. But the decisions, the irrevocable decisions, to be taken at Cairo within the next twelvemonth, are decisions which must affect the destinies of this Empire for centuries to come. In a Government which rests admittedly on the will of the people, the people have a right to be consulted on those destinies; on the most important, and not merely on the less important, of the issues on which the existence of the Government depends.

II.

INFLUENCE OF HIS JOURNEY ON REFORM OF THE FRANCHISE AND THE LORDS.

[DEESIDE, *October* 4, 1884.]

What remains is to consider Mr. Gladstone's performance in Scotland with reference to its immediate object; accepting his own point of view, and forgetting Egypt and the rest of the universe outside of these islands. It is believed that Mr. Gladstone means the carrying of the Franchise Bill to be the crowning work of his life. Among his achievements in constructive legislation, reform bills or bills for enlarging the suffrage have had no important place. It is natural and honourable to him that he should wish to leave a great franchise measure as a lasting memorial of his public life. As he said himself, he wants to broaden the basis on which the Constitution rests. It is an ambition which we Americans, at any rate, are bound to applaud. It is one more step in the Americanisation of English institutions; another stage toward that government by democracy whither England is rushing with giant strides. There is little difficulty in seeing how Mr. Gladstone might persuade himself that it is expedient to subordinate everything to this one aim. We can almost sympathise with his impatience of every obstacle, and if not sympathise with, at least understand, the mood which leads him to close his eyes for the moment to the claims of the vast Empire beyond these narrow seas, and devote himself to the immediate welfare of his nearest fellow-citizens.

Whether Mr. Gladstone's motives be simple or complex, it is obvious that he came to Scotland as to a pulpit from which to preach the gospel of Franchise, and that only. Let me drop the ecclesiastical metaphor before it becomes embarrassing or, which is worse, mixed, and say that first Midlothian, and then all Scotland, was but the platform from which he spoke to the whole kingdom. He himself has declared his conviction that England has gone as fast and as far with him as Scotland. It may be so, but in these scientific days it is safer to keep to beliefs for which sufficient evidence is forthcoming. In England the evidence has still to be strengthened. In Scotland it is already overwhelming. Scotland, however, is but the advance-guard of England in political thinking. The ideas which the Caledonian accepts to-day the Southron will proclaim to-morrow, and probably claim them as his own. Like New-England in America,

Scotland here in old England is a nursery of political ideas. It was not for nothing that Mr. Gladstone chose Midlothian as the hearthstone of the crusade which he preached in 1879. It is equally useful to him now, and the history of 1879 and 1880 explains the confidence in English support he now expresses before England has really been heard from.

Scotland, in truth, needed no kindling in favour of the new suffrage. She was ready, in Mr. Gladstone's judgment, to go too far afield in pursuit of it, and to complicate the issues which he was striving to simplify. Accordingly his first errand here was to discourage, or at least to retard, agitation against the House of Lords. Scotland, in common with Liberal England, had pretty much made up its mind that this Reform Bill, like the Reform Bill of 1832, was in peril of being wrecked by the opposition of the Lords, or of the permanent Tory majority which is encamped in the Second Chamber. It was fast approaching a state of mind in which Franchise First might cease to be its motto, and the one burning question be the House of Lords, and whether to Mend them or End them. Mr. Gladstone wants to pass the Franchise Bill, and wants, at present, neither to Mend nor End the Lords. Reform or abolition of the Lords is a problem he has not thought out. It involves an organic change from which his conservative instincts—and few men have more or stronger—shrink. Any scheme for limiting or for annulling the legislative authority of the Upper Chamber involves enormous difficulties, a prolonged struggle, probably a political convulsion beside which the present obstacles in the way of giving the vote to a couple of millions of non-voting Englishmen seem trivial.

He began, therefore, a little indirectly, but as he said of parliamentary obstruction, perhaps for that reason the more effectively, to chill the ardour of his Scotch supporters for battle with the Lords. I said at the time that he had only to utter to his audience in the Corn Exchange at Edinburgh one word of definite menace against hereditary and irresponsible power, to raise a whirlwind which even he might not afterward have been able to ride. He would not utter it. He devoted his hour and a half to an argument for the Franchise Bill—powerful and comprehensive, certainly, but so rigidly confined to the subjects long since threshed out in Parliament and the press as almost to seem hackneyed to the hardened politician or more hardened journalist. In few but emphatic words he avowed his disinclination to touch the question of reforming the Lords. He disappointed his audience, and knew he was disappointing them. Later in his speech he spoke sternly of Lord Salisbury's pretension that the House of Lords should determine the time of a dissolution of Parliament. He discussed the history of that House. He dwelt on its protracted resistance to Liberal legislation. He derided its claims to represent the whole people. He condemned its whole legislative action for fifty years. He enumerated the instances where it had set itself against the will of the people, as repeatedly declared by their true representatives in the Commons. He exposed what he called the duplicity of Lord Salisbury's dealing with the present Franchise Bill. He warned him and his majority that their veto on it could not and must not be prolonged.

But neither then nor ever during his stay in Midlothian did he swerve from his considered purpose, or let fall a word of encouragement to the great party waiting for him to put himself at their head in a great popular movement for the overthrow of the body that so steadily hindered the popular will. He tried the patience of the people, as he admitted later, but he risked everything rather than risk his bill.

Two very curious and interesting things then happened. First, the agitation against the Lords in Scotland became suddenly still. From the moment Mr. Gladstone had spoken, the waves subsided. I doubt whether people were convinced, or whether they quite agreed with him that an appeal to the reason of the Lords had a chance of being more successful or more expeditious than a threat. But they hearkened unto his words and yielded to his counsel. From that time on, the press and the platform followed him. The addresses which poured in on him might have been written by himself. Never was a more striking proof of any man's personal influence over a nation accustomed to think and act for itself.

But secondly, and more curiously still, this very submission, this loyalty, this touching devotion, reacted on Mr. Gladstone. As he went his way north he was everywhere surrounded by an enthusiastic people. They sprang from the ground to greet him as he turned southward and homeward. It is easy to laugh at railway speeches and station crowds, but no man who saw these scenes could doubt that Mr. Gladstone had Scotland at his back. He saw it, and it so far modified his mind that, for the first time, he felt it possible to use this popular agitation as a means of overawing the Lords without endangering the immediate stability of the political fabric he wished to let alone. More than once, in Aberdeenshire and in Forfarshire, he let drop sentences which foreshadowed the change. At Perth he spoke out. It is plain, he said, that the Lords have to do with the people. It is time they should understand it, time they should comprehend that we cannot always be fighting on this comparatively narrow ground. It will not do to trifle with facts. It is not to be expected that we should consent to acquiesce in a state of things in which irresponsible power is to be continually and obstinately pitted against power which is responsible. If they persist, the question will be raised whether this irresponsible power can be tolerated. "That controversy I fear would be bitter; I know it would be long, but it could end only one way, in great and extensive changes in the present balance of the Constitution."

You have only to compare those pregnant sentences with Mr. Gladstone's language and tone a month earlier to see how far, in more than one sense of the word, he has travelled, and how bracing is the political as well as physical atmosphere of Scotland. It is true that at Carlisle on his homeward journey, having once more crossed the border, and speaking on English soil, he again held out to the Lords what moderate Liberals joyfully recognised as an olive branch. No doubt he would rejoice if Lord Salisbury would seize the other end of it. There is nothing in that to impair the effect of the warning at Perth. Reasonable compromise, by all means. Reasonable concessions on both sides. But if Lord Salisbury continues to scoff at compromise and to insist, as he seems now to insist, on a Liberal surrender, the sentences at Carlisle go for nothing; the menace of Perth remains in force.

And there I leave the matter. It cannot be necessary to restate to an American audience Mr. Gladstone's argument in favour of giving votes to citizens who have none. Still less can it be necessary to debate whether fifty-nine men, who happen to be the sons of titled fathers, ought to have the power of overruling the majority of a great nation. Mr. Gladstone thinks there is much to be said for the hereditary principle, but there are few Americans of his mind. As for the franchise, that is a question we argued out for ourselves something more than a hundred years ago,—in some cases much more. Neither Mr. Gladstone nor any other leading English statesman has yet advanced to the point we then reached. Our whole political life in America is bound up in the proposition that the vote is a right of which no man can be deprived but for sufficient and exceptional cause. The Republic is built on manhood suffrage. The English Constitution rests upon the theory that the vote is a privilege to be granted or withheld in the discretion of those who happen already to possess it.

The Franchise Bill of to-day takes not one single step forward in principle. It is defended and recommended because it does not. Mr. Gladstone offered it to Parliament as a conservative measure. The Conservatives profess to accept it as such. Broadly speaking, it is only a bill for giving the vote in counties to the same class who already possess it in boroughs. In other words, it confers on the agricultural labourer the franchise which in 1867 was conferred on the artisan. But the counties with the franchise in the hands of the tenant farmer, and the tenant farmer in the hands of the landlord, have hitherto been strongholds of Toryism. This bill would disturb the Tory grip on these great constituencies, and that is the secret of the opposition to it. The probable effect of it will be to put the Conservatives of England in a minority. They have, as they think, two ways of delaying or averting that catastrophe. They may force a dissolution of Parliament on the present register, obtain a majority, and come into office. Once in office, they will pass a Franchise Bill of their own, and a Redistribution Bill of their own—or, as we should say, redistrict the country—and so preserve, or improve in their own interests, the existing balance of political power. That is the situation.

What Mr. Gladstone has done in Scotland—what he went there to do—becomes plainer, perhaps, in the light of this very elementary exposition. His mission was to save England from falling under a reactionary conservatism, under the leadership of a man whose ideas are those of his party in the seventeenth century. Franchise Bill and Reform of the Lords are but incidents in the struggle. There can be no doubt how it will end if the people see clearly what it is, and what it means. Mr. Gladstone's speeches in Scotland, and the uprising in Scotland itself, have helped them to see. The cause of Liberalism in England to-day, which is identified with the cause of Liberalism not only elsewhere in Europe but also in America, is the stronger, the nearer to its goal, for what has been said here and what has been done here during this last month. The triumph of English Liberalism means ultimately Democracy,—means, at least, manhood suffrage. Mr. Gladstone may not believe it, may not intend to hasten the approach of the day when equal political rights for all men shall be the creed of the English as it has long been the creed of the American; his practice, also, since 1870 and the adoption of the XVth Amendment. But his sympathy with the people of England is none the less profound because he prefers political changes to be gradual, and, for his own part, to confine his aims as Minister to reform of a definite and limited character.

www.ingramcontent.com/pod-product-compliance
Lightning Source LLC
Chambersburg PA
CBHW032001300426
44117CB00008B/851